DEPENDENCE AND UNDERDEVELOPMENT

JAMES D. COCKCROFT is Associate Professor of Sociology at Livingston College, Rutgers University. Before completing his Ph.D. in Latin American Studies at Stanford University, 1966, Dr. Cockcroft lived four years in Latin America (Colombia and Mexico). He is the author of *Intellectual Precursors of the Mexican Revolution* and chapters on Mexico in *Latin American Radicalism* and *The Political Economy of the Third World: Latin America*. He is presently doing research on comparative multinational corporations and the "new imperialism."

ANDRÉ GUNDER FRANK is currently Professor of Economic Development in the Department of Sociology and staff member of the Centro de Estudios Socioeconomicos (CESO) of the University of Chile in Santiago. He was born in Berlin in 1929 and educated in the United States. He has taught economics and other social sciences at Iowa State, Michigan State, and Wayne State Universities in the United States, at the University of Brasilia, the University of Chile, and at the National University of Mexico. Dr. Frank is author of *Capitalism and Underdevelopment in Latin America: Historical Studies of Chile and Brazil* and *Latin America: Underdevelopment or Revolution,* both published by Monthly Review Press; and in other languages, *Lumpenbourgeoisie: Lumpendevelopment, Dependence, Class and Politics in Latin America* and *On Capitalist Underdevelopment* (English editions in press). Besides continuing his work on Latin America, Dr. Frank is currently co-editing a two-volume anthology of analyses of the historical causes of underdevelopment and of comparison of capitalist and socialist development policies in Asia, Africa, and Latin America. Dr. Frank is married and has two children.

DALE L. JOHNSON is Associate Professor of Sociology at Livingston College, Rutgers University. Dr. Johnson received his Ph.D. from Stanford University in 1967, with a dissertation on the role of Chilean elites in economic development. He is the author of *Chilean Socialism* and articles for journals in the study of the sociology of development.

*Dependence and
Underdevelopment:*

LATIN AMERICA'S
POLITICAL ECONOMY

by

JAMES D. COCKCROFT
ANDRÉ GUNDER FRANK
DALE L. JOHNSON

ANCHOR BOOKS

Doubleday & Company, Inc.
Garden City, New York
1972

The Anchor Books edition is the first English-language publication of *Dependence and Underdevelopment: Latin America's Political Economy*. A Spanish-language edition was published in Buenos Aires by Ediciones Signos in 1970.

Anchor Books edition: 1972

EDITOR'S STATEMENT

This volume is part of a publishing program on Latin America, under the general editorship of Otto Feinstein and Rodolfo Stavenhagen. The purpose of these books is to present an inter-American dialogue on Latin American affairs, from history and culture to economics, politics, and sociology. This program is designed to make the best scholarship from Latin America available to readers in the United States.

OTTO FEINSTEIN is Professor of the Science of Society Division of Monteith College, Wayne State University. He is editor of *New University Thought*. Professor Feinstein has written articles for numerous publications, and is the editor of *Two Worlds of Change: Readings in Economic Development*.

RODOLFO STAVENHAGEN is a Mexican who studied sociology and social anthropology at the University of Chicago, the National University of Mexico, and the University of Paris. Since 1956, he has been teaching at the National University of Mexico, and is currently affiliated with the International Institute of Labor Studies in Geneva. He is the author of many articles on Latin America, including "Seven Erroneous Theses about Latin America," which appears in *New University Thought,* as well as *Agrarian Problems and Peasant Movements in Latin America,* also published by Anchor as part of this program.

Other titles in the program include *Obstacles to Development in Latin America,* by Celso Furtado, and *The Rape of the Peasantry,* by Ernest Feder.

CONTENTS

PART III

SOCIAL SCIENCE
AND STRATEGIES OF DEVELOPMENT

INTRODUCTION

We publish this work at the end of the "First United Nations Development Decade," when poverty, unemployment, and other conditions of underdevelopment in Latin America are no better and probably worse than ten years ago. One of the major themes of this work is that underdevelopment in Latin America is highly conditioned by the region's relations with the rest of the world. Gabriel Valdés, ex-Foreign Minister of Chile, suggested one reason for Latin America's continuing, even deepening, underdevelopment in his statement to President Richard Nixon at the White House on June 12, 1969:

> It is generally believed that our continent receives real financial aid. The data show the opposite. We can affirm that Latin America is making a contribution to financing the development of the United States and of other industrialized countries. Private investment has meant and does mean for Latin America that the sums taken out of our continent are several times higher than those that are invested. Our potential capital declines. The benefits of invested capital grow and multiply themselves enormously, though not in our countries but abroad. The so-called aid, with all its well-known conditions, means markets and greater development for the developed countries, but has not in fact managed to compensate for the money that leaves Latin America in payment of the external debt and as a result of the profits generated by private direct investment. In one word, we know that Latin America gives more than it receives. On these realities it is not possible to base any solidarity or even any stable or positive cooperation.[1]

[1] Cited by André Gunder Frank, "The Underdevelopment Policy of the United Nations in Latin America," *NACLA Newsletter*, December 1969, p. 1.

It is in a context of grave social and human crisis in Latin America and other underdeveloped parts of the world that we bring together the essays and analyses that comprise this book. Our aim is to develop an analytical and theoretical perspective that can be of use in the comparative study of political institutions and the problems of social change. This perspective will focus primarily on the underdeveloped nations but will also apply, ultimately, to the developed countries as well. The hypotheses we offer are not thoroughly tested propositions, but we do find the historical and contemporary evidence singularly persuasive. We hope that our criticisms of conventional approaches to underdevelopment and development, and our alternative analytical approach, will stimulate new contributions from other scholars and students of the social sciences, and that these contributions will help to deal more effectively with the central problems of development and social change, both in this country and abroad.

The fact that certain chapters in this book deal in some detail with individual countries demonstrates that we by no means reject *in toto* the recent trend in scholarship on Latin America to focus on the individual nation rather than the over-all region. However, we do feel that these "nation studies" have accumulated to such a point as to constitute a fragmentizing force, which deflects from real theoretical and empirical understanding of certain larger problems. Therefore, we present our hypotheses in more general terms and seek to place the problems of individual nations in the larger perspective of the Latin American region and its relationships to the rest of the world.

Indeed, this path of investigation has led us to take an even more global view of the problem of underdevelopment, which afflicts Asia, Africa, the Middle East, and parts of the United States and Western Europe, as well as Latin America. We see underdevelopment as intimately and causally related to the pattern of evolution of developed, industrialized societies. In brief, we investigate interrelationships between different economic, geographical, and cultural systems on a global basis over historical time. We consciously follow the general rule of social theory that states that when seeking to explain (or change) a *part* of something, in this case underdevelopment, one must look for and refer systematically to the *whole,* in terms of which that part can be understood (or changed).

It is only in this way, and with a great emphasis on historical research, that the *development of underdevelopment* can be understood. No country was ever in an original state of *under*development, although it may have been *un*developed. The processes of development and underdevelopment began when the European nations began their worldwide mercantilist and capitalist expansion. Constellations of developing metropolises and underdeveloping satellites evolved, connecting all parts of the world system from its metropolitan center in Europe, and later the United States, to the farthest outpost in the Latin American countryside.

Although throughout history the major metropolis benefits most from these interrelationships, we do not deny that economic development occurs in the more advantaged satellites (or submetropolises). Ours is not a "conspiratorial" view of history. What happens, given the dominance of the major metropolis, is that the economic development that does occur in the more prosperous of the satellites is at best a limited or "underdeveloped" development. It is constantly conditioned by relationships of dependence upon the metropolis. Economic development in Latin America, in other words, is a satellite development, which is not autonomous to the region, self-generating, or self-perpetuating.

This leads us to criticize and reject certain hallowed traditional premises. These include the following commonly accepted propositions:

(1) Underdevelopment is an *original state,* characterized by "backwardness" or "traditionalism"; underdeveloped countries have no long history of change. On the contrary, our research indicates that these countries do have a history, and that their underdevelopment has been produced by the development of mercantilism and later, industrial capitalism.

(2) Underdeveloped countries suffer from being divided into *dual societies,* one modern, urban, and integrated, the other rural, backward, and isolated, with the rural or "feudal"

society constituting a block to global modernization and economic development. The actual situation is the contrary. These rural areas have not been isolated since the beginning of the mercantile-capitalist age. The most feudal-seeming regions today are precisely those that had the closest ties to the metropolis in the past: for example, the ex-mining districts of Minas Gerais (Brazil); highland Peru; Bolivia; or Guanajuato, Zacatecas, and San Luis Potosí in Mexico; or areas of centuries of commercial agricultural exploitation for export, such as Northeast Brazil.

(3) *Diffusion* of the capital and/or culture of the developed capitalist countries is necessary for industrialization to occur. In fact the satellites have experienced their greatest industrial development when diffusion has been the least and ties to the metropolis have been weakest—e.g., during the two World Wars and the intervening Depression. When the metropolis reasserts its influence after such world crises, the recently industrialized parts of Latin America suffer renewed and sharpened strains of underdevelopment: balance-of-payments difficulties, inflation, loss of national control of the industrializing process, slow economic growth or stagnation, growing rigidity of social structure, repressive conservative governments, etc. Moreover, the diffusion or flow of capital that actually does occur in Latin America is from the poor, underdeveloped nations to the rich, developed ones.

(4) The precapitalist state of sectors of Latin American societies accounts for underdevelopment. The argument of a precapitalist stage is used by many scholars, even Marxists, to justify the supposed need for reform, or a bourgeois revolution, to bring Latin America into the capitalist stage of history. We will show, however, that the allegedly precapitalist, feudal, or backward parts of Latin America (which also can be termed *internal colonies*) both reflect and contribute to Latin America's ongoing, thoroughly capitalist underdevelopment. Since Latin America has already been shaped, underdeveloped, and misdeveloped during the capitalist stage, we maintain that the time has come for replacing capitalist underdevelopment with socialist development.

(5) *Import substitution* is the generator of economic de-

velopment. On the contrary, industrialization through import substitution fails because of the consequences of Latin America's long-term dependence upon the international system that in turn conditions permanent underdevelopment.

Part I of this book offers a conceptual foundation for explaining the economic consequences of Latin America's subordinate position in the various stages of the development of world capitalism. Here we will examine the history of Latin America from the Conquest to the present. But we also will examine the way in which this subordination conditions the evolution of the social structures, the politics, and the ideologies and culture of Latin America, which in turn further the process of economic underdevelopment. In Part II we will examine class and politics in the twentieth century, with particular emphasis on recent events, representative polities (usually those purported to be the most democratic), and the relationships between class, power, and ideology. Part III discusses the implications of our research for strategies of development and the future of social-science research.

Historically, Latin America's subordinate relationship to mercantilist and capitalist powers has resulted in the present economic, social, and political traits of underdevelopment that are internal to Latin American countries. Latin America's problems today, however conditioned or aggravated by international factors, are largely manifested in *structural underdevelopment at the national and local level*.

In its historical evolution, the process of Latin America's underdevelopment has been uneven. It has varied with world and domestic demands and prices, regional and periodic booms and busts, technological changes, and other factors, but it has been sufficiently permanent to generate a growing Latin American reaction to subordination: *nationalism*. Concomitant with this development has been the emergence of new social analyses geared to serve nationalist and class-liberation movements by disassociating analysis from metropolitan tutelage and ideology. United States scholars have much to learn from these new analyses, which we gratefully acknowledge and utilize here. Among many of the Latin

American social scientists we cite is Theotonio dos Santos. His conceptualization of dependence as a *conditioning situation,* in which specific histories of development and underdevelopment transpire, applies to our research.

In the present era, foreign capital has penetrated Latin America so thoroughly that multinational corporations no longer merely export manufactures to Latin America in exchange for primary products. Rather, they provide for the national market of a Latin American country from within by establishing enterprises located in the country itself. They also buy up medium-scale and large-scale Latin American industries, often at less than real value, and draw their operating capital from within Latin America itself. This is what we call the *de-Latin-Americanization of the industrial economy.* Whatever national industry does develop in the process of incipient industrialization inevitably suffers some form of takeover by foreigners, either directly, as here described, or indirectly, through the economy's over-all structural dependence upon the international system. The Latin American Free Trade Association and the role of multinational corporations both derive their impetus from imperialism and can only contribute to the denationalization of the Latin American economy. The ascendance of the multinational corporation is the consequence of the process of economic concentration in the industrialized countries, that is, of the development of *monopoly capitalism.* Not without reason did Lenin define *imperialism* as monopoly capitalism.

The international system of monopoly capitalism conditions the formation of class structures in Latin America. For example, the delatinamericanization of industries conditions, if not determines, the nature of Latin America's bourgeoisie. Examination of the metropolis-satellite structure, both international and national, throws into sharp relief the class structure in which the bourgeoisie is formed. The bourgeoisie develops fully or not, according to whether it is dominant or satellitized. In either case, the bourgeoisie maintains itself economically and socially on the basis of capitalism and, in order to maintain itself, has to make a political effort to preserve the same exploitative and underdevelopment generating structure that brought it into existence.

This is the theoretical framework for understanding why 25 percent of Latin America's labor force is unemployed.[2] Of this quarter of the population, 45 percent are in agriculture and the remainder in the urban economy. Even though Latin America has had relatively more industrialization than most other parts of the underdeveloped world, industrial employment is limited and (as a proportion of total employment) now stagnant or declining. The unproductive "service" and "unspecified activities" sectors have absorbed most of the growth in the urban labor force in recent decades. In other words, the exodus of the displaced poor from agriculture into Latin America's mushrooming cities has been a case of *horizontal mobility* from one situation of extreme poverty to another and not of vertical mobility from peasant to industrial worker. In both absolute and relative terms, unemployment, underemployment, and unproductive employment in petty services are steadily increasing in Latin America, as is underdevelopment of the system as a whole. Cuba alone has managed to eliminate unemployment and now has a labor shortage instead.

Development should not be confused, as it often is, with economic growth measured in annual increases of *per capita* national income or product. Growth without development[3] is a frequent experience in the past and present of the now underdeveloped countries. This is especially the case in times of raw material export booms generated by metropolitan demand: a satellite country's growth becomes manifested both

[2] Recent studies by the United Nations Economic Commission for Latin America (ECLA) and International Labor Organization provide this figure in constructing estimates for "equivalent unemployment," that is, the amount of plain unemployment plus the unemployment equivalent of those who are underemployed (Frank, *op. cit.*).

[3] To our knowledge, the term was coined by R. Clower, G. Dalton, M. Harwitz and A. Walters in their *Growth without Development: An Economic Survey of Liberia* (Evanston: Northwestern University Press, 1966), although they do not see the same implications in the term as we do.

in the product it exports and in its productive capacity but, far from generating or even permitting the structural transformation necessary for development, this growth results in the development of underdevelopment. In the present era, even substantial industrial growth, if it is of the "import-substituting" type, subordinately dependent on imperialist development, and integrated into the expansion of the multinational corporation, results in further underdevelopment.[4] Real *development* involves a structural transformation of the economy, society, polity and culture of the satellite that permits the self-generating and self-perpetuating use and development of the people's potential. Development comes about as a consequence of a people's frontal attack on the oppression, exploitation, and poverty that they suffer at the hands of the dominant classes and their system. Thus, higher GNPs in certain Latin American countries (e.g., Mexico and Peru) certainly do not constitute development in this sense. What is needed to fathom the problems raised by Latin America's obvious need for economic growth *and* development is a more profound analysis of Latin America's position in the world economy and stratification of power, as well as an appreciation of the complexity of Latin America's class structure.

Viewed internally, the key point about Latin America's class structure is its polarization into those classes with jobs, income, status, and participation in society as against those classes either without employment or in jobs of high exploitation. Among the classes that together form a "marginal mass" are most Indians, peasants, unemployed or underemployed workers, and highly exploited service workers. On the other end of the scale are the best paid of the stable working class, the entrenched middle class, and the dominant bourgeoisie of urban elites and landholders.

Viewed externally, the key point about Latin America's class structure is its place in the world system of social stratification. One specific dimension of this general phenomenon is national dependence upon *foreign bourgeoisies*, or *gran capital*. The important role of the foreign bourgeoisie in con-

---

[4] For evidence, see the U.N. studies cited in Frank, *op. cit.*

ditioning the economic and social structure of Latin America is exemplified in the history of Mexico. During the three-decade rule of Porfirio Díaz, for example, foreign capitalists achieved quasimonopolistic domination in agriculture, mining, transportation, commerce, and industry. This control was often abetted by the Mexican bourgeoisie, who were as interested as the foreign capitalists in industrialization and profit (although not as secure in times of recession or depression). In spite of latent nationalistic feelings that contributed to the *intra*class conflicts of 1907–11 and the late 1930s, Mexico's bourgeoisie tied itself in the long run to foreign capital.

Similarly, the development of Mexico's rural *latifundista* class (large landholders) was a function of worldwide economic conditions, starting in the colonial period with the exploitation of cheap labor for the mines or for direct export to the metropolises. *Latifundismo* is not a matter of a mechanical transplant of feudalism from the Old World to the New World. The *hacienda* was a notably prosperous business enterprise based on labor-repressive systems and the high value of land and its products. Even after a major agrarian reform in Mexico in the 1930s, *latifundismo* renewed its vigorous development when demand from the metropolis for food imports during World War II triggered a commercial response in Mexico's countryside. By 1970, half of Mexico's peasants were once again landless and today a small class of large landholders monopolizes Mexico's agribusiness. This retrogressive social development could happen only because the earlier agrarian reform, while temporarily alleviating Mexico's rural social problems, did not break the over-all capitalist structure of the society.

Noteworthy in our research is the interlocking character of economic investments and political power shared among landholders, mine-owners, financiers, industrialists, and merchants. These interlocking rural and urban elites ostensibly constitute a ruling class throughout Latin American history. But that class's relatively dependent character must be recognized—dependent, to one degree or another, upon foreign markets and foreign capital. This seeming cohesion in the Latin American bourgeoisie, rural and urban, is not permanent over historical time. As we document throughout this book, *intra*class as well as *inter*class conflicts often occur, and at times unusual class coalitions form. The point we emphasize, for we do not believe it has been strongly enough stated until now, is that world conditions and the behavior of the capitalist metropolises are prominent in influencing these changes in class alignments in Latin America.

Today, the foreign bourgeoisie, or *gran capital* involved in multinational corporations, is dominant at the international level, and the resident foreign bourgeoisie and their national associates are well integrated into Latin America's class and power structures. The national big businessmen, however dependent in the international economic sphere, usually retain dominant influence in national institutional spheres. Yet, the growing presence of multinational corporations signifies a trend toward a decrease in the power of these national bourgeoisies vis-à-vis the foreign bourgeoisies.

The important point is that the *fates of the two bourgeoisies are interdependent, and cannot be separated.* The close correspondence between the interests of Latin America's bourgeoisies and those of foreign investors, their dependence upon international support for survival against the forces of nationalism and revolution, and the growing importance of the multinational corporation all testify to the impact of the metropolis upon the class structures of the satellites. The so-called "national" and "progressive" bourgeoisie in Latin America is neither nationalist nor progressive—it is a dependent, *comprador* bourgeoisie. Latin America's bourgeoisies have been the active agents of foreign economic penetration—and related phenomena such as increased militarization—over the past two decades. The masses, of course, continue to produce the wealth and pay the price for this ongoing *mis*development.

Latin America's bourgeoisies show great shrewdness and strength in co-opting or repressing internal challenges to their power. They employ a sophisticated panoply of methods of control. In the chapters that follow we will try to relate the class structure and goal structure of a nation under analysis to political power relationships, whether in a one-party system like Mexico's or in a multiparty one like Chile's. Again and again, available evidence reveals that populist policies like those of the Cárdenas administration in Mexico, 1934–40, or of the Christian Democrats in Chile, 1964–70, are destined to become mere episodes in history as long as they leave the economic positions of the bourgeoisie intact.

We will try to analyze, and not just describe, the structural position of "the poor." For example, we point out that while the poor have served the function of a "reserve army of the unemployed" in the evolution of capitalism, the trend everywhere today is toward the adoption of labor-displacing technology and the growth of afunctional (i.e., marginal) labor forces. These marginal underclasses become dysfunctional for the system, both in Latin America and in the United States, when they drain off resources for their subsistence and involve large outlays of matériel, manpower, and money for preventing their revolt. We distinguish between marginal underclasses and internal colonies, since internal colonies play a functional economic role of supplying wealth to the metropolises; have a cultural or racial dimension of being dominated (also functional) as well as an economic one; and more clearly lack social mobility (because of racism and their economic role as cheap labor). The class structure within internal colonies is usually sharply differentiated, separating a small *class* of owners and middlemen, who often help administer the colony in the interest of the metropolis, against a large *mass* of people who do the work.[5] We also analyze the effects of occasional upward social mobility on individuals or groups from internal colonies—for example, Peru's *cholos*. Ultimately, all classes of a dominant society derive their relative advantage in wealth and power from the colonial population. Major struggle and conflict occur in Latin America among the classes and between the classes and the *mass*—the mass of people constituting marginal underclasses and internal colonies.

At the end of Part II we discuss the impact of modern

[5] U.S. readers will recognize here the social structure of our Afro-American or Spanish-American urban ghettos, which can profitably be viewed as internal colonies.

capitalism on oppressed classes inside the United States as well as abroad, thus emphasizing the interdependence of development and underdevelopment as processes at every level. We place special emphasis upon the accelerating advance of technology, creating a _technological gap_ not only between the United States and Latin America but also between the United States and Europe and between sectors within both advanced and underdeveloped countries. [Under monopoly capitalism, whether in the metropolis nation or the satellite nation, the structural impossibility of mass incorporation of marginals and the colonized is built into the morphology of highly technified industrial systems.] We emphasize that in Latin America, internal colonialism is part of, and intimately linked with, external colonialism, that is, imperialism. Throughout this book, we examine the various mechanisms of control utilized by modern U.S. imperialism and the forces of internal colonialism.

The chapter on the industrial bourgeoisie and other classes in Chile, reputedly South America's most "democratic" nation with the greatest social mobility, shows the rigidity of class structure and the unprogressive nature of the middle and upper classes. Our research shows that Chile's industrial bourgeoisie is divided between quiescent, nonentrepreneurial lesser figures and traditional elites; that there is little or no mobility to elite status; that elites overlap between different economic sectors; and that monopoly is a principal base of social rigidity—including the growth of a "labor aristocracy" —and highly regressive distribution of income, wealth, and power.[6] The industrial bourgeoisie as such does not view the more traditional elites in mining, agriculture, or finance as threats or rivals. [Kinship and friendship groups are more important than occupation for developing class membership and feelings of social solidarity or identification in the upper and middle classes. The industrial bourgeoisie, then, is not a

[6] Our research was completed before the inauguration of a Marxist government in Chile, but every indication since then reflects the inflexibility of the bourgeoisie in the face of serious efforts to reform society. Statements about Chile throughout this volume deal with pre-1970 Chile, unless otherwise indicated.

class-conscious, "ascendant bourgeoisie," nor is it reform-minded or highly development-oriented. The only significant vertical mobility that we have found with Latin America's national bourgeoisies is downward mobility of surfeit offspring into the *class media acomodada,* or upper middle class, and voluntary declassing of bourgeois sons and daughters (for example, in Venezuela, where they have sometimes joined the guerrillas' FALN).

The smallness of the oligarchy and lesser bourgeoisie in Chile makes it easy for word to be passed from the economic elites to their friends or contacts in any of the nonrevolutionary political parties, who take care of the necessary political work. In Chile, as in Mexico, political parties do not serve as brokers among interest groups as commonly as conventional United States scholarship would have us believe. On the contrary, our research shows that informal and personal patterns of influence, as well as political entrepreneurship, are more important in Latin America than interest-group formation and interest aggregation. Relying in the last instance on military coups, or when possible only on military threats, the bourgeoisie retains an effective veto power if reformist politicians or parties "go too far."

Today, Latin America's middle classes, far from being agents of social change, constitute a major obstacle to reform. In Argentina, Brazil, and Venezuela they are perhaps even more politically and actively reactionary than the industrial bourgeoisie. By their attitudes and behavior, the middle classes reflect and reinforce the larger economic structure. Integration into the international system divides the class structure, distributing relative privileges and social rewards to some classes and excluding others. With some important but usually short-lived exceptions, professionals, technicians, small businessmen, white-collar employees, and even occasional workers traditionally have fallen on the dependent, relatively secure, and conformist side of what Edward Boorstein has aptly termed "the imperialist divide."[7] Landless peasants, most

[7] Edward Boorstein, *The Economic Transformation of Cuba* (New York: Monthly Review Press, 1968), pp. 12–14.

workers, marginals, some small shopkeepers, and the lower stratum of salaried employees have fallen on the deprived, insecure, and precarious "other side" of that divide.

Latin American bureaucracies generally play a conservative role in administration and politics. The salaried groups near the top of the administrative apparatus, public and private (which many U.S. scholars like to think of as an upwardly mobile, progressive middle class), are in fact gaining whatever larger slice of national income they receive at the expense of the vast majority. These groups provide a source of "popular" support for reactionary military dictatorships, as in Brazil. There is no "ascendant middle class" expressing consciousness of itself in such terms. On the other hand, students of both elite universities and vocational schools have distinct causes for social protest, ranging from obstacles to upward mobility to constriction in their standard of living, as well as their indignation at what they see and learn of social injustice, which make them, when sufficiently mobilized, a progressive force for social change.

While there is a complex and intricate subsystem of stratification within Latin America's impoverished rural masses, the main point for class analysis is that _campesinos have never been feudal serfs._ If the medieval serf had land, pasture, and rights as well as obligations, the condition of most Latin American _campesinos_ has been, and is, worse. For the most part, they are landless farm workers who work on commercial farms, migrate to the cities, or fall back, when able, upon share-cropping and tenant-farming to subsist. They constitute a rural proletariat generated over historical time by the global capitalist system. In general, they reside in internal colonies whose products, natural and human resources, and wealth flow to the major cities, never to return.

The participant stable working class of union members in Latin America, usually urban-based, is small, weak, and more often than not a tool of government or some bourgeois-dominated political party. Portions of it form a labor aristocracy. Yet, as real wages of even unionized workers decline, as is the trend today, these organized workers have a greater potential for developing class consciousness and revolutionary politics. This was clearly evidenced by the heavy working-class vote for a Socialist in Chile's recent presidential election and even more so by the 1969 revolt of automobile workers in Córdoba, Argentina. Unorganized workers and the unemployed are sometimes politically more volatile, although not necessarily revolutionary.

Recognizing the powerful force of ideas in shaping the response to externally imposed change throughout Latin American history, we will try to combine our class analysis with an investigation of the underlying causes and/or concomitants of ideological shifts. This is clear in the case of nationalism, generated in great part by Latin American resentment of foreign economic domination and its political consequences. Of equal interest, however, are the cases of "liberal reform" in the second half of the nineteenth century and "democratic left" and "populist reform," even under military governments, in the twentieth century. In all cases of reform for which we have evidence, strong ideological offensives served specific interests of national and foreign bourgeoisies, always at the price of contradicting in practice the noble ideals of the "liberal," "democratic," or "nationalist" ideology in question. Only during the two World Wars and the intervening Depression, when imperialist ties were weakest, have the ideologies of bourgeois nationalism and political populism been able to flourish beyond the rhetorical level and to accomplish some autonomous industrialization and social reform.

Also of interest are the subtle and sophisticated uses of ideology made by imperialism, which have become institutionalized in such programs as the Peace Corps, Food for Peace, and the Alliance for Progress. We do not agree with those who view aggressive or militaristic policies and acts of the United States as momentary aberrations, irrational mistakes, misguided arrogance, or blind Christian idealism. On the contrary, the "welfare" ideology and foreign aid programs in which imperialism cloaks economic coercion and the direct and indirect exercise of counterrevolutionary military power are all rational policies that reflect the sophistication of hegemonic power. Finally, we are interested in the different uses of anticommunism and patriotism made by the local and foreign bourgeoisies in Latin America. We make no pretense to exhaust the complex subject of ideology and myth, wishing instead to draw attention to some of the problems as they relate to underdevelopment, class structure, politics, and imperialism.

Traditionally, the Church and the military in Latin America have been strong institutions influential in maintaining the status quo. However, in recent times minority elements of these two institutions have emerged as voices for reform, and, increasingly, even revolution. Younger priests have defended guerrilla warfare and, in some instances, taken up the gun themselves. Younger members of the military have absorbed not only the counterinsurgency training provided them by their U.S. mentors in schools abroad, but also a "developmentalist" ideology geared to reforming traditional social patterns in order to facilitate industrialization and the expansion of internal markets. An occasional U.S.-trained soldier has gone so far as to become a prominent guerrilla leader, as in the cases of ex-Army men leading guerrilla units in Venezuela and Guatemala.

In general, however, the Latin American military remains dependent upon the United States for arms, training, and political support. Its function has been to maintain "stability," to "pacify" peasant populations and urban neighborhoods on which guerrilla units depend for their survival, and to crush insurrections, whether rural, urban, or student. Napalming peasant villages became common in the 1960s. Not only the military, but also the paramilitary—police, national guard, secret-service units—became, in the 1960s, well integrated into global U.S. policy vis-à-vis revolution or insurrection, even in countries once proud of their "democratic" traditions (Mexico, Costa Rica, Uruguay, Chile). In Venezuela we note the Army's influence over the nation's politics from behind the scenes, and its historical existence as a separate power group. Evidence from Peru, however, shows greater economic and political overlaps between the officer corps and the bourgeoisie, in part a result of the growing trend toward industrialization and multinational corporations.

The military reform governments of Bolivia and Peru,[8] while anti-imperialist in their propaganda, seem unwilling to break the traditional power hold of the most advanced sectors of the bourgeoisie, national and international, but on the contrary, welcome "modernization" and "developmentalism" within the bounds of state-regulated capitalism and foreign finance. [As *The Rockefeller Report on the Americas* makes clear, support of the multinational corporation, increased military aid, agrarian reform short of "peasant control," and stepped-up dependent industrialization are very much in the interests of both Latin America's and the international metropolis's bourgeoisies.]

Up to a point, similar reforms may be welcomed even under a socialist-oriented government like that of today's Chile. Future developments in southern South America will, predictably, depend in great part upon two factors: (1) the behavior of the United States, and (2) the extent to which the economic power of the bourgeoisie, national and international, is actually challenged or broken. There, as in most of Latin America, the U.S.-trained, modernized military may be the ultimate power resource in "resolving conflict" (i.e., extending it).[9] In the meantime, so long as the United States remains bogged down with war in Southeast Asia and economic crisis at home, it will be difficult and perhaps not even desirable, *in the short run,* for the United States to reverse the reformist trend in Chile and Peru.

Recent political events throughout most of Latin America have verified the applicability of our analysis. More and

[8] This book was written before the military overthrow of the military reform government in Bolivia in late summer 1971, but those events do not contradict our analysis; rather, they reinforce the argument that imperialism and the use of the military to check reforms from going "too far" are crucial forces in preventing development and social progress.

[9] Events in Bolivia, for example, follow this pattern, at least through the autumn of 1971.

more Latin American countries have fallen under the ultimate control of their militaries. The time for a "bourgeois democratic revolution" or "democratic left" alternative has passed forever. We suggest that the immediate post-Independence period, 1830–80, was the last time such an alternative might have had a chance of succeeding. Available evidence indicates that bourgeois reformism in Latin America today is conducive to military or civilian authoritarian regimes like those of Brazil and Venezuela, tending toward a Latin American version of fascism as the contradictions sharpen and resistance grows. Even in Peru and Bolivia, significant reforms have occurred only *after* revolutionary uprisings and fierce repression—in other words, to avert revolution, not to create it. The obstacles to revolution continue to be formidable; in military terms, the counterrevolution is internationally coordinated in a deliberate manner. However, Latin Americans once before in their history, at the time of Independence, united across national borders to "throw the colonial masters out," and they may do it again.

In Part III, we will attempt to go beyond the theoretical formulations and empirical contributions of Parts I and II to confront directly the role of social science and students of economic development in the world today, especially in the Western Hemisphere. We will explain the underdevelopment of the sociology of development in the developed capitalist countries, linking it to our larger theoretical model. In discussing alternative strategies of development, policy effectiveness will be our principal criterion. This applies both to the practice of development strategy and to the underlying theory, for if a recommended policy is ineffective in practice, it renders suspect the theory from which it is derived.

Policies based upon economic liberalism, we suggest, generate wealth and power for the few and underdevelopment for the many. The same is true of many other strategies of development now fashionable in the metropolis: cultural, capital, and technological diffusion; the institutionalization of role specialization, universal standards, and achievement motivation; development by "stages"; entrepreneurship;

foreign investment and foreign aid; ctc. The very diffusion of such mistaken strategies of development is a function of the socioeconomic system in which the strategies are developed. The frustration suffered by leading United States development theoreticians, as they see more and more of their policy recommendations fail in practice, raises even more embarrassing questions, at least insofar as those who, like Walt W. Rostow, have helped shape U.S. foreign policy are concerned.

Unless they wish to be ideological and technical instruments of imperialism themselves, North American students of Latin America, we argue, must turn away from the underdeveloped development theory being formulated and used by the metropolis and take direction from the theory of underdevelopment now emerging so clearly in Latin America. In that context, the document in Chapter 11, "Declaration of Latin American Economists," takes on added significance.

Perhaps the most underdeveloped of all the social sciences is political science. We find this distressing precisely because the solutions to underdevelopment are essentially political. Political science, as an explicit attempt to be "scientific," is a product made in U.S.A. It is perhaps the U.S.A.'s most inferior export.

In Chapter 13, we elaborate upon our definition of development as the coincidence of structural change and the liberation of man from exploitation and oppression. Given prevailing conditions of underdevelopment, the only means by which structural changes that are also liberating can be brought about, is through politics. Politics are in part conditioned by theorizing about the nature of politics. Thus, the existence of an adequate theory of political development is a necessary (though hardly sufficient) condition for development itself.

Conventional U.S. theories of political development have little or nothing to say about either structural change or the development of man out of conditions of oppression. Chapter 13 suggests that the principal reason for this is that functional and pluralist theories in political science have no adequate conception of the nature of power. Power is a tangible substance rooted in the economic, social, and institutional structure of society; it is not an intangible quality available to citizens as "a facility for the achievement of societal goals." In capitalist societies (both advanced industrial and underdeveloped), a theory of political development must take into account certain basic structural facts: the conditioning of political power by economic power and the concentration of the resources of power in the hands of a comfortable minority. Approaches to political development currently in vogue simply do not face up to these structural facts.

Models of political systems evolved in the United States invariably stress, as a result of the assumptions of functional theory generally, the desirability of system stability and system integration. But genuine political development means creation of instability as a prerequisite to change and the disintegration of existing systems. Stability, it is assumed by American political scientists, permits a gradual evolution toward a modern, developed society. Needless to say, the model of the modern society toward which underdeveloped countries are expected to evolve is the United States, or rather, an image of that society (economic affluence, social fluidity, political democracy) that is mainly an ideological caricature of the North American reality.

To the degree that formalistic political science even acknowledges that systems are made up of people, the development of people out of inhuman situations is said to involve cultural rather than political solutions. In this view, the essential requirement is the adoption of proper values, conducive to social mobility within a system that has institutionalized the very values that have made the United States great. Similarly, in the political sphere the solutions to poverty and related problems involve those programs that act upon the situation of the poor, but never relate to the structural problems that create that situation in the first instance. The assumption is that the situation of the poor finds both its explanation and its solution in itself. Because political science avoids consideration of the existential situation of man and the economic and social structures that determine the situation of man, political science is a dehumanized science.

The only remedy against the causes as well as the symptoms of underdevelopment lies in the revolutionary destruction of capitalism and the introduction of socialist development. Strategically, in terms of our analysis, the principal enemy in this struggle is imperialism, but tactically in Latin America the immediate enemy is the native bourgeoisie.

We are indebted to all our colleagues in Latin America who have helped us search for greater ideological and theoretical clarity on the questions of development and underdevelopment, and we hope this book will help others to do the same. But Che Guevara and Camilo Torres, who appreciated this search, also insisted that one be first a revolutionary and then an intellectual. Their examples have inspired us throughout our work. In this spirit, we would like to dedicate our work to Che and Camilo, and to the hundreds of other martyrs of the Latin American Revolution who have given of their lives and intellects to the ever more intense struggle for freedom and development.

New Brunswick, New Jersey
January 2, 1971   J.D.C., A.G.F., and D.L.J.

PART I

DEPENDENCE, IMPERIALISM, AND UNDERDEVELOPMENT

Chapter 1

THE DEVELOPMENT
OF UNDERDEVELOPMENT*

André Gunder Frank

It is generally held that economic development occurs in a succession of capitalist stages and that today's underdeveloped countries are still in a stage, sometimes depicted as an original stage of history, through which the now developed countries passed long ago. Yet even a modest acquaintance with history shows that underdevelopment is not original or traditional and that neither the past nor the present of the underdeveloped countries resembles in any important respect the past of the now developed countries. The now developed countries were never *under*developed, though they may have been *un*developed. It is also widely believed that the contemporary underdevelopment of a country can be understood as the product or reflection solely of its own economic, political, social, and cultural characteristics or structure. Yet historical research demonstrates that contemporary underdevelopment is in large part the historical product of past and continuing economic and other relations between the satellite underdeveloped and the now developed metropolitan countries. Furthermore, these relations are an essential part of the structure and development of the capitalist system on a world scale as a whole. A related and also largely erroneous view is that the development of these underdeveloped countries and, within them of their most underdeveloped domestic areas, must and will be generated

* This chapter is a somewhat abbreviated version of Chapter 1 of *Latin America: Underdevelopment or Revolution,* by André Gunder Frank (New York: Monthly Review Press, 1969). Reprinted by permission of the publisher.

or stimulated by diffusing capital, institutions, values, etc., to them from the international and national capitalist metropoles. Historical perspective based on the underdeveloped countries' past experience suggests that on the contrary in the underdeveloped countries economic development can now occur only independently of most of these relations of diffusion.

Evident inequalities of income and differences in culture have led many observers to see "dual" societies and economies in the underdeveloped countries. Each of the two parts is supposed to have a history of its own, a structure, and a contemporary dynamic largely independent of the other. Supposedly, only one part of the economy and society has been importantly affected by intimate economic relations with the "outside" capitalist world; and that part, it is held, became modern, capitalist, and relatively developed precisely because of this contact. The other part is widely regarded as variously isolated, subsistence-based, feudal, or precapitalist, and therefore more underdeveloped.

I believe on the contrary that the entire "dual society" thesis is false and that the policy recommendations to which it leads will, if acted upon, serve only to intensify and perpetuate the very conditions of underdevelopment they are supposedly designed to remedy.

A mounting body of evidence suggests, and I am confident that future historical research will confirm, that the expansion of the capitalist system over the past centuries effectively and entirely penetrated even the apparently most isolated sectors of the underdeveloped world. Therefore, the economic, political, social, and cultural institutions and relations we now observe there are the products of the historical development of the capitalist system no less than are the seemingly more modern or capitalist features of the national metropoles of these underdeveloped countries. Analogously to the relations between development and underdevelopment on the international level, the contemporary underdeveloped institutions of the so-called backward or feudal domestic areas of an underdeveloped country are no less the product of the single historical process of capitalist development than are the so-called capitalist institutions of the supposedly more progressive areas. In this paper I should like to sketch the kinds of evidence which support this thesis and at the same time indicate lines along which further study and research could fruitfully proceed.

The Secretary General of the Latin American Center for Research in the Social Sciences writes in that Center's journal: "The privileged position of the city has its origin in the colonial period. It was founded by the Conqueror to serve the same ends that it still serves today; to incorporate the indigenous population into the economy brought and developed by that Conqueror and his descendants. The regional city was an instrument of conquest and is still today an instrument of domination."[1] The Instituto Nacional Indigenista (National Indian Institute) of Mexico confirms this observation when it notes that "the mestizo population, in fact, always lives in a city, a center of an intercultural region, which acts as the metropolis of a zone of indigenous population and which maintains with the underdeveloped communities an intimate relation which links the center with the satellite communities."[2] The Institute goes on to point out that "between the mestizos who live in the nuclear city of the region and the Indians who live in the peasant hinterland there is in reality a closer economic and social interdependence than might at first glance appear" and that the provincial metropoles "by being centers of intercourse are also centers of exploitation."[3]

Thus these metropolis-satellite relations are not limited to the imperial or international level but penetrate and structure the very economic, political, and social life of the Latin American colonies and countries. Just as the colonial and national capital and its export sector become the satellite of the Iberian (and later of other) metropoles of the world economic system, this satellite immediately becomes a co-

---

[1] *América Latina,* Año 6, No. 4, October-December 1963, p. 8.
[2] Instituto Nacional Indigenista, *Los centros coordinadores indigenistas,* Mexico, 1962, p. 34.
[3] *Ibid.,* pp. 33–34, 88.

lonial and then a national metropolis with respect to the productive sectors and population of the interior. Furthermore, the provincial capitals, which thus are themselves satellites of the national metropolis—and through the latter of the world metropolis—are in turn provincial centers around which their own local satellites orbit. Thus, a whole chain of constellations of metropoles and satellites relates all parts of the whole system from its metropolitan center in Europe or the United States to the farthest outpost in the Latin American countryside.

When we examine this metropolis-satellite structure, we find that each of the satellites, including now-underdeveloped Spain and Portugal, serves as an instrument to suck capital or economic surplus out of its own satellites and to channel part of this surplus to the world metropolis of which all are satellites. Moreover, each national and local metropolis serves to impose and maintain the monopolistic structure and exploitative relationship of this system (as the Instituto Nacional Indigenista of Mexico calls it) as long as it serves the interests of the metropoles which take advantage of this global, national, and local structure to promote their own development and the enrichment of their ruling classes.

These are the principal and still surviving structural characteristics which were implanted in Latin America by the Conquest. Beyond examining the establishment of this colonial structure in its historical context, the proposed approach calls for study of the development—and underdevelopment—of these metropoles and satellites of Latin America throughout the following and still continuing historical process. In this way we can understand why there were and still are tendencies in the Latin American and world capitalist structure which seem to lead to the development of the metropolis and the underdevelopment of the satellite and why, particularly, the satellitized national, regional, and local metropoles in Latin America find that their economic development is at best a limited or underdeveloped development.

That present underdevelopment of Latin America is the

result of its centuries-long participation in the process of world capitalist development, I believe I have shown in my case studies of the economic and social histories of Chile and Brazil.[4] My study of Chilean history suggests that the Conquest not only incorporated this country fully into the expansion and development of the world mercantile and later industrial capitalist system but that it also introduced the monopolistic metropolis-satellite structure and development of capitalism into the Chilean domestic economy and society itself. This structure then penetrated and permeated all of Chile very quickly. Since that time and in the course of world and Chilean history during the epochs of colonialism, free trade, imperialism, and the present, Chile has become increasingly marked by the economic, social, and political structure of satellite underdevelopment. This development of underdevelopment continues today, both in Chile's still increasing satellitization by the world metropolis and through the ever more acute polarization of Chile's domestic economy.

The history of Brazil is perhaps the clearest case of both national and regional development of underdevelopment. The expansion of the world economy since the beginning of the sixteenth century successively converted the Northeast, the Minas Gerais interior, the North, and the Center-South (Rio de Janeiro, São Paulo, and Paraná) into export economies and incorporated them into the structure and development of the world capitalist system. Each of these regions experienced what may have appeared as economic development during the period of its respective golden age. But it was a satellite development which was neither self-generating nor self-perpetuating. As the market or the productivity of the first three regions declined, foreign and domestic economic interest in them waned; and they were left to develop the underdevelopment they live today. In the fourth region, the coffee economy experienced a similar though not yet

---

[4] "Capitalist Development and Underdevelopment in Chile" and "Capitalist Development and Underdevelopment in Brazil" in *Capitalism and Underdevelopment in Latin America,* Monthly Review Press, 1966; revised edition, 1969.

quite as serious fate (though the development of a synthetic coffee substitute promises to deal it a mortal blow in the not too distant future). All of this historical evidence contradicts the generally accepted theses that Latin America suffers from a dual society or from the survival of feudal institutions and that these are important obstacles to its economic development.

During the First World War, however, and even more during the Great Depression and the Second World War, São Paulo began to build up an industrial establishment which is the largest in Latin America today. The question arises whether this industrial development did or can break Brazil out of the cycle of satellite development and underdevelopment which has characterized its other regions and national history within the capitalist system so far. I believe that the answer is no. Domestically the evidence so far is fairly clear. The development of industry in São Paulo has not brought greater riches to the other regions of Brazil. Instead, it converted them into internal colonial satellites, de-capitalized them further, and consolidated or even deepened their underdevelopment. There is little evidence to suggest that this process is likely to be reversed in the foreseeable future except insofar as the provincial poor migrate and become the poor of the metropolitan cities. Externally, the evidence is that although the initial development of São Paulo's industry was relatively autonomous it is being increasingly satellitized by the world capitalist metropolis and its future development possibilities are increasingly restricted.[5] This development, my studies lead me to believe, also appears destined to remain limited or underdeveloped development as long as it takes place in the present economic, political, and social framework.

We must conclude, in short, that underdevelopment is not due to the survival of archaic institutions and the existence

[5] Also see, "The Growth and Decline of Import Substitution," *Economic Bulletin for Latin America*, New York, IX, No. 1, March 1964; and Celso Furtado, *Dialectica do Desenvolvimiento*, Rio de Janeiro, Fundo de Cultura, 1964.

of capital shortage in regions that have remained isolated from the stream of world history. On the contrary, underdevelopment was and still is generated by the very same historical process which also generated economic development: the development of capitalism itself. This view, I am glad to say, is gaining adherents among students of Latin America and is proving its worth in shedding new light on the problems of the area and in affording a better perspective for the formulation of theory and policy.[6]

The same historical and structural approach can also lead to better development theory and policy by generating a series of hypotheses about development and underdevelopment such as those I am testing in my current research. The hypotheses are derived from the empirical observation and theoretical assumption that within this world-embracing metropolis-satellite structure the metropoles tend to develop and the satellites to underdevelop. The first hypothesis has already been mentioned above: that in contrast to the development of the world metropolis which is no one's satellite, the development of the national and other subordinate metropoles is limited by their satellite status. It is perhaps more difficult to test this hypothesis than the following ones because part of its confirmation depends on the test of the other hypotheses. Nonetheless, this hypothesis appears to be generally confirmed by the non-autonomous and unsatisfactory economic and especially industrial development of Latin America's national metropoles, as documented in the studies already cited. The most important and at the same time most confirmatory examples are the metropolitan regions of Buenos Aires and São Paulo whose growth only began in the

---

[6] Others who use a similar approach, though their ideologies do not permit them to derive the logically following conclusions, are Aníbal Pinto S.C., *Chile: Un caso de desarrollo frustrado,* Santiago, Editorial Universitaria, 1957; Celso Furtado, *A formaçao económica do Brasil,* Rio de Janeiro, Fundo de Cultura, 1959 (recently translated into English and published under the title *The Economic Growth of Brazil* by the University of California Press); and Caio Prado Junior, *Historia Económica do Brasil,* São Paulo, Editora Brasiliense, 7th ed., 1962.

nineteenth century, was therefore largely untrammelled by any colonial heritage, but was and remains a satellite development largely dependent on the outside metropolis, first of Britain and then of the United States.

A second hypothesis is that the satellites experience their greatest economic development and especially their most classically capitalist industrial development if and when their ties to their metropolis are weakest. This hypothesis is almost diametrically opposed to the generally accepted thesis that development in the underdeveloped countries follows from the greatest degree of contact with and diffusion from the metropolitan developed countries. This hypothesis seems to be confirmed by two kinds of relative isolation that Latin America has experienced in the course of its history. One is the temporary isolation caused by the crises of war or depression in the world metropolis. Apart from minor ones, five periods of such major crises stand out and seem to confirm the hypothesis. These are: the European (and especially Spanish) Depression of the seventeenth century, the Napoleonic Wars, the First World War, the Depression of the 1930's, and the Second World War. It is clearly established and generally recognized that the most important recent industrial development—especially of Argentina, Brazil, and Mexico, but also of other countries such as Chile—has taken place precisely during the periods of the two World Wars and the intervening Depression. Thanks to the consequent loosening of trade and investment ties during these periods, the satellites initiated marked autonomous industrialization and growth. Historical research demonstrates that the same thing happened in Latin America during Europe's seventeenth-century depression. Manufacturing grew in the Latin American countries, and several of them such as Chile became exporters of manufactured goods. The Napoleonic Wars gave rise to independence movements in Latin America, and these should perhaps also be interpreted as confirming the development hypothesis in part.

The other kind of isolation which tends to confirm the second hypothesis is the geographic and economic isolation of regions which at one time were relatively weakly tied to and poorly integrated into the mercantilist and capitalist system. My preliminary research suggests that in Latin America it was these regions which initiated and experienced the most promising self-generating economic development of the classical industrial capitalist type. The most important regional cases probably are Tucumán and Asunción, as well as other cities such as Mendoza and Rosario, in the interior of Argentina and Paraguay during the end of the eighteenth and the beginning of the nineteenth centuries. Seventeenth and eighteenth century São Paulo, long before coffee was grown there, is another example. Perhaps Antioquia in Colombia and Puebla and Querétaro in Mexico are other examples. In its own way, Chile was also an example since, before the sea route around the Horn was opened, this country was relatively isolated at the end of the long voyage from Europe via Panama. All of these regions became manufacturing centers and even exporters, usually of textiles, during the periods preceding their effective incorporation as satellites into the colonial, national, and world capitalist system.

Internationally, of course, the classic case of industrialization through non-participation as a satellite in the capitalist world system is obviously that of Japan after the Meiji Restoration. Why, one may ask, was resource-poor but unsatellitized Japan able to industrialize so quickly at the end of the century while resource-rich Latin American countries and Russia were not able to do so and the latter was easily beaten by Japan in the War of 1904 after the same forty years of development efforts? The second hypothesis suggests that the fundamental reason is that Japan was not satellitized either during the Tokugawa or the Meiji period and therefore did not have its development structurally limited as did the countries which were so satellitized.

A corollary of the second hypothesis is that when the metropolis recovers from its crisis and re-establishes the trade and investment ties which fully re-incorporate the satellites into the system, or when the metropolis expands to incorporate previously isolated regions into the world-wide system, the previous development and industrialization of these regions is choked off or channelled into directions which are not self-perpetuating and promising. This happened after each of the five crises cited above. The renewed expansion of trade and the spread of economic liberalism in the eighteenth and nineteenth centuries choked off and reversed the manufacturing development which Latin America had experienced during the seventeenth century, and in some places at the beginning of the nineteenth. After the First World War, the new national industry of Brazil suffered serious consequences from American economic invasion. The increase in the growth rate of Gross National Product and particularly of industrialization throughout Latin America was again reversed and industry became increasingly satellitized after the Second World War and especially after the post-Korean War recovery and expansion of the metropolis. Far from having become more developed since then, industrial sectors of Brazil and most conspicuously of Argentina have become structurally more and more underdeveloped and less and less able to generate continued industrialization and/or sustain development of the economy. This process, from which India also suffers, is reflected in a whole gamut of balance-of-payments, inflationary, and other economic and political difficulties, and promises to yield to no solution short of far-reaching structural change.

Our hypothesis suggests that fundamentally the same process occurred even more dramatically with the incorporation into the system of previously unsatellitized regions. The expansion of Buenos Aires as a satellite of Great Britain and the introduction of free trade in the interest of the ruling groups of both metropoles destroyed the manufacturing and much of the remainder of the economic base of the previously relatively prosperous interior almost entirely. Manufacturing was destroyed by foreign competition, lands were taken and concentrated into latifundia by the rapaciously growing export economy, intraregional distribution of income became much more unequal, and the previously developing regions became simple satellites of Buenos Aires and through it of London. The provincial centers did not yield to satellitization without a struggle. This metropolis-satellite conflict was much of the cause of the long political and armed struggle between the Unitarists in Buenos Aires and the Federalists in the provinces, and it may be said to have been the sole important cause of the War of the Triple Alliance in which Buenos Aires, Montevideo, and Rio de Janeiro, encouraged and helped by London, destroyed not only the autonomously developing economy of Paraguay but killed off nearly all of its population which was unwilling to give in. Though this is no doubt the most spectacular example which tends to confirm the hypothesis, I believe that historical research on the satellitization of previously relatively independent yeoman-farming and incipient manufacturing regions such as the Caribbean islands will confirm it further.[7] These regions did not have a chance against the forces of expanding and developing capitalism, and their own development had to be sacrificed to that of others. The economy and industry of Argentina, Brazil, and other countries which have experienced the effects of metropolitan recovery since the Second World War are today suffering much the same fate, if fortunately still in lesser degree.

A third major hypothesis derived from the metropolis-satellite structure is that the regions which are the most underdeveloped and feudal-seeming today are the ones which had the closest ties to the metropolis in the past. They are the regions which were the greatest exporters of primary products to and the biggest sources of capital for the world metropolis and which were abandoned by the metropolis when for one reason or another business fell off. This hypothesis also contradicts the generally held thesis that the source of a region's underdevelopment is its isolation and its pre-capitalist institutions.

[7] See for instance Ramón Guerra y Sánchez, *Azúcar y Población en las Antillas,* Havana 1942, 2nd ed., also published as *Sugar and Society in the Caribbean,* New Haven, Yale University Press, 1964.

This hypothesis seems to be amply confirmed by the former super-satellite development and present ultra-underdevelopment of the once sugar-exporting West Indies, Northeastern Brazil, the ex-mining districts of Minas Gerais in Brazil, highland Peru, and Bolivia, and the central Mexican states of Guanajuato, Zacatecas, and others whose names were made world famous centuries ago by their silver. There surely are no major regions in Latin America which are today more cursed by underdevelopment and poverty; yet all of these regions, like Bengal in India, once provided the life blood of mercantile and industrial capitalist development— in the metropolis. These regions' participation in the development of the world capitalist system gave them, already in their golden age, the typical structure of underdevelopment of a capitalist export economy. When the market for their sugar or the wealth of their mines disappeared and the metropolis abandoned them to their own devices, the already existing economic, political, and social structure of these regions prohibited autonomous generation of economic development and left them no alternative but to turn in upon themselves and to degenerate into the ultra-underdevelopment we find there today.

These considerations suggest two further and related hypotheses. One is that the latifundium, irrespective of whether it appears as a plantation or a hacienda today, was typically born as a commercial enterprise which created for itself the institutions which permitted it to respond to increased demand in the world or national market by expanding the amount of its land, capital, and labor and to increase the supply of its products. The fifth hypothesis is that the latifundia which appear isolated, subsistence-based, and semi-feudal today saw the demand for their products or their productive capacity decline and that they are to be found principally in the above-named former agricultural and mining export regions whose economic activity declined in general. These two hypotheses run counter to the notions of most people, and even to the opinions of some historians and other students of the subject, according to whom the historical roots and socio-economic causes of Latin American latifundia and agrarian institutions are to be found in the transfer of feudal institutions from Europe and/or in economic depression.

The evidence to test these hypotheses is not open to easy general inspection and requires detailed analyses of many cases. Nonetheless, some important confirmatory evidence is available. The growth of the latifundium in nineteenth-century Argentina and Cuba is a clear case in support of the fourth hypothesis and can in no way be attributed to the transfer of feudal institutions during colonial times. The same is evidently the case of the post-revolutionary and contemporary resurgence of latifundia particularly in the North of Mexico, which produce for the American market, and of similar ones on the coast of Peru and the new coffee regions of Brazil. The conversion of previously yeoman—farming Caribbean islands, such as Barbados, into sugar-exporting economies at various times between the seventeenth and twentieth centuries and the resulting rise of the latifundia in these islands would seem to confirm the fourth hypothesis as well. In Chile, the rise of the latifundium and the creation of the institutions of servitude which later came to be called feudal occurred in the eighteenth century and have been conclusively shown to be the result of and response to the opening of a market for Chilean wheat in Lima.[8] Even the growth and consolidation of the latifundium in seventeenth-century Mexico—which most expert students have attributed to a depression of the economy caused by the decline of mining and a shortage of Indian labor and to a consequent turning in upon itself and ruralization of the economy—occurred at a time when urban population and demand were growing, food shortages became acute, food prices skyrocketed, and the profitability of other economic activities such as mining

[8] Mario Góngora, *Origen de los "inquilinos" de Chile central*, Santiago, Editorial Universitaria, 1960; Jean Borde and Mario Góngora, *Evolución de la propiedad rural en el Valle del Puango*, Santiago, Instituto de Sociología de la Universidad de Chile; Sergio Sepúlveda, *El trigo chileno en el mercado mundial*. Santiago, Editorial Universitaria, 1959.

and foreign trade declined.[9] All of these and other factors rendered hacienda agriculture more profitable. Thus, even this case would seem to confirm the hypothesis that the growth of the latifundium and its feudal-seeming conditions of servitude in Latin America has always been and still is the commercial response to increased demand and that it does not represent the transfer or survival of alien institutions that have remained beyond the reach of capitalist development. The emergence of latifundia, which today really are more or less (though not entirely) isolated, might then be attributed to the causes advanced in the fifth hypothesis—i.e., the decline of previously profitable agricultural enterprises whose capital was, and whose currently produced economic surplus still is, transferred elsewhere by owners and merchants who frequently are the same persons or families. Testing this hypothesis requires still more detailed analysis, some of which I have undertaken in a study on Brazilian agriculture.[10]

All of these hypotheses and studies suggest that the global extension and unity of the capitalist system, its monopoly structure and uneven development throughout its history, and the resulting persistence of commercial rather than industrial capitalism in the underdeveloped world (including its most industrially advanced countries) deserve much more

[9] Woodrow Borah makes depression the centerpiece of his explanation in "New Spain's Century of Depression," *Ibero-Americana*, Berkeley, No. 35, 1951. François Chevalier speaks of turning in upon itself in the most authoritative study of the subject, "La formación de los grandes latifundios en México," Mexico, *Problemas Agrícolas e Industriales de México*, VIII, No. 1, 1956 (translated from the French and recently published by the University of California Press). The data which provide the basis for my contrary interpretation are supplied by these authors themselves. This problem is discussed in my "Con qué modo de producción convierte la gallina maíz en huevos de oro?" *El Gallo Ilustrado*, Suplemento de *El Día*, Mexico, Nos. 175 and 179, October 31 and November 28, 1965; and it is further analyzed in a study of Mexican agriculture under preparation by the author.

[10] "Capitalism and the Myth of Feudalism in Brazilian Agriculture," in *Capitalism and Underdevelopment in Latin America*, cited in footnote 4 above.

attention in the study of economic development and cultural change than they have hitherto received. Though science and truth know no national boundaries, it is probably new generations of scientists from the underdeveloped countries themselves who most need to, and best can, devote the necessary attention to these problems and clarify the process of underdevelopment and development. It is their people who in the last analysis face the task of changing this no longer acceptable process and eliminating this miserable reality.

Chapter 2

ECONOMIC DEPENDENCE, CLASS STRUCTURE, AND UNDERDEVELOPMENT POLICY

André Gunder Frank

This chapter is an attempt (1) to clarify how the historical development of the world capitalist system has subjected Latin America (as well as Asia and Africa) to an ever-increasing degree of colonial or neocolonial *economic subordination*; (2) to show how this colonial relationship with the capitalist metropolis has created and transformed, over time, *the domestic economic and class structure* of Latin American society; (3) to argue why this economic and class structure has occasioned *political, economic, social, and cultural policies* which in the past, present, and foreseeable future result in the development of underdevelopment in general, and the underdevelopment of development in particular instances in Latin America; and (4) to conclude that this historical process of underdevelopment cannot be reversed and turned into economic and social development for the majority of the Latin American people until they destroy the capitalist class structure through revolution and replace it with socialist development.

Dependence. The point of departure for any credible analysis of Latin American reality must be its fundamental determinant, which Latin Americans have come to recognize and now call *dependence*. This dependence is the result of the historical development and contemporary structure of world capitalism, to which Latin America is subordinated, and the economic, political, social, and cultural policies generated by the resulting class structure, especially by the class interests of the dominant bourgeoisie. It is important to understand, therefore, that throughout the historical process, dependence is not simply an "external" relation between Latin America and its world capitalist metropolis but equally an "internal," indeed *integral,* condition of Latin American society itself, which is reflected not only in international and domestic economics and politics but also has the most profound and far-reaching ideological and psychological manifestations of inferiority complexes and assimilation of metropolitan ideology and "development" theory. At the same time, this dependence generates reactions which are visible through nationalism, the growing class struggle against the capitalist system, and the development of scientific social analysis which places itself at the service of nationalist and class-liberation movements by disassociating itself from metropolitan tutelage and bourgeois ideology.

We may proceed, then, to examine each of the major historical and contemporary processes of the development of underdevelopment in Latin America through metropolitan, colonial economic determination of the domestic economic and class structure, and, through the latter, of the national economic and political policies that generate underdevelopment. To obtain historical perspective, we may arrange this examination more or less in chronological order, beginning with the discovery and colonization of America. If we sometimes rely on quotations, we shall (except in minor instances) take care to cite only the most unimpeachable testimony of participants in, or authoritative contemporary witnesses of, the events under examination.

Mercantile Capitalism. Christopher Columbus once declared, "the best thing in the world is gold . . . it can even send souls to heaven." Hernán Cortés, conqueror of Mexico, later said, "The Spaniards are troubled with a disease of the heart for which the specific remedy is gold." The Franciscan friars and Bishop Mota y Escobar confirmed, "where there are no Indians, there is no silver" and "where there is no silver, religion does not enter." Looking back in 1776, Adam Smith reconfirmed the same in his *Inquiry into the Nature and Causes of the Wealth of Nations,* where he wrote "Of the Motives for Establishing New Colonies":

Columbus turned his view towards their minerals; and in the richness of the production . . . he found full compensation. . . . As a result of the representations of Columbus, the Council of Castile determined to take possession of countries in which the inhabitants were plainly incapable of defending themselves. The pious purpose of converting them to Christianity sanctified the injustice of the project. But the hope of finding treasures of gold there was the sole motive which prompted them to undertake it. . . . All the other enterprises of the Spaniards in the New World, subsequent to those of Columbus, seem to have been prompted by the same motive. It was their thirst for gold . . . that carried Cortés to Mexico, and Almargo and Pizzarro to Chile and Peru. . . .

In another chapter, Adam Smith continues this thought:

The East Indies is another market for the produce of the silver mines of America, and a market which, from the time of the discovery of these mines, has been taking off a greater and greater quantity of silver. Since that time, direct trade between America and the East Indies, which is carried on by means of the Acapulco ships, has been continually augmenting, and indirect intercourse by way of Europe has been augmenting in a still greater proportion. . . . In the East Indies, particularly in China and Indostan, the value of the precious metals, when the Europeans first began to trade to those countries, was much higher than in Europe and it still continues to be so. . . . The silver of the new continent seems in this manner to be one of the principal commodities by which the commerce between the two extremities of the old one is carried on, and it is by means of it, in great measure, that these distant parts of the world are connected with one another. (Smith, pp. 528–29, 204–7)[1]

Colonial Class Structure. These witnesses attest to the early formation of a literally world-embracing mercantile capitalist system. The discovery of the New World fully integrated Latin America into the historical process of world capitalist development. The Conquest also imposed upon Latin Amer-

---

[1] A list of references appears at the end of this chapter.

ica an economically subordinate colonial relationship, whose fundamental characteristics and mechanisms survive to this day. As their religious mentors noted, the indigenous populations were primarily mobilized into the production of gold and silver, or later sugar, for export, and secondarily into the production of foodstuffs and equipment to support the export economy. For as the friars said, without Indians—or in their absence black slaves imported by the metropolis from Africa —there could be no silver production, not only because the Indians supplied the labor and generated the capital, but also because they contributed most of the necessary technology and social organization, all of which the metropolitans lacked. This process of production imposed upon Latin America necessarily gave rise to a resident commercial *and productive* bourgeoisie, which directed this process and shared its benefits in economic and political alliance with the metropolis. In the resulting Latin American economic and class structure, the fruits of the vast majority of labor were immediately appropriated by the small commercial and productive bourgeois minority. Being a subordinate and dependent bourgeoisie from the very start, the latter remitted a major part of these fruits in the form of capital transfers to the metropolis overseas, where they were eventually invested in metropolitan economic development. (We will observe later that, through exploitative exchange of raw materials for manufactures and remittances of profits and interest, this flow of capital from Latin America to the metropolis has continued to increase until today.)

And what happened to the capital surplus remaining in the hands of the resident bourgeoisie, capital that potentially could be invested in economic development? The colonial structure had created a high profitability of production for export and an unequal distribution of income at home, and the consequent class structure deprived the majority in Latin America of adequate purchasing power and rendered production for the domestic market relatively unprofitable. Therefore, the domestic bourgeoisie used the remaining capital surplus for reinvestment, to expand the export productive apparatus, or to import capital goods for the same purpose and some luxury goods for the bourgeoisie's own consumption. Thus, unlike the metropolitan bourgeoisie, the Latin American bourgeoisie did not construct or invest in a productive apparatus or create a social organization capable of generating self-sustained economic development. Instead, the colonial bourgeoisie automatically made the development of underdevelopment in Latin America into a self-re-enforcing part of the historical process of world capitalist development for as long as its metropolitan capitalist senior partner was willing and able to maintain the fundamental colonial relationship. This colonial relationship, with some local and temporal exceptions to be noted in what follows, has persisted until today.

Development of Underdevelopment. The colonial capitalist relationship, the Latin American socioeconomic structure and bourgeois political economic policy, though so far fundamentally stable, are not static. On the contrary, the uneven process of world capitalist development, the economically, technologically, and politically changing requirements of the capitalist metropolis, and the varying possibilities of Latin American responses have occasioned constant modifications in the forms of the colonial relationship, class structure, bourgeois policy, and rates, degrees, and forms of Latin American underdevelopment.

Thus, the discovery of gold, silver, copper, or other mines; the rise in world or domestic demand and price of sugar, cotton, wheat, or meat; the technological invention of better means of transportation, more efficient productive processes or bigger mills and factories; all these and other modifications of the colonial relationship have generated sudden export booms, which resulted in a new or activated regional mining and/or agricultural complex. Similarly, the subsequent exhaustion of the ores, or the increased cost of their extraction; the decline or shift in demand for an agricultural export good; the erosion or exhaustion of the soil; the decline in the labor force because of epidemics, overwork, or limited immigration; or the invasion of cheaper metropolitan manufactures, have turned the previous boom town or region into a degenerated ultraunderdeveloped social complex, whose inherited colonial class structure, not to mention its sometimes exhausted natural resources, no longer permit any sustained development. Thus, the most underdeveloped regions of Latin America today, which are characterized not only by their extreme poverty but also by their obscurantist dominant culture, fundamentalist religion, and corrupt ultra-reactionary politics, are all regions that developed during export booms of agricultural and mining products or labor —regions such as the Brazilian Northeast, the Caribbean, Central America, southern Mexico, and the former mining regions of central Mexico, Minas Gerais in Brazil, and highland Peru and Bolivia.

Latifundium Agriculture. A particularly revealing aspect of the colonial capitalist development of the domestic class structure is the growth of the *latifundium* and the formation of the modes of production in Latin American agriculture. In this regard, we may examine the example of seventeenth-century Barbados, which, after the sixteenth-century establishment of the sugar *latifundium* in the Brazilian Northeast, became the next important sugar colony. The case of Barbados is particularly instructive because, unlike Brazil, it represents the dramatic transformation of an already existing society and because we have contemporary testimony, which is cited in 1926 by Vincent Harlow in his *History of Barbados 1625–1685*.

In the days when a variety of small crops were grown, the land was occupied in small holdings by a large number of tenants. This system, usual in most young British colonies, was partly the result of the original grants of small allotments to the first settlers. . . . In this way the island was possessed of a numerous and sturdy "yeoman" class, who were indeed the backbone of the colony. With the advent of the sugar industry this healthy condition of affairs was altered. Sugar planting to be successful requires large acres of land and a plentiful supply of cheap labour; the Dutch system of long credits provided the more affluent with means to obtain both.

But the small planter with his few acres and little capital could not face the considerable initial expense of setting up a sugar factory. The land in consequence fell more and more into the hands of a coterie of magnates . . . An example of the process was to be found in Captain Waterman's estate, comprising 800 acres, which at one time had been split up among no less than forty proprietors. Emphasizing the same fact . . . is the land value belonging to Major Hilliard. Before the introduction of the new manufacture the plantation was worth 400 pounds; yet in 1643 no less than 12,000 "good men" had left the island for other plantations, and the number of landowners had decreased from 11,200 smallholders in 1645 to 745 owners of large estates in 1667; while during the same period the Negroes had increased from 5,680 to 82,023. Finally he summed up the situation by saying that in 1668 the island "was not half so strong, and forty times as rich as in the year 1645." This twofold process [comments Harlow] whereby a sturdy English colony was converted into little more than a sugar factory owned by a few absentee proprietors and worked by a mass of alien labour constitutes the main feature of Barbadian history. (Harlow, pp. 40–44, 306–10)

And, we may add, it illustrates the fundamentals of the capitalist colonial formation of the rural class structure and mode of production in all of Latin America throughout its history, including the present.

A succinct analysis of this process was provided in 1911 by Lauro Viadas, the General Director of Agriculture who had supervised much of the three decades of *latifundium* growth and mass impoverishment that preceded the Mexican Revolution of 1910–17:

Agriculture is, before and above all else, a business, and in every business the amount and safety of the profits are what determine the character of the enterprise. . . . If the large rural properties continue to exist it is because they are the logical consequence of the state of evolution of agriculture in our country, and they will have to continue to exist for the same reason, in spite of the firmest and best-intentioned plans, as long as those obstacles which hamper our agrarian progress are not removed. Large-scale agriculture asserts itself and excludes small-scale family agriculture; it takes possession of the land, attracted, and I would say strongly attracted, by economic advantages that spring from the two following causes: (1) The high price of the means of livelihood. . . . The high price of these goods leads first to a high profit for the growers and subsequently, a high price for arable land, which places it within the reach only of capitalist entrepreneurs. (2) The cheapness of labor, which reduces, relatively if not absolutely, the cost of production and produces, thereby, the above-mentioned effect of raising agricultural profits . . . (Viadas)

These two principal factors, the high price of land and its products, and the low price of labor, have been the principal causes for the growth and survival of the *latifundium*, everywhere and at all times since colonization in Latin America. The stimulus has always been the colonial relation of Latin America with the international metropolis. This occurs either directly, by instigating agricultural production for export, or indirectly, through the demand for agricultural products generated by the colonial mining or urban economy subordinated to the metropolis. Thus, in Mexico during the sixteenth and seventeenth centuries the *hacienda* and its later misnamed feudal productive relations replaced the earlier *encomienda, catequil,* and small-scale farming as the dominant mode of agricultural production, when entrepreneurs shifted their capital out of the declining mining industry and into agriculture because the rising costs of mining and the rising prices of food rendered agriculture both relatively and absolutely more profitable. But in the face of a shortage of labor created by epidemics, this potential profit could only be realized by replacing the former productive relations with the institution of the *hacienda*—which was not imported from Spain but was created by the colonial relationship. In the next chapter, we shall see how *hacienda* agriculture in Mexico perpetuated these colonial relationships, shaped rural class structure, welcomed modern capitalist techniques, and further impoverished the peasantry while extending the reign of the *latifundium* in the nineteenth century.

In Chile, the *encomienda* survived a century longer than in Mexico and Peru, and the *catequil* or *mita* was never introduced. The *encomienda* survived longer in Chile because there was no high civilization there to begin with and there were relatively few mines and little demand for labor. In Chile, then, the *hacienda* and its misnamed feudal mode of production did not become dominant until the eighteenth and nineteenth centuries, when foreign demand for Chilean wheat generated the monopolization of land in *latifundia* and the conversion of previous small holders or low-rent-paying independent agricultural producers into agricultural peons called *inquilinos*. During the nineteenth and twentieth centuries, in Argentina, Brazil, and Cuba, the concentrations of land ownership and the various modes of agricultural production were direct local responses to increasing world demand and technological progress in processing and transporting wheat and meat, coffee, and sugar, respectively. Essentially the same may be said for the sugar and cotton *latifundia* of coastal Peru, the coffee *latifundia* of Venezuela, Colombia, and Central America, and, of course, the "banana republics."

Colonial capitalist growth of the *latifundium* and its institutions is not a now-bygone historical phenomenon. This is dramatically proved by the contemporary state of agriculture in Mexico, after a revolution that cost two million lives and after the most extensive bourgeois agricultural reform in Latin America. A recent book, *Neolatifundismo y Explotación*, points out that:

> The impact of foreign demand appears clearly in the following statistics: in 1940 agricultural products were about 10.3% of total exports, whereas in 1945 this proportion was nearly 21%. . . . After 1940 when, during the war, American demand for Mexican agricultural products increases again, (1) Agricultural development depends more on external forces (demand and supply of inputs) than on the domestic market. (2) The best

lands, the irrigated ones and the other resources, like capital, labor, credit and physical inputs, begin to concentrate themselves in certain regions and in the hands of a few owners. (3) That growth opens the doors to foreign capital, which begins the process of control of national agriculture. (4) Agrarian products begin to constitute the base of Mexico's trade balance, on the side of exports . . . (5) The economic policy of the country, and especially the monetary and fiscal policy, far from contributing to the elimination of the miserable living conditions of the rural population and liberating it from exploitation, support the monopolization of the land and the exploitation of human labor. (6) This same policy helps generate the grave inequality in distribution of income. These tendencies become even stronger in the last decade. . . . "encouraged" by the Korean War, the international market maintained attractive prices on principal export crops: cotton, coffee, and tomatoes. . . . It is necessary to emphasize, then that the minifundium really constitutes 86% of the units of production. . . . In 1960, two per cent of the farms accounted for 70.1% of the value of sales. To get an idea of the acute degree of concentration suffered in agriculture, it is well to note that in the United States 10% of the farms generated 40% of the sales, and it is said that this already is a high degree of concentration.

This means that agriculture is a wonderful business for a very few people, while the large majority of the working population lives under very poor conditions. More than 55% of the farms counted by the 1960 census had sales below 1,000 pesos [80 dollars]. . . . Between 1950 and 1960 . . . the number of those employed in agriculture who do not manage their own farming increases by 60%, rising from two million to more than 3.3 million. This means that in 1960 the agricultural population without land is greater in absolute numbers than in 1930 and also than in 1910, and that it now accounts for more than half of the total agricultural population. (Stavenhagen, *et al.*, pp. 75–78, 86–87, 30–31)

The inevitable conclusion of any serious analysis such as

that of the authors of *Neolatifundismo y Explotación* is that despite the land reform

> the agricultural problem in Mexico is today more complex and in some respects undoubtedly more serious, than when the Army of the South launched into battle under the flag of Emiliano Zapata more than half a century ago. The concentration of land and of other productive resources in new forms and the foreign control exercised by Anderson Clayton & Co. are facts that converge and join each other in one single fact: the increasing exploitation of the enormous masses of peasants. . . . The neo-latifundism is not an isolated phenomenon and cannot be attributed to circumstantial factors: the peculiarities of a landowner, the dishonesty of some official, the lack of adequate personnel of this or that government department. Neo-latifundism is simply the natural result of the present structure of power, that is, of the class structure in the country. (Stavenhagen, *et al.*, back cover, p. 19)

Formal Independence. Independence came in the years 1810–20 when Spain and Portugal, occupied by Napoleon's armies, found it impossible to sustain their colonial controls over their American possessions. But this change in the colonial relationship was only the culmination of an historical process that had begun long before. Since the British destruction of the Spanish Armada in 1588 and the economic colonization and deindustrialization of Portugal through various treaties, culminating in that of Methuen in 1703, Britain had virtually eliminated the participation of the Iberian countries in world capitalist economic development. But Britain, and France until Napoleon's defeat by Britain, had increasingly come to dominate the trade not only of Spain and Portugal but also of their American colonies. This trade offered opportunities of profit to Latin American producers and exporters of raw materials and importers of manufactured goods, and they took increasing advantage of the new circumstances. In a vain attempt to counter this already inevitable historical development, and to recuperate more of the trade for themselves, Spain and Portugal liberalized their trade regulations for their colonies during the last third of the eighteenth century. But it was too late and only accelerated the tide they sought to stem.

Increased trade generated further profits from Latin American exports and strengthened the economic power and political ambitions of that sector of the Latin American bourgeoisie which produced raw materials. Simultaneously, the flood of cheap metropolitan manufactures into Latin America stifled local manufactures which had grown up during the metropolitan depression of the seventeenth century. Accordingly, when the political crisis in the metropolis offered the opportunity, some sectors of the Latin American bourgeoisie took advantage of it to capture state power and to formulate policies in their own interest. Of course, this political independence from Spain and Portugal did not automatically signify economic independence from Britain, many of whose capitalists lent aid to the Latin American fight for independence, and it did not fundamentally alter the class structure in Latin America. On the contrary, many sectors of the Latin American productive bourgeoisie had wrested state power from Iberia and eliminated its commercial intermediaries precisely in order to strengthen their trade relations with Britain.

Civil War. The ascendancy of Great Britain and the political independence of Latin America after the Napoleonic Wars left three major interest groups to define the future of Latin America: (1) the Latin American agricultural, mining, and commercial interests, who sought to maintain the export economy structure, and whose only modification would be to substitute themselves for their Iberian rivals, in privileged positions; (2) the industrial and other interest groups from the interior regions, who sought to defend their budding but still weak economies from more free trade and foreign finance, which threatened to force them out of existence; and (3) the victorious and industrializing British, whose foreign minister, Lord Canning, noted in 1824, "Spanish America is free; and if we do not mismanage our affairs, she is English." The battle lines were drawn, with the traditional Latin American import-export bourgeoisie and the metropolitan bourgeoisies in natural alliance against the weak Latin American provincial and industrial nationalists. The outcome was practically predetermined by the past historical process of capitalist development.

During the period from 1825 to 1860 the nationalist interests from the interior were still able to force their governments to impose protective tariffs in many countries. Industry, national flag shipping, and other development-generating activities showed spurts of life. At the same time, Latin Americans themselves rehabilitated old mines and opened new ones. They began to develop the export sectors in agricultural and other primary goods. To expand the internal market and promote economic development, the Liberals pressed for land and other reforms. Simultaneously, to respond to the growing external demand for raw materials, they encouraged immigration to increase the domestic labor force.

Latin America's export-import bourgeoisie and their mining and agricultural allies opposed this autonomous capitalist development because, with tariff protection, it took place at the expense of their export-import interests. They fought and defeated the provincial and industrial nationalists, who claimed the protection of federal states' rights, in the Federalist-Unitarist civil wars of the thirties and forties. The metropolitan powers aided their Latin American junior trade partners with arms, naval blockades, and, where necessary, direct military intervention. They even helped by instigating new wars, such as that of the Triple Alliance against Paraguay. This war cost Paraguay six-sevenths of its male population in the defense of its nationally financed railroad and genuinely autonomous economic development.

If we must look for bourgeois democratic revolution and industrialization efforts in Latin America at all, we should do so during the period roughly between 1825 and 1860. During this period almost all of Latin America experienced a series of civil wars. On the one side were the Federalists, provincialists, manufacturers, economic and political nationalists, and Liberals (but not free traders); on the other side,

Unitarists, domestic metropolises (usually port cities), exporters, importers, agriculturalists, free traders, Conservatives, and the English or French metropolis. The latter triumphed, first in the political and military field, then in the economic one. They crushed or deflected what might be called the bourgeois democratic revolution of Rosas in Argentina (before this Federalist changed to what in essence became a Unitarist and giveaway policy), of Francia and López in Paraguay, Rengifo and Balmaceda in Chile, Mauá and Nabuco in Brazil, etc. This frustrated the development of national capitalism in such areas as the Argentine provinces, Paraguay, parts of Chile, São Paulo in Brazil, Antioquia in Colombia, and Querétaro and Puebla in Mexico.

Free Trade. Trade and the sword were readying Latin America for metropolitan free trade. To succeed, the metropolis had to eliminate autonomous Latin American industrial development. With the victory of the outward-oriented economic interest groups over the inward-oriented ones, ever more of the Latin American economy and state had to be subordinated to the metropolis. Only then would trade become free and would foreign finance again come into its own. A contemporary Argentinian nationalist noted, "After 1810 . . . the country's balance of trade had been consistently unfavourable, and at the same time native merchants had suffered irreparable losses. Both wholesale export trade and retail import commerce had passed into foreign hands. The conclusion seems inescapable, therefore, that the opening of the country to foreigners proved harmful on balance. Foreigners displaced natives not only in commerce but in industry and agriculture as well." (Quoted in Burgin, p. 234). Another added:

It is not possible that Buenos Aires should have sacrificed blood and wealth solely for the purpose of becoming a consumer of the products and manufacture of foreign countries, for such is degrading and does not correspond to the great potentialities which nature has bestowed upon the country. . . . It is erroneous to assume that protection breeds monopoly. The fact is that

Argentina which has been under a regime of free trade for over twenty years is now controlled by a handful of foreigners. If protection was going to dislodge foreign merchants from their positions of economic preeminence, the country would have occasion to congratulate itself on making the first step toward regaining its economic independence. . . . The nation cannot continue without restricting foreign trade, since restriction alone would make industrial expansion possible; it must no longer endure the weight of foreign monopoly which strangles every attempt at industrialization. (Burgin, p. 234)

But it did.

Free trade between the strong metropolis and the weak Latin American countries produced a balance-of-payments deficit for the latter. To finance the deficit, the satellite governments accepted the offer of foreign finance from the metropolis; and in the 1850s foreign loans again began to make their presence felt in Latin America. They did not eliminate the deficits, of course. They only financed and necessarily increased the payments of deficits and underdevelopment in Latin America. It was not uncommon in those days, any more than it is today, for a Latin American country to devote 50 percent of export earnings to financing its debt to foreigners, on behalf of the continued economic development of the metropolis.

In Latin America, the foreign deficit and financing resulted in continuation of an automatic gold standard, of forced paper currency devaluation, and of domestic inflation. This increased the capital flow from Latin America to the metropolis, since Latin America had to pay more for foreign manufactures and the metropolis less for raw materials. In nineteenth-century Latin America, as today, devaluation and inflation further benefited the native and foreign merchants and property owners at the expense of those whose labor produced the wealth, robbing artisans, workers, and peasants not only of their real income but also of their small land and other property. Thus, the development of industrial capitalism increasingly opened Latin America to free trade, and transformed the economic, political, and social structure of the continent to suit the new metropolitan needs and local bourgeois convenience.

Liberal Reform. Liberal reforms in the middle of the nineteenth century are generally interpreted (by the Liberals of then and today) as a major transformation of domestic society which was stimulated by a wave of ideological enlightenment coming from the metropolis. The metropolitan influence is undeniable, but it was not simply ideological or cultural. And Latin American acceptance of this ideology, like that of free trade, was not due simply to the logic or inherent attractiveness of Liberal ideas. On the contrary, the Liberal reforms occurred at a time when new metropolitan demands were sharply accelerating the production and export of Latin American foodstuffs and raw materials to the metropolis, and not because Liberal ideas had some time earlier arrived from overseas.

Sanctified by the supposed superiority of private property over the corporate property of the Catholic Church and the communal property of the Indians, the Liberal reforms expropriated the lands of both groups. Both the Church and the Indians were deprived of their lands to a degree far greater than in Spanish colonial times. The land rapidly became concentrated into the hands of a few private farmers and land speculators and eventually into the hands of a small number of foreign and domestic private corporations. The massive loss of lands, as in white-settler Africa soon thereafter, forced the indigenous population to work as peons in the rapidly expanding agricultural and mining export enterprises.

Liberal reforms took place at different times in different countries. We may hazard the perhaps oversimplified hypothesis that the Liberal reform in any particular country did not occur simply when Liberal ideas arrived there, but when the new mono-export production of coffee, sugar, meat, wheat, cotton, or tin had expanded sufficiently to account for, say, over 50 percent of total national exports. Although some people may have long wanted the Liberal reform, for ideological reasons, it is this metropolis-stimulated expansion of Latin American export production that in each country gave certain sectors of the bourgeoisie the economic and political leverage to undertake the Liberal reform. And now the Liberals converted the word "feudalism" into a red flag with which to combat their Conservative opponents. To my knowledge this hypothesis has not been tested because it has not been previously advanced. But examination of the historical experience in Central America would seem to confirm it.

In Guatemala, coffee production began in 1856, and by 1875 coffee was already the principal export product; Liberal reform occurred in 1871–73. In El Salvador, coffee became the main export product in 1880, and the Liberal revolution took place in 1885. In Costa Rica, where coffee had become the principal export product before 1860, the Liberal dictatorship began in 1858 and lasted until 1868. In contrast, Honduras never became an important coffee exporter, and there the attempted Liberal revolution failed altogether; when Liberal reforms were introduced in 1876 they were on a very limited scale. In Nicaragua, which never became a major exporter but toward the end of the century offered the most likely route for the interoceanic canal (before it was finally built in Panama), the Liberal revolution occurred in 1892. In Mexico, export and land prices already had begun to rise in 1851, before the most famous Liberal reforms occurred in 1857. (Torres, pp. 21–50)

In each of these cases, of course, the Liberal reform served to accelerate the very economic process that had stimulated it in the first place. Once in power, the Liberals associated themselves ever more with the trade and foreign capital of the developing imperialist metropolis, which was (and is) their natural ally. This policy of alliance with the metropolis created grave economic problems of underdevelopment, which in turn generated political tensions at home and required domination through dictatorial repression. It was the Liberals themselves—who only shortly before had fought the Conservatives in the name of liberty—who now were the first to resort to repression to serve their own interests, as was most notoriously the case in the Mexico of Porfirio Díaz and in the coffee, sugar, and banana republics of the Caribbean and Central America. It would be necessary to study the Bolivian, Peruvian, Colombian, Venezuelan, and other cases to confirm or refine the hypothesis. But if it is confirmed by historical fact, it suggests that like the "reform" of independence in 1820, all significant bourgeois reformist movements in Latin America, including those of our own times, are the superstructural consequences of colonially determined economic changes, which these political reforms are designed to, and effectively do, accelerate.

Imperialism. Thus was the way paved for the emergence of imperialism and its new forms of foreign investment emanating from the metropolis into Latin America. Together with free trade, Liberal land and other reforms had concentrated land into fewer hands, had created a larger agricultural and unemployed labor force, and had brought forth Latin American governments dependent on the metropolis. These governments now opened the door not only to more metropolitan trade but also to the new imperialist investment financiers who were quick to take advantage of Latin America's increased economic dependence.

The new metropolitan demand for raw materials, and the profitability to Latin America's bourgeoisie in this area, caused Latin American governments to expand the infrastructure necessary for export production. In Brazil, Argentina, Paraguay, Chile, Guatemala, and Mexico (to the author's knowledge, but probably in other countries as well), domestic or national capital built the first railroads. In Chile, national capital opened up the nitrate and copper mines that were to become the world's principal supplier of commercial fertilizers and red metal; in Brazil, the coffee plantations that supplied nearly all the world's tables; and similarly elsewhere. Only after these proved to be booming businesses—and after Britain had to find outlets for its steel—did foreign capital enter into these sectors and, eventually, take over their ownership and management. They were able to outcompete and eventually to buy out the Latin American enterprises, often with the assistance of "smart" Latin American capital.

The significance and "profitability" of imperialist foreign investment lie not in the enormous net earnings of such investment, however calculated, but in their place in capitalist development and underdevelopment. Imperialist finance directed a large net flow of capital from the poor underdeveloped Latin American countries to the rich developed ones of the metropolis *even at the height of Lenin's "capital export" imperialism.* Cairncross estimates Britain's export of capital at 2400 million pounds and the income from its investments at 4000 million pounds between 1870 and 1913 (Cairncross, p. 180). Latin America supplied the metropolis with needed industrial raw materials and cheap food for British workers at terms of trade ever more favorable to the metropolis, which helped to depress British wages and maintain profits while providing foreign markets for capital equipment and consumer goods. Latin America thus helped the British capitalists to maintain their monopoly prices and high profits while exerting further pressure on real wages.

In Latin America, this same imperialist trade and finance did more than increase the amount of production, trade, and profit by accumulating about 10,000 million dollars (U.S.) of investment capital there. The imperialist metropolis used its foreign trade and finance to penetrate the Latin American economy far more completely and to use the latter's productive potential far more efficiently and exhaustively for metropolitan development than the colonial metropolis had ever been able to do. As Rosa Luxemburg noted of a similar process elsewhere, "stripped of all obscuring connecting links, these relations consist in the simple fact that European capital has largely swallowed up the Egyptian peasant economy. Enormous tracts of land, labour, and labour products without number, accruing to the state as taxes, have ultimately been converted into European capital and have been accumulated." (Luxemburg, p. 438).

Indeed, in Latin America, imperialism went further. It not only availed itself of the state to invade agriculture; it took over nearly all economic and political institutions to incorporate the entire economy into the imperialist system. The *latifundia* grew at a pace and to proportions unknown in all previous history, especially in Argentina, Uruguay, Peru, Cuba, Mexico, and Central America. With the aid of the Latin American governments, foreigners came to own—usually for next to nothing—immense tracts of land. And where they did not get the land, they got its products, because the metropolis also took over and monopolized the merchandizing of agricultural and most other products. The metropolis took over Latin American mines and expanded their output, sometimes exhausting irreplaceable resources in a few years. To get these raw materials out of Latin America and to get its equipment and goods in, the metropolis stimulated the construction of ports, railroads, and, to service all this, public utilities. The railway network and electric grid, far from being net- or gridlike, were raylike and connected the hinterland of each country and sometimes of several countries with the port of entry and exit, which was in turn connected to the metropolis. Today, fourscore years later, much of this export-import pattern still remains, in part because the railroad right-of-way is still laid out that way, but more importantly because nineteenth-century imperialism generated in Latin America certain vested class interests which, with metropolitan support, managed to maintain and expand the development of Western capitalism and of Latin American underdevelopment during the twentieth century.

Created in colonial times and sharpened during the free-trade eras, the class structure of underdevelopment was consolidated in Latin America by nineteenth-century imperialist trade and finance. Latin America came to be characterized by a monoculture export economy with its *latifundium* and expropriated rural proletariat, exploited by a satellitized bourgeoisie, acting through the corrupt state of a noncountry like "Barbarous Mexico" (John Kenneth Turner); the "Banana republics" of Central America, which are not company stores but "company countries"; "The Inexorable Evolution of the Latifundium: Overproduction, Economic Dependence, and Growing Poverty in Cuba" (Ramiro Guerra y Sánchez); "British Argentina"; and "Pathological Chile," of which the conservative historian Francisco Encina wrote in 1912, undcr the title of *Our Economic Inferiority: Its Causes and Consequences:*

> Our economic development of recent years exhibits symptoms which characterize a real pathological state. Until the middle of the nineteenth century, the foreign trade of Chile was almost exclusively in the hands of Chileans. In less than fifty years foreign trade has choked off our nascent commercial initiative abroad and in our own home it eliminated us from international trade and replaced us, in large part, in retail trade. . . . The merchant marine . . . has fallen into sad straits and continues to cede ground to foreign shipping in the coastwide trade. The majority of the insurance companies that operate among us have their head offices abroad. The national banks have ceded and keep ceding ground to the branches of foreign banks. An ever-growing share of the bonds of the savings institutions are passing into the hands of foreigners who live abroad. (Francisco Encina quoted in Hernan Ramirez, *Historia del Imperialismo en Chile,* p. 257.)

Bourgeois Nationalism. Twentieth-century Latin America has witnessed the perpetuation of the same colonial and class structure in its essentials, despite some important structural changes associated first with the two world wars and the intervening depression, and now with the technological revolution in the metropolis and the growth of industry in Latin America. The political problems that Latin America faces today cannot be understood without analysis of these developments. Recent changes in the class structure of Brazil, Argentina, Chile, Venezuela, Mexico, and other parts of Latin America have occurred, for the most part, in response to metropolis-generated changes in their colonial relations.

For example, it was primarily the First World War, the Great Depression, and the Second World War and its aftermath that created the international and national economic *and political* conditions that gave rise in Latin America to the industrialization attempts and the emergence of stronger national bourgeoisies, industrial proletariats, and middle sectors, and of their associated nationalist and populist ideologies and policies. That is, the First World War restricted manufacturing exports from the metropolis and weakened its colonial ties with Latin America generally, thus stimulating and permitting a significant but short-lived increase in industrial activity—mostly in the domestic manufacture of consumer goods—in Brazil, Argentina, and elsewhere. The recovery of the metropolis during the 1920s, and the beginnings of its investment in manufacturing facilities abroad (which matured after the Second World War and which will be discussed in connection with this more recent period both here and in later chapters), reincorporated Latin America into the earlier colonial relationship and transferred many of the new industrial facilities to foreign-owned enterprises.

The Great Depression drastically reduced Latin America's import capacity, metropolitan manufacturing exports, and foreign investments and loans. The onset of the Depression changed national income and its distribution so much in Latin America that the existing institutional frameworks were not able to make the necessary adjustments. Revolutions occurred in 1930, or soon thereafter, in Brazil, Argentina, Chile, and Cuba; and the Mexican Revolution activity agitated other parts of the continent. The metropolis-allied export interests were obliged to form a coalition with the still weak industrial interests and (at least in Brazil) with new regional interests, who forced themselves into the government. Counterrevolutions representing more traditional interests were successful in Cuba and Chile, though not in Brazil, Argentina, or Mexico. Throughout this period of political upheaval and class adjustment, the relaxation of economic colonial ties with the metropolis and in general (though not in Cuba) the relative paralysis of imperialist political intervention (which the metropolitan Depression produced in Latin America), provided the opportunity for new class alignments and industrialization policies. As long as the national governments protected the export interests, as the Brazilian government did through coffee-price supports, the export-import bourgeoisie was now willing and in some cases anxious to promote domestic manufacture—at a time when the Depression had ruined the export business anyway.

Consider, for example, the revealing testimony of Federico Piñedo, who was Minister of Finance in Argentina during the crucial years 1933 to 1935:

The economic life of the country turns in a gigantic master wheel which is foreign trade. We cannot replace this master wheel, but we can alongside of this mechanism create some minor wheels that permit some circulation of wealth, some economic activity, the sum of which can maintain the living standard of the people at some height. . . . It is certain that we [the export sectors, whom Piñedo represents and which were always against national industry] have always considered tariff protection self-defeating for some kinds of industry that can live only in this customs greenhouse because they lack the conditions for solid existence in the climate of our economy. But now we find that all of us agree that it is necessary to organize industries which can prosper by processing the great variety and number of raw materials that our land so generously produces. (Quoted in Murmis, p. 16)

Then Piñedo explains this sudden change of heart and political policy of the export bourgeoisie he represents:

Thus, our country has not had, as in more favourable times of its economic history, the alternative of voluntarily dedicating itself to the export of ever larger quantities of intensively developing industry and satisfying its export possibilities. For the time being the country does not have this option in its economic policy. (Murmis, p. 16)

Therefore, the Argentinian export bourgeoisie, responding to the Depression-induced change in its colonial relationship with the metropolis, itself changed its traditional economic policy. Or, more exactly, the change of policy was made by the dominant sector of the export bourgeoisie dependent on the chilled-beef trade of the Province of Buenos Aires. This sector of the bourgeoisie succeeded in having arranged the Roca-Runciman Treaty of 1933, which obligated Britain to maintain purchases of chilled beef at the level of late 1932, in exchange for which Argentina would spend the proceeds on British goods. Inland landholders, cattlemen, and smaller producers of frozen meat, whose British quota was cut in the same treaty, were sacrificed by this change of policy. Their spokesman, Lisandro de la Torre, complained:

> The theory is more or less like this: We have a limited export quota. Let us keep it for the more valuable meat, that is, let us use the quota for the relatively higher prices that it can offer for the major producers of chilled beef; and leave out of luck the small producers [of frozen meat in other provinces]. (Quoted in Murmis, p. 18)

Other representatives of these agricultural sacrificial lambs observed:

> Establishing industries that grow up in a climate of emergency measures means to create a tragic problem for the future of the country after the [World] War; it means to stimulate a struggle that we do not want between industry and the basic sources of rural production. (Quoted in Murmis, p. 26)

This prediction was, of course, borne out by history when, some years later, the export bourgeoisie, rural landholders, cattlemen, and their imperialist allies struggled against and defeated Perón and the national industrial interests he represented.

In the meantime, in Brazil, the Revolution of 1930 had brought national industrial and southern regional interests into the government to share power with the traditional coffee and mining export interests of São Paulo and Minas Gerais. Since coffee could no longer be exported because of the world depression, the export and industrial interests came to an agreement whereby the government bought the coffee from the producers (stockpiling or burning it). In exchange for this guarantee of their income, the coffee growers agreed to invest in industry instead of more coffee plantations. Despite several near divorces, this marriage of convenience lasted until the military *coup d'état* of 1964. The Second World War and Reconstruction created import shortages which gave the arrangement a new lease on life. However, after the Korean War, massive *foreign* investment maintained economic growth by so transforming the economic and political structure of Brazil into one of dependence as to finally break up the arrangement and make continued nationally generated economic development impossible.

The other major cases of bourgeois-nationalist industrial development and political populism occurred in Mexico, and to some extent, in Chile. It is no accident that in Mexico the changes in class structure and political policy associated with land reform, nationalization of petroleum, and industrial development took place, not after the Mexican Revolution, which ended in 1917, but in the 1930s and 1940s, when the Depression and the War in the metropolis had weakened the earlier colonial economic relations.

Although the Great Depression and World War II affected the whole Continent, bourgeois policies of national industrial development did not unfold in every Latin American country. Why, then, did developmentism, nationalism, and populism thrive primarily in Argentina, Brazil, Mexico, and, to some extent, Chile, and not until more recently and to a lesser extent, in Central America and elsewhere?

The answer would again seem to lie in the differences in economic and class structure that had been previously generated by the colonial relationship with the metropolis. Cardoso and Faletto have recently suggested that the determinant difference lies in the national or foreign ownership of the primary productive resources of a country, and secondarily in the immigration pattern associated with export production. In the plantation and mining export countries of Central America, the Caribbean, and parts of South America, ownership of the export productive resources had fallen into foreign hands. The consequent weak development of the local bourgeoisie did not permit it to respond to the Depression by choosing, as the Argentinian Minister of Finance had put it, between the alternatives of export or industry. Instead, these bourgeoisies were obliged to respond to the crisis by installing military dictatorships to suppress popular discontent. The Argentinian, Brazilian, and Mexican bourgeoisies, on the other hand, owned their export productive apparatus (or were in charge of a recent revolution, as in Mexico), and therefore had sufficient power and flexibility to opt for industrialization and populism. (The most difficult case to explain in these terms is that of Chile, where foreigners owned the mines but industrialism and populism appeared anyway.)

But even where it did occur, the process of industrialization through import substitution was constrained by two built-in limitations, both of which derived from the existing class structure. First, bourgeois reformers had to begin with the existing income distribution and demand structure. This meant that they had to concentrate on consumer goods, particularly for the high-income market. Without a major change in the class structure and income distribution, the internal market could not expand fast enough to sustain the import substitution process indefinitely. Second, for this reason, the industrialization programs did not produce enough industrial equipment or producers' goods, which had increasingly to be imported from abroad in order even to keep the import substitution process going. That is, they ended up only substituting some imports for others.

To have avoided these two limitations, the Latin American reformers would have had to follow the Soviet industrialization model in which the state, rather than consumer demand, determined the goods—capital goods—to be produced first. But for that they would have had to have a Soviet state, that is, a socialist class structure. The domestic political arrangements of the 1930s were able to survive the Depression for some time, because the Second World War, though it improved the export picture, still did not permit the renewal of imports from the metropolis. The end of the Korean War finally terminated this Latin American honeymoon, when declining prices for raw materials began to limit the foreign exchange available to maintain the equipment and other imports needed to sustain an autonomous industrialization process that had begun with finished consumer goods instead of basic producer goods. Thus, the only alternative left to the reformers—short of a socialist revolution—was to admit, indeed welcome, foreign investment, which supplied the needed semiprocessed material, equipment, and technology. The price, of course, was increased de-Latin-Americanization of industry and satellitization of the Latin American economy and bourgeoisie.

REFERENCES CITED

Burgin, Myron. *The Economic Aspects of Argentine Federalism, 1820–1852.* Cambridge: Harvard University Press, 1946.

Cairncross, A. K. *Home and Foreign Investment, 1880–1913.* Cambridge: Cambridge University Press, 1953.

Cardoso, Fernando Henrique and Enzo Faletto. *Dependencia y desarrollo en América Latina.* Santiago: ILPES, 1967 (mimeo.); Mexico City: Siglo Veintiuno Editores, S.A. (in press).

Encina, Francisco. *Nuestra inferioridad económica: sus causas y consecuencias.* Santiago: 1912.

Harlow, Vincent. *A History of Barbados, 1625–1685.* London: Clarendon Press, 1926.

Luxemburg, Rosa. *The Accumulation of Capital.* New York: Monthly Review Press, 1964.

Murmis, Miguel and Juan Carlos Portantiero. *Crecimiento industrial y alianza de clases en la Argentina (1930–1940).* Buenos Aires: Instituto Torcuato de Tella, Documento de Trabajo No. 48, 1968 (mimeo.).

Smith, Adam. *An Inquiry into the Nature and Causes of the Wealth of Nations.* New York: Random House, 1937.

Stavenhagen, Rodolfo, Fernando Paz Sánchez, Cuauhtémoc Cárdenas, and Arturo Bonilla. *Neolatifundismo y explotación de Emiliano Zapata a Anderson Clayton & Co.* Mexico City: Nuestro Tiempo, 1968.

Torres, Edelberto. *Interpretación del desarrollo social Centroamericano.* Santiago: ILPES, 1968 (mimeo.); Santiago: PLA (in press).

Viadas, Lauro. *El problema de la pequeña propriedad. Informe presentado al Señor Secretario de Fomento.* Mexico City: Imprenta y Fototipia de la Secretaría de Fomento, 1911.

Chapter 3

SOCIAL AND ECONOMIC STRUCTURE
OF THE PORFIRIATO: MEXICO, 1877–1911*

James D. Cockcroft

Research into the social and economic structure of San Luis Potosí at the end of the nineteenth century, together with generally available data on Mexico as a whole, suggests that many traditional assumptions about Mexican history and problems of economic development must undergo revision. Agrarian feudalism did not exist in Mexico. The single most influential economic group was neither a rural aristocracy nor an urban bourgeoisie, but rather a *foreign* bourgeoisie. The Mexican Revolution of 1910–17 was not a bourgeois one against feudalism, nor did it succeed in more than overthrowing Porfirio Díaz and changing part of the ideology of social change. Radical changes in the class structure and in the power relationships between classes did not occur as a result of the Mexican Revolution, mainly because the worker-peasant thrust of the Revolution was blunted by Venustiano Carranza's victory over Emiliano Zapata. The anti-imperialist thrust of the Revolution varied through the years, gaining strength when the workers mobilized, as during the petroleum industry crisis of 1936–38, and losing strength when the domestic bourgeoisie felt less threatened from below and more amenable to profitable arrangements with foreign capitalists, as after World War II.

* Most of this chapter appeared as Chapter One of Cockcroft, *Intellectual Precursors of the Mexican Revolution, 1900–1913* (Austin: The University of Texas Press, 1968; Mexico City: Siglo Veintiuno Editores, S.A., 1971). Reprinted by permission of the publishers. Two paragraphs from Chapter Two of the same work have been added here, as well as an introductory paragraph and concluding paragraph written for this volume.

Cliquish control of Mexico's economy and politics was a principal complaint of the Precursor Movement throughout the last decade of the Porfiriato.[1] In San Luis Potosí, a handful of elite families, often in co-operation with foreign businessmen, dominated economic, political, and social life. A system of interlocking economic interests between city, mine, and farm, tending toward increased industrialization, monopolization,[2] mechanization, profit-making, and participation of foreign capital, resulted in significant changes throughout the state's social structure. Contrary to the claims of some authorities that "feudalism" and "stagnation" characterized the countryside, social change especially affected rural areas.

Economically, railroad-building and industrialization were the two most important innovative processes generating social change in Mexico during the Porfiriato. In its railroad development, San Luis Potosí was representative of the rest of the nation. Porfirio Díaz' rail-expansion program, which added fifteen thousand miles of right-of-way to the four hundred miles completed under Presidents Benito Juárez (1867–72) and Sebastián Lerdo de Tejada (1872–76), was financed primarily by foreign capital, mostly U.S., but also British and

---

[1] The Precursor Movement is commonly defined as all political precedents (manifestoes, strikes, armed uprisings, etc.) of the Mexican Revolution of 1910–17, dating from the 1900 founding of the Club Liberal "Ponciano Arriaga" in San Luis Potosí to the 1911 overthrow of Díaz (for details, see Cockcroft, *Intellectual Precursors of the Mexican Revolution, 1900–1913*). "Porfiriato" is the word used to refer to the reign of Porfirio Díaz, 1877–1911.

[2] The word "monopoly" may be defined as "unified or concerted discretionary control of the price at which purchasers in general can obtain a commodity or service and of the supply which they can secure, or the control of price through supply, as distinct from the lack of such control which marks the ideal situation of perfect competition" (John Maurice Clark, "Monopoly," *Encyclopedia of the Social Sciences*, X, 623–30). Pure monopoly, in either a buyers' or a sellers' market, is not frequent. The principle of monopoly may be said to apply to many societies and may be extended to any pervasive control of a given area, economic or otherwise—e.g., monopoly of social status, or monopoly of political control.

French.[3] San Luis Potosí's fantastic rail expansion between 1888 and 1902 derived from the aims of foreigners in constructing railroads throughout Mexico: to extract and market mineral wealth, and to service populous industrializing areas where there existed abundant cheap labor (the state capital had nearly seventy thousand inhabitants by 1900).[4]

Railroads in San Luis Potosí ran from the state's silver, lead, and copper mines to the main north-south trunk line, to smelters, to factories, and to the port of Tampico on the Gulf of Mexico. Federal subsidies, state bonds, and concessions to prominent local businessmen and landholders like Juan B. Barragán, former San Luis Potosí governor (1869), financed the laying of the first track on the Tampico line in 1879. A year later, the U.S.-owned Mexican Central Railroad bought out all other interests and agreed to complete the railroad, which it did by 1890. Not long thereafter, Guggenheim mining interests extended this mining-transportation link by sea all the way from Tampico to Perth Amboy, New Jersey, where a new refinery completed integration of a nascent American mining dynasty from mine-mouth to the finished metal. A similar procedure of federal subsidies and business concessions was followed from 1881 to 1883 for construction of an east-west railroad connecting San Luis Potosí with Aguascalientes, site of a giant copper smelter built by the Guggenheims a decade later. President Díaz' rail policy after 1890 was strictly one of foreign concessions. U.S. business elements came to control the entire rail grid of San Luis Potosí and surrounding states. Of all foreign investments in Mexico during the Porfiriato, U.S. capital held majority control, and San Luis Potosí was hardly unrepresentative. Of total U.S. investments in Mexico, 83 percent were in rails and mining—the two principal components of San Luis Potosí's economic infrastructure.[5]

[3] Raymond Vernon, *The Dilemma of Mexico's Development*, p. 39; Fernando Rosenzweig *et al.*, *Historia moderna de México. El Porfiriato: la vida económica*, p. 1155.

[4] *Ibid.*; Dirección General de Estadística, *Censo*, 1900.

[5] Rosenzweig, pp. 493–544, 565 ff., 1066–67, 1155; Primo Feliciano Velázquez, *Historia de San Luis Potosí*, IV, 72–73, 97–100; Harvey O'Connor, *The Guggenheims*, pp. 85–101; Juan B.

Foreign economic investments were often encouraged and abetted by local businessmen of elite families, who welcomed new railroads to market their minerals and agricultural produce. In addition, a shrewd San Luis Potosí businessman who could wangle a railroad concession out of the Federal Government might sell it at a handsome profit to American investors. This was precisely what Governor Pedro Díez Gutiérrez did in 1888. The Governor, who accumulated an immense fortune while alternating the state governorship with his brother for two decades, sold his 5,500-peso-per-kilometer rail concession, which would have linked the northern mining complex of Matehuala with the agrarian hub of Río Verde, to the U.S.-owned Mexican National Railroad. Ignoring blueprints for running the line all the way to Río Verde, American engineers completed the shorter and cheaper link from Matehuala's mines to the north-south trunk line connecting Laredo (Texas) to Mexico City. President Díaz officially inaugurated the trunk line at ceremonies held in San Luis Potosí on November 1, 1888.[6]

Completion of such major railroads, together with the nationwide elimination of state and municipal import and marketing taxes in order to permit free interstate commerce, opened the gates to what most authorities agree was the period of fastest industrial growth during the Porfiriato—1895 to 1901. As Mexican economist Fernando Rosenzweig has observed: "The creation of new factories, a clear phenomenon since 1880, reached its apogee in this period, when foreign investment turned to industrial activity."[7]

Barragán, *Discurso pronunciado el 15 de septiembre de 1879 por el C. Lic. Juan B. Barragán, en la inauguración del primer tramo de Ferrocarril construido en el Estado* (pamphlet).

[6] Velázquez, IV, 72–73, 90–101, 162–63; Rosenzweig, Chaps. v, x; Isaac Grimaldo, *Gobernantes potosinos, 1590–1939;* Manuel Zepeda, *Opiniones de la prensa sobre las fiestas de inauguración del Ferrocarril Nacional Mexicano verificadas en la ciudad de San Luis Potosí los días 1°, 2, 3, y 4 de noviembre de 1888.* The Díez Gutiérrez fortune was estimated at three million pesos by Díaz braintruster Francisco Bulnes (*El verdadero Díaz y la Revolución,* pp. 165–67).

[7] Rosenzweig, pp. 314, 326.

As in Mexico's railroad-building, so in its industrial development—foreigners dominated. Foreign capital brought in modern machinery for new medium and light industries. Concurrently, even though immigrants constituted what might be called an "indigenous industrial class,"[8] foreign control of Mexico's new industries expanded and solidified during the last fifteen years of the Porfiriato. Financing of even "domestic" investments was often, at least indirectly, accomplished in significant part by non-Mexican capital. Examples of domestic financing of foreign investment, also common, reflected a high degree of co-operation between Mexican and foreign businessmen.[9] In the last nine years of the Porfiriato, new investments by U.S., British, and French capitalists exceeded all their investments of the first twenty-three years of the Porfiriato. The most spectacular increase was in U.S. investments, which more than quintupled between 1897 and 1911. As early as 1900, foreigners owned outright 172 of the 212 commercial establishments in the Federal District (Mexico City), and by 1911, foreign interests accounted for two-thirds of Mexico's total investment outside agriculture and the handicraft industries.[10]

Most influential of foreign industrial forces in the mining state of San Luis Potosí was the Guggenheim family's Sociedad Metalúrgica Mexicana, a subsidiary of American Smelting and Refining Company. By 1900, the Guggenheims already had established a thriving smelter at Monterrey, Nuevo León, and were casting about for new profitable mining ventures. Their engineers reported good opportunities throughout the North, including San Luis Potosí, which ranked seventh nationally in peso-value of mineral production (3,549,972) and second only to Zacatecas in number of men employed by the mining industry (10,767).[11] Guggenheim interests took over an incomplete and abandoned rail

8 Vernon, pp. 44–45; cf. Rosenzweig, p. 453.

9 Velázquez, IV, 155–63; Vernon, pp. 44–45; Rosenzweig, pp. 1181–84.

10 Rosenzweig, pp. 1125, 1162; Vernon, pp. 42–44.

11 *El Contemporáneo,* August 29, 1903; O'Connor, pp. 85–101.

link running east from San Luis Potosí toward Río Verde, in order to extract lead, silver, and gold from famed Cerro de San Pedro, original silver vein of the state and cause for the founding of the capital in the valley nearby in 1592. Then, on May 25, 1902, the Guggenheims' Sociedad Metalúrgica Mexicana bought the 42.3-kilometer railroad connecting Río Verde to San Bartolo on the San Luis Potosí–Tampico line, using "thousands of pesos given by large landholders . . . and fifty-cent contributions of many, many cooperating humble citizens."[12] Next, still in 1902, the Guggenheims established a multi-million-dollar smelting plant at Matehuala (lead, silver, and gold) and smaller smelters at San Luis Potosí and Wadley Railroad Station, about 40 kilometers southwest of Matehuala on the Mexican National Railroad (silver, antimony, bismuth, zinc, cobalt, and sulfur). By 1910, Guggenheim mining interests in all Mexico accounted for fifty million dollars' worth of common stock and an indeterminate amount of preferred stock. Throughout Mexico's North, the Guggenheims had "an almost complete monopoly on the metalurgical industry, upon which depended all progress in mining."[13]

In spite of a record of having collaborated with foreign capital, Mexico's bourgeoisie was not immune to the pressures of foreign competition and economic nationalism. While some Mexican businessmen profited from collaboration with foreigners, others suffered an economic squeeze. At the turn of the century, when the Liberal Clubs initiated by San Luis Potosí mining engineer Camilo Arriaga were beginning to manifest significant political opposition, there was much angry discussion about what Porfirio Díaz himself had criticized in 1876 as "selling the country to the nation next door."[14] Even

---

[12] Velázquez, IV, 162–63; A. B. González, *Album Rioverdense, colección de escritos, datos históricos y estadísticos recogidos.*

[13] Rosenzweig, pp. 283, 1092, 1184; Alfred Tischendorf, *Great Britain and Mexico in the Era of Porfirio Díaz,* pp. 72, 90.

[14] Díaz issued his Plan de Tuxtepec, January 15, 1876, to protest President Lerdo de Tejada's efforts at re-election and the sale of the national debt accumulated during the French intervention of 1862–67 to the United States (text in Jesús Romero Flores, *Anales históricos de la Revolución Mexicana,* III, 212–15).

the Catholic, Conservative San Luis Potosí newspaper *El Estandarte* was critical of "the Yankees' taking over of Mexico little by little."[15] By 1910, foreigners owned one-seventh of Mexico's land surface.[16] Few scholars would quibble with the assertion of the late Mexican economist Luis Nicolau D'Olwer that antiforeign sentiment played a pivotal role in the Mexican Revolution: ". . . all the acts for which Díaz is blamed, and the consequent loss of prestige for his regime, are connected with his policy of favoring foreign investments."[17]

Among San Luis Potosí's bourgeoisie, the end of the nineteenth century was marked by political and economic uncertainty. Many elite families were feeling the final effects of an economic slump (1892–95). Some, like the Barrenecheas and Coghlans, emerged with new strength, and others, like the Arriagas, were still staggering from the impact of the earlier crisis. These cases warrant examination because of subsequent political developments and sociological implications concerning elite families and conflicts within Mexico's bourgeoisie. Camilo Arriaga, a Liberal, was the man most responsible for initiating the Precursor Movement against Porfirio Díaz. Pedro Barrenechea, a Conservative influential in designating state governors, later lent financial aid to Madero, the moderate Liberal elected President after the overthrow of Díaz in 1911. Francisco M. Coghlan, by cooperating with U.S. businessmen, parlayed mining profits into small and medium industry, a not uncommon practice among heads of San Luis Potosí elite families.

The Arriaga family had founded its wealth on silver. It owned the state's largest silver mines, incorporated as the Compañía Minera de la Concepción. On January 16, 1893, the richest and largest mine at Concepción caved in, thus undercutting the Arriagas' fortune. Three months later, the

---

[15] *El Estandarte,* March 18, 1902.
[16] Rosenzweig, pp. 1106–15; Vernon, p. 50; Frank Tannenbaum, *Mexico, the Struggle for Peace and Bread,* pp. 140–41. Some estimates run as high as one-fifth.
[17] Rosenzweig, p. 183.

sixty-six-year-old Casa de Moneda de San Luis Potosí, major mint in the area, was closed down and its resources transferred to Mexico City. Throughout this period—from 1892 to 1895—the state of San Luis Potosí suffered a series of economic reversals: a severe slump in the silver market, drought, famine, and typhus epidemics. Consequently the economy became highly unstable. In the course of wild stock-market speculation, many mining shares traded hands. The Arriagas failed to recover fully from this economic infighting. The other major San Luis Potosí silver-mining concern at Santa Ana, directed by Coghlan and backed by U.S. capital, emerged strengthened.[18]

Before the end of the 1892–95 slump, San Luis Potosí businessmen began clamoring for political changes at the Statehouse. By 1898, they succeeded in having a new governor installed, engineer Blas Escontría. The major tactic Escontría employed to confront the state's economic crisis was the same as that being used by President Díaz on a national level: incentives for investment by foreign capital. This was the time of the concerted Guggenheim economic invasion of the state. By 1910, the United States was receiving 77 percent of Mexico's mineral exports, as compared to only 42 percent at the start of the Porfiriato.[19]

There is every indication that San Luis Potosí businessmen, with obvious exceptions like Arriaga, at first welcomed this economic shot in the arm from U.S. capital. Although well-established mining concerns like those of the Barrenecheas

[18] It was at this time that the Coghlan concern completed the installation of electricity and modern machinery provided by U.S. capital (Velázquez, IV, 103–4, 140–43); *El Estandarte*, 1892–95, *passim*; Rosenzweig, pp. 230, 794; Compañía Minera de la Concepción, *Estatutos aprobados para el trabajo y laborío de la Mina de la Concepción ubicada en el Mineral de Catorce* (pamphlet) and *Contrato celebrado entre la Junta Directiva de la Compañía propietaria y explotadora de la Mina de la Concepción y Anexas, sitas en el Mineral de Catorce, Estado de San Luis Potosí, por una parte, y el Sr. Benigno Arriaga por sí o por la Compañía o Compañías que se organicen, para la compraventa de los metales de dichas minas* (pamphlet).

[19] Rosenzweig, p. 241.

did not relish U.S. efforts to buy them out, and smaller ones even protested publicly,[20] most businessmen, shaken by the 1895 crisis, felt they stood to gain by collaboration with their foreign counterparts. Since mineral production was lagging in San Luis Potosí when compared to that in other parts of the North, San Luis Potosí mining concerns welcomed expanded export facilities provided by new rail links to the North and the Gulf. Also the establishment of U.S.-financed lead and copper smelters and small steel plants in Matehuala and San Luis Potosí facilitated local expansion in the use of mineral products.[21]

Mexican businessmen, confronted with either economic slump or the need for more capital and machinery, had to work with whatever was available. Their needs happened to occur in an economically "underdeveloped" country at a time of rapid U.S. expansion around the world. It was only natural that they resorted to collaboration with U.S. investors, when the goals of both nations' upper bourgeoisies had so much in common: economic expansion, industrialization, and profit. However, this continued collaboration with foreigners by many of the bourgeoisie coincided with the first appeals to economic nationalism being expressed by the Precursor Movement in the early 1900's. Collaboration with foreign capital, however profitable for Mexican businessmen, served to increase further the degree of monopolization and foreign

[20] E.g., Manuel José Othón, *Apuntes que, para alegar de buena prueba ante el Señor Juez 3° de Letras del Partido de Mapimí, produce Don Jesús Revilla, patrocinado por el Lic. Manuel J. Othón, y representante jurídico de la Compañía Minera "Siderita" y Anexas, S.A. de S. Luis Potosí en el interdicto de despojo promovido contra la Compañía Minera y Fundidora "Descubridora"* (pamphlet).

[21] Rosenzweig, pp. 182, 224, 230, 241, 794, 1092; Fundición de Fierro de San Luis Potosí, *Estatutos de la Fundición de Fierro de San Luis Potosí, Sociedad Anónima incorporada bajo las leyes de la República Mexicana* (pamphlet). Although mining production rose impressively throughout the nation during the Porfiriato, San Luis Potosí failed to keep up with the national pace after 1895 (Jesús Silva Herzog, *El agrarismo mexicano y la reforma agraria,* p. 104).

control of the nation's economy. At the time of the next major economic slump—1907–11—Mexico's bourgeoisie would clamor for some kind of political change. By then, economic nationalism would be making more sense to them, since foreign control would have, in the meantime, increased noticeably; national economic progress would have slowed; and the Precursor Movement would have begun to influence national politics. These factors would affect revolutionary propensities among the bourgeoisie.

A characteristic of "underdeveloped" economies in general would seem to be an ambivalent feeling among bourgeoisies about the question of collaboration with foreign businessmen, as opposed to economic nationalism. Mexico's Revolution has often been described as a "nationalistic, bourgeois revolution," aimed at freeing the country from foreign domination. However, events in the 1917–67 period would suggest that the historic ambivalence in Mexico's bourgeoisie has by no means been resolved in favor of economic nationalism. On the contrary, in spite of occasional nationalistic outbursts like that of 1938 when the petroleum industry was nationalized, the Mexican bourgeoisie today—within the broader outlines of a "Mexicanization" policy allowing the Federal Government to require a company's capital to be 51 percent owned by Mexicans—seems to be as willing as ever to collaborate with U.S. capital and less inclined than earlier in the century to support, or even tolerate, revolutionary calls for the nationalization of all industries or 100 percent Mexican ownership.[22] The roots of these discussions on economic policy go back to at least as early as the events of 1900–13, especially to the threat of an antibourgeois, revolutionary

[22] Today there is considerable evidence that, because of increased bourgeois collaboration with foreigners and opposition to revolutionary movements or proposals for nationalization of industry, ambivalence among all bourgeoisies in Latin America has diminished to the point of insignificance. Mexico's at times "anti-U.S." foreign policy should not be misconstrued, as it concerns only the ticklish question of intervention in the internal affairs of other countries ("self-determination of peoples") or occasional border disputes, and not the Mexican Government's general guidelines of co-operation with foreign capital.

worker-peasant movement spawned by the Precursor Movement. In addition, the socio-economic realities influencing developments from 1900 to 1913 included precisely this ambivalence within Mexico's bourgeoisie about economic nationalism, as well as the inexorable problem of an "underdeveloped" country's economic dependence upon a "developed" one.

During the Porfiriato, collaboration by Mexican businessmen with foreign interests included bank loans when deemed necessary. Thus, for example, the Banco de San Luis Potosí provided Edward L. Doheny with fifty thousand pesos just when the U.S. oil magnate was about to give up petroleum exploration in the Huasteca[23] region around Ebano, early in 1904. Exploration continued, and in April of 1904, oil well "Fish No. 1" gushed black gold fifteen meters high and began a fifteen-hundred-barrel daily production. Thus began Mexico's oil boom—to the profit of foreigners, but with the assistance of nationals.[24]

The Mexican group responsible for abetting the oil boom in this case, the Banco de San Luis Potosí, had been established in 1897 by prominent San Luis Potosí businessmen, led by Ramón Alcázar and Gerardo and Eduardo Meade (a wealthy landholding family), who, with J. H. Bahnsen, had been granted a federal concession to issue paper money and bonds. The bank's capital was over a million pesos. It soon

[23] Thinly populated, well-watered, jagged eastern slopes and tropical lowlands of the extreme eastern part of San Luis Potosí; part of the larger geographical and cultural section of Mexico called "Huasteca" after the Huaxteco Indians, incorporating parts of Tamaulipas, Querétaro, Hidalgo, Tlaxcala, and Veracruz.

[24] Velázquez, IV, 155–62; Tischendorf, pp. 125 ff.; Rosenzweig, pp. 1127–29; Gabriel Antonio Menéndez, *Doheny el cruel*, pp. 288–93; Joaquín Meade, *La huasteca veracruzana*, II, 135–45; E. L. Doheny, *A Brief Statement of the results accomplished by the Mexican Petroleum Company at Ebano, San Luis Potosí, México* (pamphlet). Besides Mexican bankers and large landowners, some medium-sized landholders sold property to foreign petroleum companies and came to form a provincial class of "new rich," according to Gregorio López y Fuentes, *Huasteca*, pp. 37–52, 89.

became the principal bank in the state, but collapsed during the Revolution.[25]

Families of landed wealth, as suggested by the case of the Meades and their Banco de San Luis Potosí, were quite conscious of new economic opportunities opening up with the inflow of U.S. capital and the completion of railroads and roads across the state. It was no coincidence that the first promotional organization of industrialists in San Luis Potosí was founded (May 27, 1905) as an "agricultural" and industrial center—the Centro Agrícola e Industrial Potosino. This organization was subsidized with more than fifteen thousand pesos by the state government, headed by landowner-industrialist Governor José María Espinosa y Cuevas. Its board of directors was composed of big landowners and cattlemen of the Espinosa y Cuevas, Hernández, and Barrenechea families, mining figures of the Cabrera and Barrenechea families, and industrialist Emeterio V. Lavín. Two of the state's biggest *latifundia* (large landholdings)—La Angostura and El Gogorrón, controlled by Espinosa y Cuevas, Hermanos, and miner-industrialist Felipe Muriedas, respectively—were well represented.

The new agrarian-industrial Centro welcomed such U.S. investment in local industry as the Guggenheim foundries; the Fundición de Fierro de San Luis Potosí, founded in 1904 to produce screws, nuts, and bolts; and the F. L. Schaefer Shoe Company, established in 1903–4, and sold a year later to Coghlan y Compañía. Coghlan's company also controlled shares in the Fundición de Fierro de San Luis Potosí. The massive overlap between mining, landed, and industrial

[25] Banco de San Luis Potosí, S.A., *Banco de San Luis Potosí, S. A. Concesiones, estatutos y extractos de la ley general de 19 de marzo de 1897 de Instituciones de Crédito* (pamphlet). Federico J. Meade's Haciendas Anexas was one of the biggest estates in the state, sprawling over 104,000 hectares and including part of the state of Tamaulipas (A. Fremont, *Obras de irrigación en las Haciendas Anexas y abastecimiento de la Presa de Guadalupe, San Luis Potosí* [pamphlet]). At the time of Federico Meade's death in 1909, his wealth was estimated at more than three million dollars, according to the Methodist monthly *La Ofrenda Escolar*, September, 1909, p. 134.

wealth, both domestic and foreign—a principal complaint of the Precursor Movement—was manifested by the Muriedas and Coghlan cases.[26]

Diagram 1 presents a graphic picture of the overlap between elite families in San Luis Potosí in mining, agriculture, industry, commerce, and politics. Because of the lack of adequate or complete statistical studies on estate sizes, ownership, and investment of agricultural capital in nonagricultural commercial activity, Diagram 1 is no more than a representation of what presently available evidence indicates about San Luis Potosí's social structure during the Porfiriato. It is based largely on founding statutes and annual reports published by mining, industrial, commercial, and agricultural firms in San Luis Potosí, supplemented by newspaper accounts of the time, memories of surviving citizens of the state, and the writings of contemporaries and historians. On the basis of evidence from these diversified sources, the elite families listed in Diagram 1 are not only representative; they are also the most often-cited examples of large landholders and big miners in San Luis Potosí. The Barragán, Espinosa y Cuevas, Hernández, Meade, and Muriedas families seem to have controlled the state's largest *latifundia*. As Governor Rafael Nieto pointed out in 1921, the Espinosa y Cuevas' Hacienda La Angostura alone accounted for more than one-tenth of the land area of the so-called "Central" portion of the state of San Luis Potosí, while six *haciendas* made up more than a quarter of the land in the "West" and seven *haciendas* more than a fifth of the "East."[27]

[26] Velázquez, IV, 194–97; Centro Agrícola e Industrial Potosino, *Primer Concurso de Ganadería, septiembre de 1906* (pamphlet); Fundición de Fierro de San Luis Potosí, *Estatutos de la Fundición* (pamphlet). Engineers hired by Muriedas were responsible for developing the state's system of artesian wells (1906–10), culminating with the inauguration of a hydroelectric plant in 1910. Muriedas was considered a major industrialist because of his mining interests and shipping concerns.

[27] Rafael Nieto, *Exposición de los motivos que el Ejecutivo del Edo. tuvo para pedir al H. Congreso, la expedición de la Ley Agraria* (pamphlet); Velázquez, IV, 175–77; Section II-E of the Bibliography of my book, *Intellectual Precursors of the Mexican Revolution, 1900–1913*, some seven pages of relevant pamphlets, too lengthy for inclusion here.

DIAGRAM 1
ELITE FAMILIES* IN SAN LUIS POTOSÍ

Mining	Governors	Land (Including Urban)
ARRIAGA	Barragán (1869)	Arriaga
BARRENECHEA	DIEZ GUTIERREZ	BARRAGAN
CABRERA	(1876–1898)	Barrenechea
COGHLAN	Escontría (1898–1904)	Díez Gutiérrez
Díez Gutiérrez	Espinosa y Cuevas	ESPINOSA Y
ESCONTRIA	(1905–1911)	CUEVAS
Espinosa	Hernández (1874–1876)	HERNANDEZ
HERNANDEZ		Ipiña
IPIÑA		MEADE
MURIEDAS		MURIEDAS
OTHON	Centro Agrícola e	
SOBERON	Industrial	
VIRAMONTES	Barrenechea	
ZAMANILLO	Cabrera	Small and Medium Industry
	Espinosa y Cuevas	
	Hernández	Barragán
	Lavín	Barrenechea
		BUENO
		Cabrera
		Coghlan
		Díez Gutiérrez
		Espinosa y Cuevas
		Hernández
Transportation and		LAVIN
Construction	Banking	Muriedas
Cabrera	Alcázar	Soberón
LAVIN	Bahnsen	Viramontes
Muriedas	Meade	Zamanillo

* Names printed in solid capitals indicate, insofar as it is possible to ascertain, the original source or sources of a family's wealth during the Porfiriato; names in capital and lower case indicate into what other major economic enterprises an elite family spread its interests.

This system of interlocking control by elite families in the state's economic, political, and social life alienated much of the middle class and even elements of the upper class, as in the case of Camilo Arriaga. Monolithic social control by families of the upper class blocked the advance of people from classes immediately below. Finally, elite families contributed to, and profited from, basic social changes during the Porfiriato which seriously affected expectations of the vast majority of the state's population, then living in the countryside.

To appreciate social change in Mexico's countryside, it is useful to understand how large landholders acquired and developed their wealth and how they farmed. Nearly all industralists-farmers brought together in the Centro Agrícola e Industrial Potosino had developed during the Díaz regime, or earlier, a tremendous reservoir of landed wealth through inheritance, questionable legal practices (juggling of land titles, etc.), or energetic land-grabbing under the protection of Articles 26 and 27 of the 1857 Constitution and the 1883 and 1894 "vacant-land" (baldío) laws.

The Liberal authors of the 1857 Constitution, devotees of economic liberalism and free enterprise, had called for dividing all corporately held property, which meant both Church lands and the Indians' traditional communally held ejidos. Articles 26 and 27 thus provided ideal conditions for the development of private property in Mexico, a prime goal of Liberals. Recent statistical research at the Colegio de México suggests that an inordinately large number of Liberals benefited from the Reform Laws of 1857. Most of the Church and Indian lands apparently were bought up by merchants and professionals, including bureaucrats of the Liberal government; some large landholders and land speculators also benefited. Peasants, unable to compete to begin with, were further impoverished by the 5 percent alcabala, or import and marketing tax. The 1857 Constitution thus intensified, rather than mitigated, land hunger among the peasantry.[28]

With unusual foresight, Ponciano Arriaga, great-uncle of the initiator of the Precursor Movement (Camilo Arriaga), warned of the dangerous consequences of the 1857 Constitu-

[28] Jan Bazant, "La desamortización de los bienes corporativos en 1856," *Historia Mexicana*, XVI, No. 2 (October–December, 1966), 193–212.

tion's failure to handle the land problem adequately. Although believing the right of private property to be inviolable, Arriaga nevertheless told the constitutional delegates that they had failed to define property rights precisely enough to avoid the advent of "monopolistic capitalism." Arriaga, who chaired the committee that edited Article 27 of the Constitution, proposed his own solution: elimination of *latifundia,* provision of land for all peasants, and a tax system favoring the poor. These proposals were rejected unanimously by the constitutional delegates, who by their votes showed where their own economic interests lay.[29]

The *baldío* laws of 1883 and 1894 only increased the pace of land monopolization for what Ponciano Arriaga had called "the exclusive use of the capitalists." Under this ingenious legislation, all restrictions on land sales were removed. Land-survey companies were contracted by the government to locate and measure *baldíos,* receiving one-third of all lands surveyed as compensation.

The results of such opportunities for land speculation were statistically expressed by the 1910 census. Of rural family heads in Mexico, 96.6 percent held no land at all. There were only 411,096 landholding farmers and 840 *hacendados* (large landowners). Of Mexico's total population, 80 percent depended upon agricultural wages—a sizable agrarian labor force in a country undergoing incipient industrialization. In San Luis Potosí, the percentages were almost identical.[30]

In its pattern of ever-expanding *latifundia* and more and more landless peasants and rural wage earners, Mexican agriculture was not, as often has been supposed, "feudal." Rather, it was capitalist.

"Feudalism" may be defined as that socio-economic system characterized by a closed economy unconcerned with the accumulation of capital and its progressive reinvestment for profit. The vassal owns his plot of land (fief) and in exchange provides the lord certain services, often military. The feudal

[29] Ponciano Arriaga, *Voto particular del C. Ponciano Arriaga sobre el derecho de propiedad* (pamphlet).

[30] Census of 1910, cited in various works, e.g., Silva Herzog, pp. 122–23; Nieto.

community is a self-contained, self-sustaining one founded primarily on relationships between lords and vassals rather than on kinship or an open, money-based economy or the presence of a strong State. Often, the lord's seigniory, or manor, is farmed by tenant farmers. Feudalism was prevalent during the Middle Ages in Europe, when "the absence of an easy flow of sales and purchases such as exists in present day societies prevented the formation of agricultural or industrial salaried classes and of any body of functionaries remunerated periodically in money."[31]

"Capitalism," on the other hand, may be defined as that socio-economic system in which all or most of the means of production and distribution (lands, factories, railroads, etc.) are privately owned and operated for profit, the accumulation of capital, and the progressive reinvestment of capital, with a corresponding development of wage labor, salaried classes, and regularly paid functionaries, all of whom interrelate within a relatively open, competitive market economy. Tendencies toward the formation of giant corporations and monopolistic control of sales and purchases are common to most capitalistic societies. The ruling class in a capitalistic society, as distinguished from that in a feudal society, is not simply a landholding aristocracy, but rather a bourgeoisie.

As Rosenzweig has observed, Mexican agriculture during the Porfiriato was "a new *latifundista* agriculture, oriented toward the market . . . and employment of wage labor."[32] Production of commercial commodities like cotton and sugar doubled in less than forty years under Díaz.[33] In San Luis Potosí, commercial-minded *latifundistas* like the Espinosa y

[31] Marc Bloch, "European Feudalism," *Encyclopedia of the Social Sciences*, VI, 203–10.

Recent scholarship suggests that traditional views of feudalism's closed economy may have to undergo some revision to allow for cases of market commerce that did occur (Sidney R. Packard, *The Process of Historical Revision: New Viewpoints in Medieval European History*).

[32] Rosenzweig, p. 315; Fernando Rosenzweig, "El desarrollo económico de México de 1877 a 1911," *El Trimestre Económico*, XXXII, No. 127 (July–September, 1965), 427.

[33] Vernon, p. 43.

Cuevas brothers took advantage of the recently completed rail network to develop a small-scale tomato export business via Tampico, as well as trade in cattle, hides, henequen (seventh state in henequen production in 1907), cotton, oranges (third in 1907), limes, lemons, custard-apples, plums, and peanuts. For the internal market, the state's largest farmers profitably produced basic food commodities like maize and beans, under the protective cover of a 100 percent import tariff on competitive foodstuffs undergoing price declines on the world market.[34]

A glance at Diagram 1 suggests how commercial-minded San Luis Potosí elite-family *hacendados* were. All five families listed whose wealth was founded on land were also active in industry or banking. Moreover, three of them held shares in mining companies, and two of them were represented on the board of directors of the Centro Agrícola e Industrial Potosino.

One of the Precursors' chief complaints, especially after the formation of the Partido Liberal Mexicano (PLM) in 1905, was directed against Mexican capitalism. This capitalism had a real base in the countryside. It is significant that high officials in the Díaz government wrote socio-economic analyses in precisely the same terms as those used by the PLM and in confirmation of the picture given here, especially with reference to capitalist instead of feudal agriculture. For example, in early 1911, Díaz' Development Minister Olegario

---

[34] San Luis Potosí also accounted for half of the nation's production of prickly pears (used as a vegetable or main dish, as well as in honeys and drinks), and much of the nation's *lechuguilla* fiber, extracted from a cactus-like plant for use in handbags, sacks, and coarse rope; both items were produced commercially on *haciendas* (Rosenzweig, *Historia moderna,* p. 57; Eugenio Martínez Núñez, *Juan Sarabia, apóstol y mártir de la Revolución Mexicana,* I, 32). There were two railroad stations within the borders of the Espinosa y Cuevas' Hacienda La Angostura (Silva Herzog, p. 124). On crop production, including exports, see Rosenzweig, *Historia moderna,* pp. 46–49, 57–58, 74, 123–24; Eduardo Chávez, *Estación Agrícola Experimental de Río Verde, San Luis Potosí* (pamphlet). On internal food market, Rosenzweig, *Historia moderna,* p. 47; Tannenbaum, pp. 140–46; Henry Bamford Parkes, *A History of Mexico,* p. 306.

Molina described Mexican agriculture as "capitalist exploitation." Lauro Viadas, General Director of Agriculture and a chief collaborator of the Development Minister, contributed a statistical study confirming Molina's conclusions. Viadas described land hunger, a steady rise in prices on consumer goods and in rural and urban land values, "concentration of all kinds of production in the hands of a few," the rising cost of food staples, low cost of labor, and consequent "reduced production costs and increased profits" as "capitalist agriculture . . . lacking a noncapitalist farmer element."[35]

The major structural change in Mexico's countryside under this system of capitalist agriculture was not the entrenchment of alleged feudal patterns but rather the considerable expansion of a rural working class, as the Development Minister asserted and the 1910 census confirmed. Viadas expressed a corollary to the Minister's analysis when he wrote that, except for "capitalist" farmers, the Mexican countryside no longer contained "the farmer element, furnished with the indispensable resources necessary for family farming." The only remedy to the sharpening conflicts between rural "proletarians" and "capitalist" farmers, according to both the Development Minister and the Director of Agriculture, was to convert "as great a number as possible of the proletarians into property holders."[36]

Concurrent with this structural change in Mexico's countryside was the introduction of modern machinery and transportation. This was the case not only in San Luis Potosí and other mining states but also in more traditional farming areas, such as Morelos, native state of Emiliano Zapata. There the railroad, which reached Tepoztlán in 1897, opened up new commercial possibilities, and mechanization was introduced on large modernized farms. Trade flourished, the charcoal-making industry was launched, wire fences and steel plows were introduced, and even a cultural renaissance occurred. Private-property holders like the Zapata family lost their lands,

[35] Silva Herzog, pp. 161–63; text in Jesús Silva Herzog (ed.), *Colección de folletos para la historia de la Revolución Mexicana: la cuestión de la tierra*, I, 112 ff.
[36] *Ibid.*

as did the communal-land holders (*ejidatarios*), to big commercial farmers, interested in expanding the sugar industry in Morelos by developing large plantations with cheap labor and by constructing sugar mills on the plantations themselves. These mills were connected by railroad with urban industries (e.g., rum distilleries). Thus at the turn of the century sugar mills sprang up in the rural communities of Tepoztlán, Tlalneplantla, Cuautenco, and Jonacatepec (scene of Zapata's first major battle in the Revolution). The expansion of capitalist agriculture soon converted Morelos into what John Womack has called "a network of rural factories. By 1908 the seventeen owners of the thirty-six major *haciendas* in the state owned over 25 percent of its total surface. . . . Investment in irrigation works probably went as high as that in milling machinery. . . . After Hawaii and Puerto Rico, Morelos was the most productive cane-sugar region in the world."[37] Except for the Federal District, Morelos was by 1911 the most commercialized state south of Coahuila and west of Veracruz in all Mexico (based on per capita retail sales).[38]

Because of structural changes introduced by this increased pace of capitalist agricultural development in Mexico's countryside during the Porfiriato, a relatively static situation became highly dynamic. Social relationships on the farm were changing from relatively co-operative communal organization (*ejido*) to owner-foreman-worker-peon hierarchies. Many peasants experienced economic frustration and downward mobility—from small property holder or *ejidatario* to rural proletarian. For a few, there was social progress to foreman, miller, mechanic, or administrator. For economically deprived subsistence farmers and landless peons, employment on large

[37] John Womack, Jr. *Zapata and the Mexican Revolution* (New York: Alfred A. Knopf, 1969, p. 49; Mexico City: Siglo Veintiuno Editores, S.A., 1970).
[38] Rosenzweig, "El desarrollo," *El Trimestre Económico,* pp. 415–17; Moisés González Navarro, *Historia moderna de Mexico. El Porfiriato: la vida social,* pp. 144, 211; Oscar Lewis, *Life in a Mexican Village; Tepoztlán Restudied,* pp. xxv, 433–37; Gral. Gildardo Magaña, *Emiliano Zapata y el agrarismo en México,* Vol. I; Alberto Morales Jiménez, *Hombres de la Revolución Mexicana,* p. 210.

plantations may have offered some slight—at best seasonal—economic relief.

This is not to say that there did not exist hierarchical patterns of social organization in the countryside and within *ejidos* prior to the changes implemented during the Porfiriato. Rather, the degree and nature of hierarchical organization underwent change resulting in a more formalized and permanent division of labor and greater distances separating groups. As the peasants assumed more regularized working schedules and routines, superimposed from above for the profit of others instead of from within for their own *ejido*, they became at least dimly aware of new conditions, new exploitation, and new demands. Most peasants felt a strong sense of resentment about the changes being introduced into their lives. In an economy of rising prices on basic staples, the landowners' offer to the peasants of low wages in exchange for their labor on land that often originally had been theirs seemed unfair. Sociologically, an increasingly unbalanced structure, characterized by unfair exchange, was developing in Mexico's countryside. Earlier examples of unbalanced rural structures in Mexican history, in spite of ostensibly "stable" or "balanced" conditions, had resulted in violent peasant or Indian revolts, as in the case of the so-called "caste war" of 1847 in Yucatán. Behind the façade of the Paz porfiriana, there existed in the countryside a state of considerable social imbalance, worker resentment, and potential violence.[39]

Two kinds of appeal were to be made to landless peasants and rural proletarians during the Revolution. The first was simply to return lands to the peasantry. This appeal took different forms, ranging from the cautious and unfulfilled promises of upper-class leaders like Madero to the militant demands of peasant revolutionaries like Zapata. Falling between those two extremes was revolutionary leader Alvaro Obregón, who often spoke out for peasants and workers within a broad political coalition led by *hacendado* Venustiano Carranza. Both Zapata and Obregón came from families with small landholdings and a generally petty-bourgeois outlook. Zapata's

[39] Nelson Reed, *The Caste War of Yucatan;* Andres Molina Enríquez, *Los grandes problemas nacionales.*

status was on the decline, having had his lands taken away from him during the Porfiriato and having been forced to serve in the Army. Obregón, on the other hand, was on the way up. He had advanced from the rank of employee on a Sonoran chickpea *hacienda* to that of owner of a small piece of former government land. If sociologists are correct in their view that severe social dislocation—whether involving rapid upward (if blocked) mobility or rapid downward mobility—has often produced heightened social-psychological tensions, then it should come as no surprise that revolutionary leadership was produced, as in the case of Zapata and Obregón, by individuals moving in opposite directions on the social continuum. Zapata was clearly more radical and charismatic in his handling of the agrarian problem than was Obregón, perhaps because he was more disillusioned than Obregón. Moreover, Zapata did not share Obregón's esteem for capitalist agriculture. Obregón had made an auspicious start toward large-scale commercial farming in Sonora through his cultivation of chickpeas for the growing export market.[40]

The second kind of appeal made to the peasantry was that of the PLM, which demanded that rural proletarians "seize all the means of production," which meant both land and machines. These two appeals—to return farm land to the peasants, on the one hand, or to seize all means of production, on the other—were distinct in social derivation. By comparison with the Zapata movement, the PLM derived more from industrial workers, small merchants, and petty-bourgeois intellectuals than from peasant workers, *ejidatarios,* and small property holders. Nevertheless, the two appeals ultimately had much in common so far as the peasantry was concerned, judging both from the later Zapata-PLM alliance and from the

[40] Gral. Gildardo Magaña, *Emiliano Zapata y el agrarismo en México,* I, *passim;* Alberto Morales Jiménez, *Hombres de la Revolución Mexicana,* pp. 183–91, 207–18; Antonio Díaz Soto y Gama, *La revolución agraria del sur y Emiliano Zapata, su caudillo;* Djed Bórquez (pseud. of Juan de Dios Bojórquez), *Forjadores de la Revolución Mexicana,* pp. 26–35, 45–53; John W. F. Dulles, *Yesterday in Mexico,* pp. 4, 24, 26; Alvaro Obregón, *Ocho mil kilómetros en campaña.*

tendency for peasants to grab lands and mills spontaneously during the Revolution.

Thus, the process of social change taking place during the Porfiriato went beyond the new industries springing up in the cities and, by means of railroads and new farming techniques, reached into the remote confines of Mexico's supposedly "feudal" countryside. Agriculture became an eminently capitalistic enterprise, as land was bought and sold on an open land market and peasants were further incorporated into the wage labor system. The existence of this capitalistic social structure, dominated by bourgeois elite families, makes it difficult to conclude, as many writers have done, that the Mexican Revolution was in its essence a bourgeois (antifeudal) revolution. In the sense of economic nationalism, or protest against undemocratic politics, or anticlericalism, or dissatisfaction with economic slow-down, the Revolution to some degree did command at least tentative bourgeois backing. The structure of Mexico's society, however, implied an eventual confrontation between proletarians and capitalists. It therefore should come as no surprise that the main political force of the Precursor Movement—the PLM—as well as major political movements that emerged during the Revolution, brought together workers and peasants to fight against the bourgeoisie. For these participants, this was an anticapitalistic revolution.

How the Mexican peasants and workers fought, and eventually divided, in that proletarian revolution is a subject for another book. That they did indeed fight around relatively common, anticapitalist, antiimperialist issues, I have shown elsewhere.[41] History has shown that, after dividing among themselves, they were defeated, initially by the military setbacks suffered by the army of Pancho Villa and by the assassination of Zapata, ultimately by organized labor's dependent relationship to the government, the corruption, inadequacy, and uneven record of agrarian reform, and foreign capital's renewed thrust into the national economy. That Mexico's peasants and workers remain conscious of their

[41] Cockcroft, *Intellectual Precursors of the Mexican Revolution, 1900–1913.*

revolutionary heritage, the gains they did win (at least on paper) in the 1917 Constitution, and the need to reassert themselves in an effort to revolutionize society and determine their own destinies was manifested in 1968 by the fact that many of them rallied to the protest movement of the students, an event whose internal dynamics have yet to be completely understood and whose consequences are still being felt.

Chapter 4

DEPENDENCE AND THE INTERNATIONAL SYSTEM

Dale L. Johnson

THE NATURE OF DEPENDENCE

Colonialism and imperialism are concepts associated with the historical and contemporary analysis of European and U.S. capitalism. As actual phenomena, colonialism and imperialism result from the imperatives generated in the structure and functioning of capitalism, as the system grows and changes. The concept of dependence, as it has been elaborated in recent years, refers to the situation that the history of colonialism has left and that contemporary imperialism creates in underdeveloped countries. Dependence is imperialism seen from the perspective of underdevelopment.

Theotonio dos Santos has provided the clearest conceptualization of dependence. He suggests that "dependence is not an 'external factor,' as is often believed." Rather, dependence is a "conditioning situation" in which the specific histories of development and underdevelopment transpire in different regions and countries.

Dependence is a situation in which a certain group of countries have their economy conditioned by the development and expansion of another economy, to which the former is subject. The relation of interdependence between two or more economies, and between these and world trade, assumes the form of dependence when some countries (the dominant) can expand and give impulse to their own development, while other countries (the dependent) can only develop as a reflection of this expansion. This can have positive and/or negative effects on their immediate development. In all cases, the basic situation of dependence leads to a global situation in dependent countries that situates them in backwardness and under the exploitation of the dominant countries. The dominant countries have a technological, commercial, capital resource, and social-political predominance over the dependent countries (with predominance of some of these aspects in various historical moments). This permits them to impose conditions of exploitation and to extract part of the domestically produced surplus.[1]

Historical situations of dependence have shaped present-day underdevelopment in Latin America, Asia, and Africa. Underdevelopment is not an original state.[2] In Latin America, the early roots of the economic and social structure of underdevelopment are located in Spain's and Portugal's cultivation of Spanish America and Brazil as colonial dependencies. But political independence from colonial domination in the first decades of the nineteenth century did not mean independence to emulate Europe and North America in developing modern industrial societies. The reason for this lies principally in the character of the relationships between the Latin American countries and the industrializing countries of Europe and the United States. In the nineteenth century, Latin American countries developed as *de facto* colonies of the industrializing Center, with first England and then the United States serving as the heart of the imperial Center. This process brought about results more or less equivalent to

[1] Theotonio dos Santos, *La crisis de la teoría del desarrollo y las relaciones de dependencia en América Latina* (Santiago: "Boletín del Centro de Estudios Socio-Económicos, No. 3, 1968, Universidad de Chile), pp. 26–27. Dos Santos also elaborates upon these themes in his *El nuevo caracter de la dependencia* (Santiago: *Cuadernos del Centro de Estudios Socio-económicos,* No. 10, 1968) and *Socialismo o Fascismo: Dilema Latinoamericano* (Santiago: Editorial Prensa Latinoamericano, 1969).

[2] Latin America is not *un*developed. The region has been underdeveloping for several centuries. The concept of "developing countries" is misleading to the degree that it implies a self-sustained process of industrialization or a process of economic and social development similar to Europe and North America in the nineteenth and twentieth centuries.

those observable in European colonies elsewhere in today's underdeveloped world. Latin American economies became oriented to the export of primary products, normally under the control of foreign capital, and constituted as markets for imported manufactures. Foreign capital developed transportation facilities and utilities complementary to the export sector. The combined economic and military power of the imperial countries became instrumental in keeping Latin American nations as *de facto* colonies. Given this conditioning situation there has always been a weak impulse in Latin America toward economic growth in general and industrialization in particular. National governments or private national businessmen have had little or no control over international markets for primary goods, the prices of which are unstable and frequently subject to unfavorable terms of trade in relation to imports. Increasingly in the modern era, Latin America is losing control of its manufacturing sector to multinational corporations.

Dependence relations also shape the social structure of underdevelopment. A principal factor in the development and perpetuation of underdevelopment was (and is) the coincidence of interest between national oligarchies and the economic structure of underdevelopment. National businessmen grew up with and benefited from their nations' position as *de facto* colonies, as evidenced in the case of Mexico under Porfirio Díaz, described in the preceding chapter. Today, influential national businessmen still gear much of their investment to the export sector or activities complementary to foreign industrial capital, and they are interlocked in noncompetitive relationships with foreign investors.

Such are the general outlines of the situation of dependence. The objectives of this chapter are: 1. to demonstrate that incipient industrialization in Latin America has changed the character of dependence relations without fundamentally altering the basic fact of dependence itself; 2. to describe the changing pattern of foreign investment corresponding with incipient industrialization and the significance of these changes; 3. to portray briefly the institutional structure of the international system; and 4. to analyze the impact of the international system and the increasing presence of the multinational corporation upon the social and power structures of the more industrialized Latin American countries.

IMPORT-SUBSTITUTION, INDUSTRIALIZATION, AND DEPENDENCE

There are a variety of specific conditions of dependence, which include:

1. Secular tendencies toward deterioration in the terms of trade involving
   a. inelasticity of demand for primary exports;
   b. instabilities and gradual relative decline in quantum and prices of exports; and
   c. secular rise in prices of imports.
2. Chronic deficits in balance of payments
   a. caused by factors in (1);
   b. accelerating costs of services; and
   c. transfers of capital abroad.
3. Rigidities in the composition of imports provoked by
   a. the necessity of importing raw materials and intermediate goods to supply newly established industries;
   b. the necessity to import food because of crises in agriculture; and
   c. the chronic shortage of foreign exchange.
4. Progressive decapitalization involving
   a. the delatinamericanization of industry;
   b. payments of royalties, franchise costs, etc.;
   c. a net flow of private capital to the exterior; and
   d. services on foreign transactions and the foreign debt.
5. Political dependence generated by
   a. the close correspondence between the interests of national oligarchies and national bourgeoisies and the structure of the international system;
   b. dependence of national oligarchies upon international support for survival against the forces of nationalism and revolution;

   c. specific alliances of national businessmen and foreign investors;

   d. the development of foreign businessmen as independent loci of power within Latin American nations;

   e. extent of coercive power in the hands of agents and agencies of imperial power: the multinational corporation, the World Bank and International Monetary Fund, and United States agencies and military power; and

   f. power of the Latin American military forces strengthened by United States assistance and training.

A number of Latin American countries, particularly Argentina, Brazil, Chile, Mexico, and Uruguay, have experienced a modest degree of industrialization. It could be argued that the general situation and several of the specific manifestations of dependence represent a model of underdevelopment prior to incipient industrialization, and that economic and sociopolitical changes in the more industrialized countries have reduced dependencies. The weight of the evidence, however, supports a contrary hypothesis. The UN's Economic Commission for Latin America has presented voluminous evidence and thorough analyses of the secular tendency toward deterioration in the terms of trade, of the factors involved in balance of payments crises, and of the decapitalization which results from the net outflow of private capital, services on foreign transactions, and services on the large and growing foreign debt.[3]

---

[3] Progressive decapitalization has received less attention than the terms of trade and the balance of payments difficulties. Between 1950 and 1961, 2,962 million dollars of U.S. private capital flowed into the seven principal countries of Latin America, while the return flow was 6,875 million dollars. Due to pricing methods and illegal transfers, these figures underestimate the outflow of private capital from Latin America. Between the United States and all underdeveloped countries, the net inflow of private capital to the United States, according to the U. S. Department of Commerce, was 16.6 billion dollars between 1950 and 1965. Latin America's contribution to this sum was 7.5 billion dollars. André Gunder Frank ("Servicios extranjeros o desarrollo nacional?," *Comercio Exterior* XVI, Febrero de 1966) has shown for Latin

The process of import-substitution industrialization which has occurred or is beginning to occur in a number of Latin American countries does not, then, necessarily entail a reduction of dependence upon the international system. Economics remain highly dependent upon foreign trade. Exports and imports in Latin American countries represent proportions of the gross product that are higher than in the advanced industrial countries, and the Latin American countries are consequently highly subject to patterns of international commerce over which they have very little control. Exports and imports as a proportion of gross product are reduced very slowly. National manufacture of previously imported finished products often involves the importation of raw materials and intermediate parts (some industries, particularly foreign-owned, essentially assemble imported parts) and almost always

---

America as a whole that over 60 percent of current foreign exchange earnings from exports are consumed in the payment of services and usages other than imports of goods (about 15 percent of exchange earnings in profit repatriation, 15 percent in debt service, 10 percent in freight and insurance, 6 percent in foreign travel, and 16 percent in "other services," "donations," "funds transferred abroad," and "errors and omissions"). These data are for the early 1960s—if anything, the situation has deteriorated subsequently, especially in terms of services on the foreign debt, which also has serious implications in addition to exchange depletion and capital drain. Every country except Venezuela has a serious foreign debt problem. Argentina, for example, has average annual exports valued at about one billion dollars. In short-term foreign debts alone between 1962 and 1966, Argentina was scheduled to repay between a quarter billion and one-half billion dollars annually, for a five-year total of 1.7 billion dollars. The long-term debt totaled about one billion dollars. In 1964, Brazil had an external debt of nearly three billion dollars, with much of it payable. After the April 1964 coup the military government succeeded in refinancing the debt, and by 1965 had gained 873 million dollars through the Alliance for Progress and international agencies. In exchange, Brazil administered the favorite stabilization policies of the IMF, yielded an iron concession to Hanna Corporation, repealed laws governing repatriation of profits on foreign investments, participated in the Dominican Republic pacification of 1965, and gave support to the United States in international affairs.

requires the importation of the machinery and equipment necessary to establish production.

Brazil, Argentina, Mexico, and Colombia import goods and services that represent 9 percent to 12 percent of gross national product. The other Latin American countries have much higher import coefficients; for example, imports represent about 20 percent of gross national product in Chile, Peru, and Venezuela. During recent decades, import-substitution industrialization has been one factor in the reduction of import coefficients in several countries. (The principal factor, of course, has been that the quantum of exports has expanded modestly in most cases while the value of exports has declined relative to the price of imports.) But import substitution has caused a great rigidity in the composition of imports. Consumers' goods once accounted for a large proportion of imports. Now, imports of raw materials, intermediate goods, capital goods, and food claim most of the available foreign exchange. Colombia is a case in point. In the late 1940s, Colombian imports represented over 12 percent of gross national product. Import-substitution manufacture and unfavorable conditions for exports had reduced the import coefficient to about 10 percent by the early 1960s. Over the decade of the 1950s, imports of consumer goods dropped from 21 percent to 11 percent of total imports, while imports of raw materials and intermediate goods increased from 30 percent to 46 percent of total imports. Some national manufacture of capital goods (particularly construction materials and simple machinery) reduced their importation from 46 percent to 40 percent of imports. The rigidity of this composition of imports lies in the fact that one-fourth of all machinery and equipment needed by Colombia must be imported, and in the fact that a disruption of the supply of raw materials and intermediate goods would severely affect the economy.

In Latin America, there is little expectation that significant markets can be found for exports of manufactures that might loosen dependence upon primary exports. In Chile, for example, exports of manufactures, at 46.7 million dollars in 1950, gradually declined from that date to 32.4 million dollars in 1963.[4] At the same time, manufactured imports increased from 185.9 million dollars in 1950 to 477.9 million dollars in 1963. Food imports more than doubled to a 1963 level of 49.3 million dollars and continue to rise; chemical imports nearly tripled, as did machinery and tools (which account for one-half of all imports) and transport equipment. In general, the nature of the dependence upon primary exports and large quantities of imports changes with import-substitution industrialization but the dependence itself tends to continue, and in some ways even to become greater.

The crisis of traditional agriculture and the development of the urban economy (which are interrelated and causally dependent upon each other) has meant that increasing amounts of scarce foreign exchange are utilized for imports of foods in nearly all the Latin American countries. Countries undergoing industrialization shift their resources to urban centers and to commercial agriculture for export, and this is a principal factor in declining or lagging food production. Peru is a case in point:

. . . in 1964, 70 per cent of all agricultural products were destined primarily for export. Meanwhile, agricultural production for the domestic market, carried on mainly in the mountains, tended to stagnate and deteriorate more and more. As a result, importation of food products rose 'explosively' from close to 40 million dollars' worth in 1960 to more than 134 million dollars' worth in 1965. In 1966 alone, imports of food increased by 27 per cent.[5]

The agricultural crisis is aggravated by the continuation of concentration in the ownership of land and the pattern of

[4] On the structured obstacles to exports of manufactures in Latin America see Albert Hirschman, "On the Political Economy of Import-Substitution Industrialization" in Charles Nesbit (ed.) *Latin America: Problems in Economic Development* (New York: The Free Press, 1969).

[5] Aníbal Quijano Obregón, "Tendencies in Peruvian Development and in the Class Structure," James Petras and Maurice Zeitlin, eds., *Latin America: Reform or Revolution?* (New York: Fawcett, 1968).

changes in the mode of utilization of agricultural labor and capital. The modernization that has occurred in agriculture consists mainly in a shift from production for the national market to production for export, departures from "precapitalist" forms of labor servitude toward wage labor, and increasing adoption of farm technology. The effect of this modernization is to create a highly exploited rural proletariat and to force large members of peasants off the land into urban slums where they are relegated to marginal status in the growing underclasses of Latin American societies.

In general, incipient industrialization has meant that primary production (including mining) declined in weight in terms of contribution to the national product. Commercial and traditional agriculture and the export sector, however, have survived incipient industrialization more or less intact organizationally, particularly with respect to the position of the corresponding classes in control. The social forces of the old order—foreign and national capital in primary production, big export merchants, and *latifundistas*—are still firmly entrenched in their respective sectors and have accelerated the diversification of their activities into the urban economy as well.

Crises of the export sector, created by depression and war, induced industrialization. It is also true, however, that the process required foreign exchange earned by exporting in order to import raw materials, intermediary inputs, and machinery and equipment, particularly in the later stages. Moreover, part of the capital for industry depended upon the continuation of labor-repressive techniques of surplus appropriation in commercial and traditional agriculture (and nationally owned mining, which is technologically backward) in order that *latifundistas* and merchants trafficking in agricultural commodities could shift some of their investment to industry and related urban activities. The primary sector could not provide *both* capital and working classes with sufficient income to incorporate into a mass market for products of the urban economy.

Incipient industrialization depends upon the transfer of capital from all sectors to the urban economy, but it also has depended upon the exploitation in depth of existing markets, and the vegetative growth of these markets, among urban middle- and upper-income classes. This is the key to both the stagnation phase of incipient industrialization and the growing polarization of society between the affluent and the poor. The former have jobs, income, status, and participate in society and politics. The poor, on the other hand, composed of marginal underclasses, Indians, peasants, and workers either without employment or in jobs of high exploitation, are deprived of minimal and regular income, social status, and participation in education, politics, and other institutions of civilized societies.

CHANGING PATTERNS OF FOREIGN INVESTMENT

Foreign investments have played a key role in the development of underdevelopment. Traditionally, foreign investments in Latin America have been located in mineral production and tropical agriculture for export and in transportation facilities constructed to move primary exports out from the interior to the seaports. Foreign investors soon branched out into utilities and urban, nonindustrial activities. This pattern of foreign investment created the original model of the Latin American neocolonial economy based upon an international division of labor, in which the region exported primary products and imported manufactures. In the case of mineral and petroleum production, this created "enclave economies" that were viewed as extensions of the metropolitan industrial economy and assumed to function independently of the national economies. This model postulated national economies as consisting of a "feudal" agricultural sector and production of limited goods for urban markets by artisanry and light manufacture. In the case of sugar, tropical fruits, and other commercial crops, the situation was assumed to be similar except that what national economic surplus became available (particularly in coffee-producing countries) was diverted to commercial agriculture under the control of companies like United Fruit or of national *latifundistas* and powerful merchant-exporters. Actually, enclave economies did not function independently of local economies, and commercial agriculture (not "feudal" agriculture) absorbed much of the available land and capital and gave direction to the entire path of development. Other versions of the "enclave economies" model, formulated more recently, recognize that primary production tends to orient national investment toward activities complementary to the neocolonial economy and to create an extreme structural dependence upon international trade and upon export taxes and import customs as governmental budgetary sources. This type of structure, created by foreign investment and extreme dependence upon foreign trade, constituted classical underdevelopment.

The sociological model of class and power structure associated with this conception is that of a peasantry in servitude, a small working class in mining and light industry, an artisanry, and a small urban middle class. These classes were all dominated socially and politically by an oligarchy of feudal lords and big commercial interests in league with foreign investors. Although these economic and sociological models are based upon some dubious theoretical assumptions,[6] as descriptions of the neocolonial economic and social structure they bore at least some superficial similarity to the actual state of affairs—several decades ago. The best that could be said for the models today is that they crudely fit those Latin American countries that have not yet begun a process of incipient industrialization.

Latin American countries, of course, still function as suppliers of petroleum and strategic raw materials needed by the United States industrial and war machines (the protection of strategic mineral supplies still preoccupies U.S. policymakers) and they continue to constitute markets for United

---

[6] See especially André Gunder Frank's critique of "dualism" in Chapter 12. See also the debate over "feudalism" in Latin America: Frank, Chapters 1 and 2; Rudolfo Stavenhagen, "Seven Fallacies about Latin America," and Luís Vitale, "Latin America: Feudal or Capitalist?" both in Petras and Zeitlin, *Latin America: Reform or Revolution?*

States manufactures. What has changed significantly is the *form* in which countries are constituted as a market for manufactured products. Foreign exchange shortages and exchange controls in Latin America no longer permit imports of large quantities of consumer goods. The new pattern is for multinational corporations to provision the national market from within through the establishment of enterprises located within the country itself.

The facts on recent foreign investment in Latin America are clear. The trend is toward investment in manufacturing and other urban activities (department stores, retail outlets of corporate subsidiaries, chain markets, banking, and the communication media).[7] In manufacturing, the value of United States investments increased from 8 percent of total investment in 1950 to about 25 percent in 1968. This investment is now heavily concentrated in Brazil, Mexico, and Argentina, but has also been increasing during the 1960s in Peru, Venezuela, Uruguay, Chile, and Colombia. Sales of United States manufacturing affiliates increased 70 percent between 1957 and 1962 (compared to a 17 percent sales increase for manufactures in the United States). Production capacity of American manufacturing companies abroad increased 31 percent in 1965, 17 percent in 1966, and 23 percent in 1967 (many now work with excess capacity while still managing to repatriate large profits).

Since the end of the Second World War, direct investments abroad of U.S. corporations have zoomed from five billion dollars to over sixty-five billion dollars in 1969 (about twenty billion dollars in underdeveloped countries). Between 1960 and 1965, twenty-two hundred corporations undertook six thousand separate investments. The key institution in the new wave of foreign investment, however, is the giant multinational corporation, controlled from North America or Europe. Considering just North American investment, less than one hundred firms account for over two-thirds of all U.S. investment abroad. Foreign investment by the multinational corporation has profound significance for the Amer-

[7] Jon Frappier, "U.S. Media Empire: Latin America," *NACLA Newsletter* II (January 1969), pp. 1–11.

ican economy and even greater significance for the handful of giants for whom the United States represents a home office and half or less of their total business. Michael Locker aptly illustrates this:

> Statistics for foreign sales by U.S. firms provide another indicator of increasing U.S. dependence on overseas operations. For example, in 1950, foreign sales totaled approximately $37 billion (13 per cent of GNP). Domestically produced exports accounted for one-third of these sales; goods produced by U.S. subsidiaries abroad accounted for the other two-thirds. By 1964, foreign sales had climbed to $110 billion (18 per cent of GNP), with only one-fifth supplied through exports. Twenty-two per cent of total profits are presently derived from foreign sales—as compared with 10 per cent in 1950. The larger corporations in several key industries are especially dependent on overseas markets and profits. Several leading U.S. firms (including Standard Oil of New Jersey, Colgate-Palmolive, Singer, National Cash Register, Texaco and Burroughs) are deriving *more than half* of their profits from foreign sales, much of it produced overseas; a long list of other giants (e.g., Eastman Kodak, Pfizer, Caterpillar Tractor, Corn Products, St. Joseph Lead, Minnesota Mining and Manufacturing, Goodyear and Coca-Cola) derive between 30 and 50 percent from these sales.[8]

The consequence of the upsurge and pattern of foreign investment in the region is a trend toward delatinamericanization of the industrial economy. An Argentine journalist of considerable analytic skill has observed that the process of deargentinization is proceeding among both medium-size firms, which are being brought up by foreign corporations, and large enterprises:

> . . . Some firms began to pass into foreign hands through a mechanism at once simple and dramatic: the suppliers of machinery and equipment that remained unpaid or

[8] Michael Locker, "Overseas Expansion and Government Contracting: The Story of Kaiser's Global Empire," *NACLA Newsletter* II (April 1968), p. 1.

creditors by royalties began to hold stock in these firms. Then, generally in a second step, they began to buy up the majority package. This has occurred at the level of medium-sized firms.[9]

This phenomenon of buying up smaller firms in the process of creating vertical integration is particularly acute in Argentine industries supplying parts for motor vehicles, textiles, chemicals, and tobacco (Philip Morris recently acquired a monopoly of the market for cigarettes). The process is also proceeding in banking. The same has been happening in Brazil since 1964. The credit squeeze of the anti-inflationary program starves Brazilian firms of capital and gives foreign companies with access to more extensive capital resources the opportunity to buy up Brazilian industries at less than their real value. In 1963, subsidiaries of U.S. corporations accounted for about 30 percent of total manufacturing sales. By 1965, foreign firms had half or more of the market in machinery and electrical equipment, transport equipment, rubber products, drugs, cosmetics, and tobacco, and 20 percent or more of the market in all other Brazilian manufacturing sectors except food and beverages.

In the sector of large enterprise in Argentina:

. . . in 1956, 75 of the 100 largest firms censused were Argentine; in 1966, the participation had fallen to only 50.[10]

The fifty largest firms in Argentina include the giant state petroleum company and four state-operated transport and utility enterprises (34 percent of the capital of the fifty largest), European firms (29 percent of capital of the same fifty firms), North American companies (22 percent of capital), and private Argentine firms (22 percent of capital). In

9 Julian Delgado, "Industria: el desafío a la Argentina," *Primera Plana* No. 297, 3 de setiembre de 1968, p. 56. *Primera Plana,* an outstanding magazine, was closed down by Argentina's military government in 1969.

10 *Ibid.,* p. 56.

effect, foreign capital dominates large enterprise, while the state provides low-cost fuel, power, and transportation.[11]

Foreign investment normally takes the form of the importation of machinery and equipment by multinational corporations into the recipient country. It is not unusual for foreign capital to retain entire control of the subsidiary or firm established. On the other hand, there are cases, which appear to be on the increase in some countries, of joint ventures and mixed enterprises that are negotiated directly with big national investors and/or the state; stocks and bonds of some international companies are sold in national capital markets; development and investment banks mobilize private and state capital for collaborative undertakings. Both national businessmen and foreign capital find security and profit in these associative arrangements. In Mexico they are encouraged by law.

The fact that foreign investors bring machinery and equipment with them on undertaking a new investment does not mean that foreign capital is necessarily entirely foreign in origin or that it represents capital that would not otherwise be available to the recipient country. In fact, there has been a *new outflow* (after a net inflow in the 1950s to manufacturing in several countries) of private capital from most Latin American countries for about a decade. Often national capital is involved in the operation of enterprises under complete or effective foreign control. It is not uncommon for foreign-controlled firms to raise national currencies for operating capital. Banks, insurance companies, and financial corporations, foreign[12] and national, draw upon local savings and loan to foreign corporations and sometimes purchase their stock. Also, profits on sales within the country represent national capital. At least part of the net outflow of capital, then, is generated within the recipient country itself.

It is not my intention here to become involved in the

[11] See also Jaime Fuchs, *La penetración de los trusts yanquis en la Argentina* (Buenos Aires: Editorial Cartago, 1969).

[12] However, the biggest depositors in foreign banks are usually foreign businesses.

conventional analysis of the pros and cons of foreign investment, but a quote from an internal document of the Argentine Unión Industrial (hardly noted for its economic nationalism)[13] may be useful. The Unión Industrial summarizes
the positive and negative aspects of foreign investment in
Argentina:

The positive would be:

Substantial improvement of the financial position of
numerous important firms.
Renovation of the methods of management, administration, commercialization, etc.
Incorporation of new productive technologies and improvement of equipment.
Improvement in the balance of payments.

The negative effects would be:

Transfer of control to foreign hands.
Monopolistic or quasimonopolistic control of important industrial markets by strong foreign firms.
Narrowing of the future possibility of overcoming
technological dependence.
Decreasing possibility for Argentine executives of upward mobility within the firms, particularly to highest executive class.
Weakening in the formation of a national entrepreneurial class.
Disadvantageous competitive situations for Argentine
firms that subsist in the market.
An increase in the deficit of the balance of payments

[13] To my knowledge the Unión Industrial has never opposed
Law 14.780 of 1958, which provides: "1) foreign capital enjoys
the same rights that the law accords to national capital; 2) investments can be channeled toward the installation of new plants
or toward the amplification of existing plants; 3) the incorporation of capital can be made indistinctively in foreign exchange,
machinery or equipment, semi-elaborated products, or raw materials; 4) repatriation of capital will have no more limitations
than those that are agreed upon at the moment of authorization
of the investment; 5) in order to encourage investment the Government will extend import custom and tax concessions . . ." (and
other provisions favoring foreign investments).

beyond the short term; the possibility of the insertion of the development of acquired Argentine firms within a world market strategy of foreign firms in control.

Diversion of national financial resources toward more solid, solvent, and profitable foreign firms.[14]

Rather than discuss the pros and cons of foreign investment in a specific country, which are, to be sure, interesting and illuminating, it is important to examine the present meaning and future significance for Latin American economies and social structures. The theoretical significance is noted with clarity by Theotonio dos Santos:

It is the specific conditions of the world economy in which the process of industrialization in our continent is realized—and perhaps of the countries in development in general—that essentially changes the meaning of this process. Industrialization in these countries transpires within the context of the process of world capitalist integration under the control of monopoly capital.[15]

The following conclusions can be drawn from dos Santos' careful research on the recent trends and general significance of foreign investment, especially in Brazil, which he takes to represent the future of Latin America:

(1) Large scale enterprise is now the predominant form of economic organization in the urban economy. Foreign capital, particularly U.S. based multi-national corporations, have achieved a high degree of control over large enterprise, notably in manufacturing.

(2) This has led to an increasing degree of economic concentration, monopoly of markets, and high profit levels. Repatriation of profits, together with fees for royalties, technical services, interest, and other services on foreign capital represents a net outflow of capital.

(3) An "administrative stratum," representing the interests of foreign capital emerges. There is increased syn-

---

[14] Cited by Delgado, *op. cit.*

[15] Theotonio dos Santos, *El nuevo caracter de la dependencia* (Santiago: Centro de Estudios Socio-Economicos, *Cuadernos,* No. 10, 1968), p. 10.

dical and political organization of foreign capital, leading to a high degree of influence over politics and state policies.[16]

Under present circumstances the future can only mean further delatinamericanization of underdeveloped economies. Sectors where foreign capital is involved continue to grow, while sectors under national control lag behind or stagnate. This appears to be as valid for countries in which, like Argentina and Brazil, the multinational corporation is omnipresent, as it is for rapidly industrializing countries like Peru. According to the Peruvian sociologist Aníbal Quijano, writing before the ostensibly nationalist policies of the military government took effect in 1969–70: "Of all the economic sectors . . . only those that are directly connected with and controlled by foreign capital continue to develop, regardless of their degree of participation in overall production."[17] Quijano notes that by the early 1960s the ascendance of foreign capital had become clear; about 80 percent of all investment in the industrial sector by then was of foreign origin. The current Peruvian government is pushing industrialization. It is becoming clear, as our next chapter will show, that the government still favors foreign investment in the industrial sector.

This is not to say that national investors are being entirely eclipsed in Latin America, though this possibility always exists if trends continue. National capital is, however, already integrated into a dependent relationship with foreign industrial and finance capital. This is true not only in associative ventures, but also in the sense that foreign capital has access to technical, financial, and power resources, as well as other competitive advantages, that national capital cannot match. Also, where foreign capital has control of basic industry, national capital finds outlets for investment in associative arrangements, in supplying industries to basic industry, and in light industry producing ordinary consumer goods, real estate, and speculative financial activities. The dependence

[16] *Ibid.*

[17] Aníbal Quijano Obregón, "Tendencies in Peruvian Development and Class Structure," Petras and Zeitlin, *Latin America: Reform or Revolution?*, pp. 294–95.

relation, however, is one that is also advantageous to national businessmen, as will be elaborated upon shortly.

The direction of foreign control of national economies is clear. Where foreign capital has traditionally operated, there is likely to be continuation of control over primary sectors. Foreign capital will no doubt continue as an important factor in transportation, power, and communication, and is rapidly achieving control of the motor vehicle industry, consumer durables, capital goods, and other large-scale or highly technological industries. These are principal growth sectors in countries undergoing incipient industrialization and constitute practically the only growth possibilities, under existing governments and institutional arrangements, in those countries, such as Argentina and Uruguay, where over-all economic development is stagnant. This pattern can easily degenerate into a system under predominant foreign control producing television sets, cars, and gadgetry for the middle- and upper-income groups and Coca-Cola for the workers. Meanwhile, subsidiaries of Madison Avenue firms and American communication media sell the populace on the happiness to be found in the consumption of superfluous goods,[18] produced with the latest labor-saving technology; on the virtues of free enterprise; and on the goodness of whatever military dictator or antinational authoritarian regime happens to be in power.

An analysis of foreign investment in Latin America would not be complete without a commentary upon the position of the multinational corporation vis-à-vis the Latin American Common Market. Here we may let *Fortune,* a magazine that carefully reflects the latest trends and thinking among North American big businesses, tell the story:

> For U.S. private enterprise, the common market spells enticing new opportunity. Apart from the traditional mining (Anaconda, Creole Petroleum) and farming (United Fruit, W. R. Grace), U.S. investment until now

[18] Such consumption can only be considered a crime against humanity, and perhaps national suicide, when millions of people lack a minimum diet, a roof, education, medical care, employment, and any hope for the future.

has mostly gone into manufacturing for "import substitution"—producing for a national market under protective tariffs. But U.S. businessmen are beginning to see in the Latin American common market the advantages that they seized upon in the European Common Market: the chance to move to the broader, more competitive, and potentially more profitable task of supplying a market big enough to be economic on its own terms. . . .

In many a boardroom, the common market is becoming a serious element in planning for the future. Ford Motor of Brasil, which makes Galaxies, thinks it could mesh nicely with Ford of Argentina, which makes Falcons, thus deriving economies of scale by producing both cars for larger markets. Kodak, which now makes photographic paper in Brazil, would like to make exportable film in Mexico and cameras and projectors in Argentina. I.T.T., with telecommunication-equipment plants in Argentina, Brazil, Chile, and Mexico, wants to "rationalize production, interchange parts, and raise production high enough to export from Latin America to other parts of the world," says Vice President Gerhard Andlinger, the company's group executive for Latin America. Other corporations interested in rationalizing or expanding operations include G.E., Remington Rand, Otis Elevator, Worthington, Firestone, Deere, Westinghouse Air Brake, American Machine and Foundry.

This may sound like a U.S. take-over of the whole Latin-American economy, and plenty of Latin-American businessmen believe that's just what's afoot. But the fear is not necessarily valid. As things stand now, most foreign-owned enterprises in Latin America reinvest a lot of their profits, thus tending more and more to be part of the landscape. Yet if they are really going to take up residence and avoid the take-over charge, U.S. subsidiaries will have to admit Latin Americans more readily to an ownership role. Telling them to buy stock in the parent company on Wall Street is so far not the answer, since getting the dollars, and getting them out, is balked by currency restrictions and tax law.

A quick sentence in the Punta del Este declaration hints at a long-range solution: a common market stock market, which would let an Argentine buy stock in a

Venezuelan brewery, or a Colombian buy stock of Brazil's Willys-Overland.[19]

In the absence of viable institutions for coordinated regional planning of development programs by the Latin American nations involved[20] and the control or outright exclusion of foreign capital with superior capital, technology, organization, and marketing resources, the Common Market will only contribute to furthering the process of delatinamericanization of underdeveloped economies.

THE INTERNATIONAL SYSTEM

If dependence is the basic conditioning situation of underdevelopment, then it is the international system upon which Latin American nations are dependent. This concept implies a structure—a structure of institutions, classes, and power arrangements. The dynamic process that occurs within that structure is rightfully termed imperialism. Imperialism is an institutionalized system of control which systematically shapes the institutions and structures of dependent, dominated countries and limits their freedom of action, if they are to avoid the system's sanctions, to system-defined alternatives.

The international economy is the fundamental aspect of a larger system that is complex in structure, expansive, and viable. But, as implied in the definition of imperialism, the international system is not simply economic. It is also a stratified system of power relations.

At the core of the nexus of power relations within the international system is the integrated, multinational corporation. Particularly important are the oil companies, some utilities and transportation companies, certain financial institutions, and the industrial giants in consumer durables, chemicals, and

[19] *Fortune,* June 1967 as cited by Edie Black, "Who's Common Market Is It?" *NACLA Newsletter* I (August 1967), p. 3.
[20] See Miguel Teubal's excellent analysis of the unfeasibility of regional planning in his "The Failure of Latin America's Economic Integration," in Petras and Zeitlin, *op. cit.,* pp. 120–44.

capital goods. These expansive corporate enterprises operate in a growing world market that they divide among themselves just as they have the markets of the industrial countries. Investments are oriented toward expansion of markets, toward guaranteeing sources of raw materials and other inputs, toward profit maximization, and toward the establishment of monopoly positions. All these factors, of course, are interdependent. Profit maximization would be impossible without expansion of markets, the control of supplies, and the establishment of monopoly (or monopolistic competition within an oligopolistic structure).[21]

The ascendance of the multinational corporation is a consequence of the process of economic concentration in the industrial countries. Economic concentration is a continuous process in all capitalist economies, developed, developing, and underdeveloped. In the developed United States, it has reached a point in which five hundred industrial corporations —one-tenth of 1 percent of all such corporations—account for about one-third of all production. The top fifty industrials do as much business as the next 450 in size, and the biggest ten have profits that equal half that of the next 490 corporations.[22] And these data obscure the degree of concentration of corporate control among the giants themselves and in relation to big United States banks by way of interlocking directorates. (The latest example of concentration of economic power, the quickened pace of corporate mergers and the surge of the conglomerate phenomenon, mainly, though not entirely, exclude the giants.)

It also happens that the big foreign investors that have been termed the multinational corporations are found prin-

[21] It is quite erroneous to establish growth itself or corporate goals other than profit maximization as the guiding principle in the analysis of corporate behavior, as John Kenneth Galbraith has attempted to do in his celebrated book, *The New Industrial State* (Boston: Houghton Mifflin, 1967).

[22] See Robert Heilbroner, *The Limits of American Capitalism* (New York: Harper Torchbooks, 1966), Gabriel Kolko, *Wealth and Power in America* (New York: Frederick Praeger, 1962), and Paul Baran and Paul Sweezy, *Monopoly Capital* (New York: Monthly Review, 1967).

cipally among the largest concerns, which are also the United States' biggest exporters of manufactures and importers of raw materials mined in underdeveloped countries. Military production is an avaricious consumer of strategic metals, and these corporations are also among the major recipients of defense contracts with which the U.S. military establishment protects the international system from the presumed threats of the Soviet Union and China and the real threats of nationalist, populist, or socialist revolutions in underdeveloped countries. Moreover, these same corporations receive a large share of government subsidies for research and development in new technologies under the guise of defense and space contracts.[23]

Documentation for these generalizations is not lacking. Only forty-five U.S. corporations, each with investments in excess of one hundred million dollars, account for 57 percent of all American foreign investment. One hundred sixty-three firms account for 80 percent of all American foreign investment. In manufacturing, between 20 percent and 50 percent of output in nearly all sectors is exported or purchased by the government for defense purposes. Fifteen percent of raw materials consumed by all industry goes to defense. Nearly all the U.S. supplies of manganese, chromite, cobalt, nickel, tin, and bauxite are imported and most of these metals are consumed by the big industries.[24]

Multinational corporations are rapidly expanding export sales and foreign operations in a wide range of sectors. In chemicals, for example, exports nearly doubled between 1957

[23] Theoretical treatments with specifics relating to Latin America are Harry Magdoff, *The Age of Imperialism* (New York: Monthly Review Press, 1969), James O'Connor, *The Meaning of Economic Imperialism* (pamphlet by the Radical Education Project, Ann Arbor, Michigan), Celso Furtado, "La concentración del poder económica en los Estados Unidos y sus proyecciones en América Latina," *Estudios Internacionales* I (Octubre de 1967 y Marzo de 1968), Paul Baran, *The Political Economy of Growth* (New York: Monthly Review Press, 1956).

[24] Heather Dean, *Scarce Resources: The Dynamics of American Imperialism* (pamphlet of the Radical Education Project, Ann Arbor, Michigan).

and 1965 to a value of 2,402 million dollars, while sales by affiliates of U.S. chemical corporations abroad tripled to a level of 6,851 million dollars; in nonelectrical machinery, exports increased about 40 percent between 1957 and 1965 to 5,158 million dollars, while sales of foreign affiliates tripled to a level of 5,257 million; the same trends are evident in metals, rubber products, paper, transportation equipment, and other manufactures.[25]

These corporations operate under an imperative to grow.[26] They seek to assure sources of raw material supplies abroad, to promote exports, to open up investment opportunities abroad for their enormous accumulations of capital, and to guarantee the security of existing investments.[27]

Thus (a) the growth imperative, (b) expansion abroad by way of foreign investment, (c) vested interests in maintaining export markets and assuring supplies of raw materials, and (d) vested interests in government contracts for defense and research and development related to defense and the space race with the Soviet Union, make the multinational corporations, and the classes that control and serve them,

[25] Harry Magdoff, "The Age of Imperialism," *Monthly Review XX* (June 1968), pp. 11–53.

[26] On the growth "imperative" stemming from oligopolistic accumulation see Paul Baran and Paul Sweezy, *Monopoly Capital* (New York: Monthly Review Press, 1967); on the "technological imperative" see John Kenneth Galbraith, *The New Industrial State* (Boston: Houghton Mifflin, 1967).

[27] There is a certain contradiction between the investment-seeking capital accumulations of the large corporations that find a resting place abroad and the fact that the return on these investments soon amounts to more than the original investment. Between 1950 and 1965, U.S. direct investments in Latin America increased from 4.5 billion dollars to 10.3 billion dollars. At the same time, income on this investment transferred to the U.S. during this period amounted to 11.3 billion dollars. The capital inflow from investments in other underdeveloped regions was 9.1 billion dollars greater than the flow to these regions. Only in Europe and Canada has the flow of direct investments been greater than the return on existing investments. This level of capital inflow would seem to create an even greater imperative toward foreign expansion.

the principal beneficiaries of the status quo within the international system.

The multinational corporations, however, do not operate by themselves, but within the context of a set of modern international institutions, and among power groups whose interests are interrelated with those of the corporations. The expansions of multinational corporations to underdeveloped countries has in part been made feasible by the rationalization of international capital flows and monetary transactions carried out by the World Bank and the International Monetary Fund—international agencies that rather strictly serve the interests of the multinational corporations, exporters of the industrial nations, and international financial circles. These agencies can and do exercise enormous pressure upon underdeveloped countries to keep their financial houses in order and to promote a favorable climate for private business.[28] The favorite mechanism of control by the IMF and World Bank is setting conditions on loans—creditor governments must follow certain monetary, fiscal, and tariff policies that are consistent with the interests that the international agencies represent. The adoption of these policies usually means economic contraction, unemployment, and reduced real salaries and wages in the country that applies them. Underdeveloped countries find it difficult to avoid external borrowing due, in good part, to their dependent position in the international economy in the first instance. This is not a conspiracy. The policies of international leaders are rational and flow from the structure of the international system. Harry Magdoff notes:

> By its structure and administrative procedures, the IMF acts only to enforce the rules of the game that govern the existing power relations among countries—*rules that evolved in the very process by which some nations be-*

[28] See Andrew Shonfield, *The Attack on World Poverty* (New York: Random House, 1962); David Felix, *Monotarists, Structuralists and Import Substitution Industrialization* (New Brunswick, N.J.: Rutgers University Monograph Series "Studies in Comparative International Development" I, No. 10, 1965); I. Marcus Fleming, *The International Monetary Fund, Its Form and Functioning* (Washington, D.C. 1964).

came the rich nations and other nations became the poor nations.[29] (emphasis in original)

U.S. agencies and foreign policy are perhaps the crucial buttresses of the international system. The Export-Import Bank and the Agency for International Development actively promote U.S. business interests abroad as well as U.S. exports. The various programs of the Alliance for Progress are supportive of the same ends.[30]

United States aid programs, which typically are extended in the form of credits for imports from the United States (about 90 percent of U.S. aid has been thus "tied," though a loosening up is in process) transported in U.S. ships are geared to the promotion of American exports in general and apparently to the exports of multinational corporations in particular. In iron and steel products, fertilizers, and railroad transportation equipment between 25 percent and 30 percent of exports are financed by U.S. economic aid; in rubber products, nonferrous metals, and petroleum products, the percentage financed by aid is between 8 percent and 11 percent; about 5 percent of exports are thus financed in machinery and equipment, chemicals, motor vehicles, engines and parts, and basic textiles.[31]

Under the altruistic-sounding "Food for Peace" program, the U.S. government acquires national currencies from the sale of U.S. agricultural surpluses that are retained or, whenever possible, used to promote U.S. goals of strengthening free enterprise and American conceptions of freedom. About 30 percent of all U.S. agricultural exports are financed by

[29] Magdoff, 1968, *op. cit.*, p. 49.

[30] As President John F. Kennedy once put it, "Foreign aid is a method by which the United States maintains a position of influence and control around the world, and sustains a good many countries which would definitely collapse, or pass into the Communist bloc." Committee on Foreign Relations, U.S. Senate, *Some Important Issues in Foreign Aid* (Washington, D.C.: Report prepared by the Legislative Reference Service of the Library of Congress, 1966), p. 15.

[31] Charles D. Hyson and Alan M. Strout, "Impact of Foreign Aid on U.S. Exports," *Harvard Business Review* (January–February 1968).

aid programs. Through the Food for Peace program in India, the U.S. has come to hold about 20 percent of the national currency and in Pakistan about 15 percent. Thus, to the degree that these funds are used (most are held in reserve), the United States is in a position to strengthen the foreign and private sectors in countries committed to state planning of national development.

If each individual aid program in Latin America were examined, most would be found to be of apparent benefit to the recipient countries, free of strings except that materials and their transport and any contracts let abroad be American in origin. Some aid programs, however, are far from disinterested and relate directly to U.S. business interests and/or military policy. Tobis cites such a case in Guatemala:

> An example of how this "aid" works is seen in the roadbuilding project sponsored by USAID in Guatemala. USAID and the Export-Import Bank are each providing about $6 million for the Rio Hondo Road Project. This road will connect Puerto Barrios (the major Atlantic port, owned by IRCA) with Honduras. The $14 million principal plus roughly $5 million in interest has to be paid back to the United States in dollars. . . . The machinery for the construction must all be bought in the United States. The engineers, the contractors, and the supervisors are all from United States companies. Three United States Firms . . . are constructing the road. . . . It is interesting that Thompson-Cornwall is the same company that constructed the United States airbase at Retalhuleu. This was the base from which United States planes left Guatemala for the Bay of Pigs invasion. . . .
>
> The United States government claims that the road which is being built to connect Puerto Barrios with Honduras will aid Guatemala and Central America in two ways. First, the project will create jobs in the Oriente portion of the country where the *guerrilleros* are concentrated and "will show the *campesinos* in that area that we are doing something to help them."
>
> Second, the United States claims that the road will increase Common Market trade between the Central American countries. But Puerto Barrios is primarily used

as the port entry for United States products which are to be sold in Central American countries. The other Central American countries have little use for the Atlantic port in Guatemala. The road will therefore be of greatest benefit to the United States companies that export to Central America.[32]

This by no means exhausts the instruments of domination, which also extend to the sphere of nongovernmental institutions. The American labor movement, as we will elaborate in the next chapter, has long helped national businessmen and international capital, allegedly with CIA money, to fight political unionism that could make the working classes in underdeveloped countries a force for social change. Increasingly, U.S. universities and private foundations, which are becoming heavily involved in education in Latin America, are becoming a facet of the system of international domination.

Foreign policy flows naturally, and by and large rationally, from the structure described. The basis of United States foreign policy is a conception of national interest as inherently involved in the strengthening of international capitalism against the threats of socialism and nationalism. The 1965 United States invasion of Santo Domingo and the genocidal war that the United States perpetrates upon the Indochinese people indicate the lengths to which the imperial colossus will go wherever nationalism or socialism achieve a strong foothold. But counterrevolutionary warfare is a last resort to stem the forces of change. It is preferable that "Free World" governments police themselves. In Latin America, the key to the subversion of nationalism and socialism and the promotion of "internal security" has been United States military aid programs. Military aid to Latin America between 1953 and 1966 totaled 1,135 million dollars. Aid in recent years has been running about one hundred million dollars annually, and since 1963 most of it has been channeled into the training and equipping of Latin American armed forces for action in internal security, counterinsurgency, and civic action.

[32] David Tobis, "Foreign Aid: The Case of Guatemala," *Monthly Review* (January 1968), pp. 43–44.

The array of military training facilities and bases designed specifically to deal with military contingencies in Latin America are impressive:

In the Panama Canal Zone are located (1) the U. S. Army Forces Southern Command, which oversees all military programs in Latin America including counterinsurgency training programs by Special Forces units, the civic action programs of Latin American armies, any combat or "stability operations" in Latin America (such as the Dominican Republic invasion and the Bolivian operation against Che Guevara's guerrillas), the forty-three military advisory missions in seventeen countries, as well as the hardware involved in the Military Assistance Program; (2) The U. S. Army School of the Americas, which has trained over twenty thousand Latin Americans in counterinsurgency, civic action, and other military skills; (3) Albrook Air Force Base, which provides flight training and training in the virtues of napalm; (4) The U. S. Army Jungle Warfare School, which offers training programs in jungle survival and combat; (5) The 8th Special Forces contingent, which consists of some eight hundred Green Berets, who travel throughout Latin America offering special instruction in counterinsurgency; (6) The U. S. Army Tropic Test Center, which is involved in the application of sophisticated technology to counterrevolutionary strategy.

Puerto Rico harbors vast U.S. naval facilities designed to protect the U.S. sphere of influence to the South, including the Headquarters of the Commander South Atlantic Force and Roosevelt Roads. The Strategic Air Command has Ramey Air Force Base. Counterinsurgency training facilities are located at the Salinas Training Area.

In the United States, the Agency for International Development runs the International Police Academy, which has trained two thousand police officers, 60 percent of whom come from Latin America, in the most efficient methods of population control and paramilitary operations; an Inter-American Defense College exists for high-ranking Latin officers. In addition to the CIA, there are a number of intelligence-gathering, research, and contingency planning agencies such as The Center for Research in Social Systems and The Atlantic Research Corporation.[33]

United States private investment, aid programs, foreign policy, military assistance, military interventions, and international agencies, under the influence or control of the international business community, are interwoven and oriented toward the promotion and maintenance of influence and control in other countries. These are the dimensions of imperialism. There is one further dimension that bears brief examination: the ideological.

Economic aid is good business. It is not a gift, nor does it necessarily have to involve an imperialist plot. There certainly is nothing wrong with a nation promoting its own economic interests. Japan, several Western European nations, Canada, the Soviet Union, and Eastern European countries extend economic and technical aid in different forms without thereby achieving a high degree of control over the recipient country. The problem with U.S. aid is that it is used as an instrument of control at the same time that the "welfare" ideology that underlies it legitimizes the control structures.

There is a constant growth of internal administrative structures influenced or controlled by U.S. officials (or by thoroughly "Americanized" national administrative and technical experts). In some countries, this has proceeded to the extent that the Agency for International Development—sometimes working closely with a team of experts from American universities and backed by a large American foundation, as in recent tax reform proposals in Chile, Colombia, and El Salvador—virtually writes legislation, subsequently involving itself in the administration of the program. Latin American countries certainly need a thorough reform of tax structures (and any agrarian reform may be better than none), but it impresses me as exceedingly perverse when a foreign power attempts or actually arranges to write and implement tax laws in another country. That such a phenomenon strikes

[33] This kind of information is reported in various issues of *NACLA Newsletter*.

many others as an example of American nobility and generosity is a tribute to the power of ideology.

In addition to funds, the many programs of the Alliance for Progress have brought a flood of American experts into advisory and administrative positions in agricultural programs, community development, labor bureaus, development projects of all kinds, police training—practically every government administrative agency and many private institutions. In some Latin American countries (Brazil, the Dominican Republic, and Chile and Bolivia up to 1970), this has proceeded farther than in others, while some nations (e.g., in Central America) are more vulnerable with even less administrative presence. I am not suggesting that United States personnel control administration in Latin America (as was the case with American "advisory" personnel in Vietnam prior to the outbreak of large-scale hostilities there), but only that presence implies some degree of influence.

The result is a strengthened system of imperialism, because the day-to-day administrative influence that the United States has in Latin American countries is greater than ever before and because built into the system is a set of ideas—a complex of doctrines that serve, rather effectively in most cases, to rationalize and legitimize the structure. Ideology is a distinguishing characteristic of this system, and this new face might justifiably be termed "welfare imperialism."[34] It is not the vulgar racism of "manifest destiny" characteristic of early phases of American expansionism. The legitimating ideology states that U.S. aims are altruistic; that the nation seeks not to dominate but to liberate; that aid programs are developmental . . . and the American citizens who pay the cost and the Latin Americans who suffer the consequences accept these ideas. Everywhere people believe that President Kennedy's Alliance is indeed an Alliance for *Progress;* that aid programs are disinterested; that the Peace Corps is admirable . . .

An analysis of the relationship of the Alliance for Progress

---

[34] The term "welfare imperialism" was coined by Steve Weissman and John McDermott in unpublished works.

and patterns of military assistance previously described sheds further light on the nature of welfare imperialism. In the conventional critique, it is argued that the United States increase in military aid and the emphasis upon an active role for the military in internal politics is counterproductive because it encourages military coups and strengthens authoritarian regimes, and therefore is subversive of United States proclaimed goals of support for reform, democracy, and development in Latin America. Yet these military programs evolved with the Kennedy Administration *simultaneously* with the Alliance for Progress. It is not that these two programs of the United States are at cross-purposes and self-defeating, as suggested by Barbar and Bonning[35] and other liberal critics of U.S. policy in Latin America. Seen from this perspective, the grand rhetoric of the Alliance for Progress is but another weapon in the arsenal.

No, American power and the means of implementing it are not simply arrogant; nor are they irrational, or motivated by hysteria conditioned by a paranoid Christian anticommunism, as various persuasions of critics have it. Welfare imperialism, economic coercion, and the exercise of counterrevolutionary military power are rational policies that reflect the sophistication of hegemonic power.

THE INTERNATIONAL SYSTEM AND NATIONAL CLASS AND POWER STRUCTURES

The literature on the impact of colonial domination in Asia and Africa shows much more clearly how colonialism shapes social structures than does the literature (which has generally suffered from a severe economic bias) on Latin America. A recent example of such analyses of experiences in other underdeveloped regions is Barrington Moore's book *Social Origins of Dictatorship and Democracy,* which contains chap-

---

[35] Willard F. Barbar and C. Neale Bonning, *Internal Security and the Military Power: Counterinsurgency and Civic Action in Latin America* (Columbus, Ohio: Ohio State University Press, 1966).

ters on India, China, and Japan. Although colonialism is not his focus (and I believe he underestimates its impact) Moore manages to show how British colonial policy and practice undermined the development of an Indian national bourgeoisie while creating strong landlord and moneylender classes. Thus, India was left with a social structure which, combined with its new neocolonial status and severe internal problems, probably condemns this unhappy nation to perpetual underdevelopment. While China escaped India's fate of total colonization—and the traditional ruling class, independently of the obstacles placed by imperialism, helped to keep the lid on industrialization—the effects of imperialist encroachment were no less effective in shaping the direction of development and the structure of classes. Specifically, imperialism created a merchant *comprador* class, strengthened and made alliances with decrepit bourgeois warlords, and prevented the emergence of a national bourgeoisie.

> After the conclusion of the Opium War in 1842, the *compradores* spread through all the treaty posts of China. These men served in a variety of capacities as intermediaries between decaying Chinese officialdom and the foreign merchants. . . . By shady methods they could accumulate great fortunes to live a life of cultivated ease. . . .
> Not until 1910 did the Chinese business class begin to show some definite signs of emerging. . . . But the whole indigenous commercial and industrial impulse remained puny. By the end of the Imperial regime, there were said to be some 20,000 "factories" in China. Of these, only 362 employed mechanical power.
> Thus China, like Russia, entered the modern era with a numerically small and politically dependent middle class. This stratum did not develop an independent ideology of its own as it did in Western Europe. . . .[36]

Latin America is another case. Historically, the situation in the region may be described, in Frank's terminology, as a

[36] Barrington Moore, Jr., *Social Origins of Dictatorship and Democracy: Lord and Peasant in the Making of the Modern World* (Boston: Beacon Press, 1967), pp. 176–77.

process of the "development of underdevelopment." This is a sociological as well as economic process. Underdevelopment is *structured* by the patterns of historical movement of the international economy; underdevelopment is cemented by the dependent position of national oligarchies in international stratification. Claudio Veliz explains the manner in which this process occurred in late nineteenth-century Chile, a process repeated with variations elsewhere in Latin America. According to Veliz, Chile was dominated by the "three legs of the national economic table":

> In the first place, there were the mining exporters of the north of the country; then there were the agricultural and livestock exporters of the south; and finally there were the large import firms. . . . These three pressure groups were in entire agreement about what economic policy the country should follow . . . and the three totally dominated national life, from the municipal councils to diplomatic representation, economic legislation and the horse races. . . .
> The mining exporters of the north of the country were free traders. This policy was not fundamentally due to reasons of doctrine—though they also had these—but rather to the simple reason that these gentlemen were blessed with common sense. They exported copper, silver, nitrates, and other minerals of lesser importance to Europe and the United States, where they were paid in pounds sterling or dollars. With this money they bought equipment, machinery, manufactures, or high quality consumer goods at very low prices. It is hard to conceive of an altruism or a far-sighted or prophetic vision which would lead these exporters to pay export and import duties with a view to the possible industrialization of the country.
> The agricultural and livestock exporters of the South were also emphatically free traders. They sent their wheat and flour to Europe, California and Australia. They clothed their cowboys with ponchos of English flannel, rode in saddles made by the best harnessmakers of London, drank authentic champagne and lighted their mansions with Florentine lamps. At night they slept in beds made by excellent English cabinet-makers, between

sheets of Irish linen and covered by blankets of English wool. Their silk shirts came from Italy and their wives' jewels from London, Paris and Rome. For these *hacendados* who were paid in pounds sterling, the idea of taxing the export of wheat or of imposing protective duties on imports was simply insanity.

The big import houses of Valparaíso and Santiago also were free traders. Could anyone imagine an import firm supporting the establishment of high import duties to protect national industry!

Here, then, is the powerful coalition of strong interests, which dominated the economic policy of Chile during the past century and part of the present century. None of the three had the least interest in Chile and industrialization. They monopolized the three powers at all levels: economic power, political power, and social prestige; and only in a few instances did they see the absolute control they exercised over the nation endangered.[37]

The table toppled when it lost two of its legs: foreign capital displaced national capital in northern mining and the *hacendados* of the South lost their export markets. In the twentieth century, incipient industrialization transpired and reshaped the social structure. But the contemporary situation in Chile (until 1970 at least) and elsewhere in Latin America is still characterized by national class and power systems that mesh smoothly with the international system. The new urban-based oligarchies and national bourgeoisies, though essentially dependent, even client or *comprador* classes, profit from the structure of the international system and from their close financial and political relations with multinational corporations and those who hold power internationally. The Latin American middle classes, strengthened by industrialization at one time, played vaguely nationalist and progressive roles as classes in ascendance. Now they engage in what Claudio Veliz terms "the politics of conformity"[38] and have developed a close ideological affinity with

[37] Claudio Veliz, "La mesa de tres patas" *Desarrollo Economic* III, No. 1–2 (Seb.–Abril 1963), pp. 237–42.
[38] Claudio Veliz (ed.), *The Politics of Conformity* (New York: Oxford University Press, 1968).

the precepts of the political and social thought promoted by established interests within the international system and national oligarchies.

Modern imperialism systematically generates and shapes dependent national class and power structures. The extreme of this situation in Latin America was perhaps found in pre-revolutionary Cuba. The unusual clarity and drama of the analysis make Edward Boorstein's words concerning Cuba worth quoting at some length.

> The class structure of Cuba was not just a matter of the traditional division into bourgeoisie, proletariat, and peasantry, but also of relations with imperialism. Cutting across the traditional divisions was the line between those who benefited from imperialism and those who suffered from it. The richest, most powerful groups derived their wealth and power from imperialism. Those groups which did not enjoy the favors of imperialism tended to be poor and weak.
>
> All but a small part of Cuba's upper classes were dependent on activities tied to the United States. There were the magnates of the sugar industry, owners of the sugar centrals and *latifundia*. The big importers, the core of the urban oligarchy, had a magnificent source of income in the hundreds of millions of dollars worth of goods imported each year. The bankers depended for most of their business on the export of sugar and tobacco and on imports. The real estate operators depended on the oligarchy and the government for most of their business and on the United States for equipment and many construction materials.
>
> Most retail stores other than the small ones in wooden shacks, depended on imports.
>
> For whom did the financially successful professionals work in Cuba? Where were the jobs and the money? The most expensive lawyers worked for the big companies, the big importers and commercial speculators, the real estate operators. The engineers and chemists worked for the large foreign-owned or foreign-oriented sugar companies, manufacturing plants, or mines. The architects worked for the real estate companies, the rich, or the government. And the doctors, dentists, and

nurses served the rich and middle classes, most of whose income was tied directly or indirectly to imperialism.

Many employees and even some workers in the foreign companies got salaries and wages which by Cuban standards were high. In the capital-intensive, automated plants the cost of granting good pay was small. Many of these employees and workers developed a strong interest in their own favored position.

Now let us cross the imperialist divide in Cuban society. What can be considered a national bourgeoisie was weak and small; it did not have enough of a base in national industry and commerce on which to rest. The owners of the little—often family-operated—shops and factories turning out bread, shoes, dresses, furniture, etc. were not really in the same class as the sugar magnates, the big importers and the bankers. And there were not enough of them to make up for their individual weakness, to make them in the aggregate into a force that could worry imperialism and its local partners.

There were thousands of small retail enterprises in Cuba—in wooden shacks or outdoor stalls and stands. Many of them had lower incomes and a more precarious economic position than the higher-paid workers in the foreign plants.

Most city workers, in the cottage industries and small shops, on the docks, and in the transportation system received much smaller wages than the elite in the large foreign companies. Nevertheless, they were better off than the vast majority of those engaged in agriculture.

About two-thirds of Cuba's farmers were tenants, sharecroppers, and squatters. Historically, the peasants had been thrown off the land when the cattle ranches and sugar estates were formed. They had an interest in land reform, in the expropriation of the large estates, including the choice lands of the large foreign sugar companies.

Finally there was the largest, most homogenous, and poorest bloc of the Cuban proletariat: the workers in the cane fields—a proletariat created by the sugar industry. Although the workers in the cane fields and those in the electric power industry were both proletarians, their positions differed greatly. The electric power workers enjoyed privileges which the foreign corporations had found it expedient to grant in order to soften the opposition to imperialism. But there could be no privileges for the sugar workers. The profits of the large companies and the functioning of the sugar industry required that they be kept in misery.[39]

Of course, Cuba was an exceptional case. Perhaps only Puerto Rico and the Dominican Republic (and the client states of Asia such as South Korea, Taiwan, and Thailand) approximate the status of full-fledged economic colony and political protectorate that once characterized Cuba. The extreme case, however, serves to accentuate the fundamental forces at work in the various countries of Latin America. Each Latin American dependence has specific qualities and dimensions; each nation has developed underdevelopment according to unique economic, social-cultural, and political factors and events in their separate histories. But the unique qualities, factors, and events should not be allowed to obscure the fundamental conditioning situation of dependence. Under present circumstances, dependent states under control of local oligarchies and their allies among the military and middle classes can only negotiate the conditions of dependence.

In the case of the industrialized countries of Latin America, several general and specific aspects of class relations across national frontiers have already been discussed in the examination of dependence and foreign investment. In subsequent chapters, special attention will be given to the role of nationalist ideology and support for national development policies among the national bourgeoisies and middle classes of Latin America. Generally speaking, the middle classes and the national bourgeoisies are not nationalist in orientation, while the structure of dependence has been a critical factor in determining the political shift (and the support that these classes have lent to the shift) toward a politics of conformity everywhere and a politics of reaction especially notable in key countries like Brazil and Argentina. It remains here

[39] Edward Boorstein, *The Economic Transformation of Cuba* (New York: Monthly Review Press, 1968), pp. 12–14.

to seek to clarify the issue of whether or not international *gran capital* has usurped the position of dominant class from the oligarchies.

The degree to which the presence of multinational corporations in countries such as Brazil, Argentina, Uruguay, and Mexico, and increasingly Chile, Peru, Colombia, and Venezuela, has caused a shift in the internal structure of the dominant classes, is difficult to analyze in the absence of careful empirical research. What is certain in the most industrialized countries is that national oligarchies are in close interconnection with foreign industrial and finance capital and that the wealth and power of both the core of national oligarchies and foreign businessmen are now primarily based upon finance and industry (rather than the earlier base of primary production and export-import). Theotonio dos Santos has argued that the extreme significance and economic weight of large enterprise in basic industries which are subsidiaries or otherwise integrated with multinational corporations, has brought those in control, *"gran capital,"* to the position of the dominant core of the class holding the reigns of economic power, and ultimately of political power. Dos Santos takes Brazil as the case in point, but argues that the same process is occurring in the other industrialized or industrializing countries of Latin America. Perhaps dos Santos' case is overstated. Undoubtedly, international *gran capital* is an influential interest group within the uppermost circles of national class and power structures. But it seems more likely that the national multisector oligarchies happily accede the larger and more risky investments to the multinational corporation and cooperate with foreign capital in joint ventures, while still retaining control of key sources of national economic and political power.[40]

[40] The Editors of *Monthly Review* suggest: ". . . while multinational corporations do not, as so often claimed, internationalize their managements, they do *de*nationalize a section of the native bourgeoisies in the countries they penetrate. This of course weakens these native bourgeoisies and makes it that much harder for them to resist demands and pressures emanating from more powerful countries." "Notes on the Multinational Corporation," *Monthly Review* XXI (October 1969), p. 6.

It is not that foreign businessmen form a corporate group exercising power as an enormously influential interest group in Latin American societies, which is certainly the case of national oligarchies. Nor is it that foreign businessmen are integrated into the social circles and political intrigues of national oligarchies. As Baer and Simonsen observe of the American business community in Brazil,

> United States executives and their families do not expect to settle there permanently; often the man sees his period of work in Latin America as simply one rung in a ladder of success most of which is to be climbed elsewhere, and his family are not necessarily the most willing camp followers. They do not learn Portuguese, the children do not attend local schools, the parents keep to their own clubs and social activities.[41]

On the other hand, what Norman Bailey has referred to as "neo-liberal groups"[42] (conservative propaganda and action organizations of businessmen) active in various countries have the financial backing of the U.S. capital and participation by American executives in Latin America. In Brazil, the Instituto de Pesquisas Estudos Sociais (IPES), which played an important role in creating the conditions for the Brazilian military coup of 1964, had the participation of 297 U.S. firms operating in Brazil.[43]

The case seems to be that at the international level *gran capital* is dominant; at the national level, *gran capital* is highly integrated into national structures; but national oligarchies are dominant in most institutional spheres. If indeed national oligarchies still retain predominant control of the

---

[41] Werner Baer and Mario Henrique Simonsen, "American Capital and Brazilian Nationalism," in Marvin D. Bernstein (ed.), *Foreign Investment in Latin America* (New York: Knopf, 1966), p. 279.

[42] Norman Bailey, "The Colombian 'Black Hand': A Case Study of Neo-liberalism in Latin America," *Review of Politics* XXVII (October 1965); Theotonio dos Santos, *El nuevo caracter de la dependencia* (*op. cit.*) offers some evidence of the direct political role of U.S. capital located in Brazil.

[43] Dos Santos, *ibid.*, p. 63.

economy and the principal social and political institutions within Latin American societies, then the development alternatives and the political choices that they can make with this power are defined and circumscribed. This is evidently the case when development takes place within a context in which the Latin American economies are integrated into a dependent position in the world economy, and national power is subordinated in the international stratification of power.

The points of articulation between the interests of the dominant classes in Latin America and class interests in the imperial Center reside in their position at the apex of structures of wealth, privilege, and power, in distinct yet closely interrelated worlds, neither of which could continue to exist without the other. Imperialism could not sustain itself as a dominant force in the world, were it not for support among client classes in underdeveloped countries. And oligarchies would fall one by one to national revolutions if they did not get international backing.

PART II

CLASS AND POLITICS

Chapter 5

LAST RITES FOR THE REFORMIST MODEL IN LATIN AMERICA

James D. Cockcroft

In Part I, we examined the process of underdevelopment in Latin America as it relates to hegemonic external forces which, operating over historical time, condition the shape of Latin American class structures and the formulation of national policies. These policies, except in times of world-wide war and/or depression, reinforce the growth of the capitalist metropolis, the underdevelopment of Latin America, and the symbiotic ties of dependence between the two. In Part II we will investigate examples and models of political dependence, political ideology, class formation, internal (and increasingly international) class strife in Latin America, and increased militarization of Latin America, generated by this historically conditioned relationship.

An overview of Latin America today reveals a high development of repressive military apparatuses, heightened underdevelopment, greater U.S. penetration into the economies and political structures than ever before, and ostensible "contradictions" between the ideology of reform and the practice of repression, which, upon closer examination, are mutually supportive parts of an integrated international system. A country count shows that of nineteen republics, not counting Cuba, Trinidad-Tobago, and Guyana, three nations continue to maintain long-standing military dictatorships: Haiti, Nicaragua, and Paraguay. Ten have suffered antireformist military *coups d'état* since the launching of the Alliance for Progress, and some of those ten have already begun the second go-round of *coups* (from 1962 to 1968, there were fourteen *golpes del estado* by the military in Latin

America). Three countries—Venezuela, Colombia, and Costa Rica—have remained or fallen under the domination of military or paramilitary elements. Only three have sustained any pretense of a "democratic" tradition—Mexico, Uruguay, and Chile—and closer examination of those cases will reveal crueler realities.

This trend toward the militarization of Latin America received major impetus during the Presidency of John F. Kennedy, at the very time when the Alliance for Progress and its talk of reform were receiving such exaggerated publicity. Few people at the time recognized the integrated nature of U.S. military aid programs and the Alliance for Progress. The entire panoply of U.S. "aid" techniques discussed in the preceding chapter—everything from police academies to AID sanitation projects, from counterinsurgency training and military missions to World Bank loans and IMF credits, from CIA agents to the Peace Corps—served then, as they serve today, to integrate yet further Latin America's economies and markets into an international system dominated by the United States.

Whenever seriously enough endangered, the classes benefiting from this integration have resorted to the most extreme measures of repression, marked by direct U.S. military intervention, as in the cases of the CIA-sponsored invasions of Guatemala (1954) and the Bay of Pigs (1961), or, more desperately, the U.S. invasion of Santo Domingo (1965). Less direct—but often as repressive and violent—forms of military intervention by the United States have emerged with the use of U. S. Special Forces (Green Berets), aircraft, and napalm in at least six other Latin American countries during the 1960s, to say nothing of the use of Latin American militaries and police trained and armed by the United States to crush frequent internal insurgencies. In addition, as noted earlier in the case of U.S. advisers drafting tax programs and establishing parallel (or often integral) administrative structures in some Latin American countries, there are numerous nonmilitary violations by the United States of the principle of nonintervention in the internal affairs of other nations. The result of all of these U.S. interventions has been not only to produce among the general populace of Latin America an intensified "Yankeephobia," but also to harden feelings there into a legitimate cynicism about U.S. intentions, as *The Rockefeller Report on the Americas* has conceded.[1]

The 1965 invasion of Santo Domingo was not so much a throwback to gunboat diplomacy as it was a logical consequence of modern U.S. policies. There has been a subsequent development of huge troop-transport planes for instant dispatch to any part of the globe, not to mention the perfection of techniques of electronic warfare and aerial bombardment in Southeast Asia and Latin America (infrared "sensors" detected and followed Che Guevara in Bolivia, while U.S. pilots have reportedly flown combat missions from Panama over Guatemala). The United States is prepared, then, to resort to direct military intervention if necessary to preserve its interests, even while preferring to have "Latin Americans fight Latin Americans," or "Asians fight Asians," as the so-called Nixon Doctrine has so quaintly put it. At one point in

[1] Bolivia, Peru, Colombia, Venezuela, Honduras, and Guatemala have been napalmed. Evidence ranges from testimony of Che Guevera (*Bolivian Diary*) to that of U. S. Army General Robert W. Porter, Jr. (before the *U.S. House Committee on Foreign Affairs, 90th Congress, 1st session*, 1967, pp. 535–62). As Richard J. Barnet points out, however, the United States places its main reliance upon Latin American military forces: "U.S. policy is to avoid the use of American personnel where possible for combat, reserving them for training and advice" (*Intervention and Revolution*, New York, 1968, p. 58). The Miami *Herald* (May 21, 1970) has reported the use of napalm in Brazil, and returning Peace Corps volunteers, journalists, and clergy have spoken of the use of Green Berets and napalm in almost every Latin American country. After the 1964 military *coup d'état* in Brazil, a Jungle Warfare Training Center was established in the heart of the Amazon near Manaus, staffed by the Brazilian military and U.S. advisors. For examples of cynicism involved in modern "Yankeephobia," and its justification, consult Juan José Arévalo, *The Shark and The Sardines* (New York: 1961), *Anti-Kommunism in Latin America* (New York: 1963), and Juan Bosch, *Pentagonism: A Substitute for Imperialism* (New York: 1969). Also cf. *The Rockefeller Report on the Americas, The Official Report of a United States Presidential Mission for the Western Hemisphere*, by Nelson A. Rockefeller, New York *Times* edition (Chicago: 1969).

May 1965, U.S. troops in and around the Dominican Republic outnumbered those in Vietnam by two to one. This show of muscle reflected the U. S. Government's irrevocable commitment to a policy of "anticommunism" and protection of established U.S. economic interests in this hemisphere even at exorbitantly high costs. During the Cuban missile crisis of October 1962, Theodore Sorenson later recalled, President Kennedy was willing to risk a probability of anywhere from one in three, to one in two, of all-out thermonuclear war.[2]

Clearly, though, the lesson of the 1965–66 occupation of the Dominican Republic is not that "communism" will be fought wherever it occurs, but that revolution or the *risk* of revolutionary change will be turned back whenever the United States can so affect developments. International treaties are subject to unilateral abrogation by the United States at even so slight a pretext as the *possible* resumption of power by a constitutionally elected President who earlier had received 60 percent of all votes cast (Juan Bosch).

In the face of this reality, Latin Americans are left with only two *viable* alternatives for establishing their political identities: revolutionary nationalism or pro-U.S. militarism. The first alternative involves a process of violent revolution, even under an elected government like that of Chile today, which leads to the expropriation of large landed and corporate properties to provide a radically more equitable distribution of income and political power and rational use of economic resources. The second alternative, even when cloaked in the name of "nationalism," involves the violent maintenance of the status quo and military suppression of large numbers of people.[3] The military regime of Brazil

[2] Theodore Sorenson, *Kennedy* (New York: 1965), p. 705.

[3] Because of their twentieth-century revolutions, Mexico and Cuba are not included in most of the generalizations of this chapter; their relevance, however, becomes clear in what follows. "Neutralism," for which there is considerable latent sentiment in Latin America, is not a feasible alternative. "Neutralism" can emerge only after an intensely nationalistic, anticolonial struggle, as in the case of India. Even in that case, however, "neutralism" has more surface than substance. When confronted by its dif-

exemplifies this latter alternative. The Brazilian military have jailed or outlawed so many former Presidents and important figures of the "reformist," "centrist," "moderate," and even "conservative" political sectors that the only effective wielders of political power still extant are those of the right and extreme right, while the only effective organized political threat to the status quo is posed by those of the underground left, the exiled left, and the few Church and student radicals which the "colonial-fascist" state has not been able entirely to suppress. Widespread use of prison tortures of the most brutal kind further serves to intimidate people favoring change in Brazil. The military regime there is unabashedly pro-United States, not only in its economic and foreign policies, but also in its internal propaganda (for example, the prevalence of the slogan "Cristianismo sim, comunismo não," which is more political than clerical).

To realize the inexorability of the choice between revolutionary nationalism and pro-U.S. militarism in Latin America today, one must first recognize the passing from the scene of yet another, often heralded alternative: reformism. Traditionally, reformism has been referred to in the United States as "the democratic left," although Latin American

---

ferences with China over the disputed international border, India, in spite of its earlier disdain for the Cold War, returned unequivocably to the British-U.S. side of international politics. Actually, India's "return" had begun much earlier, as Hamza Alavi has documented in his insightful essay "Imperialism Old and New" (*Socialist Register*, 1964, reprinted in pamphlet form by Radical Education Project, Box 561-A, Detroit, Michigan). Indeed, the Congress Party, had it not maintained its practical, working alliance with the Western powers and permitted continued Western economic penetration and influence, but instead moved left, would more than likely have faced the unsavory prospect of being overthrown by more conservative, pro-West forces (cf. events in Ghana and Indonesia). In Latin America, with the exception of Cuba, which chose the first alternative of revolutionary nationalism, those countries that have moved toward "neutrality" in world trade and aid (i.e., increased economic exchange with the Socialist world on any significant scale) have been swiftly brought back "into line" by the assorted pressures of the United States and domestic political-economic forces.

sociologists have been quick to point out that the reformers are neither democratic nor left. More recently, reformism has shed its "democratic" pretenses and become directly military, as in the cases of today's military dictatorships of Bolivia and Peru. The United States has tolerated or encouraged the reformist alternative to revolution (and continues to do so today), although simultaneously it has encouraged the more reactionary alternative exemplified by Stroessner's Paraguay or today's Brazil. Where United States tolerance of reformism breaks down is precisely when a *risk* of revolutionary change seems too great to permit and resources for its elimination are readily available—as happened with the occupation of Santo Domingo in 1965–66, and as may yet happen in today's Chile, Bolivia, or Peru, whether directly, or indirectly through military *golpe del estado*.[4] (United States military involvement in Southeast Asia, economic stagnation at home, and geographical distances make it less likely, *in the short run,* that the United States will invade one of the southern South American nations.) Curiously, following the landing of U.S. troops in Santo Domingo, spokesmen for the "democratic left" like the U.S. magazine *The New Leader* and Juan Bosch himself openly acknowledged the demise of the reformist alternative as a viable model for Latin America.[5]

[4] As happened in Bolivia in August of 1971, after this book was written.

[5] Sam Halper, "The Dominican Upheaval," *The New Leader,* May 10, 1965 ("Win or lose, however, the Communists will emerge after a while in their own right as the men who will really make the promised revolution, for the Bosches are finished"); Juan Bosch, "A Tale of Two Nations," *The New Leader,* June 21, 1965; Bosch, "An Anti-Communist Manifesto," *New York Review of Books,* October 26, 1967 (a review of Regis Debray's *Revolution in the Revolution,* in which Bosch views the Castro strategy for Latin America as a "nationalist" one, which, in spite of its egalitarian goals and use of the word "communism," is "anti-Communist" in its denunciations of Moscow's foreign policy and most Latin American Communist Parties; the Castro strategy, according to Bosch, expresses "a historical process that for years has been at work at the very heart of the Latin American left. . . . Fidel Castro knew—and knows—that what has kept the democratic reformist parties in our countries from gaining the support of young people are the close relations between their governing offi-

Ideologically, the reformist model has shared much with the revolutionary model in twentieth-century Latin America. Both reformers and revolutionaries have championed equality of opportunity, political democracy, and state protection of basic economic rights (minimum wage, the strike, workers' compensation, housing, health, land for the landless, "social justice"). The reformist constitutions of Mexico (1917), Cuba (1940), Venezuela (1960), and the Dominican Republic (1963) all drew heavily on the work and ideas of left movements of preceding decades; all included provisions for agrarian reform. What made those constitutions reformist and not revolutionary was not merely the failure of national leaders to implement them. The constitutions themselves provided for either the inviolability of private property or the inalienable right and desirability of private ownership in most areas—a characteristic sign of reformism rather than revolution. In turn, these constitutions represented the expression of those groups holding political power at the time—the national bourgeoisies and the middle classes, in coalition with portions of the unionized working class. However similar in certain respects to revolutionary programs (e.g., in agrarian reform), the reformist ideology was, and still is, a buttress for capitalism and the bourgeois state in Latin America, rather than a threat.

Indeed, the principal difference between a reformist model and a revolutionary one is that a reformist model does not provide for a frontal and coordinated assault upon the landholding, capitalist, and foreign elites in Latin America—the kind of assault launched by Bolivian miners and peasants in 1952–53 or "26th-of-July" revolutionaries in Cuba, 1956–60. Reformers tinker with the economic machinery and its social and political superstructure, literally seeking to "re-form" them through specific adjustments and compromises. Revolutionaries overhaul the economic machinery and social sys-

---

cials and the United States."); Bosch, *Pentagonism;* Bosch, interview, *The New Leader,* February 28, 1966 ("I believe that in the Dominican Republic Latin America has been given a lesson: the lesson is that it is not possible to establish a democracy with the help of the United States, and neither is it possible to establish a democracy against the United States").

tem, literally seeking to "revolutionize" them through radical change. Revolutionaries, no matter what their personal class background (e.g., Fidel Castro, a *déclassé* "aristocrat"), build their movements with the support and on behalf of the lower and property-less classes. Reformers, on the other hand, develop their ideas and politics in terms of retaining the support and enhancing the long-term interests of the ownership classes—the national and foreign bourgeoisies—by appealing to segments of the lower classes for support and trust.

Most reformers would accept this basic distinction between the two models, hastening to condemn the revolutionary one for its "destructive," "nihilistic," or "violent" dimension. However, most reformers would object to the supposition that their approach to social change does not confront vested economic interests in Latin America. Quite the contrary, the reformer argues, the "democratic left" is "left" precisely because it seeks to change the status quo, to provide for a more equitable distribution of income, to reform the land system, to gain part interest, usually on a fifty-fifty basis, in foreign economic monopolies like oil, copper, iron ore, steel, and so on. Moreover, the Latin American reformer does not merely talk about agrarian "reform." Today, he uses the very language of "revolution" (especially in the case of the Christian Democrats of Chile).

It was President Kennedy who said, for example: "Those who make pacific *revolution* impossible, make violent *revolution* inevitable" (emphases added). President Kennedy of course followed the policy of supporting reformers like Juan Bosch in the Dominican Republic (1963) while simultaneously training and equipping the antireformist Army and police forces that overthrew the Bosch regime. This adds an ironic dimension to the bankruptcy of the reformist model in Latin America today.[6]

[6] For details and further references, consult Fred Goff and Michael Locker, "The Violence of Domination: U.S. Power and the Dominican Republic," in Irving Louis Horowitz, Josué de Castro, and John Gerassi (eds.), *Latin American Radicalism* (New York: Vintage, 1969), pp. 249–91.

Reformism's failure in Latin America cannot be explained solely by the incompetent, interventionist, and often Machiavellian machinations of U.S. policy-makers—although large-scale economic, political, and military interests of the United States in Latin America ultimately constitute the main obstacles to "pacific revolution," as other chapters in this book make evident. Much of the failure of the reformist model may be attributed to the inadequacy of the model itself and of its Latin American practitioners. Indeed, the failure of reformers to live up to their idealized self-image, and their betrayal of many of their own stated goals, suggest the increasing irrelevance to Latin Americans of the reformist model as a viable tool for breaking out of underdevelopment.

The decline of reformism can be traced back to many events in twentieth-century Latin American history. The Dominican intervention of 1965 was, in the sweep of history, not an exceptional event. Either through invasion, support of antireform military and police elements, or the dispatch of gunboats and troops, the United States has for many decades prevented reform, even when paying it lip service in Latin America. Not without profound political intuition did the great Latin American "Liberator" Simón Bolívar conclude in 1829 that "The United States appear to be destined by Providence to plague America with misery in the name of liberty."

One could argue that reformism was strangled in its cradle. Certainly by 1933, when so many hopes were raised by President Franklin D. Roosevelt's endorsement of the "Good Neighbor" policy of Herbert Hoover, the record should have been clear for those who cared to look. In 1933, the Roosevelt Administration dispatched gunboats to the coastlines of Cuba to stand ready to "protect" human lives and property against the threats of the revolution taking place on that island in the aftermath of the overthrow of dictator Gerardo Machado. This military show of force, combined with U.S. diplomatic and economic pressures exerted inside Cuba, cut short the four-month life of the reformist government of Ramón Grau San Martín and ushered in the long direct and indirect dictatorship of Fulgencio Batista, the unintended fruit of whose policies is the revolutionary model offered to Latin America today by Fidel Castro and the Cuban Revolution.

In more recent times, one has only to consider the rash of military *coups d'état* in Latin America during the administrations of Kennedy and Lyndon B. Johnson, who, in the tradition of Roosevelt, also trumpeted a "new" and "reformist" concept, the Alliance for Progress, to see how repeatedly the reformist model has failed, even when it has the public patronage of its U.S. supporters. For these reasons, when the Dominican intervention of 1965 is placed in historical perspective, one must speak of "last rites for the reformist model in Latin America." The younger generation in Latin America —today's politically active students, many of whom accept the basic tenets of Marxism-Leninism, and today's ever more class-conscious young workers and peasants—realizes the impossibility of reform. This generation is not blind to the long historical record of reformism's failure. Therefore, it increasingly views revolution as the only realistic, satisfactory, and ultimately lasting and humane solution to the problems of poverty and underdevelopment. A brief review of reformism's latest failures in Latin America will help explain why this is so.

Two kinds of reformers have been prominent during this latest period of military *coups d'état* and U.S. support for military repression (President Kennedy's symbolic delays of diplomatic recognition of new military regimes did not alter the long-run U.S. support of these regimes). The first kind of reformer derives historically from the Marxist-oriented, student-dominated Peruvian *Aprista* movement and its sister movements throughout Latin America in the 1920s and 1930s. This group of reformers includes the founder of APRA, Víctor Raúl Haya de la Torre, who in the 1960s aligned with the political right wing in Peru. Included in this group or inspired by it, and also moving to the right in the 1960s, are the following important political figures: former Venezuelan Presidents Rómulo Betancourt and Raúl Leoni; President-maker José ("Pepe") Figueres of Costa

Rica; Puerto Rican political boss Luis Muñoz Marín; Guatemala's ex-President, Juan José Arévalo; Juan Bosch of the Dominican Republic (whose leftish statements began only after the 1965 invasion and his 1966 electoral defeat); Argentina's overthrown President Arturo Frondizi; deposed Bolivian President Víctor Paz Estenssoro; and Prime Minister Eric Williams of Trinidad-Tobago.

The second kind of reformer is not as directly linked with the Marxist-oriented movements of the 1920s and 1930s. He is less ideologically consistent than the first kind, which, as we have seen, is hardly noteworthy for its consistency. He is a political product of growing revolutionary pressures in Latin America, engendered by economic stagnation or decline, population growth (the highest rate in the world), increased economic dependence upon monopolistic business concerns (mostly U.S.), and the language of political debate following upon the aborted agrarian reform in Guatemala (1953–54) and the revolutions in Bolivia (1952–56) and Cuba (1959 to date). This kind of reformer, not unlike the first kind, is highly pragmatic; sophisticated in his handling of domestic politics; cooperative with U.S. business interests; and anxious to lead what everyone seems to agree is the inevitable "revolution." These reformers vary in style. Several are the messianic, persuasive, and well-financed Christian Democratic or "Popular Action" types, as exemplified by Chilean ex-President Eduardo Frei; Venezuelan President Rafael Caldera; the recently deposed President of Peru, Fernando Belaúnde; Ecuador's overthrown President Carlos Julio Arosemena; and Brazil's ousted President João Goulart. Others are paternalistic, oligarchic, more traditional types, as represented by Colombia's former Presidents Alberto Lleras Camargo and Carlos Lleras Restrepo (they are cousins) and Honduras's deposed President Ramón Villeda Morales. Often, at election time, within the rather narrow confines of the bourgeois "democratic" electoral arena of most Latin American countries where illiterates are either prohibited from voting or bribed to vote the "right way," this second kind of reformer becomes the "rightist" or "moderate" alternative to the "left" or "liberal" candidate, the first kind of reformer.

Despite differences in rhetoric and style, none of these reformers, when in power, significantly changed the status quo, but instead maneuvered to retain power. They all repressed much of the left; gave in to the constricting economic guidelines of the IMF and similar U.S.-dominated agencies upon which most Latin American nations depend for loans (and past debts); suppressed strikes; sent the military into traditionally "autonomous" universities; jailed troublesome elected congressmen or public officials; distributed some lands; built few houses; killed some workers; and in general moved to the right. Also, these reformers' rigid "anticommunism," exaggerated along U.S. lines, further served to maintain the status quo and economic dependence upon the United States. Any hint of weakening in his anticommunism has been enough to cost a reformer his political job. President Arosemena's trip to the Soviet Union, unlike Richard Nixon's, made him suspect in the eyes of the U. S. Government and the many anticommunists among Ecuador's U.S.-supplied Armed Forces, who eventually overthrew him. Trade with Russia or the Soviet "bloc," on however small a scale, has with rare exceptions been unthinkable for a Latin American reformer if he wishes to stay in power, no matter how much the United States trades with Socialist countries. Each of the Latin American reformers, then, has cooperated with, and received the enthusiastic (if not lasting) support of, the United States.

For example, in the 1950s and 1960s all of these reformers supported the efforts of the AFL-CIO to influence Latin America's labor movement, often with the assistance of funds from the Central Intelligence Agency. The main organization used by the AFL-CIO and the CIA in these efforts has been the American Institute for Free Labor Development (chaired by J. Peter Grace, President of W. R. Grace and Company and a director of the First National City Bank, and funded by U.S. businessmen, AFL-CIO, CIA, and, to the amount of nearly 90 percent of the Institute's declared income, the U. S. Agency for International Development—

AID). President Frei of Chile retained as his Minister of Labor until February 1968 a former board member of the American Institute for Free Labor Development, William Thayer, whose support of the AFL-CIO campaign against Social Christian unions in Latin America caused grave consternation within more radical segments of Frei's own Christian Democratic party. These Latin American reformers also supported and contributed to anticommunist student movements linked hemispherically with the U. S. National Student Association, another conduit for CIA funds and agents. People like Betancourt, Bosch, Muñoz Marín, and Figueres were key participants in the International Institute for Political Education, set up with CIA funds in San José, Costa Rica in 1959 as a training institute for young Latin American political organizers and administrators.[7]

Nevertheless, faced with the example of revolutionary Cuba, whose leader was himself initiated into politics through such reformist movements in the late 1940s and early 1950s,

[7] Goff and Locker, pp. 267–70; George Morris, *CIA and American Labor: Subversion of the AFL-CIO's Foreign Policy* (New York: 1967); Serafino Romualdi, *Peasants and Peons, Recollections of a Labor Ambassador in Latin America* (New York: 1967); Sidney Lens, "American Labor Abroad: Lovestone Diplomacy," *The Nation*, July 5, 1965; New York *Times*, February 16–24, 1967; Subcommittee on American Republic Affairs of the Senate Foreign Relations Committee, "Survey of the Alliance for Progress-Labor Policies and Programs," July 15, 1968, in *Congressional Record*, September 25, 1968; Susanne Bodenheimer, "Stagnation in Liberty—The Frei Experiment in Chile," *NACLA Newsletter*, March 1969, p. 3. Also used in these U.S. efforts to control Latin America's labor unions, and supported by the Latin American reformers, has been the Organización Regional Interamericana de Trabajadores (ORIT), the operating budget of which is only one-twentieth that of the more influential American Institute for Free Labor Development. U.S. journalist John Gerassi, who visited and wrote about the International Institute for Political Education before it was known to be CIA-funded, thought it resembled a "Capitalist Comintern." According to Gerassi (*The Great Fear in Latin America* [New York: 1963], p. 209), "It seemed to me as if the whole purpose of the school was not so much how to get reforms without revolutions—as it claims—but rather how to convince Latin Americans that the best road to development is more United States investment."

and fearful of the growing sentiment for revolutionary change
in Latin America, the United States played an important role
in causing the overthrow or replacement of almost all of
this latest generation of Latin American reformers. Only two
of the eighteen men named above are still heads of government today: Williams (Trinidad-Tobago) and Caldera
(Venezuela). Both men have moved slowly, or reneged, on
their promises of reform; both have encouraged or tolerated
vastly increased strength among their militaries and paramilitaries, the agencies most often utilized in replacing the
other sixteen reformers named; both have declared "states
of siege" in order to "pacify" insurgent populations; and
Williams has ruthlessly crushed a "black power" revolt that
in fact is part of a larger Caribbean nationalist movement
for revolutionary change and equality for *all* colored peoples
(including East Indians). The removal from power of so
many reformers does *not* mean that the bourgeois groups that
back these reformers cannot (or do not) at another time
provide new reformers in place of those who have been overthrown or discarded. It *does* suggest how inadequate the reform model is when put to the test of "re-forming" the social
and political structures of Latin America.

Only three countries can pretend to some vague honoring
of their claims of utilizing the democratic process so rhetori-
cally championed by supporters of the reformist model. The
first is Mexico, which could not even begin talking of democracy until after having had a violent revolution (1910–
17). Yet Mexico's "democracy" is generally recognized as
a sham. Minority parties receive only token representation.
Voter apathy is widespread. The Partido Revolucionario Institucional (PRI) always wins. When citizens try to protest
the sham nature of Mexico's alleged democracy, or other
grievances are expressed, Mexico's military and police step
in with considerable force, as evidenced in the October 2,
1968, "massacre" of Tlatelolco, when some five hundred
men, women, and children were killed, another two thousand
wounded or injured, and some fifteen hundred arrested in a
downtown plaza of Mexico City by troops and police during
an assembly for a rally organized by the student movement.

Such massacres and militarization of society make Mexico a dubious example of "successful reformism." Because of its revolutionary rhetoric and earlier nationalization of oil, railroads, and electricity, however, Mexico is a particularly complicated case, which we analyze elsewhere in this volume.

The second nation pretending to some form of democracy is Uruguay, the misnamed "Swiss democracy of Latin America." Uruguay faces the threat of a military *coup d'état* and possible outside military intervention (from the strong "gorilla" militaries of Brazil and Argentina, upon which the United States would prefer to depend should Uruguay's worsening economic crisis and growing left-nationalist ferment cause another Dominican Republic). In October of 1965, a state of siege was declared in Uruguay. Uruguay's strong labor movement and independent press were suppressed by the police and the military. The United States welcomed these developments, and later ones, because Uruguay had taken a relatively independent stand at the United Nations during debates on the U.S. intervention in the Dominican Republic. Also, Uruguay represented a clear obstacle to Latin American support for a U.S.-sponsored inter-American "peace-keeping" force.

The economic source of Uruguay's crisis was the decline in the meat and wool market from 1957 to the present, which led to recession, inflation, dependence upon the United States and international loan agencies, and a cutback in the standard of living for not only workers but also Montevideo's prospering middle classes and petty bourgeoisie. After 1965, unemployment, underutilization of factory capacity, currency devaluation, a spiraling cost of living, and repression of striking meat and banking employees led to the end of the fifteen-year experiment in a multi-Executive (the nine-man *colegiado*). Symbolic of the decline in democratic traditions in Uruguay was the inauguration as President in March 1967 of a military man: retired Air Force General Oscar Gestido.

Workers and students mobilized in 1968 but were crushed by the repressive forces of the strengthened Uruguayan state. U.S. aid poured into Uruguay to strengthen the Army and the police. Left-revolutionary parties, press, students, workers, and priests were killed, jailed, or outlawed. In response, a band of urban commandos known as the Tupamaros carefully coordinated a series of reprisals against conservative businessmen and the government in Montevideo, where almost half of Uruguay's population resides. An FBI agent on loan to Uruguay to help train the local police was kidnapped and, because the government refused to release political prisoners rounded up during earlier states of siege in exchange for the release of the FBI agent and other foreign officials kidnapped, the FBI man was executed. This execution was viewed by many Uruguayans as justified when placed in the context of earlier government violence and preventive detentions of "suspicious" citizens, as well as the international context of U.S. training of Latin American police forces and cooperation with such local right-wing terrorist organizations as Brazil's "Death Squad" and Guatemala's "White Hand," which have taken the lives of thousands of innocent people. The Tupamaros, like similar organizations in Brazil, Guatemala, and elsewhere in Latin America, have a strong internationalist consciousness. They seek to free hundreds of political prisoners, to save the lives of many who are killed, jailed, or tortured without cause, to go beyond the bounds of bourgeois, repressive law, and to establish a legality based on universal responsibility: that of revolution. Ideologically, they have chosen the first alternative raised in this chapter, that of revolutionary nationalism. They see their struggle as long-term, waged against the forces of U.S. imperialism and the dependent Uruguayan bourgeoisie, and on behalf of the lower classes, with the aim of establishing a socialist state in solidarity with other socialist and revolutionary movements around the world. Drawing many of their members and much of their support from the middle and even disenchanted segments of the upper classes, the Tupamaros have chosen the urban "sea of people" as their theater of guerrilla operation, although they also make occasional forays against large landholders in the countryside. Massive military buildup inside Uruguay, the use of U.S. advisers and military personnel, and repeated house-to-house searches and preventive arrests have failed to "uncover" or destroy the Tupamaros. If anything, they have made the Tupamaros more popular than ever before.

The third and last country with the most legitimate claim to some semblance of democracy is Chile, where the Christian Democratic "revolution in liberty" fizzled. The Christian Democrats' efforts to undermine the socialist left through revolutionary and nationalist rhetoric and social reform did not succeed. The attempt to break the Socialist-Communist majority in organized labor failed. Agrarian reform only whetted the appetites of peasants. Programs of "popular promotion" did not keep the urban poor from exerting increasing pressure on the system. As the inadequacy of the reform model became ever more manifest for all to see, the Christian Democrats divided among themselves. Left-nationalist members deserted the party in droves, criticizing President Frei for his compromises with the United States (one reason the U.S. copper companies did not complain very much about the Chilean Government's purchase of shares in their subsidiaries—a process called "Chileanization" which, because of reduced taxes, tripled the U.S. companies' profits in four years). One of the original Christian Democrat "rebels," as they are sometimes called, Congressman Patricio Hurtado, described Frei's Christian Democracy in the words of Fidel Castro: "shop window of imperialism." It should have come as no surprise to anyone familiar with the Latin American reformist model that Hurtado was arrested on charges of forgery.

Yet, as in the cases of Mexico and Uruguay, Chile's original reputation for democracy was itself ill-founded. As one U.S. scholar has observed: "What we have praised as democracy in Chile since 1920 has amounted to little more than a system in which a small, privileged class has been gentlemanly in determining, through very limited electoral processes, which of its members would rule the country. . . . Chilean democracy and Chilean capitalism have gone hand in hand toward producing outrageous social injustice."[8] The Frei Government's failure to effectively challenge this tra-

8 Frederick B. Pike, *Chile and The United States, 1880–1962* (Notre Dame, Indiana: 1963), pp. XXV, 296.

ditional pattern of injustice led many of its top political figures to withdraw from the Christian Democratic Party in
May 1969, taking with them key elements of labor and the
peasantry and most of the youth movement. As one of these
"popular unity" figures, Senator Rafael Agustín Gumucio,
said upon leaving the party, after his colleagues barely missed
outvoting the Frei "officialist" forces at a meeting of the
party's national committee: "The ideal which always united
us was the struggle against the injustice of capitalist structure. . . . Now things are different. The advanced currents of
Christian thought are no longer taken up by us and in fact
we are less an instrument for the revolutionary changing of
society, than one of social status, a force administering the
system, guaranteeing the established order."[9]

Increasingly, President Frei's government resorted to the
use of troops to put down strikes, peasant land seizures, and
student unrest. Scores of workers, peasants, and students
were shot in the process of the Christian Democratic reformers' misnamed "revolution without an execution wall."
Such was the bankruptcy of the reformist model in its last
civilian outpost in Latin America. The 1970 election of a
Socialist President supported by a coalition of left-wing and
small middle-class parties was a popular response to the inadequacy of the U.S.-backed, Christian Democratic reform
model. How far President Salvador Allende will be willing
to go in reclaiming the Chilean economy for Chileans and
granting the just demands of workers and peasants, or how
far he will be *permitted* to go by the Chilean bourgeoisie and
its U.S. supporters, remains, at the time of this writing, to be
seen.

However, the precedent of the much-publicized "Project
Camelot" is ominous. That scandalous project linked U.S.
university professors with a U. S. Department of the Army
intelligence-gathering and contingency-planning study focused on Chile for the purposes of military and civilian coordination in the event of a "Communist takeover" (i.e.,
electoral victory). Such a "takeover," in fact, subsequently

[9] *Airmail Latin America* (London), May 9, 1969, p. 146; *El
Mercurio* (Santiago), May 1–4, 1969.

occurred, at a time when U.S. interests were seriously diverted in the areas of the Cambodian invasion and planned Laotian invasion, as well as a stagnant economy and rising unemployment at home. Nevertheless, political assassinations occurred right after the election in Chile, and CIA operatives were rumored to be everywhere. Chile received more U.S. military aid *per capita* by far than any other Latin American country between 1953 and 1966, and its military ranks third behind Brazil and Peru in terms of number of soldiers trained in the United States. The Chilean military has intervened before at critical moments in modern Chilean history, and may yet be used to overthrow Allende. Much will hinge on whether Allende acts fully and without compromise on the radical program under which he ran for election. If he does, Chile will indeed begin the construction of socialism—and that is a risk that the ruling national and international elites are not eager to run.[10]

The only other pseudodemocratic cases requiring further elaboration for the purposes of our analysis here are those of Venezuela, Colombia, and Costa Rica. In Venezuela, the military historically has been the determinant power, whether behind a civilian façade or not. As in Colombia and the rest of Latin America (except Cuba), the Venezuelan military is today "modernized," "advised," and supplied by the United States to preserve "the peace" (i.e., the status quo) against revolutionary guerrillas or excessively reformist politicians. Venezuela's traditional conservative party, the

[10] James Petras and Maurice Zeitlin (eds.), *Latin America, Reform or Revolution?* (Greenwich, Connecticut, 1968), pp. 202–48; *The Minority of One,* November 1967; Irving Louis Horowitz, *The Rise and Fall of Project Camelot: Studies in the Relationship Between Social Science and Practical Politics* (Cambridge, Massachusetts, 1967). Among various social-science intelligence projects sponsored by the Pentagon that became public knowledge after the exposure of "Camelot" and yet received no significant publicity were "Project Role" (for Latin American military personnel), "Project Resettle" (agrarian population in Peru), and "Project Simpático" (affecting attitudes in Colombia). An indefinite number of such projects have quietly, without fanfare, succeeded. For a discussion of the Chilean military and Allende's program, see *Monthly Review,* January 1971.

Church-supported COPEI (the so-called "Christian Socialists"), is today barely distinguishable from Betancourt's and Leoni's Acción Democrática (AD)—so far to the right have the reformers of the 1930s moved in the 1960s. AD's failure, combined with unofficial U.S. support for COPEI in the electoral campaign, may explain in part why COPEI won the Presidency in the 1968 elections. But COPEI represents no rebirth of reform in Venezuela. Its campaign slogan was "law and order." Caracas's workers and unemployed, whose neighborhoods have repeatedly been occupied by troops under AD governments, know what that means. They voted for losing coalition candidates opposed to COPEI and AD, causing these two reformist parties to do poorly in the nation's populous capital.

Colombia's agrarian reform is generally recognized as a fraud. The oligarchy rules supreme in Colombia, while the military occupies the universities and patrols the countryside, well supplied with U.S. advisers, guns, helicopters, and napalm in its fight against revolutionary guerrillas. So desperate did conditions become in Colombia in the 1960s that even the centuries-old conservative hold of the Catholic Church became challenged from within by progressive, younger priests. One of them, Camilo Torres, to whom this book is dedicated, eventually took up the gun to join the guerrillas in their battle against the government and the oligarchy. Torres, a professional sociologist and scion of one of Colombia's oldest and most distinguished oligarchic families, eventually was captured and later executed by the Colombian Army; but his example continues to inspire others throughout Colombia and, indeed, the hemisphere. Meanwhile, tear gas, Mace, small arms, communications and transportation equipment provided by the United States continue to be used by the Colombian police and military to "control" urban unrest, as former U. S. Secretary of Defense Robert McNamara has proudly acknowledged.[11] In early 1971, a nationwide stu-

---

[11] McNamara, testimony before joint session of the Senate Armed Services Committee and the Senate Subcommittee on Department of Defense Appropriations on the Fiscal Years 1967–71 Defense Programs and 1967 Defense Budget, cited in Petras and Zeitlin, *Latin America, Reform or Revolution?*, pp. 353–54.

dent and urban workers' revolt against the regime led to a number of deaths at the hands of the U.S.-advised military and yet another of Colombia's many recent "states of siege."

Costa Rican politics follow the pattern in Venezuela, except that the reformist "revolution" occurred ten years earlier and did not provoke, through its failures, significant guerrilla warfare. In addition, Costa Rica's reformers outlawed the Army, making it more difficult for the military to rule either overtly or covertly, as in Venezuela. No matter. Costa Rica sent troops to the Dominican Republic; Venezuela did not. In Venezuela, a strong military could afford to permit a reformist President a semblance of independence by not sending troops to Santo Domingo as part of the inter-American "peace-keeping" force. In Costa Rica, a weak paramilitary (national police and civil guard) asserted its voice in mediating national politics by pressuring a reformist President (Figueres' man) to send troops to Santo Domingo. Thus, a reformist-model country with a "democratic" tradition, Costa Rica, contributed troops to put down reformers in a traditionally undemocratic country, the Dominican Republic, as part of an inter-American force that included soldiers from dictatorships like those of Brazil, Honduras, and Nicaragua. Few American scholars at the time could fathom these ostensible "contradictions," mainly because they did not yet fully grasp the bankruptcy of the reform model itself.

Figueres had led the 1948 reform-revolution in Costa Rica. As late as 1953 he had written: "It would be wise if the United States withdrew economic occupation." Yet during his five-year Presidency of Costa Rica (1953–58) he renewed contracts with United Fruit (for 30 percent of profits) and extended concessions to Standard Fruit Company "to establish plantations all over Costa Rica's Atlantic Coast (which United Fruit had abandoned in the 1920s)."[12] By 1965, Costa Rica's left-nationalist movements had become thoroughly harassed or crushed. A new, unprecedented (since 1948) threat from the right had emerged.

This resurgent radical right consisted of such elements as the following: soldiers of fortune, including Cuban exiles

12 Gerassi, *op. cit.,* p. 208.

who established a military base in Costa Rica in 1965 only to have it closed down when international pressures mounted; frustrated politicians; conservative political parties; smugglers and criminal elements; the rapidly expanding, U.S.-supplied national police and civil guard (Article 12 of the Costa Rican Constitution outlaws an army); and assorted police and political goon squads and terrorists, including the paramilitary organization called Free Costa Rica Movement. In the 1966 elections, a three-party coalition dominated by conservatives defeated the "reformist" presidential candidate, hand-picked by Figueres.

It should be pointed out that the development of strong militaries and paramilitaries in such traditional "democracies" as Costa Rica and Uruguay has been part of U.S. foreign policy for many years now. The results of this policy have been illustrated not just by the frequent *coups d'état* in Latin America but specifically by the failure of the Bolivian Revolution of 1952. Unfortunately for the armed, revolutionary miners and peasants, the Presidents of post-1952 Bolivian governments followed the reformist model, permitting the defeated military to re-establish itself and gradually disarming the people's militias. Over the years, often under the guise of "civic action" programs, the United States built up a strong Bolivian Army and Air Force that overthrew President Paz Estenssoro, murdered hundreds of miners, and established a military dictatorship. (We shall analyze below the more recent "military reformist" models developed in Bolivia and Peru.) The United States is pursuing a military reinforcement policy throughout Latin America, including Mexico, Uruguay, and Chile, the three "democratic" countries mentioned earlier and the only three to oppose with any frequency U.S. interventionist measures passed by the rubber-stamp Organization of American States.

Similarly, the United States has created militaries where none had existed before (except for foreign troops) in parts of Latin America traditionally controlled by European powers. In British Guiana (now Guyana), where the United States and Great Britain in 1964 avoided a leftist and constitutional victory by providing for revised constitu-

tional and electoral procedures, a new "Guiana Defense
Force" was built up prior to the granting of "independence",
which, after many postponements, was finally accomplished
in 1966 under Prime Minister Forbes Burnham. Burnham
had edged out Socialist Cheddi Jagan by means of a revised
electoral code. Burnham's government made a binding agreement that allows the United States to erect military installations and to land military aircraft, equipment, and supplies
in Guyana. While not yet a U.S. military base and colony,
like Puerto Rico, whose ruling party in the 1950s and 1960s
also was in the "reformist" tradition, Guyana does follow the
contemporary pattern of the "successful" (surviving) reformist model: retention of power behind bayonets, a country made "independent" by means of military occupation—
by its own "defense force."

What alternatives, then, are there for people seeking reform in Latin America today? Naturally, they have to, and
want to, at least pay lip service to nationalism—but this does
not necessarily mean revolution. Brazil's military dictatorship
is quite nationalistic on the surface, believing its propaganda
to the effect that it is "saving the nation from communism." However, such right-wing pseudonationalism as Brazil's, which strengthens the status quo, tortures political
prisoners, rationalizes the giving of more of the nation's resources and wealth to U.S. monopolies (the famed Hanna
mining deal, among others), and justifies the building of U.S.-
provided rocket-launching pads up and down the Brazilian
coast, is clearly counter to the reformist's *ideology,* if not
his practice.[13]

One model, then, is that of a right-wing, military-
dominated, anticommunist, pro-U.S. regime, practicing
pseudonationalism. As we have seen, even when the military
does not dominate overtly, a reformer is expected by the

[13] For an analysis of the right-wing Brazilian alternative, which
is praised so highly by such Senators as J. William Fulbright,
consult André Gunder Frank's well-documented articles in *El Día*
(Mexico City), October 8, 1965, and *The Minority of One,* July
1965.

United States to conform to each dimension of this model, in which case he can continue to *talk* about revolution. If a reformer shows signs of weakening on any one of the dimensions of this model—for example, if he attempts to nationalize more than a single natural resource without compensation, or if he proposes legalizing a Marxist, leftist, or nationalist party (Argentina's *Peronistas*)—then he is very likely to find himself removed to a distant ski resort or offshore island, as were Argentina's Frondizi and Peru's Manuel Prado and scores of other post-Kennedy chief executives in Latin America. With luck, he might end up teaching at Harvard, as in the case of Peru's latest deposed reformer, Belaúnde.

This is the supreme lesson of Santo Domingo, where U.S. troops served as honor guard for the funeral of the reformist model. Not only is the reformist model inherently defective; it cannot even operate on its own terms. It is, in brief, defunct. As if in militaristic mockery of its shattered dreams, its language alone survives.

That is why so many of the "new" reformers in Latin America, called upon by the ruling national and foreign (U.S.) bourgeoisies to bring "stability and progress," are younger men from the military (e.g., the late and little-mourned General René Barrientos of Bolivia), whose performances reflect no greater success than those of their predecessors. In fact, the record of the latest generation of reformers in Latin America—and the next one, should there be one—demonstrates conclusively that reformism in Latin America is conducive in the long run to military fascism, as in Brazil or Argentina, or to civilian neofascism (enforced by a well-armed, "modernized" military), as in Venezuela. To survive, reformism must not introduce any real reforms.

As an alternative to outright revolution, the military reformist regimes in pre-1971 Bolivia and Peru represent a kind of reform model that the United States may now be beginning to tolerate, if not, perhaps, to encourage. Both regimes emerged as a response to increased revolutionary pressures from below. Both regimes nationalized oil, declared an amnesty for political prisoners, turned over at least one major newspaper to workers' cooperatives, and, with partial success, called for large "anti-imperialist" street demonstrations on their behalf. The military personnel of both governments received training in the United States and participated earlier in the 1960s in the napalming of peasant villages, the repression of peasant, student, and guerrilla revolts, and, in the case of Bolivia, the killing of hundreds of tin miners and the execution of Che Guevara.

It has been often alleged that Che's death "proved" that guerrilla warfare was no longer possible in Latin America. In that case, one wonders what Vietnam, Cambodia, and Laos "prove." One also wonders what the continuation of guerrilla warfare in other Latin American countries and the emergence of Tupamaro-style urban guerrillas "prove." Finally, Che's sacrifice must be placed in the context of ongoing developments inside Bolivia.

Che's guerrilla movement was not wiped out. On the contrary, it survived, gained new recruits, and moved part of its armed contingents northward, leading the government to declare a state of siege in early 1969. There followed another military coup, more repression, and then nationalization of Gulf Oil in late 1969. As guerrilla resistance escalated, progressive elements within the military found it necessary to launch a coup-within-a-coup in 1970, to establish a Bonapartist regime, and reportedly to initiate secret negotiations with the guerrillas. Many peasants, miners, and students mobilized to force the new government in a revolutionary direction. Revolutionary elements of society objected to the government's reported offer of compensation to Gulf. In June of 1970, many of the top leaders of Bolivia's national student organization resigned their positions to join the guerrillas. A subsequent national convention of Bolivian students endorsed their example, while mourning the capture of some of their comrades in the jungle and their subsequent "murder" by Bolivian Army and alleged CIA guards. The Bolivian national student convention concluded that "armed struggle is the only way to liberate the country."[14] Later in 1970, some

[14] Report on the Nineteenth National University Convention of the Confederación Universitaria Boliviana (CUB) in *El Diario* (La Paz), November 10, 1970.

of the guerrillas reportedly accepted an arrangement with
the government to obtain safe transfer to exile in Chile. In
exchange, the government supposedly promised further
revolutionary changes in Bolivia, but it did not deliver beyond
the level of its radical rhetoric and the release of most political prisoners, including French journalist Regis Debray.
CIA operatives and U.S. military personnel continue to maneuver inside Bolivia to control and reverse the forces of
revolution unleashed by the earlier 1952 revolution and subsequent mobilization of guerrillas, miners, and students. The
United States continues to protest the nationalization of Gulf,
but has not, as of early 1971, "arranged" a settlement, or
another *coup d'état* from the right (which, in fact, it did succeed in assisting in August of 1971, after this sentence was
written). Meanwhile, U.S. investors are seeking new concessions in other areas of natural resources and, more importantly, in new manufacturing industry.

Next to the United States' obvious preoccupation with
events in Southeast Asia, it is the trend of new foreign investment patterns, described in the preceding chapter, that
best explains this relative tolerance of the U. S. Government
for agrarian reform and modified nationalism in Bolivia and
Peru. According to *The Rockefeller Report on the Americas,*
U.S. direct investment in Latin American manufacturing
industry has increased in the last decade from one fifth to
one third of all U.S. investments in Latin America. UN figures show the rise of the proportion of U.S. private investment directed toward the industrial sector in Latin America
to almost 60 percent in 1962. The reasons for this shift have
been explained in the preceding chapter, but are made even
more obvious in *The Rockefeller Report.* The United States
is moving into a computer-cybernetic stage of industrialization. More traditional U.S. manufacturing concerns are suffering from the need to hide behind high tariff walls, inefficiency, the high cost of labor, and a shortage of skilled labor.
The Rockefeller Report spells out the strategy for the 1970s,
which actually already has been implemented in the 1960s:

National productivity would be enhanced by shifting

workers and capital out of protected industries into industries where advanced technology and intensive capital
investment permits the United States to pay high wages
and still remain competitive in world markets. The goods
the United States is now producing inefficiently would
be imported, mainly from less developed countries. Consumers would gain through lower prices. . . . The less-
developed countries would also gain. With abundant supplies of labor and wage levels well below those in the
United States, they could export processed foods, textiles, apparel, footwear, and other light manufactures,
as well as meat and other farm products. . . . Such nations would become better customers for the high-
technology products of the United States. (pp. 102–3)

In other words, the United States now has a vested interest
in *encouraging* economic development in Latin America, so
long as it follows general guidelines consistent with U.S. corporate interests. Common markets serve to lower outmoded
tariff barriers and to increase the flow of trade, dominated
by U.S. and multinational corporations, and so *The Rockefeller Report* endorses not only the Latin American Free
Trade Association and the Central American Common Market but also the idea of a Latin American dollar market similar to the Eurodollar market. Moreover, *The Rockefeller
Report* argues for easing the pressure on Latin America's foreign debt and stretching out the amount of time to pay off,
setting aside equivalent amounts of postponed payments for
the purposes of:

(*a*) financing exports of capital goods within the region, (*b*) financing expanded economic development
through national and regional development banks, and
(*c*) financing local private participation in local *joint
ventures with foreign capital*. . . . The United States
is but one partner in a development effort which is about
90 percent financed by the other American republics.
(pp. 66 and 88; emphasis added)

Agrarian reform such as that in Peru now becomes advantageous since it serves not only to alleviate the force of
rising revolutionary impulses among the peasantry but also

to broaden the consumers' market for manufactured goods and agricultural machinery. Peru's agrarian reform serves to rationalize and mechanize agriculture, and clearly favors the commercial sector of the landholding elite, except in the case of the large sugar estates, which are to become peasant co-operatives run by the state (sugar interests like W. R. Grace and Company had earlier begun to transfer their investments to other parts of the economy). Under the new agrarian reform law, compensation to the large landholder is paid in bonds immediately convertible to cash if they are invested in enterprises selected by the government, thus encouraging industrialization. Workers are somewhat pacified by a new profit-sharing law, which gives them a small, but significant, "part interest" in the new (and old) manufacturing enterprises. The U. S. Government declared Peru's agrarian reform law in line with the Alliance for Progress, and the Inter-American Development Bank advanced an eighty-million-dollar loan to Peru.

Partial nationalization of foreign-owned oil fields serves further to "steal the thunder" of left-wing and nationalist political forces. The damage done to one foreign company, Standard Oil of New Jersey, is more than offset by the benefits offered to it and other U.S. corporations in the form of new oil-exploration concessions and investment grants and tax exemptions in other sectors of the economy, which in turn become ever more dominated by foreign capital. Peru compensated indirectly, but handsomely, for partial nationalization of oil when it extended to the U.S.-owned Southern Peru Copper Corporation the vast copper deposits of Cuajone, with a promised U.S. investment of over 355 million dollars. The government has made similar concessions to foreign investors in manufacturing industry, with guaranteed tax exemptions and other forms of protection well into the 1980s. The Peruvian Government's advertisements in leading U.S. newspapers seek increased private investment in an economy described as favoring "economic freedom" and "private enterprise." Meanwhile, U.S. corporations continue to transfer their factories abroad to exploit cheap labor and to develop expanded markets—usually with the help of local capital—at the very locale of colonialism, without the cost of export-import taxes or the need for middlemen, and with extra tax write-offs and benefits for "investing in development."

Peru's bourgeoisie has good reason to support the new military regime. The university reform abolishes university autonomy and makes political activity by students subject to severe punishment, thereby limiting the revolutionary potential of that traditionally troublesome sector. Even large landholders are rewarded under agrarian reform to the extent that they are "compensated" by increased shares of stock holdings in the growing urban sector of the economy. Most of them already had begun the shift into urban investment before the new agrarian reform. Title IX of the new law provides for partitioning of property through private initiative, thus permitting large landholders to divide up their estates among friends and relatives, and thereby preserve their monopolization of the best lands. In any case, the land reform has not proceeded rapidly and has been kept in the hands of the government bureaucracy and therefore out of the flammable area of "peasant control." Bourgeois elements discomforted by the reforms of the new military government are reassured by its swift repression of students in Cuzco and Lima, peasants in Juanta and Ayacucho, and mine workers of the U.S.-owned Cerro de Pasco corporation.

For two decades now, the Peruvian economy has been showing handsome economic growth rates, as foreign capital has increased its investment in the industrial sector (it accounts for over 80 percent) and even in the financing of government development programs. The majority of foreign capital continues to flow into the rich mining sector of the economy. Foreigners have turned increasingly to investment in intermediate basic industries—metallurgy, chemicals, cement, paper, wood, etc.—rather than merely to the traditional light consumer goods manufacture. Rapid economic growth in Peru has precipitated an expansion in the internal market for manufactured goods, a trend now encouraged by agrarian reform.

But Peru has "grown" by means of borrowing from abroad, as its foreign debt of nearly $1,000 million indicates, and by permitting increased foreign penetration of its economy. The standard of living of the masses has remained poor or has declined; unemployment and underemployment continue at nearly 30 percent. The long-range trend is already evident: foreigners bringing in the latest technological advances and large quantities of capital, buying out small and medium-size Peruvian businesses, interlocking with the richest local companies and banks, using small but skilled labor forces, as well as large and unskilled ones for certain kinds of assembly work, and, through the administrative adjunct implanted in a stronger centralized government (AID officials, Peace Corps, technical advisers, engineers, etc.), coming to guide the "development" process from within. Foreigners, mostly Americans, already have obtained majority control of the world's biggest fishmeal industry—originally Peruvian, today Peru's leading nonmineral export.

Thus, as the economy progresses toward an urban, industrialized stage, dependent on foreign markets and international corporations doing the financing and investing, Peru's industrial and financial bourgeoisie welcome limited reforms introduced by the military junta. Members of the junta themselves, by making public their financial holdings, are known to be personally involved in urban properties, industrial concerns, and investment companies, foreign as well as national. Trained not only in counterrevolutionary warfare by their U.S. advisers, the new military "technobureaucrats" of Peru have also been schooled in "civic action" and "community development" programs and thereby have absorbed a "developmentalist" ideology. *The Rockefeller Report* tacitly endorses this ideology when it foresees for the 1970s "continuation of the trend of the military to take power for the purpose of guiding social and economic progress" (p. 36). While wary of dictatorial, "nonpluralist," and even Marxian tendencies in this new type of Latin American military personnel, *The Rockefeller Report* nevertheless welcomes "a new type of military man coming to the fore . . . [as] a major force for constructive social change in the American republics" (p. 32). At the same time, the report recommends increased military aid and training programs for the Latin American military (p. 63).

Peru's new military government may be reformist or developmentalist, but like earlier reform models it can be tolerated and even encouraged by the U. S. Government so long as it remains subordinate to foreign investment and foreign debt-holders. As for the Peruvian bourgeoisie, it is already suffering internal splits between those advanced, urban, industrial sectors, tied to foreign capital and experiencing rapid growth, and more conservative, rural, traditional sectors. However, the bourgeois class as a whole is not eager to have the political situation become so unstable as to permit renewed peasant revolts, such as those earlier in the 1960s led by the Quechua-speaking Trotskyist, Hugo Blanco. The military has been far more successful in stabilizing the majority of the population through its current practices, than by its earlier resorting to napalm and armed occupation of the countryside. That kind of violence will come again only as a last resort.

But come again it may, along with likely civil war, should populist elements within Peru's military seek to move the government sharply to the left, or should students, workers, and peasants unite their energies for the making of a true revolution instead of the fraudulent kind now being engineered behind the mask of the regime's "anti-imperialist" and "nationalist" rhetoric. The Committees for the Defense of the Revolution, formed to defend Peru's claim to a two-hundred-mile offshore fishing rights limit, have the potential of becoming popular mass organizations, leading one general to comment: "They ought to boost production and not meddle in politics." In the meantime, Peru's bourgeoisie is cognizant of the fact that it derives more advantages from its subservient role to foreign capital and U.S. military aid than it would were it to try to go it alone in defiance of foreign interests. The ultimate threat to its survival remains that of the predominantly Indian masses.[15]

[15] On Peru, consult James Petras and Nelson Rimensnyder, "What Is Happening in Peru?," *Monthly Review,* February 1970; Karen Spalding, "Peru: the Military Managers," *Leviathan,* July-

Given the inability of the reform model, whether civilian or military, to reverse the trend of foreign takeover of Latin America's "development," there remains only one alternative for Latin Americans seeking sustained economic development and independence: that of anti-U.S. nationalism, involving violent revolution, a radical redistribution of income and political power, and rational use of economic resources. This should come as no surprise, since few have denied that violent revolution was bound to occur in Latin America sooner or later and since the bourgeoisies and militaries in Latin America have recently moved so overwhelmingly to consolidate their control, and that of the United States, under the Alliance for Progress. Moreover, even to the skeptical, forty thousand U.S. troops in and around the Dominican Republic in less than seventy-two hours is pretty persuasive evidence.

That this second, revolutionary alternative, though difficult, is practicable, is indicated by the example of Cuba, especially in its post-1959 phase. While a quick guerrilla success is out of the question now, precisely because of Cuba's success and the U.S. reaction hemispherically since 1960, long-term guerrilla struggle and development of urban, mining, and peasant cadres are already occurring in much of Latin America. Now that the reformist model has been exposed for what it is, the revolutionary forces in Latin America come face to face with the main internal enemy, the principal class opposed to serious reform. That class is the national bourgeoisie, once thought to be "progressive," but now best understood as reactionary. And the bourgeoisie includes in its ranks most of the large landholders, export-import businessmen, bankers, merchants, miners, industrialists, and manufacturers. Because this bourgeoisie in turn has grown ever more dependent upon the foreign (U.S.) bourgeoisie, in a long historical process with brief respites during war or depression, it has come to

August 1969; Aníbal Quijano Obregón, "Tendencies in Peruvian Development and Class Structure," in Petras and Zeitlin, *Latin America, Reform or Revolution?*, pp. 289–328; Shel Stromquist, "Peru: Nationalist Reform or Anti-Imperialist Revolution," *2 . . . 3 . . . Many . . .* , Winter 1970.

perform an ever more anti-nationalist role. The Latin American bourgeoisies have been the principal agents of increased militarization and foreign economic penetration over the past two decades.

Even where a self-declared socialist is elected President, as in Chile, the process of revolutionary change cannot occur without large-scale mobilization of the masses, which is bound to provoke counterrevolutionary violence. For progressive Latin Americans, there can be no doubt that the revolutionary alternative is more consonant with the reformist model's proclaimed *goals* than the alternative of right-wing military rule or counterrevolutionary violence.

Meanwhile, where are the reformers today? They are either in power and moving toward the political right, in jail, in exile, or attempting electoral comebacks. José Figueres has been re-elected President in Costa Rica and now openly calls for an inter-American invasion of Cuba, while at the same time protesting CIA meddling in the internal affairs of his country. Bolivia's Paz Estenssoro has flirted off and on with the idea of moving left and regaining power through violent revolution, while not ignoring the possibilities of linking himself to one or another military coup (which, in fact, he did in August of 1971, thus showing once again the last resort of bourgeois reformers—use of the army as the ultimate bourgeois "party" in Latin America). Other reformers, like Bosch, are considering the idea of either an electoral or violent political comeback; Bosch has given increasing ideological support for revolution in Latin America. He is especially indignant about the reign of terror in the Dominican Republic since 1965, which has claimed over six hundred victims. Bosch once believed the main terrorist group to be La Mano (The Hand), an organization he claimed was formed by members of the local bourgeoisie working in close collaboration with the CIA. Bosch himself has been a target of terrorist attacks. Since the 1971 publicity given "la banda," an anti-Communist terrorist organization in the Dominican Republic, Bosch has told the New York *Times* that it and similar right-wing terrorist groups in Guatemala, Argentina, Uruguay,

Brazil, and Mexico "all form part of a continental plan of U.S. origin."[16]

It is well known that some civilians in the Dominican Republic are still armed. A political comeback by a reformer, *if* it is to succeed, nowadays necessitates either a total embrace with U.S. imperialism as in the case of Figueres, or: (a) the presence of an armed populace and/or (b) the support of a significant portion of the military [unlikely without (a), as the Dominican case illustrated in 1965]. Such civilian *armed presence* in turn necessitates either a political move to the right and military suppression of that presence (this occurred in Venezuela after dictator Marcos Pérez Jiménez was overthrown in 1959), or a move to the left and tolerance of that presence (this occurred in Cuba in 1959 after Batista was overthrown).

The U. S. Government apparently realized this when it refused to let Bosch return to the Dominican Republic and militarily suppressed the April 1965 Dominican Revolution. In a very real sense, the Dominican uprising *did* pose the threat, ultimately, of "another Cuba"—at least in the sense of expropriation of U.S. properties, legalization of leftist parties, and mobilization of the people. Thus, the United States found itself obliged to act with massive military might and unilaterally—as it will continue to do if necessary, with or without the diplomatic fig leaf of the Organization of American States.

The United States may insist on sending troops to every Latin American country experiencing revolution; or it may ultimately succeed, as it is succeeding today, in arranging *de facto* regional "multilateral intervention" armies similar to the one sent to Santo Domingo.[17] If these events occur, progres-

[16] *Intercontinental Press,* September 14, 1970, p. 741; *Guardian,* September 15, 1971.

[17] General William C. Westmoreland, "Generals of the Americas Unite," Address to the Eighth Conference of the American Armies, Rio de Janeiro, Brazil, September 25, 1968, reprinted in *NACLA Newsletter,* October 1968. For a model of a U.S.-controlled regional multilateral military force, *de jure,* already in full operation, advised by the CIA, and *de facto* incorporating Costa Rica and Panama, where there are national guards instead of

sive Latin Americans, including those reformers who have not opted for the right-wing trajectory traced by their most prominent representatives, will probably have to unite in transnational revolutionary armies to oppose such reactionary international military machines, even as Bolívar and San Martín did against Spain during the Independence movement a century and a half ago.

---

armies, consult John Saxe-Fernández, "The Central American Defense Council and Pax Americana," in Horowitz, *et al.* (eds.), *Latin American Radicalism,* pp. 75–101.

Chapter 6

VENEZUELA: CLASS STRATIFICATION AND REVOLUTION*

James D. Cockcroft

In recent years, Venezuela has experienced intensified political divisions, reaching even the family level. A wealthy Venezuelan recently wrote to the Minister of Justice as follows:

> I address you in your capacity as Justice Minister and personal friend . . . In these lines you will see the anxiety of a father, but also the profound grief and indignation of a Venezuelan. . . . As you perhaps already know, one of my sons, Gastón, in spite of the beliefs, convictions, and traditions of the family, identifies with the parties that we in Venezuela call leftist. . . . In Gastón's case, such a decision produces in me the grief and anxiety that any father must experience when his son follows a mistaken path. . . .
>
> My son was taken prisoner in Puerto Cabello during the recent revolt in that city [launched by the Navy, June 2, 1962], without anyone's being able to tell me of the circumstances surrounding the arrest. . . . In Valencia, where he is now, he has been held completely naked in a cell. The clothes and parcels we had sent him from the house had never been delivered to him. Such treatment resulted in his contracting a skin disease. To this moral and physical maltreatment was added primitive, savage, bodily torture: for two entire days he was submitted to it, dunking his head in water until he lost consciousness and later, upon regaining consciousness, repeating the procedure continuously, interjecting blows and taunts. . . .

* This chapter is a slightly revised version of an article that originally appeared in *Mexico Quarterly Review*, Vol. II, No. 3 (July 1965).

The defeat of Communism is vital for Christian civilization. . . . You and I sustain principles which Communism denies and aspire to a life altogether different from that which Communism offers us. But the goal of defeating Communism is not attained by applying to Communists, contrary to Christian ethics, inhuman methods of violence which make us equal to beasts and make us no better than our very adversaries. . . .

With the fall of Pérez Jiménez, and the ascent of a regime said to be democratic—and it is in its origin—we came to think that the nightmare of prison tortures had ended once and for all. But our affliction has not ended, since, in spite of the principles that underlie the regime and the sacred constitution, tortures and mistreatment continue to be applied. . . .[1]

In addition to describing traditional Venezuelan police brutality, this letter poignantly reflects the division that has grown between the generations. Indeed, a Venezuelan Turgenev might today compose a *Fathers and Sons* modelled on such famous fathers as congressman Jóvito Villalba and Supreme Court Justice Ignacio Luis Arcaya, leaders of the once leftist, now moderately rightist Unión Republicana Democrática (URD), whose sons, arrested in October 1963, are ardent revolutionaries.

These rebellious sons of a new generation, still a minority except in student politics, do not form a revolutionary vanguard in Lenin's sense of a small, united, and determined political party leadership. However, as Venezuela's established leftist parties are now underground[2] and their older leaders in jail, these youths are emerging as a militant, tight-knit movement, acting under the banner of the guerrilla-led Fuerzas Armadas de Liberación Nacional (FALN) and on behalf of the "exploited proletariat."

What is the state of Venezuelan society—to have bred such

[1] Published in Caracas's conservative daily *La Esfera,* June 29, 1962.

[2] Since this article was written, the Venezuelan Communist Party regained its legal recognition and release of its leaders from prison by denouncing the guerrilla movement and defending participation in the established political framework.

widespread disillusionment and revolutionary fervor? Have the poverty and unemployment, the murders of students, the suppression of parties and press, and the corruption in high places reached the extent of deterioration characteristic of Cuban society in 1958? Although such headline-making factors as the Cuban Revolution and U.S. "imperialism," and the lesser-known Venezuelan tradition of student participation in revolutionary politics, are surely parts of the causal matrix, the thesis of this short paper is that the revolutionary activity of numerous middle-class youths in Venezuela is in great part the result of the longstanding injustices of a highly stratified class system, a system which has challenged the moral honesty and intellectual integrity of each younger generation.

In this system, the power elite that rules over the impoverished majority of the population[3] includes three main sectors: foreign capitalist, domestic oligarchic, and state.

The principal foreign element is that of the United States, led by Standard Oil of New Jersey and backed by the U. S. Government.[4] Also active in Venezuela are Gulf Oil Company, Standard of California, Socony Vacuum, Bethlehem Steel Corporation, United States Steel, General Motors, Du Pont, General Electric, Sears Roebuck (a luxury chain outside of the U.S.), and 300 other U.S. corporations. Of all foreign investments in Venezuela, 67 percent are U.S.; moreover, 87 percent of U.S. investments in Venezuela are in oil or iron, the source of 97 percent of the nation's export earnings. Of all U.S. investments in Latin America, 38 percent are in Venezuela. U.S. companies not only have set up assembly plants and new factories in Venezuela, exploiting cheap labor, but also have used the banking structure to raise local currency for their investments. According to its own adver-

[3] Pages 14 through 18 of Edwin Lieuwen's *Venezuela* (London: Oxford University Press, 1961) provide an excellent description of how "over half the population lives at bare subsistence levels."

[4] A clear explanation of this complicated arrangement is Harvey O'Connor's *World Crisis in Oil* (New York: Monthly Review Press, 1962), pp. 128–71.

tisements (e.g., *Wall Street Journal*, February 23, 1966), the Morgan Guarantee Trust Company, through its sixteen correspondent banks in Venezuela, holds 55 percent of all privately owned commercial bank resources and helps foreign firms raise local funds.

The domestic, oligarchic power elite in Venezuela is composed of large absentee landholders, industrial capitalists, big bankers and investment financiers, insurancemen, import-export monopolists, and similar types who have established a profitable, working alliance with foreign operators subject, however, to occasional tensions caused by Venezuela's economic nationalism. This domestic elite is referred to as the "Fuerzas Vivas" (economic power elite) even by its political representatives, like ex-President (1959–64) Rómulo Betancourt.

Interlocked, but not always cooperating, with the vested foreign and domestic interests is the powerful, conservative Venezuelan state, with its established institutions: the military, police, national guard, clergy, judiciary, bureaucracy, and legal political parties.

The military, largely armed and advised by the United States and its military mission in Caracas, is the real power in today's Venezuela, just as it has been throughout history.[5] Ruling behind a civilian façade, the military—mainly the Army, some 30,000-men strong—is itself a separate oligarchy, led by traditional army families from the conservative region of the western, Andean states of Táchira, Mérida, and Trujillo.[6] When the Army crushed the navy barracks revolts of May and June 1962, led by dissident navy families (especially that of Captain Jesús Teodoro Molina Villegas) and

[5] Lieuwen, *op. cit.*, p. 160. Lieuwen devotes much of his other major work to the role of U.S. military missions in Latin America —see *Arms and Politics in Latin America* (New York: Frederick A. Praeger, Inc., 1961).

[6] In spite of the overthrow of dictator (1949–58) Marcos Pérez Jiménez, many officers of his Army resumed top leadership posts in 1959–64, along with men loyal to the government party Acción Democrática (AD). See the *Hispanic American Report*, v. XV (1962), pp. 427 and 526.

not the extreme left as commonly reported, all the military joined to force President Betancourt "to suppress the leftist opposition and to roll back some of his social and economic reform policies."[7] In this manner, as well as by frequently occupying workers' neighborhoods with troops in order to prevent physical expression of unrest, having political leaders come on regular visits to the bases to confer, and judging political and civilian cases in military tribunals, the Armed Forces play a key role in maintaining the status quo in Venezuela. Finally, civilian presidents like Betancourt and Raúl Leoni are confronted with the constant historical reminder that when their party has aggressively pushed social reforms, as in 1945–48, it has been overthrown by the military.[8]

The police and national guard are especially active in putting down opposition. "Goon squads" of the Dirección de Policía (DIGEPOL) periodically invade Caracas's Central University (in violation of university autonomy) or smash opposition printing presses (now practically extinct except on a clandestine basis). For example, on May 15, 1964, a DIGEPOL goon squad raided Central University in what the University's most anti-leftist president in the past five years labelled "the worst invasion the University has suffered in recent years . . . wounding various students . . . a new and brutal aggression."[9] Earlier, a more independent but still moderate president of Central University had denounced "the reactionary campaign against the University being waged by oligarchic groups, against the people and representing interests foreign to the nation."[10]

The clergy and judiciary further aid the power elite in Venezuela. Their progressive rhetoric is belied by their actions. For example, in June 1964, the Church won its battle to have the 19th-century anti-clerical legislation of dictator Antonio Guzmán Blanco modified to allow the Vatican once again to make appointments without prior consultation of lists

[7] *Ibid.*
[8] Lieuwen, *Arms and Politics . . . ,* p. 52.
[9] *El Nacional* (Caracas), May 16, 1964.
[10] See interview with Francisco de Venanzi, *El Nacional,* May 31, 1962.

of candidates proposed by Congress. The Supreme Court, when confronted with the necessity of ruling on the legality of President Betancourt's May 1962 outlawing of the Communist Party and extreme-left Movimiento de Izquierda Revolucionaria (MIR), begged the question by simply acknowledging that "the two parties would be considered 'inactive' so long as the presidential decree were not rescinded."[11] Meanwhile, Communist and MIR congressmen (16 percent of the Chamber of Deputies and large numbers of state-level legislators) were jailed; the judiciary did nothing about these violations of congressional immunity, or the usurpation of its authority by military tribunals.

One of the most selfish, ambitious, and conservative groups that bolster Venezuela's power elite is the bureaucracy, which numbers 300,000 and drains about 45 percent of the national budget. Both President Betancourt and President Raúl Leoni (1964–69) have publicly acknowledged widespread corruption in their AD-dominated bureaucracies.

Also fighting for the spoils are Venezuela's legal political parties, which under Betancourt became especially violent in their efforts to gain greater power. While the Communist and MIR were driven underground by the state machine of violence, each political party and AD's organized labor movement developed efficient "goon squads" to rout the left and fight one another. A typical case of interparty war was that of the goon-squad attacks exchanged between AD and its dissident "Ars" faction (AD-Ars) in 1962–63. AD-Ars commanded the services of "Sotopol" (abbreviation for police of Hugo Soto Socorro, AD-Ars congressman—"Soto-policía") which in 1960–61 had served AD in assaulting the labor, press, and political offices of the URD, Communists, and MIR. Upon returning to power in 1959 (after ruling briefly with the military, 1945–48), AD had attempted to solidify political control through violence and threat; today, AD, its labor-union militants, and DIGEPOL continue to employ goon-squad tactics.[12]

[11] *Hispanic American Report*, v. XVI (1963), p. 979.
[12] The AD party organ *A.D.*, September 17, 1960, admits the existence of such "goon squads." Political columns by various

Finally, extra-legal terrorist groups contribute to the violent political struggle in Venezuela. Although publicity in the foreign press has focused on the FALN, which could not be mentioned in the Venezuelan press following the government's April 1963 absurd assertion that it "does not exist,"[13] rightist terrorism flourished in the chaotic conditions of 1958–64. In the Caracas workers' neighborhood of 23 de Enero, a Pérez Jiménez-launched housing project of 150,000 people, 50 percent of whom are under 15 years of age, a clandestine, rightist group called "Cobra Negra" has gained a reputation for sniping from rooftops.[14] Other groups, mostly loyal to ex-dictator Pérez Jiménez and in some cases possibly allied with the government's secret service have received occasional publicity.[15]

Leftist terrorism, led by the urban guerrilla branch of the FALN, was avoided during the initial year of the guerrilla movement (1961–62). However, as government suppression increased, and open political propagandizing for revolutionary reforms became impossible, the FALN resorted to terroristic tactics, mostly aimed at U.S. oil installations. This terrorism was exaggerated in the U.S. press, leading many to believe that olive-green uniformed agents of Fidel Castro were machine-gunning innocent citizens in Caracas's streets. The fact is that the FALN avoided bloodshed, and Havana had little to do with terrorism, by the Venezuelan Govern-

---

journalists in the independent, anti-leftist daily *El Nacional*, 1960–64, make frequent reference to Sotopol and DIGEPOL, as well as to other political-party goon squads. That pro-government labor unions have their goon squads was finally confirmed by the *New York Times* in a Caracas dispatch by Richard Eder, February 21, 1963.

[13] *Hispanic American Report*, v. XVI, p. 168.

[14] *Ibid.*, p. 1075.

[15] Rightist revolts by ex-military men and discovery of rightists arms caches are periodically reported in the *Hispanic American Report*, vs. XI–XVI (1958–63). A typical extreme-right terrorist group is "PROFAN" (Pro-Fuerzas Armadas Nacionales), described in *El Nacional*, June 6, 1962.

ment's own admission,[16]—although the notorious and un-proven "arms cache" case did lead to the O.A.S. censure of Cuba, with Mexico's abstention, in 1964.

Venezuela's three-pronged power elite (foreign capitalists, domestic oligarchs, and the state and its institutions), although not always working in perfect harmony, rules over an impoverished mass. Caracas's gaudy skyscrapers, hotels, and night clubs are surrounded by a bathtub ring of tumble-down shacks with no sanitation and inadequate water, in which subsist 440,000 of the Federal District's 1,257,515 population (1961 census). Unemployment is at least 13 percent of the labor force, or more than 300,000. Underemployment is an even worse problem, as "many hundreds of thousands hold part-time jobs only."[17] The economy is sluggish,[18] so that

[16] Inside Venezuela, the government repeatedly stated that Havana was not giving orders to Venezuelan terrorists (*Hispanic American Report*, v. XV, pp. 930 and 1028). "Except for the shooting of policemen and sniping attacks—which may be effected by other less organized groups—the National Liberation Army has avoided bloodshed"—*New York Times*, December 9, 1963.

[17] *Rundt's Market Reports* (New York), January 8, 1964, p. 28.

[18] According to the International Monetary Fund, public and private investments dropped from 6.34 billion bolívares (3.35 bolívares equaled $1, pre-1964 devaluation) in 1959 to 5.16 billion bolívares in 1962. This figure recovered to 6.98 billion bolívares in 1968. Central Bank gold and dollar reserves plummeted from $1395 million in 1957 to $576 million in 1962 (with help of U.S. loans, up over $900 million in 1970). The public debt increased from 2.1 billion bolívares to 4.6 billion bolívares between 1965 and 1969 (4.5 bolívares=$1). From 1958 to 1960 flight capital approached $2000 million. Dependence on oil and iron export earnings increased from 95.6 percent in 1952 to 96.8 percent in 1967. The government's share of oil earnings dropped from $1873 million in 1957 to $1435 million in 1958, held level at about $1550 million a year following that. The number of oil rigs in operation dropped from 115 in 1957 to 30 in 1962 to 25 in 1963 (average). The number of exploration wells drilled fell from 598 in 1958 to 34 in 1969. New investment in petroleum dropped from $536 million in 1958 to $144 million in 1967 (back up to $290 million in 1968). Crude oil production, main source of Venezuela's economic survival (two-thirds of crude oil refining is done outside of Venezuela), fell below the government goal of a 4 percent-per-annum increase when it rose only slightly between 1965 and 1969, from

poverty worsens each year. The annual Gross National Product increase barely keeps pace with a population growth rate variously estimated from 3 percent to 4.5 percent a year, and often falls behind.[19]

In spite of its limited recovery from the 1960 depression, Venezuela's economy can not confront the fresh demands for jobs (more than 100,000 a year). Although business activity is relatively vigorous, and even as upper bourgeois elements engage in speculative and industrial activities, and government, foreign aid, and private foreign investment contribute to new profit opportunities, employment in industry (operating at only 50 percent capacity) is actually dropping—as the following table indicates:

EMPLOYMENT INDEX OF SELECT INDUSTRIES PROVIDED BY CENTRAL BANK
BASE YEAR, 1958 = 100.

Year	Petroleum	Iron	Metallic Mft.	Automotive Assembling	Textiles[20]
1959	96.9	103.6	111.2	112.4	106.7
1960	91.1	104.4	103.9	102.2	108.6
1961	82.8	98.3	100.1	94.2	117.7
1962	76.8	93.2	95.5	93.1	117.7

Machines are replacing men, and much-heralded new industries like textiles and automotive assembling are not creating enough new jobs. The high cost of living (Caracas has

1268 million barrels to 1312 million barrels. See Banco Central de Venezuela, *Informe económico, año 1962; Informe económico, año 1967; Boletín Mensual,* August 1970; *Rundt's Market Reports,* January 8, 1964; The Economist Intelligence Unit, *Quarterly Economic Review. Venezuela Annual Supplement, 1970* (London: 1970).

[19] Central Bank figures show the following annual GNP increases: 1960: 1.4%, 1961: 1.7%, 1962: 6.3%, 1963: 4%, 1964: 8%, 1965: 5%, 1966: 2.1%, 1967: 4.3%, 1968: 5.8%.

[20] Banco Central de Venezuela, *Informe Económico, año 1962,* Appendix (no p.). The gain in textile-factory employment is small if one considers the claimed 150 percent increase in production capacity, 1959–62.

the highest of any city in the world with the possible exception of Guatemala City) further oppresses Venezuela's masses.

Organized labor is, as in most of Latin America, a political tool of the government. The Confederación de Trabajadores de Venezuela (CTV) claims a membership of 1.3 million workers. Assuming that figure to be correct, if the CTV had followed AD instructions and voted for Leoni in the December 1963 presidential elections, then the votes of those workers and their wives would have totalled about 2 million. Yet Leoni received only 957,699 votes total (AD down from 49 percent in 1958 to 33 percent in 1963)—suggesting that more than half of the union members were disillusioned with AD-style leadership, or that the CTV's claim of 1.3 million workers is exaggerated. Villalba's URD, through its left wing in 1962, had sparked the formation of an opposition labor movement (including Communists and MIR) which lost strength in the face of government competition and suppression and today controls less than 10 percent of national union membership. Nevertheless, many organized workers resent AD leadership, and those that are not unionized usually suffer the ills of at least underemployment.

Venezuela's peasantry is, as Lieuwen points out, even worse off than the urban workers.[21] Some 45 percent of the workers are on the farms, where less than 8 percent of the national wealth is produced.[22] Agrarian reform has not adequately confronted the accumulated evils of absentee landlordism, market monopolies and speculation, debt peonage, and scarcity of credits, tools, seed, and land titles. According to the government, 60,000 families received land during the Betancourt administration, in spite of less and less budgeting each year.[23] In 1955, an estimated 350,000 peasant families were without sufficient land to cultivate.[24] The opposition claimed that only 10,000 families received land under Betancourt.

[21] Lieuwen, *Venezuela*, p. 15.
[22] *Rundt's Market Reports*, January 8, 1964, p. 28.
[23] See the *Hispanic American Report*, v. XV, pp. 430–31, 530, and v. XVII (1964), p. 51.
[24] *Ibid.*

Spontaneous peasant land grabs were, in fact, common. In spite of whatever land-reform efforts have been made by the government, the fact is that Venezuela continues to import one-fourth of its total food requirements[25] and that thousands of peasant families leave the countryside and swarm into the cities each year. Venezuela's overcrowded cities mushroomed to 62.5 percent of the population by 1961, compared to 46.2 percent in 1960; rural population plummeted from 46.2 percent in 1950 to 32.5 percent in 1961.[26]

Per capita income in Venezuela is $812 a year, but its grossly unequal distribution contributes to a cruel struggle for survival among the majority of the population. Government figures reflecting maldistribution of income normally do not even provide income brackets for families earning less than $2,000 a year. But they do indicate that the larger a family is, the lower is its income:

Monthly per capita income	% of population	people in family[27]
$750 and up	3%	3.5
$360–$750	7%	4.
$180–360	20%	4.5
less than $180	70%	6.5

More and more babies amidst greater poverty constitute part of the demography of poverty. Some 60 percent of Venezuelan births are illegitimate.[28] Two-thirds of the 1961 population of 7,524,000 is under 25 years of age, while half is under 18. By mid-1969, population was estimated at 10 million peo-

[25] Milk and dairy products, wheat, barley, oats, maize (corn and cornmeal), beans, dry edible peas, oil seeds and derivatives, fish meal, fruits.

[26] According to 1950 and 1961 censuses. "Intermediate" accounted for remaining percentages (c. 5 percent) in each case. "Urban" defined as more than 2,500 inhabitants in a concentrated area; "intermediate" as between 1,000 and 2,499; and "rural" as less than 1,000.

[27] *Rundt's Market Reports.* January 8, 1964, p. 28.

[28] According to Dr. Gustavo H. Machado, founder and ex-president of the apolitical Consejo Venezolano del Niño (*Hispanic American Report*, v. XVI, p. 272).

ple, of whom 46 percent were under 15 years of age and 56 percent under 20, with over 70 percent of the population urban. Slums are mushrooming, and government-financed housing has not even come close to keeping pace with demand. To make up the 1962 national deficit of 575,000 living units, and without taking into account population growth, 125 houses an hour every working day would have to be constructed for two years, according to the state-planning agency Oficina Nacional de Coordinación y Planificación (CORDIPLAN).[29]

In brief, because of the rising cost of living, increased unemployment and underemployment, and a rapidly expanding population, much of which migrates to already overcrowded cities, Venezuela's impoverished masses are getting poorer every year, and the present power elite seems unwilling or unable to do much about it.

Meanwhile, the bourgeoisie is divided and confused. While upper bourgeois business elements prosper and interlock and bureaucrats fight to preserve their vested interest, smaller shopkeepers, tradesmen, and merchants are becoming antagonistic, frightened, and desperate. However, the plight of the petite bourgeoisie is not sufficient to make it an active force for revolution, since its representatives fear that the "Fidelista"[30] leadership of the FALN will provide a sweeping revolution similar to that in Cuba, where small merchants lost control to the proletariat. Some middle-class professionals, often underemployed, enter the politico-economic establishment, while others resign in protest,[31] and others join the revolutionary left.

Sons of the bourgeoisie generally enter business, the bu-

[29] *Rundt's Market Reports*, January 8, 1964, p. 40.

[30] A term used in the world's press to refer to persons who believe in the revolutionary line of Fidel Castro and act accordingly.

[31] For example, Judge Joaquín Gabaldón Márquez, in his youth known as "the poet of the Generation of 1928" (that of Betancourt, Leoni, Villalba, and other rebellious youth), who resigned from the Supreme Court in June 1962, in protest against the government's arrests of congressmen.

reaucracy, or politics, some of them polarizing to the revolutionary cause where they find a role appropriate for the times and consistent with the nation's long history of student revolt.[32]

In view of this kind of social stratification, which tends to perpetuate poverty among the majority of the population, it is little wonder that instability and alienation permeate the political-social scene in contemporary Venezuela. Even though one might hesitate to hazard a guess about the future chances of any sweeping social revolution, we can already detect the signs of both revolution and civil war.

[32] See James D. Cockcroft, "Venezuela's Fidelistas: Two Generations" (Stanford University: Institute of Hispanic American and Luso-Brazilian Studies, 1963, mimeo.).

Chapter 7

THE NATIONAL AND PROGRESSIVE BOURGEOISIE IN CHILE*

Dale L. Johnson

Though the terminology and moral implications differ, both Marxist and conventional academic social analyses posit the existence of a progressive bourgeoisie in the transition process from non-industrial to industrial societies. The presence of this self-conscious, politically active class is assumed to be a necessary prerequisite for the social and political transformations that must accompany, or even precede, economic development. Marxist and conventional thought agree on the critical nature of the formation of progressive classes, particularly a new entrepreneurial class, in the experience of Western industrialized countries. Regarding the situation in presently underdeveloped countries, the thesis states that nationalism is a force promoting development and modernization. Orthodox Marxists refer to the formation of a national bourgeoisie. Liberal American academicians and Alliance for Progress policy formulators refer to the democratic middle groups, of which urban commercial and industrial elites constitute an important sector.

This essay constitutes an analysis and empirical examination of the ideological position and political roles of industrial managers in one of the more industrialized countries of Latin America: Chile. In order to place the politics of Chilean industrialists in a wider perspective, some general findings of

* Originally published in *Studies in Comparative International Development*, Vol. IV, No. 4, 1968–69. Reprinted by permission of the publisher. A list of references appears at the end of this chapter. As throughout this volume, statements about Chile may be assumed to refer to pre-1970 Chile, unless otherwise indicated.

my research project "Industry and Industrialists in Chile" are first summarized (Johnson, 1967).

I. INDUSTRY AND INDUSTRIALISTS IN CHILE

Chile is a troubled nation. The economy suffers from a stagnation-inflation crisis. For fifteen years the expansion of production has barely exceeded the rate of population growth, while the currency devaluates from 20 to 80 per cent annually. The country has a rigid social structure: social classes are clearly demarcated and there is little mobility between strata. Distribution of income data indicate that the rich are getting richer and the poor poorer. Society is torn by social conflict, violence, and constant political turmoil, which so far have failed to produce structural changes. Politics now consists of a sharp struggle between three powerful forces; the intransigent political right whose basis of power is the control of vast economic resources; the socialist and militant left representing an alliance of the materially or socially disadvantaged and the revolutionary intellectuals; and Christian Democracy, a populist movement which now occupies the seats of governmental power and promises to carry out a "revolution in freedom."

The nation did experience a period of incipient industrialization (1933–53) which considerably increased the total of national wealth, caused transformations in social structure, and moved politics out of the realm of struggle between factions of the oligarchy toward modern mass politics. Nevertheless, many of the traits of underdevelopment remain; in fact, these traits have become accentuated in the period of stagnation. While a sustained rate of development toward an industrialized society may not make Chile a less troubled nation, it would at least relieve some of the most pressing and urgent human problems of underdevelopment. The possibility for achieving development is the principal subject matter of the research. The analysis focused upon one sector of the economy, manufacturing industry, and upon a key group in society, industrialists.

METHODOLOGY OF THE EMPIRICAL RESEARCH

The major portion of the information and data for the project were gathered by the author in Santiago, Chile in 1964 and 1965.[1] A sample of manufacturing firms, stratified according to size and type of industry, was drawn from the Industrial Census of 1957 and one and one-half to two hour interviews were conducted with each of the general managers of firms selected.

The criterion of size utilized was the number of persons employed by the firm. "Medium-sized" firms employ between 50 and 199 persons, and "large" firms have 200 or more employees. At the time of the interviews, there were about 500 legally constituted medium-sized manufacturing firms and 150 large industrial corporations in the country. The sample drawn included 146 medium-sized and 105 large firms. Interviews with the general managers, or in a few cases with other higher executives, of 69 concerns of each size in the sample, were obtained between January and June of 1965. These are approximately 14 per cent and 46 per cent of the total number of medium-sized and large firms, respectively. While the sample was drawn at random, the firms interviewed are underrepresentative of the smallest enterprises (50–100 employed).

The criterion for sample selection in terms of type of industrial production was the United Nations Industrial Classification, which includes 20 distinct lines ranging from processed foods to diverse manufactures. In relation to the total

[1] The research was made possible by an initial grant from the Doherty Foundation covering travel and living expenses. Other assistance from the *Centro de Estudios Socio-Económicos* of the *Universidad de Chile,* and the Latin American Research Center of the University of California, Riverside is gratefully acknowledged. I am particularly indebted to Professor Eduardo Hamuy of the University of Chile and Fernando Henrique Cardoso of The Latin American Institute for Economic and Social Planning for their aid and advice. The Social Science Research Council is supporting the final stages of the research.

number of firms in each line of production, the sample over-represents several of the heavy industries and underrepresents the printing and leather industries.

Geographically, the sample is underrepresentative of manu-facturing establishments in Concepción and Valparaiso.

Nearly two hundred questions—many of them elaborate and most structured to include fixed alternative responses—were asked of 138 industrialists. However, not all the questions were asked of the entire sample, so that the number of responses to an item is usually less than the total number of interviews. At the end of the interview, a lengthy question-naire was left with the manager. Questionnaires containing many of the interview items were also collected from thirty-seven young professionals (mostly graduates in economics and sociology) working in university and governmental eco-nomic research institutions and thirty-three industrial work-ers. Unfortunately, only twenty-eight questionnaires were col-lected from industrialists before the repercussions of the United States Department of the Army sponsored "Project Camelot" forced the premature cancellation of the research.[2] The industrialists responding to the questionnaire are not rep-resentative of the larger group interviewed (politically, they stand to the left of the majority of the managers). The sample of unionized workers, which was not drawn in a sys-tematic manner, seems to have a much higher proportion of "traditional" and conservative workers than is found in the organized working class generally.

AN OVERVIEW OF THE RESEARCH FINDINGS

The investigation and analysis so far undertaken in Chile can be divided into three interrelated parts. (1) The growth of production since 1930, the changes in forms of organiza-tion and structure during incipient industrialization, and the

[2] I feel much concern and indignation regarding Camelot and similar projects (Johnson, 1966: 206–7). Irving Louis Horowitz (1967) has performed a useful service for the social science pro-fession by editing the volume on Project Camelot.

present growth possibilities of the industrial sector. (2) Industrialists as a social group, their position in the social structure, their roles in enterprise and society, and their ideological make-up. (3) The political economy of economic development and social change.

(1) The possibilities for "breakthroughs" based upon economic conditions in the industrial sector that would form the basis for a self-sustaining process of industrialization, create a more fluid social structure, and diminish social conflict are not present in Chile. This conclusion is arrived at after an analysis of major aspects of industrial organization and structure. These include: (a) *The size of manufacturing firms.* There has been a marked bifurcation of industrial structure. A sharp differentiation has developed between the limited number of larger, modern corporations, and the thousands of smaller, less efficient firms. Small firms are unable to cross the line to become medium-sized enterprises and finally grow to large industrial corporations. (b) *The different sectors of industry.* The traditional sector, largely composed of industries producing goods for ordinary consumption, seems to have very little growth possibility. Plants in the sector operate with considerable excess capacity. Lagging growth of national income and the increasingly regressive distribution of income prevents the expansion of internal demand and there are few export possibilities. The dynamic sector, producing durable consumption and capital goods may have further growth possibilities. However, growth in this sector is not likely to offset the existing equilibrium of stagnation in the economy. (c) *The type of organization of firms and the patterns of ownership and control.* Over one-half the medium-sized and many large enterprises in Chile are family-run operations. This has distinctly unsaluatory effects for industrial development. An economic oligarchy primarily involved in banking and little concerned with industrial development controls a significant proportion of the largest industrial corporations. No more than one firm in five are corporations relatively free from family or extra-sectoral control. This has significant consequences for growth and the manner in which industrialists perform their roles. (d) *The degree of industrial concentra-*

tion. Conditions in the industrial sector are far from competitive. This has manifold, mostly adverse, consequences for prices (which are high), efficiency (which is low), and income distribution (which is highly regressive).

In short, analysis of industrial organization and structure and economic conditions during the period of incipient industrialization and the later period of stagnation suggests that development is not likely to proceed simply through the dynamic workings of the economy. Accordingly, an attempt is made to determine if the ways in which industrialists carry out their entrepreneurial roles constitute or may constitute factors in achieving a breakthrough toward sustained industrialization.

(2) The results of the investigation forced the conclusion that industrialists cannot be considered "dynamic entrepreneurs." There is a propensity for high levels of consumption, an exceedingly low level of investment in industrial production, and a transfer of capital from industry to other, less productive activities. But industrialists are prisoners of the institutional and structural context in which development must unfold. The essence of entrepreneurship would seem to lie in breaking out of the institutional and structural rigidities such that private decisions and individual rationality more closely coincide with the developmental needs of the economy. Insofar as entrepreneurship in this sense depends upon the presence of certain social characteristics or personality traits among entrepreneurs, the possibilities are not very encouraging. Industrialists are not a socially marginal group, outstandingly achievement oriented, nor creative in personality structure—which are factors theoretically linked to entrepreneurship.

The growing literature on development places considerable emphasis on the need for certain social and political changes to precede economic development. In Chile, the institutions and structures which impede development are not likely to be changed through the political process to the extent that these changes depend upon political action undertaken by industrialists. They do not constitute a self-conscious, progressive or nationalist bourgeoisie—as this essay will document in some detail. At the present time, they are largely conservative, passive spectators of Chilean politics.

(3) Change and growth will not necessarily proceed, then, from spontaneous developments in the economy, from the dynamic performance of the occupational roles of entrepreneurs, or on the basis of social and political action undertaken by a key group in society. Finally analyzed in the research summarized here, is the possibility of the state itself replacing the private sector as the driving force behind development. The new reformist, Christian Democratic government is state-interventionist and oriented toward a certain degree of economic planning. The government proposes a concentrated attack upon the many problems which confront Chilean economy and society. The success of the Christian Democratic effort depends to a considerable degree upon two factors: (a) the extent to which the cooperation of businessmen in development plans can be attained; and (b) the willingness and the ability of all Chileans to undertake significant reforms of the features of the nation's social and institutional structure incompatible with sustained economic development and social change. In the face of imminent change, industrialists will likely join with other social and political forces acting to keep Chile as it is rather than promoting what the country might be.

II. NOTES ON THE FORMATION OF THE INDUSTRIAL BOURGEOISIE

In *The Communist Manifesto,* Marx wrote:

The bourgeoisie finds itself involved in a constant battle. At first with the aristocracy; later on, with those portions of the bourgeoisie itself whose interests have become antagonistic to the progress of industry; at all times, with the bourgeoisie of foreign countries. . . .

The Chilean industrial bourgeoisie does not possess the characteristics Marx ascribed to the classic European bourgeoisie. Chilean industrialists are not the modernizing elite of which one reads so much in the current literature on development. Neither do they constitute a progressive group within the middle sectors of society, as implied by noted North American analysts of Latin American society and politics, such as John J. Johnson (1958). Analysis and documentation of these propositions are contained in subsequent sections of this essay dealing with several aspects of industrialists' ideology and with their position in the structure of influence. First it is necessary to summarize research findings regarding entrepreneurial social origins and the formation of the industrial class in Chile as these findings relate to the problem of the formation of progressive classes in the middle and upper ranks of society.

The formation of social groups and classes, the kinds of ideologies and sociopolitical roles which these groups and classes evidence, and their position in society at any point in time can be traced back to particular historical processes. The historical analysis of industrialization and its social effects in Chile reveals very different patterns than in the experience of the Western industrialized countries.[3] It is particularly significant that the transformations in social structure accompanying incipient industrialization in Chile have not had the effect of creating a fluid society with high rates of social mobility and the ascendance of groups of "new men" to places of prominence. The mobility of the industrial class provides evidence in support of this generalization.

In the earliest years of incipient industrialization (the 1930's), entrepreneurial mobility is *not* properly seen as a process of rapid vertical mobility through business activity. Rather, the establishment of new industry constituted a transfer of function, personnel, and capital from commerce, agriculture, and services into industrial pursuits. Although the

[3] This is analyzed in greater depth elsewhere (Johnson, D. L., 1967–68: 127–51). In a comparative and historical context, this work attempts to provide conceptual links between (a) industrialization process, (b) social change as the impact of economic transformations upon occupational structures, (c) individual mobility as a social process, (d) the formation of new classes and relations between classes, and (e) the class and group conflict theory of social change.

entrepreneurs gradually improved their economic position in the process of shifting their activities to manufacturing, few experienced a fundamental change in their position in the class structure. The fathers, even the grandfathers, of the present generation of industrialists were members in modest to substantial standing of the business, professional, and landowning classes—and this is as true of immigrant entrepreneurs as those native to the country for generations. Not one of the fathers of the managers interviewed was an artisan or industrial worker. Only one of the 138 firms in the sample was established as a small plant. Nor have the managers of Chilean manufacturing firms been intra-generationally (occupationally) mobile. Most began their work careers as executives or professionals in private practice and their education compares favorably with that of the North American corporate elite. At the present time, given the existing difficult economic conditions and a high degree of economic concentration, it is practically impossible to establish a successful business enterprise of a respectable scale of operation. All these facts indicate—and this is very different from what one finds in most of Western Europe and the United States—that business activity has not been and does not now constitute a significant avenue of social mobility.

In general there has been a considerable expansion of the Chilean middle- and upper-middle classes as a consequence of urbanization and industrialization accompanied by political modernization. Technical and administrative positions in private enterprise have multiplied and the public bureaucracy has expanded in the last decades. Yet, the middle- and upper-middle classes may simply have expanded largely on their own base (large families combined with a much lower death rate than the masses') and through the integration of persons from the immigrating European middle classes. The mobility that has taken place seems to be lateral or vertical between class levels that are most proximate. There is considerable horizontal movement of individuals, especially young people into newer occupations, but these are not necessarily more nor less remunerative, prestigious, or influential than their previous jobs or those of the parent. Educational opportunities at the secondary and university levels are largely limited to the economically privileged and culturally advantaged, and the educational system functions more to close than to open ranks. This does not mean that there are not individual cases of mobility. Particularly ambitious, talented, or lucky individuals do sometimes improve their social position, especially if they can manage a college education and work themselves into the pattern of influence and patronage at the upper levels of society.

The implications of these mobility patterns for class formation are readily apparent. In the absence of mobility of reasonably large numbers of individuals with common origins from lower to substantially higher positions in the hierarchies of class, status, and power, it cannot legitimately be said that a new class has ascended. A new class, be it a new elite, a new middle class, or an ascendant bourgeoisie implies more than a functional shift in work roles.

The class origins of the men who perform new economic functions are a key to the explanation of their relations with other classes in society. Particularly important are the relations between the major classes of a nascent industrial society: a maturing industrial bourgeoisie, the established upper rural and urban classes, the urban working class, and the peasantry. The focus on class relations and class conflicts, in turn, is at the core of a study of social change. While the group and class conflict approach to social change[4] often assumes inherent progress through the operation of a metaphysical dialectic or a Darwinian evolutionary process, it remains nonetheless true that structural contradictions which form the context of class relations and conflict in society are central elements in the total process of change.

In Chile, there is no doubt as to the intensity of the struggles between employers and employees and landowners and peasants—these struggles are mediated by political mechanisms or take on the character of major encounters between

[4] Historically, I am referring especially to Marxian and Weberian theory and to certain varieties of evolutionary doctrine. The better modern works include that of Bendix (1956) and Dahrendorf (1958).

urban or rural workers and the state. This conflict is the principal direct cause of the current (mid-1960's) political crisis in the country. On the other hand, the relations between the industrial bourgeoisie, the established upper classes, and the extremely wealthy and powerful economic oligarchy (Escobar, 1961; Johnson, D. L., 1967: ch. 2; Bourricaud, 1966: 17–31; Imaz, 1964; Lipset and Solari, 1967) have been and remain rather pacific. One of the reasons for this should already be clear: industrialists are not a class of new men out to usurp the privileges of established classes. They began as relatively privileged members of society and have improved their position by increments as their businesses gradually expanded. The entrepreneurs of foreign origin (Lebanese, Jews, Germans, Italians, and others of European origin) and their descendents seem to have found comfortable niches in society. They cannot be considered classes of socially marginal or new men.

There are several other factors which determine the relations between the industrial bourgeoisie and established upper classes which I have analyzed in the previously cited monograph. In summary, it can be stated that the "struggle for supremacy" thesis flowing from Marxian and traditional sociological doctrines is not accurate in describing this complex of class relationships. Nor is what might be termed the "fusion thesis" correct. (Analyzing the relationship of German junkers and the bourgeoisie, Max Weber termed the phenomenon "amalgamation"; Schumpeter referred to "an active symbiosis of bourgeoisie and feudal protecting strata.") Industrialists have not fused with the established economic elite to form a new oligarchy or ruling class. Industrialists cannot match the wealth and power of the fifty or so traditional families who control a sizeable proportion of the nation's wealth. There is little or no mobility of new wealth into the various cliques which together form an oligarchy of the economically powerful. Industrialists apparently do not invest extensively in land or marry their daughters off to the sons of oligarchical families. As subsequent analysis will show, the "fusion" is a symbolic one: the industrialists have absorbed important aspects of the system of values and ideology of the economic oligarchy. The ways in which similar values and ideology become translated into action, however, are differently structured by occupancy of distinct positions in society and by the very different degree of group consciousness and interest organization of the oligarchy on the one hand and the industrial bourgeoisie on the other.

III. IDEOLOGY

The manner in which persons occupying new functional positions in the economy perform their economic, social, and political roles is influenced by prevailing economic and social structures. The patterns of role performance by a key group like industrial entrepreneurs, in turn, have definite implications for the social changes experienced, or yet to be experienced, by the country. Thus, of primary concern in the analysis of ideological perspectives among Chilean industrialists are those aspects of thought which most directly relate to role performance and most readily translate into action.

There is a high level of public consciousness concerning the difficult economic situation and "the social question," as injustice, inequality, and class conflict are referred to in Chile. The political situation is in a state of flux, and a shift in the level or direction of political action by a key group has great significance. The future rate of industrialization and the nature of social and political changes yet to transpire will in part be determined by the posture adopted by industrialists in promoting or resisting change. This can be predicted on the basis of their current ideological stance.

INDUSTRIALISTS: RIGHT, CENTER, OR LEFT?

Chilean industrialists like to view themselves as positioned from the center to the left in the spectrum of political ideologies. In response to an interview item requesting political self-classification as "right," "center," or "left," half placed themselves in the middle and 27 per cent as either "center-left" or "left." About one-fifth identified with the political right or center-right. Strangely, when asked to classify "the majority of industrialists" politically, it turned out that nearly every manager conceives of himself as to the left of the majority! According to self-identification industrialists are center-left; according to classifications by each industrialist of other industrialists, the predominant orientation is center-right.[5]

Other data confirm that managers have an accurate perception of the political position of other managers and considerably exaggerate their own progressiveness. About 40 per cent identify with one of the parties of the traditional right, the Liberal or Conservative, or the Radical, a party now holding a generally center-right orientation. Among those not identifying with a political party (about one in four), the predominant orientation was a passive conservatism. A general classification of the industrialists into two groups, "Rightist" and "Christian Democrats" (based upon party identification, voting in congressional and past presidential elections, and other non-attitudinal data) finds the rightists constituting a two-thirds majority. Many identifying with the Christian Democratic Party, however, do not share the reformist orientation of the Party. About half the rightists consciously identify their political thought as closest to that of liberalism or radicalism, two varieties of rightist ideology that are now nearly indistinguishable when dealing with adherents from the upper ranks of society.[6] This position

[5] In the alternative version of the interview schedule (two partially distinct schedules were used), the question on self-identification was put in its most workable form, in terms of right, center-right, center, center-left, and left. Combining 105 responses from both interview schedules shifts self-identification somewhat to the right: right 4 per cent, center-right 36 per cent, center 46 per cent, center-left 11 per cent, and left 3 per cent.

[6] The radicals have a left-of-center minority, apparently largely drawn from the public bureaucracy and the middle classes who have not shifted their allegiance to the Christian Democrats. A

TABLE 1
POLITICAL CLASSIFICATIONS OF CHILEAN
INDUSTRIALISTS (Percentages)

	Self-Classification[a]	Classification by each of majority
Right	15	40
Center-right	07	13
Center	50	42
Center-left	17	—
Left	10	02
Don't know	—	04
Total	100	100
Number	59	55

[a] The question called for classification as right, center, or left, but some amended the scheme to find mid-way positions (see note 4).

departs from the ideology of the Conservative Party in terms of the issues of clericalism and anti-clericalism and the "modernness" of the respective world views. Liberals and radicals representing "modern conservatism" are traditionally anti-clerical (though the Church-State issue has little salience now, there is still a residue of conflict on the political right over problems associated with the growing secularism of urban society). Followers of the Conservative Party are promoters of the institutions of family, church, and social hierarchy, and represent the traditionalism of pre-industrial society. In its most modern form, this variety of conservative ideology in Chile, and in much of Latin America, is similar to Spanish fascism.

On basic questions of political ideology, industrialists are conservative but not reactionary (in the strict sense of the term, reactionary thought is not very common in Chile, and

section of the Radical Party threw their support to FRAP candidate Allende in the crucial presidential election of 1964 rather than support the Radical candidate, Julio Durán, who expounded views of the far right.

probably less prominent within the uppermost classes than within certain sectors of the middle classes). On the constantly recurring issue of property rights, for example, 38 per cent of the sample believe "private property is a sacred right," while over one-half believe that the state has a right to define the social function of property:

(One of 11 multiple choice questionnaire items based upon prevailing attitudes on different issues that constantly recur in Chilean politics. Instructions are to choose the alternative that most closely represents the respondent's thinking. Administered to twenty-six industrial managers, thirty-six research professionals, and twenty-nine industrial workers.

1. Private property is a sacred right and nothing should impede its free exercise. (Industrialists 39 per cent, researchers 0 per cent, workers 38 per cent.)

2. Under certain circumstances, the state should limit and control property rights in the interest of the common good.[7] (Industrialists 53 per cent, researchers 56 per cent, workers 38 per cent.)

3. The state should be the owner of all the sources of wealth that have to do with the well-being of the population and the economic security of the country. (Industrialists 8 per cent, researchers 44 per cent, workers 24 per cent.)

Attitudes toward the prevailing democratic order in Chile are distributed in the following manner:

1. Many of the ideas concerning existing democracy in Chile are mistaken. What the country needs is *an honest and authoritarian regime* that represents less the majority than the best elements of society. (Industrialists 27 per cent, researchers 17 per cent, workers 7 per cent.)

2. The country is very fortunate in enjoying an *almost perfect democratic life.* (Industrialists 27 per cent, researchers 6 per cent, workers 21 per cent.)

---

[7] Alternative two has more ambiguity built into it than was the case for the other ten issues and alternatives. Both intelligent conservatives and reformist Christian Democrats, for example, would be in agreement but would interpret the phrase "under certain circumstances" in quite different ways.

3. In order to improve democracy in Chile, it is necessary to give all the sectors of society a *greater degree
of participation.* (Industrialists 38 per cent, researchers
47 per cent, workers 32 per cent.)

4. The only way of improving democracy in Chile
is *to limit the power of the oligarchy.* (Industrialists 8
per cent, researchers 6 per cent, workers 14 per cent.)

5. There is no democracy in Chile. Only *when the
people conquer power by means of revolution* will there
be true democracy. (Industrialists 0 per cent, researchers
25 per cent, workers 25 per cent.)

The assumption involved in the design of these and nine
other multiple choice questionnaire items is that the positions of the various groups in society can be described and
compared to the positions of political parties and movements.
The alternatives were carefully written to reflect, in
commonly-used terminology, the points of view typical of
extreme rightists, rightists, Christian Democrats, socialists,
and revolutionary leftists. Items were written on the following
issues: education, tax burdens, state and private enterprise,
role of the Church, social classes, property rights, monopolies, agrarian reform, democracy, social mobility, and the
Alliance for Progress. As a preliminary device for analyzing
and comparing responses, the alternatives on each item are
scored from "1" for the extreme right to "5" for the extreme
left; to the left of the mid-point at "3" are the responses
characteristic of Christian Democracy and "4" represents
the reformist position of the FRAP socialist-communist
coalition (*i.e.,* a left-right continuum). When scores on the
eleven items are aggregated,

14 represents the extreme right position
24 Chilean liberalism[8]
36 the Christian Democratic reformist position[9]
43 the FRAP position
46 revolutionary socialism

[8] The liberal position in Chile is not liberal in United States
usage of the term. A liberal in Chile is what might be termed in the
United States a "moderate conservative."

[9] In a few cases, the Christian Democratic and FRAP positions
are the same, in which case the alternative was coded "4."

The small—and in the case of industrialists and workers, unrepresentative—samples of the three groups achieved mean scores as follows:

29 industrialists (N=25; *i.e.*, number responding to all
    11 items)
34 workers (N=25)
38 researchers (N=35)

Although the 25 industrialists responding are decidedly to the left of the larger sample interviewed, only one scored up to or to the left of the Christian Democratic reformist position. In contrast, only 8 of 35 researchers scored to the right of the Christian Democratic position.

The above findings are based upon historical factors influencing the politics of industrialists up to 1965. These political orientations could conceivably change with circumstances. It is now appropriate to consider some underlying or dynamic aspects of ideology—such as nationalism and basic attitudes toward change—in order to examine the possibility that industrialists could adopt a more progressive political posture.

NATIONALISM IN THE BUSINESS COMMUNITY

Business nationalism, in any meaningful sense, consists of powerful sentiments within the business community in favor of national economic development and the means necessary to achieve it. In the context of underdeveloped countries, *it is divorced from the ideology of economic liberalism*—free trade and laissez-faire—and attempts to influence or control state policies in ways which contribute to industrialization while utilizing national resources under the control of indigenous businessmen (Seton-Watson, 1964; Johnson, H. G., 1965: 169–85). To the extent that (a) the underdeveloped economy is highly dependent on the outside; (b) there is considerable foreign investment; and (c) the resident foreign business community and the guardians of its interests in Washington or elsewhere constitute centers of power with interests divergent from those of the local businessmen, the national bourgeoisie will express anti-foreign sentiments. Chile, like other Latin American countries, occupies a fundamentally dependent position in the world economy and in the international stratification of power. There is an increasing degree of foreign investment in manufacturing. Since the advent of the Alliance for Progress, United States government agencies have dramatically increased their involvement in the economy, in the government administration, and in the educational system. In the face of this situation, a strong nationalist reaction has developed within some sectors of society.

Research by Sanford Mosk (1950) and Raymond Vernon (1963) reveals some degree of business nationalism in Mexico. Vernon, for example, examines the opposition of the *Confederación Patronal de la República Mexicana* to the doctrines of economic liberalism espoused by other powerful employer organizations. This trade association made some impact among Mexican industrialists and government circles in the critical period of development policy formulation in the post World War II era of incipient industrialization. It propounded social doctrines based upon the corporative and cooperative economic philosophy of the Catholic Church as well as policies protecting and promoting national industry. Fernando Henrique Cardoso also noted the existence during Brazil's incipient industrialization of smaller industrialists unconnected with foreign capital who were actively engaged in pressuring the state toward the adoption of policies favoring development in general and the growth of nationally-owned industry in particular. Cardoso (1965: 72) also suggested that, once successful, these industrialists substitute an "entrepreneurial ideology in the North American style . . . defense of property, free initiative . . . for the belief in the necessity of state intervention in order to impede . . . foreign capital."

A variety of information concerning nationalistic thinking among Chilean industrialists was obtained in interviews. To begin with, they are not at all opposed to foreign investment nor are they anti-American. Opinion is nearly unanimous that "the nation needs more capital in order to develop industry and means should be adopted to encourage private foreign investment in Chilean manufacturing" (Lauterbach, 1962). In contrast, a majority of the sample of young professionals working in research institutions believe that "there is considerable foreign investment in national manufacturing and means for its control should be adopted." From a list of 41 diverse "problems of development" administered to 60 industrial managers in interviews and to 35 researchers in questionnaires, the latter emphasized the following three: "export and repatriation of capital by foreign mining companies"; "the pressures of the International Monetary Fund and other international organizations"; and "the excessive power of imperialism." While the majority of researchers believe these constitute significant problems for the nation's development, only small percentages of industrialists hold such views. Researchers view "external indebtedness" (which in 1965 was over two billion dollars) with great concern; relatively limited numbers of the industrialists think it is a major problem. Industrialists are opposed to nationalization of the American-owned copper mines and nearly all are in favor of the government's new policy of Chilean "association" with the mining companies. The copper program requires a huge investment by the Chilean government while effective control of the mines and the marketing of copper remain in the hands of the companies.

The phenomenon of anti-Americanism from the right in Latin America, as suggested by Frederick Pike (1962) in his excellent book on Chile, does not seem to be true of Chilean industrialists. This anti-Americanism, to the extent that it exists, may proceed in part from the reformist sentiments stirred up among the populace by the propaganda of the Alliance for Progress, and in part from a clash of the supposed spiritual values of Latin Americans as contrasted to the reputed crass materialism of North Americans. However, less than one in five agree that "the United States is a rich and powerful country, but materialist and lacking in spiritual values." Nearly half the industrialists believe that the Alliance for Progress "will bring great benefits for Chile and Latin America"; none believe it is "another imperialist scheme."

The Christian Democratic government is attempting to pursue an independent foreign policy with respect to the United States without straying from the Western bloc. While relations with Cuba have not been re-established after their rupture under pressure from the United States and the Organization of American States in August of 1964, diplomatic and commercial relations with most of the Socialist bloc countries were re-established in 1965 (there was an 18-year break in relations with the Soviet Union). Sixty-three per cent of the industrialists favored this move and 40 per cent would not be opposed to diplomatic and commercial links with China, even though the government has not indicated such plans. Opinion is about equally divided that the establishment of commercial relations with the Socialist bloc will signify a "moderate expansion" of markets for Chilean industrial products, on the one hand, or "no expansion" of markets on the other hand.

Up to this point, about the only elements of industrialist thought which could properly be considered nationalistic were their attitudes on policy matters which have to do with aspects of Chilean foreign relations. However, these are passive attitudes; the *Sociedad de Fomento Fabril*, or other industrial trade associations, is not, nor is it likely to be, agitating for trade with China or for taking an active role in the movement by Third World countries within the United Nations to restructure international trade (as in the 1964 Geneva Conference on world trade matters). The managers interviewed were rather pessimistic that underdeveloped countries can improve their trade position vis-à-vis the industrial countries through agitation in international organizations. Over one-third believe that "future markets for industrial products will be almost entirely absorbed by the already developed nations, but underdeveloped countries like Chile will find limited markets for a few products for which they enjoy comparative advantages." They were more optimistic about the possibilities for Chilean exports of manufactures with the establishment of the Latin American Free

Trade Association. However, *not one firm* had made concrete plans for placing their products on the Latin American market.

Nationalism in Latin America (Jordan and Whitaker, 1966)[10] is a phenomenon quite distinct from the relatively coherent formulations current in the ex-colonial countries of Africa, Asia, and the Middle East. In parts of the Third World, other than Latin America, nationalism is often manifestly ideological; it constitutes a political force of considerable magnitude by providing a rallying point for national unity and a means for the mobilization of the collective energies of disparate groups and masses behind national programs of economic development and sociopolitical modernization. There is no Latin American equivalent to Arab or African nationalism, Nkrumahism, or even De Gaullism that receives wide adherence.

Chile and other Latin American countries are highly economically dependent upon the outside and subservient to foreign political pressure. Their national interest could be served by pursuing policies designed to diversify exports and solve the foreign exchange problem, raise the level of domestic capital formation to put an end to foreign indebtedness, restrict private foreign investment to activities consistent with national needs which could not otherwise be met, implement a dignified foreign policy promoting national advantage, etc. In other words, nationalism could conceivably provide a justification and means for the transfer of power from foreign interests and domestic classes linked to foreign interests to national groups—including sectors of the business community—while promoting national independence and development.

In the world anti-colonial revolutions of the 1940's and 1950's, the most vocal nationalist elements were those groups

[10] I am principally concerned with nationalism as ideology, and in a subsequent part of the essay, with the functions of patriotism. Nationalism as a social value is widely held in Chile. Most Chileans have an "internalized feeling of national community," and the state is usually seen "as the impersonal and ultimate arbiter to human affairs" (Silvert, 1963: 18–19).

whose interests were not directly tied up with colonial domination or who stood to gain by national independence; namely, intellectuals, administrators, technicians, professionals, military officers, organized workers, and segments of the business class held back by the colonial pattern. None of these groups, including the national business class since new policies fomented a private sector, had a vested interest in Western-style free enterprise as a system. The identification of colonialism and imperialism with Western capitalism, therefore, became readily accepted and a form of "state capitalism" ("socialism" in such countries as the UAR, Algeria, Guinea—and Ghana and Indonesia until recently), as the social and power base of the essentially "new" middle class became the most feasible alternative to the liberal capitalism of the West. But the differences between ex-colonial and Latin American countries are great. Latin America *developed* under liberal capitalism, and the social equivalents to most of the national revolutionary groups of Asia, Africa, and the Middle East have, in Latin America, grown up with and benefitted from the maintenance of liberal capitalism. Latin American oligarchies are urban big businessmen, not tribal chieftains or feudal landlords who can be removed from power with relative ease, or educated professionals and administrators who can be swung over to support a nationalist movement.

The business nationalism which may exist in isolated cases in Latin America, and apparently, not at all in Chile, is not generally tied to a developmental ideology, such as that stimulated by the Economic Commission for Latin America (Hirschman, 1965 and 1961), much less to any progressive political movement. In Mexico, business groups with some nationalist sentiments now constitute a strong pressure group on the government and the PRI (Institutional Revolutionary Party) from the right. Indeed, the growing, conservative *Partido de Acción Nacional* sometimes invokes fascist-type nationalist slogans and is receiving increasing support from industrial groups in the manufacturing center of Monterrey and business elements throughout Mexico. It seems likely that any successful nationalistic movement in Latin America which enjoys the support of significant sections of the business community will be highly militaristic with strongly conservative, if not fascistic, overtones—as in Brazil and Argentina.

Elsewhere in the Third World, a dialectic has taken place between socialism and nationalism. As David Apter notes: "Each of these ideological forces emphasizes different attachments, meanings, and evaluations of solidarity, identity, and motivation. Socialism is more universalistic and secular in tendency. Nationalism incorporates specific elements of tradition and employs them to bring meaning to the establishment of a solidly rooted sense of identity and solidarity" (Apter, 1964: 26). In Latin America, the dialectic moves between patriotism and reaction. Patriotism provides neither personal nor national identity; it may ameliorate class conflict to a degree, but does not bring about national unity behind development programs. Ordinary patriotism is backward-looking and not a vision of a future (Michelena; Gerassi, 1965: 181–94).

PATRIOTISM AND ANTI-COMMUNISM IN SOCIOLOGICAL PERSPECTIVE

In certain segments of Latin American society, nationalism (in the sense of patriotism) and anti-communism are inextricably linked as aspects of ideology. Most Latin Americans from the middle ranks of society upward have always been adamantly opposed to ideas implying profound social reforms, and quick to condemn and repress those who propound such ideas. *Anarquista, revolucionario, agitador, communista* are terms applied, often indiscriminately, to advocates of social reform. However, it has only been in recent decades—since the rise of mass politics internally and the Cold War internationally—that the use of these and related concepts has become part of a highly developed political strategy and a major aspect of conservative ideology.

Both nationalism and the philosophy of anti-communism are related to processes of legitimation. The symbolic process involved in legitimizing existing institutions and social structures can take on positive or negative overtones. In the positive sense, the *status quo* can be rationalized and justified on whatever substantive merits it may have or be said to have. Comparisons may be made between the complimentary nature of existing social arrangements and natural law or human nature. And, all else failing, there is the ultimate appeal to patriotic unity behind the legitimate institutional procedures (such as constitutional democracy) for effecting adjustments in the social system in order to accommodate society to the immediate social or economic problems that confront it. In the negative sense, the *status quo* can be defended by conditioning the populace to emotionally react to certain symbols and to regard certain ideas as inherently evil and the people who expound them as dangerous, subversive, or traitorous. While anti-communism (or "anti-revisionism" in another context) performs these conditioning functions, the use of nationalism in legitimizing institutions and structures is more complex.

Common to all forms of nationalism is the notion of anti-patriotic ideas. But nationalism, particularly in many ex-colonial countries, is by no means entirely "negative." In special circumstances, the possibility of bringing about social change can be increased by the constant promulgation of symbols of the old order. Japan after the Meiji Restoration is the classic example. Apart from their xenophobic aspects, several varieties of Arab, African, and Asian nationalism contain elements which emphasize the desirability, within the context of building a modern society, of reconstituting (idealized) elements of the traditional order which existed before imperialism and colonial domination deformed economy and society. Mexico and Cuba, however, are probably the only Latin American nations in which nationalist appeals of this type have been used in a way visibly complementary to bringing about social change.

In Latin America, the *status quo* has been justified through various forms of ideological influence and manipulation such as the projection of an image of material and social progress for all. This is combined with the frequent evoking of all manner of primitive patriotic symbols. These symbols are essentially the national heroes, legends, customs, and belief systems established by the nineteenth-century elite. Most Latin Americans, and certainly the Chileans, are patriotic people who are relatively unconcerned with what goes on in the world outside national boundaries.

Leftist nationalistic propaganda in Chile, which has no appeal to businessmen, has emphasized a militant anti-Americanism and, to a degree, Chilean chauvinism.[11] American imperialism in Chile, however, has been too remote from the immediate experience of most Chileans (at least until the recent explosion of the United States Army's Project Camelot) to raise many emotions, and chauvinism of the left tends to complement traditional symbols and foment an attitude of mind more favorable to the *status quo* than to profound changes in the social order.[12] One of the real weaknesses of the Chilean left is its inability to evolve patriotic symbols independent of those established by the nineteenth-century elite. The left's political effectiveness is severely limited by the propaganda which defines socialism as anti-national and unpatriotic, even treasonable. Recently, the combined effects of an increasingly developing social and economic crisis and the increase in strength of political forces calling for reform,

[11] The Chilean Socialist Party is the center of the militant and positive nationalism (as distinct from a purely doctrinaire anti-Americanism).

[12] This generalization requires some qualification. The reform and revolutionary movements are not without powerful ideological weapons drawn from the traditional culture. Chile has an enchanting popular folk culture, much of it of popular protest against social ills. Though not as rich as some other Latin American countries such as Brazil and Mexico, the folk music and the literature written by socially conscious intellectuals, even poetry by workers, cannot but move anyone with humanistic sentiments to protest of social injustice if not to revolutionary action. Truly great novels with a dramatic and moving social content have been written in the context of the development of the North as a mining center; one of the greatest poets in the Spanish language, Pablo Neruda, is on the Central Committee of the Chilean Communist Party. Violeta Parra and her children, Angel and Isabel, brilliantly preserve and promote the revolutionary emotion of folk music.

have brought about a situation in which positive ideological appeals emphasize *the legitimate procedures* for initiating change, namely, a glorification of existing democratic forms and "legalisms." The entire arsenal of the traditional ideals embodied in the philosophic basis of Western liberal democracy and traditional patriotic symbols have recently been dusted off and put into effective use. In the critical 1964 presidential election, one observed the effectiveness of these legitimations, not only in the outcome of the elections, but in the very fact that presumably[13] revolutionary political groups, socialists and communists, felt forced to deny revolutionary intentions and to profess unqualified allegiance to the procedural forms which have always functioned to direct, order, and (especially) to limit change.

The manipulation of symbols extolling the virtues of the society as it is and emphasizing the inherent rightness and goodness of the values which underlie it, the careful writing of constitutions and laws which specify the procedures and limits of change, are frequently complemented by promulgation of emotional-laden and virulent attacks on ideas—or persons and social groups espousing such ideas—contrary to the existing order of things. One function of this is to achieve a consensus on values and ideas associated with the legitimizing ideology by creating unfavorable attitudes and emotions toward ideological alternatives. Another function is to provide a convenient focus for discontent which elements in the society may feel in such a way as to cement the social fabric of the *status quo* or, in such a way that discontent is directed away from attachment to an ideology opposed to the existing order.

Anti-communism is such an ideology. In Latin America, the virtues of free enterprise, freedom, and individualism

[13] The word "presumably" is used advisedly as both the Communist and Socialist Parties are really reformist rather than revolutionary. I found it rather amusing and clever propaganda to observe every reference by Santiago's conservative paper, *El Mercurio*, to the FRAP (the initials are almost always used) fully written out not as *Frente de Acción Popular*, the real name of the left's electoral coalition, but as *Frente Revolucionario de Acción Popular*.

are buttressed by constant comparison with the evils of socialism, tyranny, and collectivism. The propaganda which emphasizes the virtues of democracy versus the evils of dictatorship has notably diminished in quantity everywhere as military dictatorships in Brazil and Argentina have displaced populist regimes and dismantled political parties. Concomitantly, communism and communists rather than the powers that be, frequently become the favorite target of social groups —many of them adhering to demagogic populist movements which rise and fall and never accomplish much—who have real grievances with the *status quo*. Anti-communism in Latin America also serves to direct discontent in non-political directions, quiets or tones down criticisms of the *status quo* by persons who fear being labeled communist, and smears and limits the effectiveness, moderates the programs, and creates divisions within reform movements.

ANTI-COMMUNIST IDEOLOGY AND CHILEAN INDUSTRIALISTS

A more or less coherent anti-communism—and by implication anti-reformism, a conspiratorial view of politics, and an aversion to ideas involving social change—has been absorbed by many of the industrialists. *It is a natural complement to the absence among Chilean businessmen of nationalist sentiments beyond simple patriotism.* It is also a tribute to the power of ideas emanating from AP and UPI wires, the Latin America Desk of the State Department, and the United States Information Service.

For over one-third of the industrialists interviewed, anti-communism appeared to be of an emotional strength nearly equal to that of staunch American "patriots" for whom the conspiracy assumes such a proportion that reason becomes inoperative. This estimate of the degree of anti-communism felt by the interviewees is based upon their responses to a dozen items, some of them reported below, which are directly related to the issue. Forty-four per cent were judged "anti-communist" on the basis of reasonable ideological reservations given that they are businessmen, 15 per cent "not very anti-communist," and 3 per cent "not anti-communist" (N=108).

About 60 per cent see "the communist threat" as a "problem of development". Most have an "unfavorable" opinion of the Soviet Union; only 4 per cent and 9 per cent have a "favorable" opinion of China and the Cuban Revolution, respectively. Those who thought it "inconvenient" to open diplomatic and commercial relations with China were mostly in agreement with a list of possible reasons for *not* establishing relations provided to them. The prepared list included:

1. There would not be advantageous trade possibilities for Chile. (86 per cent in agreement.)
2. It would be undesirable in view of our economic dependence on the United States. (53 per cent.)
3. China represents a danger to world peace and therefore is better left isolated from the world community. (67 per cent.)
4. Relations with China would encourage the extreme left in Chile. (81 per cent.)

Only a few are in favor of Chilean support for United States direct military intervention in Cuba, on the one hand, or of Chile's re-establishing diplomatic or commercial relations with Cuba on the other; but most favor "supporting United States and OAS measures tending to isolate the Cuban regime, short of military intervention." In sum, it seems evident that anti-communism is inconsistent with the major criteria of nationalist policy: the need to carry out an independent foreign policy, which as noted, is the only avenue on which there exists some degree of potentially nationalistic sentiment.

Logically, not one industrialist has a "favorable" opinion of the Chilean Communist Party, only 2 out of 66 are "indifferent" to the Party, while the remainder hold different degrees of "unfavorable" attitudes. Responses to several items borrowed from an "anti-communism scale" developed by Professor Eduardo Hamuy and the research assistants at the *Centro de Estudios Socio-Económicos* and administered to industrialists in the questionnaire also give an idea of the depth of anti-communist feeling:

1. Communist governments maintain themselves in power by the will of the majority and do not need terror. (Industrialists in agreement 26 per cent, researchers 63 per cent, workers 55 per cent.)

2. Communists are not concerned with our country and only want power to utilize it in favor of Russia. (Industrialists 72 per cent, researchers 31 per cent, workers 68 per cent.)

3. The principal task of Chileans is to impede the triumph of Marxism, demolishing international communism. (Industrialists 73 per cent, researchers 28 per cent, workers 68 per cent.)

It would be wrong, however, to oversimplify this matter and write off industrialists as a reactionary group opposed to any kind of change and ready to label any type of reform "communist." A distaste for changes advocated by communists and others of the socialist left can also provide the ideological basis for advocacy of significant reform. The anticommunist Christian Democratic reform movement in Chile owes its ascendance to political power precisely to the threat of a socialist Chile and its advocacy of reforms that stop just short of socialism. Might industrialists be anti-communists of the center or center-left, ready to move solidly behind a reform and development program that presents an answer to communism, that pulls the political ground from underneath the left? The answer seems to be no. Industrialists are little inclined toward significant reform, though not adamant in the face of all programs calling for change, and apparently not disposed to accede to the argument that social reform is the only answer to communism. The next section discusses the support given to programs of economic, social, and political reform.

INDUSTRIALISTS AS REFORMISTS

If Chilean industrialists do not constitute a nationalist bourgeoisie, neither do they form a progressive group within the middle sectors. The respondents were asked their opinions concerning various policies of the administration of President Frei who had been elected just months previously. Considerable publicity had been given the new government's program to combat inflation, President Frei's request for extraordinary executive powers, the agrarian reform, an important new tax law, and other proposals. In general, there is but limited support for these measures among industrialists. A summary index to support for government reform, which weights opinions on the issues mentioned and several others, finds only 4 per cent solidly behind the government, 14 per cent giving moderate support, and 26 per cent a limited degree; 47 per cent are generally opposed and 8 per cent totally opposed.

The anti-inflation program consists of four aspects: (1) an increase in agricultural prices; (2) an increase in wages and salaries equal to 100 per cent of the year's previous rise in the price level; (3) a relative reduction in profits in the urban economy; and (4) a continuation of the system of price controls.

TABLE 2

ATTITUDES OF INDUSTRIALISTS TOWARD ASPECTS OF THE GOVERNMENT ANTI-INFLATION PROGRAM
(Percentages)

Attitude	1 Agric. Prices	2 Wage Increase	3 Profit Reduction	4 Price Controls
Very favorable	25	32	09	06
Favorable	52	53	32	51
Unfavorable	11	11	39	34
Very unfavorable	04	03	18	09
Do not know	08	01	02	—
Total	100	100	100	100
Number	75	74	66	47

This aspect of government policy receives greater support than any other program. (Chronic inflation is an enormous problem for businessmen, though they benefit from the inflation-induced regressive trend in the distribution of income.) Three-fourths or more are willing to see prices paid to farmers rise (which benefits big landowners and means higher food prices) and consider it just that workers and salaried employees receive wage increases commensurate with the previous year's rate of inflation (40 per cent in 1964). There is less favorable sentiment, however, for the implication of these price and wage increases, namely, that the government use its powers for controlling price increases for products such that businessmen's profits rise at a rate less than that of the overall price index.

Agrarian reform: While not everyone in Chile is concerned with such problems as social injustice in the countryside, the integration of impoverished and oppressed peasants into the national community, or the political power of the landowning class, most now recognize lagging agricultural production as a very serious problem. Over 60 per cent of the industrialists say that "a backward agriculture" is a "very important" development problem. Over one-half are in agreement with the original proposal of the Christian Democratic agrarian reform which was "to install 100,000 new proprietors in six years." Less than one-fourth, however, were in favor of "the government having powers to expropriate *latifundia.*" Without such powers, the reform could not be realized. Only 17 per cent were in favor of both the reform and powers of expropriation. In late 1965, however, the Frei Administration submitted a detailed agrarian program to the Congress which went beyond the implications of the original proposal. The principal industrial trade association, the *Sociedad de Fomento Fabril,* joined the *Sociedad Nacional de Agricultura,* which represents the landowners, in denouncing it.

Tax reform: A number of the industrialists believe that the regressive distribution of income and the conspicuous consumption of upper-income groups place limitations upon national savings and investment. Also, over one-half said that the regressive distribution of income constitutes "a development problem." In 1965, the government proposed the *impuesto patrimonial,* a tax on property and visible capital, designed to hit middle- and upper-income groups. Quite a furor was raised before the legislation was drastically modified by congressional and executive action. About one-third of the interviewees professed a favorable attitude toward the *impuesto patrimonial,* a high percentage considering that industrialists would have felt a greater tax pinch.

IDEOLOGICAL DIFFERENTIATION AMONG INDUSTRIALISTS

Ideologically, industrialists are a fairly homogeneous grouping. This does not mean that they constitute a definite group that articulates a particular ideological position. On the contrary, the absence of passionately-held, well-formulated political beliefs (and, as will be shown, the absence of group consciousness and effective organization to propound the views of industrialists in the public sphere) means that their world view and potential influence remain unexpounded and unexercised. Rather than being a sophisticated world view of a new, ambitious group in society, or even the self-interested rationalizations of a special interest group, the thinking of most industrialists simply mirrors the value premises of the staid and conservative, the class prejudices current in the upper ranks of society, and the ideas—drawn from traditional legitimizing doctrines and international wire services—skillfully propounded in the media controlled by the economic oligarchy.

There are differences in ideological thought between industrialists who occupy distinct positions in the industrial sector and in the social structure. While these differences do not overshadow the generalizations of the above paragraph, it is interesting to note that the data are at least minimally consistent with the hypothesized effects of social marginality (Hagen, 1962). Such a phenomenon does not exist as a powerful social and psychological force in Chile. A minor degree of insecurity regarding social position, however, may be influencing some members of Chilean minorities and those of lower social origin in the nation's rigid class structure toward acceptance of a more critical view of society and moderate social reform measures.

There are slight tendencies (most not statistically significant) for managers of Middle Eastern and Jewish origin to favor Christian Democracy, the government program, and agrarian and other social reforms. While the Spanish industrial minority, who operate light industries of limited scale, did not identify with the Christian Democratic Party, they tended to support government reforms. The Spanish, as were those of lowest social origin, also were significantly less anti-communist than other managers—and by implication, less taken in by the legitimations of the *status quo* propounded by the established powers. Industrialists of lowest social origin also supported government, agrarian, and other reforms to a significantly greater degree than those of highest social origin. In no sense, however, can a progressive minority be identified.

No social group or class can articulate its interests and express its ideological position in the wider society in the absence of a certain degree of group cohesion, dedication to collective expression of interests and political ideas, and organization to propound them. Are the industrialists a self-conscious bourgeoisie?

IV. CONSCIOUSNESS AND POLITICAL ROLES

CONSCIOUSNESS

The degree of class or group consciousness which persons occupying a particular position in society may develop is determined by a number of factors. Two of these are the realization by individuals that they have something in common with others (a similar role to perform, a greater or lesser participation in the sharing of society's social rewards, etc.) and the ready communication of mutual concerns and interests between individuals occupying the same or similar social positions. If a degree of identification with others develops around common concerns and interests, a feeling of solidarity may result. In these circumstances, the group or class could be said to be conscious of itself. In social theory, however, analysis does not, or should not, end here. We are also concerned with the wider roles which groups and classes play in social conflict and social change, or (to turn the coin over) in social integration and stability. That is why one examines the patterning of the distribution of social rewards and the conflicts which flow from this, the development of common interests among groups, and the ideas, action-programs, and interest associations which may become characteristic of self-conscious groups and classes.

A practical means of ascertaining the extent to which persons occupying a similar position in the social structure identify with each other and feel a sense of solidarity is simply to ask them. Two such questions were included in one version of the interview schedule. First, industrialists were asked if they had "good friends" among the seven different occupational groupings listed below.

Has friends among:	% Yes		% Yes
Industrialists	91	Bankers	42
Professionals[14]	86	Ministers, senators,	
University professors	58	and deputies	36
Agriculturalists	49	Military officers	31
			(N = 55)

There is a good deal of social interaction between the various groups in the upper ranks of society. Nearly all had good friends among other industrialists. When asked to identify the grouping in which the interviewee preferred to have his friends, however, only 25 per cent indicated industrialists; over 40 per cent said they had no preference; 15 per cent preferred professionals, and the remaining groups gained scattered responses. Presumably, if group identification and solidarity were present, there would be a decided preference for association within the industrial circles.

[14] "Professionals" refers to doctors, lawyers, dentists, and other graduates of professional schools such as architects and civil engineers.

TABLE 3

GROUPS OF IMPORTANCE AS IDENTIFIED BY
INDUSTRIAL MANAGERS (Percentages)

Group	Most Important	Second in Importance	Third in Importance
Family	54	40	04
Chile as a nation	39	35	07
Circle of intimate friends	05	18	24
Industrial association	02	02	18
Other industrialists as a group	00	00	13
People of your same social position	00	00	11
Religious organization	00	00	11
Members of social club	00	02	02
Political party	00	00	02
Other	00	02	09
Total	100	100	100
Number	57	57	55

A general absence of industrial group identification is indicated in responses to the question, "Which of the following groups has more importance for you? Or, put in another way, to which group do you owe your maximum loyalty?" As first or second choices from the list of nine only two out of fifty-seven chose his "industrial association." Relatively few respondents chose this alternative and "other industrialists as a group" as third among groups of importance to them. "Family," "Chile as a nation," and "circle of intimate friends" are clearly the most important sources of identification for industrialists. In the interview item following this, the same list less the three first choices was presented. Few respondents identify with or even belong to a political party and only a small minority find any identification in social clubs. "People of your same social position" received about the same number of choices as "industrial association" and "industrialists as a group" when the shortened list was employed.

There are many reasons why industrialists do not form a

self-conscious industrial bourgeoisie. Perhaps the most important of these are the historical factors involved in the growth of the manufacturing sector, the patterns of recruitment and mobility of entrepreneurs, and the development of Chilean political economy in response to externally-imposed crises. These factors have already been briefly commented upon and are discussed in some depth elsewhere (Johnson, D. L., 1967–68: 127–51). Suffice to say here that the international crises of depression and war, not agitation on the part of an ascendent industrial bourgeoisie, forced economic policies of state intervention fomenting industrialization. In Chile there never has been a struggle of manufacturing groups to promote their interests vis-à-vis the oligarchy rooted in finance and commerce. Industrial structure developed in a manner which has divided industrialists rather than brought them together. By the time stagnation had overtaken the economy (about 1953), the industrial sector had bifurcated into a few hundred larger, modern enterprises on the one hand and thousands of smaller firms and artisan shops on the other. Industrial concentration has gradually proceeded, limiting the entrepreneurial activities of the industrialists to their particular lines. Each of the industrial minority communities specializes in certain types of production. The minorities, especially the Arabs, Jews, Spanish, and Germans, constitute sources of community which militate against a wider identification within the industrial community as a whole. The family firm is still the predominant mode of organization in the sector. Both the minority and family industrialists seem to have found comfortable niches in society and are not strongly motivated toward dynamic occupational role performance—even if prevailing economic conditions and the structure of industry were propitious for entrepreneurship, which they are not. A number of the largest industrial corporations have fallen under the control of powerful economic elites whose primary interests reside in finance, commerce, and politics, rather than the pursuit of industrial progress.

In short, industrialists are a fragmented group performing a common function. Historically, individual manufacturers or special interest groups have never come together to form a class with a set of common interests and a particular conception of the nation's political economy opposed to another class with different interests and ideology. Conflicts over economic interests and issues of economic policy have not created an historical basis for the development of a self-conscious industrial bourgeoisie.[15]

Up to this point it has been shown that Chilean industrialists do not constitute a nationalist, progressive, or self-conscious bourgeoisie. The analysis of the next section demonstrates that industrialists live within limited social circles and that trade associations do not represent industrialists as a group nor effectively articulate collective interests in the political arena.

SOCIAL PARTICIPATION AND INTEREST AGGREGATION

One of the most surprising findings of the research is the low level of participation in activities beyond the firm and family. Only 15 per cent are active in the principal industrial trade association, *La Sociedad de Fomento Fabril*. As few as 25 per cent are active in social clubs, about one out of three attend church regularly, only a handful of the 138 industrialists interviewed belong to a political party, none are active in parties, while fewer than one in five reported being "active" or "moderately active" in the presidential campaign of 1964—an election in which nearly all industrialists feared the victory of the socialist-communist candidate.

It is quite clear that the source of community for industrialists lies primarily in the family, followed at some dis-

[15] What I have found in Chile and the general findings of Cardoso (1965: 68; 1964) in Brazil, which also indicate an absence of group consciousness, seems to be generally true in Latin America. Cardoso states an important factor very succinctly: "If we consider each industrialist in particular, we see that he is situated in society as a function of other statuses, besides that of industrial entrepreneur, that he possesses."

tance by intimate friendship circles. Social clubs, religious organizations, trade associations, and political parties seem to hold little importance in the lives of industrialists. Consider first some of the information available on social and religious participation.

When questioned, twenty-one out of seventy-two managers said that they hold a membership in the exclusive *Club de la Unión*, which in recent years has begun to open its doors to those of lesser credentials. However, only six managers in the sample visit the stately mansion a block from the Presidential Palace with any frequency. A larger proportion, 25 per cent, frequent one of the other exclusive social clubs with some regularity. About half the sample do not belong to one of these clubs. Apparently, there is no clamor of "new wealth" for entrance to gathering places of the socially prestigious. (A substantial number of Arabs and Jews, however, hold inactive memberships in exclusive clubs.)

About three-fourths of the industrialists of foreign origin (most second generation) belong to the *Club Español, Club Árabe*, or one of the other social clubs grouping the members of national minorities. Of those belonging, one-third are active. The industrialists, in spite of being the wealthiest members of a minority group, probably do not exercise a decisive influence in the ethnic communities. Rather, it is likely that the professionals and persons in government service are leaders of the communities.

As is very common among Latin American males, there is not, among industrialists, a great deal of religious sentiment. Fifteen per cent say they have no religion; over one-third rarely or never attend church; somewhat less than one-third attend church weekly. None are active in religious organizations.

Since the principal focus of this paper is upon the political roles played by industrialists, the degree to which industrial trade associations aggregate the various interests within the sector and articulate the position of the industrial group in the political arena becomes an important area of investigation. The results of research into this question reveal that the principal industrial trade association is not actively supported by most industrialists. The association is not representative of many firms in the sector and apparently does not constitute a powerful special interest group in Chilean politics.

La Sociedad de Fomento Fabril (SFF) was founded in 1883 by the *Sociedad Nacional de Agricultura.* The first president was Don Agustín Edwards Ross. The descendents of both the Edwards and Ross families continue to be among the most influential elite figures in Chile (Chileans usually retain paternal and maternal family names). The first vice-president, Don Antonio Subercaseaux, was a member of an aristocratic family distinguished in letters. In short, the SFF was founded by the oligarchy which at that time was primarily involved in agriculture, mining, and commerce. In 1884, as one of its first official acts, the newly formed society worked to assure free entrance of Chilean products to Bolivia, which Chile had just defeated in the War of the Pacific.

In an important article on public policy and organized business in Chile, Constantine Menges identifies the functions of business associations:

> They are in part social clubs and offer the *camaraderie* of the typical technical-professional association. More importantly, they perform three principal functions in Chile: they provide various *technical services* for their members; they occasionally serve as *internal regulators* of their economic sector: and they represent the sector's *economic interest* in national politics (Menges, 1966: 347; *Sociedad de Fomento Fabril,* 1962).

This is an accurate general stipulation. However, the associations undoubtably vary in the extent to which they succeed in fulfilling these functions. The industrialists do not, as revealed in the item on "groups of importance" to the industrialists, identify with their trade association or derive in any way a sense of camaraderie from membership. Regarding the provision of technical services, two other associations, the *Instituto Chileno de Administración Racional de Empresas* (ICARE) founded in 1955 "by a dynamic group of young and successful businessmen" (U. S. Department of Commerce, 1960; Alexander, 1962) and the *Instituto de*

Organización y Administración de Empresas (INSORA) of the University of Chile, function better in the provision of many services than does the SFF. The SFF no doubt acts as an internal regulator of industrial activities when conflict over division of the market arises. Menges (1966: 348) comments,

> . . . it is customary that no major new capital invest-ment is made in a line of production where facilities already exist until the association has investigated whether the Chilean market can "support" competitive production. On one such occasion, two prominent po-litical personalities were locked in conflict within the SFF over the intention of one to open up competitive production facilities. The compromise solution arranged by the Executive Council of the SFF permitted the new-comer to produce—but for export.

However, not all firms are SFF members and some powerful textile interests have withdrawn from the organization. It is unclear what regulative powers the association has over non-affiliated enterprises. The SFF, and to a lesser extent other industrial associations, also represent the sector's economic interest in national politics. But the facts seem to be that the SFF does not aggregate, represent, or effectively articulate the interests of all industrialists. Only a minority are active in the SFF and half of those interviewed did not hold a favor-able opinion of the association.

The SFF was founded by the economic oligarchy—the basis of which remains mainly non-industrial—to further their interests. Although only a proportion of present-day indus-trial enterprises are controlled by the oligarchy, the top busi-nessmen apparently are disproportionately influential in the determination of SFF policy. The governing Directive Council of the organization is composed of Honorary, Elec-tive, Associative, and Provincial Councils. A substantial pro-portion of the names listed as Elective and Honorary Council members are persons of considerable influence in Chile. There are 28 representatives on the Elective Council, where the most important decisions are made. Eighteen of those representatives occupy directorships in four or more industrial and non-industrial corporations (the definition of "economic elite" or "oligarchy" employed in the study) or are members of oligarchical families (based upon the 1962 list of SFF office holders). Nine of 11 Honorary Council representatives are members of the oligarchy. Provincial Council members or representatives from affiliated industrial associations, however, are not usually from the oligarchy. Also, Menges' study indicates that there is a regular four-year turnover in SFF officials, who tend to be the most "successful persons," suggesting that a self-perpetuating clique is not directly in control of the association.

ITEM: In terms of representation of industrialists' in-terests, effectiveness of their work, etc., what opinion do you have of the SFF and the principal trade associa-tions of your sector? (Very good, good, regular, bad, very bad; if less than good opinion, why?)

In response to this item, only one-half said that they had a "very good" or "good" opinion of the SFF (N=56). The reasons stated for the less than favorable opinions did not usually have to do with the facts on elite influence pointed out above, but one-third of those critical of the SFF said that the organization is "controlled by a minority" or "represents special interest groups." (*"Intereses metalúrgicos"* were men-tioned with some frequency; the metal industries have a high proportion of the larger firms integrated into oligarchic eco-nomic groups.)[16] Most of the criticisms expressed had to do with SFF's effectiveness: that is "inefficient," "badly or-ganized," "does not provide adequate services," etc. A few think that the association is neither representative of indus-trialists as a whole nor effective in representing industrial interests.

Whatever the reasons, the fact is that many industrialists do not view their principal interest association favorably, or even participate in it. Over one-fourth of those questioned do not even belong, fully 42 per cent hold inactive mem-

16 The term "economic groups" is employed by Ricardo Lagos Escobar (1961) to describe the constellations of corporations in all sectors of the economy tied together through interlocking di-rectorates and ultimately controlled by the members of the oligarchy.

berships, 15 per cent participate rarely or occasionally, while only 15 per cent actively participate. In contrast, 57 per cent of those interviewed actively participate in the principal trade association of their particular line of production; 36 per cent do not belong or belong without participating in their sector's association (small service associations). Two-thirds of the members say they have a good opinion of the association in their line. A few sector organizations, notably the *Asociación de Industriales Metalúrgicos* (ASIMET), have developed a reputation for being effective in providing services to members.

Except for the SFF which has been carrying on a running battle with the Christian Democratic government over credit policies and agrarian and other reforms, the trade associations and the great majority of individual industrialists do not perform political roles—though apparently family and friendship relations serve individual industrialists and small, special interest groupings to influence political decisions affecting their immediate interests. Organized expression of common interests or beliefs is not a frequent occurrence either through trade associations or political parties.

These findings again challenge prevailing notions concerning the political roles of an industrial bourgeoisie in a nascent industrial society. Further analysis concentrates in greater depth upon the place of industrial organizations and industrialists in the structure of influence in Chilean society.

THE STRUCTURE OF INFLUENCE AND THE INDUSTRIALISTS' PLACE IN IT

These conclusions as to the political influence of Chilean industrialists are valid whether one assumes a pluralistic or elitist model of power structure in the country. Even in a society dominated by a classic oligarchy or ruling class, any major social grouping of lesser status can make its weight felt if it is well organized and effectively mobilizes its resources (Bourricaud, 1966: 17–31). But Chile is not a society dominated in economical, social, and political spheres by an oligarchy in the same sense as, say, Colombia. Political forces have considerable room to maneuver and can, when fully mobilized, influence the course of events, at least to the point where basic institutions and structures are threatened. A number of groups—labor unions, unionized salaried employees, certain professional associations, for example—play active roles in defense of their interests. Usually a strike or political action by such groups is defensive: they are forced to take a defensive position against some adverse economic trend or governmental action. Some groups, particularly students, play wider political roles of offense as well as defense, and effectively express themselves on broad ideological issues. There are quite a number of political parties and factions within parties which tend to represent the interests and ideological positions of particular social classes. This does not mean that Chile is a pluralist society in which power is widely dispersed, or that a minority of the truly powerful do not dominate politically. One of the fascinating things about Chile is that politics goes on but nothing much changes. This is not because the political arena is composed of veto groups who cancel each other out in such a way that no group dominates and nothing can happen. It is a rare occasion in which public power—long months or years after turmoil and conflict over an issue have raged—does more than bring about minor adjustments in an effort to face the problems at hand. The reasons for this are that the prevailing institutional network is very strong and that power, like wealth and social prestige, are unequally distributed. The interesting situation which exists at present in the country for the first time in its history (possibly excepting a brief period in 1938–40), is that the pinnacles of economic power are occupied by a privileged oligarchy whose direct representation in the political sphere has been lost. There is a heavy concentration of economic power in the hands of a small, tightly-knit class. Yet, political office is occupied by those pledged to bring about changes which are bound to affect the very institutions and configurations of social structure from which the oligarchy derive their privileges, wealth, and influence. The question becomes what political roles industrialists are or will likely be playing in this situation.

The interests and ideals of different classes, groups, and

individuals in Chile are represented in the political sphere
in basically three ways: through formal institutional mechanisms of public corporations and government agencies,
through informal interpersonal relations of influence, and
through the medium of political parties.

The quasi-corporative relationship between government
agencies and business associations described by Menges seems
to give organized business groups a great potentiality for
influence over both the minor and major governmental decisions which affect the interests of businessmen. The SFF,
the National Agricultural Society, Central Chamber of Commerce, National Mining Society, and the Confederation of
Production and Commerce, as well as business associations
of lesser importance, have formal representation on several
key semi-autonomous financial policy institutions and many
specialized government agencies concerned with the functioning of the economy. In 1964, the SFF had 43 representatives
in public and private institutions: "26 were voting members
of government policy-making boards and 8 were voting
members on government advisory councils" (Menges, 1966:
349).

There are limitations to the corporative pattern, however.
Menges notes that: "The access of business associations to
membership on such committees, however, is not an institutionalized right and by no means automatic, even if the government seems generally favorable to business interests. The
SNA (*Sociedad Nacional de Agricultura*) did not even
formally participate in, much less dominate, the government
committee which drew up the 1961 agrarian reform law"
(Menges, 1966: 353). This is in sharp contrast to earlier periods in Chilean history when the SNA formulated practically
all legislation and policy that had to do with agriculture.

This corporative institutional arrangement is more formal
than operative (although this may be changing as will be
shortly pointed out). The predominant pattern of political
influence seems to lie in informal personal relations between
private interests and government officials. The second major
pattern of political influence is the contact between private
interests and political parties. These contacts, however, are

not formal in the sense that a group interested in an issue presents its point of view to the governing council of the party. Parties or factions within parties, which rather closely represent the interests of different groups and classes, tend to have a high degree of ideological affinity with their constituents, which minimizes the need for contacts. When an issue arises of interest to a particular constituent, a word to an influential person in the party suffices to bring the matter to the attention of the appropriate persons in government. As Menges (1966: 356) prudently puts it: "A . . . plausible, though not proven, possibility is that in a small, stratified society the range of informal contacts with party leaders is so great and policy disputes between some parties and the business associations so few that there is little need to make any elaborate arrangements for contact."

Though Menges (1966: 354) emphasizes the formal influence of business associations in the quasi-corporative institutional system, he also succeeds in illustrating the importance of the informal pattern of influence. He notes that ". . . the really important contact with the legislature involves informal relations with individual congressmen." The liaison between business interests and prominent politicians, however, usually occurs directly and not through the medium of political parties. There are no formal contacts between business associations and parties, and the parties do not serve as brokers among business groups.

The general ideological position of a major social group is not directly represented in the political arena except through political parties. Thus, until the Congressional elections of 1965, the Conservative Party reflected the position of landowners and the very Catholic sectors of the middle class; the Liberal Party spoke for the oligarchy and larger business interests; the Radical Party and factions within it represented the public bureaucracy, certain sectors of the middle class, regional agricultural and business interests, and segments of the urban business community; and the Socialist and Communist Parties reflected the position of the labor bureaucracy and the intellectuals (Guilisasti, 1964; Gil, 1966). These patterns are changing as a consequence of the recent electoral victories of the Christian Democratic Party which now enjoys broad support in all social classes (though its real basis is the middle class and youth, its votes come from women of all classes and the unorganized urban mass). No party or faction represented industrialists. Nor does Christian Democracy reflect the ideological position of an ascendent industrial bourgeoisie.

The formal, quasi-corporative pattern existing may become more operative under the regime of the Christian Democratic Party. The theoretical journal, *Espíritu y Política,* illustrates the fact that Christian Democracy has a rather elaborately formulated corporative theory of social organization and functional democracy which forms part of the movement's broader ideological perspective (Petras, 1967). The utopia of some influential intellectuals in the movement is a society in which all functional groups are highly organized and effective participants in institutional decision-making. They advocate organization of rural education units and Christian peasant unions, popular promotion for the marginal urban mass, a reform of enterprise in which workers are formally consulted in management decisions, and representation of all groups and classes in governmental institutions and the political process.

Strong factions of the Christian Democratic movement would like to reduce the influence of economic power over public policy while raising the level of influence exerted by the middle class, workers, and peasants.[17] Up to now, the influence of middle- and working-class groupings in the political process lies in their vote and ability to disrupt the *status quo* through strikes and violence. They have never had meaningful institutional representation in government except through political parties. Business organizations like the SFF may eventually find themselves sitting across the table from

[17] The government has attempted to reduce the power of private banking interests over Central Bank policy by reducing their representation on the Board of Directors. Christian action groups are attempting to organize peasants and the government is trying in every way to bring more unions, now mainly communist or socialist, under Party control.

labor representatives and other unfamiliar faces in executive meetings of public corporations and government agencies— if the Christian Democrats are successful in organizing working- and middle-class groups under its political control (groups under control of socialists and communists are unlikely to be coopted into decision-making structures).

Menges' study (1966: 359) notes relatively frequent conflicts of interest between and within business associations. At the same time, the associations sometimes take joint political action. "As might be expected, such instances seem almost entirely restricted to *redistributive* issues and most often only those we have labeled *multisector*." A general wage increase or a reform of the constitution changing the definition of property rights can bring about cohesion and direct political intervention by associations in all sectors. To the extent that the various sectoral associations are ideologically sympathetic to or influenced or controlled by the economic oligarchy, one would expect a greater degree of total mobilization to the extent that the oligarchy's interests are threatened.

At the present time, the congress and administration are less friendly to the general interests and ideological position of the oligarchy and business interests of lesser weight. Since these are now not as able to effect their policies through their influence with prominent individuals in government or in political parties, it is probable that the interest aggregation and articulation functions of business associations will become more prominent. The positions which the SFF and other sectoral associations now hold on the Boards of the Central and State Banks, the Development Corporation, and other public institutions and agencies give business interests great influence over the kinds of policies which these corporations and agencies can begin to adopt under the aegis of a reform government. To the extent that the principal trade associations are influenced or controlled by the economically powerful, the Chilean oligarchy retains as a veto group some of the power it has lost in the structure of interpersonal influence, the political parties, and the formal political process. The position held by the economically powerful in Chile is similar to the position of the military in several other Latin

American countries: unfriendly constitutional governments can go just so far and no further without bringing on a major crisis.

Also, there is every reason to believe that the pattern of political influence ("having friends in high places") will continue under the new government. Private interests, however, may not receive quite the sympathetic hearing they have received in the past. Under the previous Democratic Front government of President Alessandri, some individual industrialists (about one-third of those interviewed) had ministers, deputies, or senators as friends. New informal patterns of influence will undoubtedly develop between Christian Democratic politicians and businessmen. For specific needs the bureaucratic maze may continue to be partially set aside for businessmen by relatives or friends strategically located in administrative or political spheres.

There are, then, two basic means by which industrialists exercise political influence. By far the most common is for a particular individual or a special interest group to fit themselves into the pattern of informal, interpersonal relations of influence. The other involves the activities of the trade associations. The SFF, as noted, is not representative of all industrialists. In the past, the association has tended to articulate the interests of those it does represent through informal relations within government circles. Given the present situation, the SFF may increasingly utilize its position in the quasi-corporative institutional system to make its weight felt and may act in the public sphere with other business organizations on multisector, redistributive issues of concern to employers and the propertied.

Lacking group consciousness, effective trade organizations, or a political party representing manufacturing interests as a whole, industrialists have influence as individuals, particularly regarding matters that directly affect their firms. But the interests and ideology of the industrial group as a whole are largely unrepresented. The potential power which industrialists as a group enjoy in terms of their position in the national economy, their wealth, and their occupational prestige is not usually translated into direct political power.

There is a certain degree of realization of this relative lack of political influence among the respondents. About half replied negatively when asked "Do you think that, in the last two or three decades, industrialists have been capable of influencing the policies of the state in order to promote industrial interests and the economic development of the country?". According to responses to a related item, the influence of industrialists was stronger under the Alessandri administration (1958–64) than under the Ibañez (1952–58) or Radical Party (1938–52) administrations. One-third believe that industrial interests will be "better represented" under the Frei government than under the Alessandri administration. The managers were also asked: "During the administration of President Alessandri, which sector of the national economy was most favored in terms of government development and aid policies?" Among seven sectors on a prepared list, construction was identified by over one-half as the most favored. In the estimation of managers, industry was little favored by government policy, in spite of the fact that President Alessandri himself was president of the *Compañía de Papeles y Cartones* (paper company), one of the largest industries of the country. (Alessandri represents a traditional oligarchic family active in manufacturing and politics for some time.)

There are no present indications that industrialists will organize to better promote the interests or development of the industrial sector through attempts to influence state policy or to more vigorously propound their ideal interests in the political sphere. There is a trend in their voting behavior toward limited support for Christian Democracy, a movement which espouses development ideas with a great deal of vigor (28 per cent voted for Christian Democratic candidates in the 1965 congressional elections). However, this support seems to reflect a "bandwagon effect." In the 1958 elections, industrialists showed little enthusiasm for Eduardo Frei's candidacy to the presidency and there is no reason to suppose that industrialists will become caught up in the sentiment for development and reform characteristic of many Christian Democrats. If the attitude of the SFF toward the

Frei government's credit policies and agrarian reform is any indication, changes in the long-standing relationship between the private sector, including manufacturing, and public power is likely to be met with a vested interest reaction. There is little dissatisfaction among businessmen with the *status quo* in any major respect; and no indication that a nationalist and progressive bourgeoisie is ascendant.

IV. CONCLUSIONS

If there is any country in Latin America that can carry out a "revolution in freedom," that country is Chile. But the evidence presented here makes it quite clear that the revolution cannot depend upon the support of the industrial bourgeoisie. Nor is there a shred of evidence that other sectors of the entrepreneurial and propertied classes possess a nationalist, developmentalist, or reformist orientation.[18] Reform sentiments within the non-propertied sectors of the middle and upper ranks are largely confined to the intellectual and professional groupings and parts of the lower middle class hardpressed by inflation and unable to make it socially. The bulk of the middle class in Chile now votes for reform candidates only out of fear of the more revolutionary changes that the socialist left advocates. Elsewhere in Latin America, the middle classes, fearing the populism of demogogues and mass agitation, are increasingly moving in support of strong-armed and conservative dictatorships.[19] "Men of goodwill" are every-

[18] Evidence is quite to the contrary. James Petras analyzes attitudes on reform issues on the part of several sectors of the middle classes. His data are from Professor Eduardo Hamuy's survey research on political attitudes among the population of Greater Santiago.

[19] There is a prevalent notion that the middle sectors constitute democratic and reformist forces in Latin American countries (Johnson, J. J., 1958). This thesis seems clearly demolished by both the force of events (e.g., the middle class-supported rightist military coups in Brazil and Argentina) and the theoretical and empirical analyses of Latin American social scientists (Veliz, 1966; Nun; Ratinoff, 1967; Petras and Zeitlin, 1968).

where, but it remains true that privilege, status consciousness, and favorable class position breed a fondness for the *status quo.*

Those who sincerely desire to see Latin American countries make the break from the oppressive stagnation of the *status quo,* ought not to be deluded into thinking that substantial reforms tending to create "pre-conditions" for development are going to be brought about by ascendant elites or newly formed classes in the middle ranges of society. The class basis of political movements willing and able to effect substantial reform will be intellectuals, organized workers, peasants, an aroused and mobilized urban *lumpenproletariat,* and small segments of the middle class. Neither should one be surprised by the ideology of movements genuinely favoring change—revolutionary populism or socialism with strong nationalistic strains. As the *status quo* is more effectively propped up by United States aid and intervention, *Fidelista* guerrilla forces come to the fore. The next Vietnam may not be Chile, but it probably will be a Latin American country.

REFERENCES

Alexander, R. (1962) Labor Relations in Argentina, Brazil, and Chile. New York.

Apter, D. E. (1964) Ideology and Discontent. Glencoe, Ill.: Free Press.

Bendix, R. (1956) Work and Authority in Industry: Ideologies of Management in the Course of Industrialization. New York: Wiley.

Bourricaud, F. (1966) "Structure and function of the Peruvian Oligarchy." Studies in Comp. Internatl. Dev. 2 No. 2: 17–31.

Cardoso, F. H. (1965) El empresario industrial en América Latina. United Nations, Economic Commission for Latin America.

——— (1964) Empresario industrial e desenvolvimento econômico. Rio de Janeiro, Brazil.

Dahrendorf, R. (1958) Class and Class Conflict in Industrial Society. Stanford, Calif.: Stanford Univ. Press.

"Declaración de los economistas latinoamericanos." Desarrollo 1 (Sept.).

Escobar, R. L. (1961) La concentración del poder económico. Su teoría, realidad chilena. Santiago, Chile: Editorial del Pacifico, S.A.

Frank, A. G. (1967) Capitalism and Underdevelopment in Latin America. New York: Monthly Review Press.

Gerassi, M. N. (1965) "Argentine Nationalism of the Right." Studies in Comp. Internatl. Dev. 1 No. 12: 181–94.

Gil, F. (1966) The Political System of Chile. Boston: Houghton Mifflin.

Guilisasti, (1964) Partidos políticos chilenos. Santiago, Chile: Editorial Nascimento. (Second ed.)

Hagen, E. (1962) On a Theory of Social Change. Homewood, Ill.: Dorsey Press.

Halperin, E. (1965) Nationalism and Communism in Chile. Cambridge: M.I.T. Press.

Hirschman, A. O. (1961) "Ideologies of economic development in Latin America." In A. O. Hirschman (ed.) Latin American Issues: Essays and Comments. New York: Twentieth Century Fund.

Horowitz, I. L., ed. (1967) The Rise and Fall of Project Camelot: Studies in the Relationship Between Social Science and Practical Politics. Cambridge: M.I.T. Press.

Imaz, J. L. de (1964) Los que mandan. Buenos Aires, Arg.: Editorial Universitaria de Buenos Aires.

Johnson, D. L. (1967–68) "Industrialization, Social Mobility, and Class Formation in Chile." Studies in Comp. Internatl. Dev. 3 No. 7: 127–51.

—— (1967) Industry and Industrialists in Chile. Stanford, Calif.: Stanford Univ., unpub. Ph. D. dissertation.

—— (1966) Comment in The American Sociologist 1 (Aug.): 206–7.

Johnson, H. D. (1965) "A theoretical model of economic nationalism in new and developing states." Pol. Sci. Q. 80 (June): 169–85.

Johnson, J. J. (1958) Political Change in Latin America: The Emergence of the Middle Sectors. Stanford, Calif.: Stanford Univ. Press.

Jordan, D. and A. P. Whitaker (1966) Nationalism in Contemporary Latin America. Glencoe, Ill.: Free Press.

Lauterback, A. (1962) Managerial Attitudes in Chile. Santiago: Univ. of Chile, Institute of Economics.

Lipset, S. M. and A. Solari, eds. (1967) Elites in Latin America. New York: Oxford Univ. Press.

Menges, C. C. (1966) "Public Policy and Organized Business in Chile: A Preliminary Analysis." J. Internatl. Affairs 20: 347.

Michelena, J. A. S. "Nationalism and Political Participation in Venezuela." Massachusetts Institute of Technology, unpub.

Mosk, S. (1950) Industrial Revolution in Mexico. Berkeley: Univ. of California Press.

Nun, J. "La crisis hegemónica y el golpe militar." Berkeley: Univ. of California, Institute of International Studies, unpub.

Petras, J. (1967) Chilean Christian Democracy: Politics and Social Forces. Berkeley, Calif.: Univ. of California, Institute of International Studies Monograph Series.

—— "Reform and the Middle Class in Chile." Berkeley: Univ. of California, Institute of International Studies, unpub.

—— and M. Zeitlin, eds. (1968) Latin America: Reform or Revolution? New York: Fawcett.

Pike, F. (1962) Chile and the United States. South Bend, Ind.: Univ. of Notre Dame Press.

Ratinoff, L. (1967) "The New Urban Groups: The Middle Classes." In S. M. Lipset and A. Solari (eds.) Elites in Latin America. New York: Oxford Univ. Press.

Seton-Watson, H. (1964) Nationalism and Communism: Essays 1946–1963. New York: Praeger.

Silvert, K. H. (1963) Expectant Peoples: Nationalism and Development. New York: Random House.

United States Department of Commerce (1960) Investments in Chile. Washington.

Veliz, C., ed. (1966) Obstacles to Change in Latin America. New York: Oxford Univ. Press.

Vernon, R. (1963) The Dilemma of Mexico's Development. The Roles of the Private and Public Sectors. Cambridge: Harvard Univ. Press.

Chapter 8

CONTROL AND CO-OPTATION IN MEXICAN POLITICS*

Bo Anderson and *James D. Cockcroft*

INTRODUCTION

This chapter will attempt to describe and account for some basic features of the Mexican political system. The analysis is structural rather than historical. That is, we have not tried to narrate how the Mexican system came into being, but have rather attempted to set forth a somewhat abstract formulation, which we believe can account for certain broad tendencies in Mexican politics in the sense that many concrete policies and changes in policies and political events are more or less direct manifestations of the principles our formulation contains. The formulation consists of (1) a description of what we believe is the basic and enduring *goal structure* of the Mexican political system, and (2) a set of structural principles which seem to determine, broadly speaking, how the elements in the goal-structure are implemented, and what the relations between different groups in the system will be like. Hence, we believe that some basic tendencies of the Mexican polity can be made meaningful by our formulation. However, we do not attempt to analyze the question why in Mexico there gradually developed a polity having these properties; nor do we try to answer the somewhat more

* This article originally appeared in the *International Journal of Comparative Sociology*, VII, 1 (March 1966). Reprinted by permission of the publisher. A list of references appears at the end of the chapter.

fundamental and general question about what the conditions are for a political system to develop these properties. (We do believe that these questions are important, however; if we knew the answer we would know more about the problem of how to combine basic democracy with rapid economic growth, starting from a state of rather extreme underdevelopment, than we now know.)

We do not claim to have isolated all the major principles which determine the structure of Mexican politics. We also regard our present formulation as a first tentative statement, although we believe it to be essentially correct.

Also our formulation is intended to apply *only to modern* Mexican *national* politics. Economically and culturally Mexico is a very heterogeneous society. In many local areas grassroots politics is structured by "traditional factors" like kinship (including ritual kinship or the *compadrazgo*); and sometimes indigenous or Indian political forms of organization have survived in some modified form. (Sieverts, 1960; Friedrich, 1965.) This is more common in some states of the Mexican Union than in others. Politics in some southern states, Guerrero is often mentioned as a prime example, is very much traditional. In some of the economically more developed states, like Sonora and Baja California, politics seem less traditional. There are a host of important general questions that could be raised about the way that such traditional subsystems operate within the context of the national polity and economy. One could ask, for instance, how the power position of local bosses (*caciques*) is changed by the welfare and development policies that are carried out by the federal government or the regional commissions, modelled on the TVA (for instance, the Papaloapán Commission, Poleman 1964). Such a study of political subsystems will not be undertaken in this paper, however.

We will attempt to illustrate our model with descriptions of concrete cases drawn from contemporary Mexican politics. The information about these comes from accounts in books and newspapers and also from interviews we have conducted in Mexico at various times during the period 1963–

64. These cases are only assumed to be illustrative of the mode of analysis used in this paper.

THE GOAL STRUCTURE OF THE MEXICAN POLITY

An adequate understanding of the structure of a political system presupposes an analysis of its *goal structure*. Therefore in this section we shall attempt to characterize the major goals of the Mexican polity and the relations that hold between these goals. The term "goals" refers to aims that are consciously being promoted by those in the polity that make major decisions. There is, in fact, a great deal of consensus in Mexico about what the goals are, and how they relate to one another, although groups and individuals differ a great deal with respect to the weights and priorities to be given to the different goals. The following picture of the goal structure of Mexican politics has been pieced together from official speeches and statements, newspaper editorials and interviews with politically active persons.

The following major goals are present in the Mexican polity: political stability, economic growth, public welfare and mexicanization. Let us now first characterize what we mean by these terms.

Political stability refers to a state where (1) the basic political institutions are seen as legitimate by the bulk of the population, (2) the incumbent decision-makers are granted the right to make binding decisions, even by those who do not always agree with their decisions, (3) the succession of office-holders, proceeds according to rules specified in advance, that are accepted by most people as binding. After the overthrow of the regime of Porfirio Díaz in 1911, Mexico went through more than a decade of frequent insurrections, civil wars and general fragmentation of the political system. Beginning in the twenties, however, the system has gradually gained a considerable degree of stability. A rather dramatic and much publicized example of change toward stability arose right after the 1964 elections, when Gonzáles Torres, the unsuccessful candidate of the main rightist opposition party (PAN),[1] publicly acknowledged that the candidate of the ruling party (PRI),[2] had won a clear majority of the popular vote. Prior to this, the PAN typically used to attribute PRI victories in elections to large-scale fraud.

Economic growth, in the sense of industrialization and modernization of agriculture, was promoted by the Díaz regime and was encouraged by the revolutionary regimes in the 1920s, following the economic chaos of the civil wars. A very determined effort to make Mexico a modern industrial country has been underway since the end of the Second World War. (For descriptions of different aspects of the Mexican Economic Modernization program see Vernon, 1963, 1964; and Flores, 1961).

Public Welfare. The revolutionary program stressed heavily the need for raising the material and cultural level of the Mexican masses. In the agrarian sector, a massive land reform program has been carried out in order to help the peasants to obtain ownership of their land, and to enable landless laborers to acquire some land of their own. (Whetten, 1948; Flores, 1961). For the urban workers low-cost housing, subsidized staple foods and a federally determined minimum wage level (it varies from state to state) are among the welfare policies. The middle class, especially that sector which consists of government employees, also has available low-cost housing, cheap vacation plans and other benefits.

Mexicanization refers to the policy of securing control over the major economic companies and activities in the country for either private Mexican citizens or public agencies. Before the revolution, and for a substantial time after the revolution, foreign companies controlled many aspects of the Mexican economy. Since the 1930s the Mexican government has by expropriation or purchase obtained control over many enterprises that used to be foreign-owned. The most famous case is, of course, the expropriation of the oil companies in 1938, which led to a bitter conflict with the United States. (See Cronin, 1960, Chaps. 7–10.) There are also many other less well-known cases, like the nationalization

[1] Partido de Acción Nacional.
[2] Partido Revolucionario Institucional.

of the electric power industry (see Vernon, 1964) and land-holdings. (See Cronin, 1960, Chap. 6; Flores, 1961, Chap. 17.) Nationalism is certainly a driving force behind these measures. More important, however, is the belief that if national economic planning for growth is to be successful (and the Mexican government is committed to a policy of rather centralized economic planning), it is necessary that Mexican authorities be able to make all major economic decisions about investments, allocation of resources and so on. Mexico has encouraged foreign capital to invest in Mexico, but sometimes demands that the majority of the shares be under Mexican control.

Let us now turn to the question of how these goals are related to one another. For the purpose of this analysis we shall concentrate on *short-term* relationships. We are going to use the goal structure to analyze political decision-making, and in Mexico, as in most other systems, political and economic planning seems to be conceived over periods of five to ten years. A president is elected for six years; he cannot constitutionally be reelected, and policies often change somewhat when a new administration comes in, so it is often not worth it to plan ahead in detail for longer periods than a presidential period.

Our conception of how the major goals of the Mexican polity are related to one another (goal structure) is as follows:

(1) Political stability clearly facilitates investments and other means toward economic growth. Stability and order makes economic planning feasible, both for private entrepreneurs and public agencies. An unstable regime would have difficulty attracting foreign and domestic capital. Loss of work hours due to political strikes, damage done to equipment, buildings and other facilities during disorders would also impede the growth of the economy.

(2) Economic growth is clearly a prerequisite for the maintenance and extension of welfare services and policies. If a country wishes to industrialize and at the same time undertakes to construct a welfare state, then the economic growth rate has to be substantial if both sets of goals are to be met. It has been remarked that serious political problems

are created in countries that attempt to build extensive welfare services before they have reached a high enough level of wealth. (Dore, 1964.) Even in countries with a certain amount of wealth and a steady growth rate, welfare policies may slow down industrialization and economic growth. Wage increases and benefits for the workers may mean less capital available for critical investments. Land reform measures might sometimes lead to fragmentation of land-holdings into economically unviable units.

(3) Following a line of thought that goes back to Durkheim (1933), we also assume that industrialization contributes to political stability by creating "organic solidarity," that is, interdependence due to division of labor between the various parts of the country. Localism, the traditional individual's sense that he owes his primary allegiance to "La Patria Chica" rather than to the nation, may be expected to diminish in importance as a result of this. The mobility of the labor force that industrialism tends to create, should work in the same direction.

(4) Welfare policies contribute to political stability. In Mexico no regime would get much popular support that did not try to improve the lot of the poor masses, maintain a minimum wage level, give land to at least some of the landless, provide cheap housing and subsidized staple foods, and organize public works and other welfare facilities.

(5) Mexicanization has, we believe, contributed a great deal to political stability in Mexico. Apart from satisfying nationalistic sentiments, mexicanization has provided ambitious and competent Mexicans with access to important economic command posts, whether as private owners or public officials. (To a similar end, Mexico requires foreign companies that operate in Mexico to train Mexicans for managerial positions in the companies.) The opportunities thus given to aggressive, competent individuals to acquire power, wealth and prestige within the system, prevents them from joining restless strata that might be a threat to the regime. (Emerson, 1960; Zelditch and Anderson, 1965.)

(6) It also seems clear that the mexicanization program has contributed a great deal to economic development in

Mexico. Through control over the petroleum industry, for instance, the Mexican government has gotten a whole industry of synthetic fibers and other chemical products well under way. (Bermúdez, 1963, 21 f.)

This analysis has shown, we believe, that the relationships between the goals are rather complicated. All goals cannot be maximized simultaneously. Compromises are made necessary, especially between the goals of industrialization and public welfare. Both these goals affect that of political stability, which in turn is seen as a main responsibility and concern of the power-holding political groups. And in Mexican history political stability has never been something to be taken for granted. In Mexico, therefore, the political elements will have to take the major share of the responsibility for how compromises between economic growth and public welfare are achieved. The state, represented by the federal government and the top organs of the ruling party, exercises a great deal of influence over business, as well as over labor unions and agrarian organizations, to this end. (The business community has considerable political influence, but how this is exerted falls outside of the scope of this paper.)

Well organized interest groups exist in Mexico which attempt to promote one or the other of the goals in Γ[3]. Interest groups differ from one another in the priority ordering they want to see given to the goals in Γ. The agrarian organizations demand a rapid completion of the land reform at the expense of those landholders who still own or control more land than the *Código Agrario* allows. The middle class, including many governmental officials, seems to regard land reform measures, and especially economic aid to marginal farmers, as welfare measures that should be given low priority in order that capital not be diverted from more profitable enterprises. The labor organizations demand wage increases and other benefits for the urban working classes. Business groups demand freedom from government regulations.

[3] The symbol refers to the goal-structure of the Mexican polity. It is used throughout this chapter.

(For description of several of these organizations, see Scott, 1964; Brandenburg, 1964; and Kling, 1961.)

The national political leadership in Mexico is strongly committed to the goal-structure Γ and is cognizant of the interrelations between the various goals.

Mexican presidential administrations have differed with respect to the emphasis given to the different goals, but we think it is fair to say that every regime from around 1920 and on has pursued the goals in Γ, and been fairly well aware of their interrelations. In fact, certain changes over time in the political climate in Mexico can be interpreted as reflections of changes in priorities given to the elements in Γ. The Cárdenas administration (1934–40) was very much concerned with agrarian reform (to a large extent a welfare issue) and mexicanization. (The oil industry was nationalized in 1938.) This regime, governing during the world-wide depression, could hardly have stressed economic growth and industrialization. In contrast, the Alemán regime (1946–52) stressed industrialization. The heavy emphasis on industrialization necessitated, or was seen to necessitate, holding back wage increases and other welfare measures. This took the form of repressive measures against militant labor union and agrarian agitation, and accounts for the bad name of Miguel Alemán in left-wing circles in Mexico.

THE OLIGARCHIC PATTERN

The Mexican national leadership seems, by choice or necessity, to be committed to tolerating a substantial amount of political pluralism. It is taken for granted, and indeed sometimes encouraged, that occupational groups attempt to promote their interests and demands through organizations. Political parties, other than the ruling PRI (Partido Revolucionario Institucional) are also tolerated, although not allowed to challenge effectively the PRI monopoly on power.

The political leadership in Mexico is committed to a

substantial amount of pluralism, but is determined to preserve for the foreseeable future the *de facto* power monopoly of the PRI.

Our next two principles deal with conflict between interest groups.

> The top decision-makers in Mexican national politics act so as to minimize the overt conflicts between interest groups giving different priorities to the elements in Γ.
>
> If conflict arises between interest groups involving priority ordering of goals in Γ, the top leadership of the PRI and the government reserves for itself the right to make final and binding decisions.

Several writers about Mexican politics have emphasized that interest groups play an important role in the political system. The ruling party, the PRI, consists of three segments: the agrarian (peasants and agricultural laborers) sector (CNC, Confederación Nacional Campesina), the labor sector (CTM, Confederación de Trabajadores Mexicanos), and the middle class sector (CNOP, Confederación Nacional de Organizaciones Populares). The only major interest groups that are excluded from the party are certain business groups. (For further organizational details, see Scott, 1964.) In the party policy-making and executive bodies on the local, state and national level, there will always be representatives from each one of the three sectors. The various interest groups therefore have a voice in the nominations for public offices like federal and state deputies, senators, state governors and president of the republic. (He who gets the PRI nomination, then, can be virtually sure of getting elected.) There is no doubt that in the pre-nomination struggle the various interest groups try to promote candidates sympathetic to their causes. It seems to be clear, however, that the top leadership of the party maintains rather tight control over who gets the actual nominations. Nominations are made at party conventions, but before the name of an aspirant is put before the convention, he will have to be approved by the national committee (Comité Ejecutivo Nacional), the top group of the PRI. Thus, the national committee has effective veto power.

We interviewed a representative of the National Committee of the PRI, who had been sent to a northern state to supervise the selection of candidates for the 1964 elections. He told us that there had been six aspirants for the two Senate posts from the State. The National Committee allowed only two names to be placed before the convention which then had the option of accepting or rejecting these two men. During the discussion he maintained that this procedure should not be called imposition of candidates by the national committee; the committee passes on candidates that have been made available on the local scene. He also emphasized that Mexico, because of its turbulent history, needs a party that maintains "La paz social" by seeing to it that equilibrium is maintained between the various special interest groups. He also said that, in his opinion, the middle class sector of the party, the CNOP, can be said to represent the "national interest" more than the more specialized agrarian and labor sectors. The CNOP represents a "more varied collection of interests" than the other sectors, according to him.

We interviewed the representative from the National Committee in the presence of high PRI officials on the state level (including the president of the state committee). Everybody was very deferential toward the national committee man. The latter did not hesitate to interrupt the others and was addressed by the honorific title "Don." (Anderson and Cockcroft, *Field Notes*. Summer 1964).

The national committee consists of seven members and is one of the most powerful political bodies in Mexico, second only to the office of the president of the republic or the secretary of the Interior (Gobernación).

While we agree with Robert Scott and others that interest groups are very important in Mexican politics, we believe that they play an essentially secondary role, and that the real power lies in an inner circle of the ruling party. (It is hard to say how large this group is or how it is structured.) The interest groups *articulate* demands and needs, but the decisions how to combine and harmonize these demands on the national level in the light of long-term goals are made by the ruling circle. The leaders are, however, at the same time, very much concerned with getting to know the points of view of various interest groups. The decisions of the top leadership are carried out by a bureaucracy, staffed by professionals of various kinds. They often seem to have a "middle class" orientation, but they hardly act in their professional roles as representatives of any interest groups. The "técnicos," strongly committed to *dirigismo*, seem concerned with efficiency and economic modernization, often viewed in a long term perspective. That the bureaucrats and politicians consult with representatives of the interest groups is obvious, but consultation is not necessarily acquiesing to pressures and demands; as we shall see, it can be purely for purposes of information and co-optation. Leaders of interest groups on the local and national level are very busy trying to influence *administrative* decisions and seek redress for grievances and local problems, like shortage of water for irrigation, maltreatment of peasants by local officials and so on (compare La Palombara, 1960). Thus, several of the peasant leaders we interviewed make regular trips to Mexico City on behalf of the members of their organizations. This holds both for leaders of the official CNC and those representing dissident groups. It is obvious that some detailed empirical studies of political and bureaucratic practice need to be done before we can say anything beyond these generalities about the role of the interest groups in the formulation of long-term policies on the one hand and administrative implementation on the other.

There have been some very recent developments that suggest that the oligarchic control over nominations may change. The regime has lately been experimenting (in Baja California) with a nomination procedure based on direct primaries. In these "elecciones internas" the members of the PRI, by direct and secret ballot (see for instance *El Día*, April 14, 1965, and *Política*, April 15, 1965, 24), selected candidates for various offices. These elections were reported to have proceeded quietly. The leader of the PAN in Baja California declared that the chosen PRI candidate for governor is "an honorable man" and he expected that the coming constitutional elections will "be clean."[4] (*El Día,* April 14, 1965.) This experiment with direct internal election was explicitly set up in order to select candidates with popular support. It was conceded that the old system, still practised in the other states, often led to the selection of candidates with little support among the population. (See for instance *Excélsior,* April 17, 1965.)

THE CO-OPTATION PATTERN

The ruling party in Mexico was built up during the 1920s and 1930s to provide a political instrument for the modernization and nationalization of the polity. It was from the very beginning ideologically and socially very heterogeneous. Apart from an adherence to the principles of the revolution, as set forth in the constitution and various other documents, membership required no specific ideological commitments. Marxists and other socialists became members, as did traditional liberals and people without any coherent political beliefs at all. The party has by and large continued to be pragmatic and ideologically vague. At times strongly ideologically oriented groups have split away from the PRI. In the late 1940s, for instance, the former leader of the labor sector, Vincente Lombardo Toledano, split away to form his own Partido Popular Socialista, (PPS), which claims to be Marxist. (We shall have more to say about this party and its peasant organization later.) In the last 5 years or so, there has been a great deal of unrest in the peasant sector of the ruling party. An independent peasant organization, (CCI, that is Central Campesina Independiente) was formed by people who used to be active in CNC, the PRI peasant sector. This group is especially strong in Baja California and is led by a rather charismatic leader named Alfonzo Garzón. Both the PPS and the CCI are very critical of the PRI and "the ruling

[4] A PAN leader in Baja California later bitterly alleged that the elections held in the State in August 1965 were fraudulent.

oligarchy." The two organizations have organized mass demonstrations in favor of radical agrarian policies in their strongholds (the PPS and its peasant organization in the Yaqui and Mayo valleys in Sonora, and the CCI in Mexicali, Baja California). Several of their leaders have been jailed and the authorities have used rather harsh methods to "restore order." (*Hispanic American Report*, November, 1962.) However, and here we have to anticipate later sections of this chapter, in spite of their bitter criticism of the PRI, both the PPS and the CCI *give the PRI a kind of qualified support,* especially at election times. The dissidents do not attempt to build political parties that could aspire to become serious rivals of the PRI. (It is true that elements of the CCI supported the uncompromising Frente Electoral del Pueblo in the 1964 elections, but this was an exception to the main trend and later caused the CCI to split.) The PPS openly supported the PRI presidential candidate, Gustavo Díaz Ordáz, in this election, and Alfonzo Garzón seems lately also to have found that he has something in common with the PRI. In a report of a meeting between Garzón and the new president of the PRI (head of the Comité Nacional) agreement was said to have been reached about certain issues (. . . con respecto a los destinos de Baja California; *Siempre,* March 31, 1965, 57.) The PPS and CCI are not the only dissident groups that have kept or built ties with the PRI. In the 1960s left-wing groups inside and outside the PRI formed an organization called Movimiento de Liberación Nacional (MLN). This group was very critical of the PRI, but its majority did not break with the party in 1964. Its chief sponsor, ex-president Lázaro Cárdenas, endorsed Díaz Ordáz, the PRI candidate. We were told by a man who had been a local leader of the MLN in a northern state, that the best thing for him and people like him would be to support the PRI and work inside the party for a more radical line. In return, he and others seemed to expect that the left would get some influence; that maybe some cabinet post would be given to a person sympathetic to their point of view. (Anderson and Cockcroft, *Field Notes,* Summer, 1964.)

A change in the electoral system, put into effect for the

first time in 1964, guarantees that some officially "approved" opposition groups get representation in the federal Chamber of Deputies. Twenty-five seats are divided between the legally registered opposition parties in proportion to their total showing in the elections. Since the total number of deputies is 200, the PRI retains a comfortable majority.

We believe that the leadership of the PRI rather systematically attempts to make dissidents give at least qualified and partial support to the party, and that the PRI is willing to give dissidents a hearing and certain concessions in return for such limited support.

This mechanism of control has been called co-optation. "The process of absorbing new elements into the leadership or policy-determining strata of an organization as a means to averting threats to its existence or stability is called co-optation" (Selznik 1949, 259). In the Mexican case the *intent* of the PRI is certainly to avert threats to the stability of the polity and the co-opted dissident groups certainly *come to believe* that they will get a measure of influence but the extent to which they get any real influence, that is get some parts of their programs enacted, is hard to determine. Co-optation is an exchange process, and can thus hardly be an enduring phenomenon unless the co-opted groups, led by rather astute politicians, receive some concessions. Our data do not allow us to penetrate this process any further.

> The top leadership in the ruling party in Mexico systematically attempts to co-opt dissident groups into at least partial support of the PRI. The PRI is ready to make limited policy concessions to such groups in return for limited support.

The co-optation principle reflects, we think, a very basic concern that goes back to the times right after the revolutionary wars: the need to "nationalize" politics in the country. After the wars, politics in Mexico was very fragmented. Local bosses (called *caudillos* or, on a smaller scale, *caciques*) controlled many areas of the country, maintained their own armies or bands of strongmen, and acted often independently of or in defiance of the national authorities. Ideologically most of these bosses seem to have claimed to be representatives of "the true" revolution. Some combined anarchism with what little was known of Russian Communist practices into extreme left-wing ideologies (Friedrich, 1965). The party that began to be built in the 1920s had as one of its tasks to overcome this fragmentation, to build an organization which, although ideally sensitive to local needs and demands, could be an instrument in the construction of a modern, rather centralized state and the maintenance of social peace. As we have already said, the party chose to be ideologically pragmatic and vague, in order to accommodate the various different groups. Groups of different persuasion were offered rewards and concessions in return for loyalty to the party and the regime. It was also, however, made very clear that the party would not tolerate any strong centers of power that were outside of the party or not allied with the party. If co-optation failed strongarm methods were used. Many of the local caudillos and caciques were assassinated, on order from the regime. Gradually there emerged the pattern we have seen: the PRI attempts to co-opt dissident groups and these know that in order to have any impact at all it is wise for them to maintain friendly relations with the PRI. Repression of unco-optable groups is nowadays most of the time less harsh, but it still exists. While the PRI and its presidential candidate won support from many of the leftists, bitterly critical of the "oligarchy," in the 1964 elections, some leftist groups formed the Frente Electoral del Pueblo (FEP). This organization was hostile to the PRI and had its own candidate for the presidency. The FEP was *not* allowed to register as a legal political party. It was also regarded as ineffectual and unrealistic by many people sympathetic to its views on issues. (A strong split developed, for instance, within another dissident group, the MLN, over whether or not to support the FEP.) Thirty members of the FEP, the CCI and the Mexican Communist party were arrested in April 1965 in Mexico City and many documents were confiscated (*Política*, April 15, 1965, 5).

We thus have another principle of politics in Mexico.

If co-optation of dissident groups fails, then repression is likely to occur.

The measures taken against the FEP and the Communists presumably represent premeditated decisions by the national authorities. There is also another type of repression in Mexico which represents survivals of earlier political forms. Local political and military authorities sometimes resort to violence against dissident groups, especially, it seems, in the country-side.[5]

In Baja California, for example, an agrarian settlement, not far from Ensenada, is ruled by a cacique, who seems to base his power on his connections with the CNC and the state government. Opponents to him within the settlement have been assassinated by his alleged "pistoleros."

As we have already said, politics in the state of Guerrero has the reputation of being controlled by traditional bosses. In the late 1950s there occurred violent and bloody clashes between soldiers and demonstrators in the cities of Iguala and Chilpancingo. The governor responsible for these measures of violence was later removed by the president of the republic. (Anderson and Cockcroft, *Field Notes,* 1964.)

The PRI has been more concerned with co-opting left-wing than right-wing dissidents. The reason for this is partly that the PRI regards itself as the only legitimate heir to the Mexican revolution. This revolution was made in order to accomplish large-scale social change. The conservative and clerical groups which were bitterly opposed to the revolution had no place in the revolutionary party. They had to be reckoned with but could not be coöpted. Left-wing dissidents, however, could challenge the PRI on its own ground. The regime has tolerated a conservative opposition party, the Partido de Acción Nacional (PAN). The PAN voters come from different social strata. There are the big businessmen,

[5] For accounts of politically inspired violence in different parts of Mexico, see the weekly *Política,* the section entitled "La Nación."

the members of the small town clerically oriented middle classes and also the religious peasants in some parts of the country. (See for instance Foster 1948 for a description of peasant conservatism). The party also attracts workers and peasants who are discontented with the ruling PRI, which is often seen as corrupt and inefficient. The PAN won some local elections, for instance in Mérida, Yucatán in 1964, but has never been able to challenge the power of the PRI in any serious manner. It used to accuse the PRI of large-scale fraud in the counting of ballots. Recently the PAN has accepted the legitimacy of the basic gains of the revolution and a Christian Democratic faction of the party is making itself noticed. In talking with PRI officials one sometimes gets the impression that the PAN is regarded as a legitimate opposition party which fulfills an important role in Mexican politics (the revolution was among other things made in the name of democracy), but which is not expected to seriously challenge the role of the PRI, sometimes referred to as "el partido oficial", as representative of the mainstream of Mexican politics.[6]

To summarize, then, the PRI seems to be ruled by an oligarchy which, using both the carrot and the stick, keeps dissident groups under control. The ruling group considers and arbitrates the conflicting demands of many, often rather militant, interest groups, but also has rather explicit long-term plans for how Mexico is to develop economically, politically and socially. The oligarchy perpetuates itself. The incumbent president of the republic, for instance, has the decisive voice in determining who his successor is to be and he selects the president of the Comité Nacional of the PRI. As we have seen, the top leadership of the party maintains tight

[6] We said earlier that in Mexico a rather modern political system on the national level coexists with remnants of a traditional system. This is well illustrated by the contrast between the Baja California direct primaries with the following incident observed by an anthropologist in the state of Oaxaca: On election day in 1964 in a Zapotec community nobody cast a vote. In spite of that some 500 votes were recorded for both the PRI and the PPS. The count was made by the two officials from the lists of residents. Nobody in the town seemed to mind. (W. H. Geoghegan, *Field Notes,* Summer, 1964.)

control over nominations and elections. The minority party seats in the Chamber of Deputies and the Baja California direct primary experiment demonstrate, however, that the oligarchy also thinks ahead toward a more democratic polity, when the "political maturity" (Madurez Cívica) is greater than it is now. (It is, of course, no coincidence, that the experiment with direct primaries was undertaken in Baja California, one of the most modernized states in the country.) In fact, some public pronouncements by the PRI president suggest that the oligarchy sees democratization of Mexico as proceeding in set stages. A new stage was said to have been entered with the institution of the direct primaries and the minority party seats.

THE PARTIDO POPULAR SOCIALISTA
AND ITS PEASANT LEAGUE

The purpose of this section is to illustrate further the main argument about the structure of Mexican politics that is set forth in the preceding sections. The information comes from printed sources and from interviews conducted in 1964 with leaders in the Unión General de Obreros y Campesinos Mexicanos, the peasant league of the PPS.

Vincente Lombardo Toledano was head of the labor sector of the PRI up until 1941. In the late forties, after having been pushed aside by the ruling Alemán group in the PRI, he founded the Marxist Partido Popular Socialista. In collaboration with Lombardo a peasant leader, Jacinto López, who had earlier been active in the CNC, founded the agrarian organization, Unión General de Obreros y Campesinos Mexicanos. This organization has branches in more than a dozen states, but has its main strength in Sonora, primarily in the Yaqui and Mayo river valleys. The organization comprises both members of agricultural collectives (*ejidos;* for the meaning of the word "collective" here see, for instance, Whetten, 1948) and landless laborers who demand land (*solicitantes de tierra*).

In the Yaqui valley the Unión General claims to have

some 11,000 members (700 *ejidatarios* and some 10,000 *solicitantes*), organized in 117 local groups. The organization has a democratic structure: decisions are made by an assembly of the chairmen of the locals. A secretary coordinates the activities from a small office in Ciudad Obregón, the main city of the region.

The main activity of the organization consists of putting pressure on the political authorities on the municipal, state, and national levels to obtain full compliance with the agrarian reform laws. The valley has good, irrigated land, suitable for cotton, wheat and some corn. There are many ejidos in the Yaqui valley, but much land is also in the hands of private families. Maps of the land tenure situation show that members of some families of revolutionary fame and families related to these by marriage (Obregón, Tapia, Calles) own large, sometimes continuous holdings. In order to comply with the letter of the law, the land a kin group owns is divided up between quite a few members. This is regarded by the peasant organization as a violation of the spirit of the land reform laws.

The Unión General demands a change in this situation. A substantial part of the privately owned land should, the organization claims, be made into ejido land, so that at least some of the many landless solicitantes can get titles to land of their own. The organization has sponsored mass demonstrations and land invasions in order to put pressure on the authorities.

In spite of its agrarian militancy, the Unión General maintains somewhat strained, but not unfriendly relations with the PRI. Our informant characterized the relations between the organization and the state government at that time (1964) as "cordial." It had been worse earlier when the son of Alvaro Obregón, the revolutionary leader and later president of the Republic (a member of one of the great landholding families), was governor of Sonora. When Díaz Ordaz was nominated as the PRI presidential candidate, the Unión General followed the decision of Lombardo Toledano to support him. Díaz Ordaz met with Jacinto López and the Yaqui valley leader of the Unión General in Hermosillo, the capital of

Sonora. At that time the peasant leaders turned over to him a detailed account of the land tenure situation in the Yaqui and Mayo valleys. (This meeting was given some national publicity, see *Siempre,* May 6, 1964.) Díaz Ordaz was very concerned with the situation (our notes from interviews with Jacinto López and Yaqui valley informant). He used language to the effect that the situation is a scandal (*es un desmadre*) and indicated that he would try to do something about the situation. The Unión General leaders were evidently rather impressed with Díaz Ordaz, who used to be regarded as a member of the right-wing of the PRI. "He matured during his campaign, came to understand domestic and agrarian problems," they said. (*Our field notes, 1964.*)

Lombardo Toledano seems, in spite of his Marxist ideology and leadership of an opposition party, to retain some access to and influence in the inner circle of the government. The PPS got a number of the minority party seats in the national Chamber of Deputies after the 1964 elections, and Jacinto López was seated as a representative of the party. López clearly seemed to regard this as a gain. He and his organization now have a national platform from which they can make their views heard. López and our other informants from the Unión General are clearly gradualists. They believe that change can only come slowly in Mexico as a result of pressures and organization work. The organization was, nevertheless, denounced as Communist by some PRI leaders from the middle-class sector we interviewed in Hermosillo, Sonora.

THE CCI EXPERIENCE:
DISSENT FOLLOWED BY CO-OPTATION

The CCI received its initial impetus from Alfonso Garzón of Baja California, after a left-leaning state governor there (1953–59) had named the charismatic peasant leader head of the state branch of the CNC, the PRI's peasant sector. However, when the CNC and PRI failed to meet adequately the demands of Baja California peasants, already aroused by the dumping of saline water from the U.S. Colorado River which killed off their crops (*Hispanic American Report,* XV, 989–90), Garzón broke from the PRI to form his own peasant movement, the nucleus of the national CCI, which was officially founded about a year later (*Hispanic American Report,* XVI, 14–16). He took an overwhelming majority of Baja California's peasants with him (our interviews).

As the salinity problem worsened, as new CCI locals formed in other states, Communist-oriented members of the CCI (less so Garzón's group) openly backed the "illegal" presidential candidate of the FEP. In 1964, the PRI stepped up its pressures on Garzón and his followers to "re-enter the fold." Garzón had vainly essayed the tactic of political candidacy against the PRI in 1962, when he ran for mayor of Mexicali but was refused recognition as a candidate. The failure of FEP candidate Ramón Danzós Palomino, himself a peasant leader from the north (the impoverished La Laguna area), in the 1964 presidential elections, may have further disillusioned Garzón with the efficacy of political dissent. In any case, repression of CCI demonstrations continued apace, and by 1964 Garzón seemed willing to reconsider his relationship with the PRI.

The CCI people we interviewed emphasized that their organization was working solely for the interests of the campesinos. They seemed determined not to let their organization be used for any broader political purposes, and expressed rather strong resentment against the Communist Party, which they accused of being more interested in broad political questions than in the problems of the peasants. Within the CCI, friction between the Communists and their sympathizers and Garzón and his group has occurred from the time the organization was founded.

The CCI, then, is clearly a dissenting group, but it is important to note that its dissent, although very vigorous, has been limited to a sharply limited set of issues. This strategy, of course, makes a reconciliation with the official party, once the issues that brought about dissent have been attended to, much easier than a line of more diffuse and less delineated dissent. In the interviews, the CCI men often condemned certain groups within the PRI, but indicated that there were others that they respected. For example, speaking about a peasant leader in Mexicali who had chosen to stay in the official CNC where he led a dissident faction, they emphasized that he is "clean and honorable." The PRI on its part kept lines of communication open with the CCI, at least with its branch in Baja California, the Liga Agraria Estatal. Before the 1964 elections, one of the PRI candidates for senator from this state contacted leaders of the Liga, in order to hear their points of view on current issues.

The Díaz Ordaz administration concluded an agreement with the United States which promises to end the dumping of salt water into the Colorado River. It has also been announced that large sums of money will be used by the government to rehabilitate the Mexicali valley land that had been ruined by salt water. (*El Día*, March 26, 1965.) At least some of the goals that the CCI had been agitating for have thus been achieved. In September 1964, Garzón declared Communist members of the CCI *personae non grata* (*Política*, October 15, 1964). Danzós, his followers from the Laguna, and all Communist members of the CCI in turn declared Garzón and his group expelled from the CCI. In effect, a second CCI was formed behind Danzós.

Garzón, meanwhile, began to cooperate more openly with the PRI. Demonstrations by Garzón's CCI became less common, although various of his followers continued to be smeared as "Communists" and jailed from time to time. Garzón and his group seemed to have made their peace with the PRI at the time of the gubernatorial election in Baja California in August 1965. Garzón was photographed frequently with the PRI candidate, and according to at least the PAN, Garzón openly campaigned for the PRI among the peasantry (*El Día*, July 30, 1965). Thus, Garzón and the CCI seemed to be following the same road toward co-optation by the PRI as Jacinto López and the Unión General did in Sonora a year earlier.

The PRI still had to reckon with the unco-optable Danzós faction of the CCI, however. As we would expect, repressive measures were used toward them. When small-scale milk producers in Puebla protested a new pasteurization law which threatened to encourage large monopolies in October 1964, they invited Danzós to address a rally. Danzós and other "Communists" were jailed. The PRI labor movement, and the CTM rallied behind the state governor in a show of unity. This may have been a mistake, for among Puebla's students and workers the occasion of the milk-producers' protest and severe repression of demonstrators was a perfect pretext for expressing their own complaints about the relatively unprogressive and stagnant administration of the governor, an Army General accused of nepotism. When massive demonstrations demanding the governor's resignation mounted, and a few labor unions began to cancel their affiliation with the CTM, (some observers say that worker soviets were even formed in some cases), the problem assumed national proportions. The President of Mexico called in high national and local PRI officials and worked out an immediate solution. The demands of the dissidents were swiftly met. The Puebla governor stepped down behind the facade of "a leave of absence." The people who booed him turned out the next day to cheer the new governor, who was flown in from Quintana Roo where his progressive administration had been described by PPS leader Lombardo Toledano as "an example for all governors to follow." (*Política,* Nov. 1, 1964, also, *Excélsior* & *El Día,* Oct. 15 through Nov. 1, 1964.)

The Puebla experience was one of dissent, followed by repression, followed by a kind of co-optation. When repression failed, co-opting the demands of the dissenters by naming a new governor with a more liberal program succeeded.

MEXICAN POLITICAL PATTERNS
AS FUNCTIONS OF THE GOAL STRUCTURE

The two broad tendencies in Mexican politics that we have tried to demonstrate in the previous three sections, the oligarchical and the co-optation patterns, should be related to the nature of the goal structure that we described at the outset. In an underdeveloped society with sharp latent and

often manifest conflicts between interest groups, regions and
to some extent ethnic groups, and a tradition of political
violence, a regime that is strongly committed to political
stability, substantial economic development and social welfare,
faces a task that must often seem insurmountable. If the regime, by choice or necessity, is *also* committed to a certain
amount of political pluralism, then it cannot choose the way
of Communist one-party states. Under conditions of economic backwardness increments in welfare policies and wages
and other benefits must be controlled carefully, if there are
to be resources available for economic growth. The demands
and expectations of the population have to be met to some
extent to ensure the necessary amount of political stability,
required for continuous economic growth. Dissident political
groups, based on substantial or important social strata which
believe that their demands have not been met adequately,
will tend to develop. If the regime is unable to or does not
want to suppress these, then it has to develop ways of co-
existing with them, but in such a way that they do not
threaten the stability of the polity. The regime will very likely
tend to develop mechanisms like the control and co-optation
pattern described in our analysis.

If our analysis is right, the Mexican polity provides an
example of a complicated system of exchanges between interest groups and an oligarchy that provides decisive and
sometimes rather ruthless leadership. It is what Shills (1962)
calls a tutelary democracy. Political "interest group" theory,
which has had a tendency to view politics solely as shaped
by contending interest groups, and hence to ignore the role
of leadership on the national level, should have much to learn
from the study of this system.

In conclusion we shall mention, but not analyze here, one
important cost that may be inherent in this type of political
system. The absence of a real contest between opposing political parties breeds political apathy and indifference. We
know that popular participation in Mexican politics is quite
low compared to more advanced democracies (Almond and
Verba, 1963, Chaps. 3–9). We are referring to real involvement in politics, not the kind of sham participation that oc-

curs when a busload of peasants is brought in to cheer a candidate in return for beer and food. It is quite clear that the top leadership desires active citizen participation in public affairs, but the basic structural features of the polity may make it impossible to reach this goal. The minority party seats in the Chamber of Deputies and the experiment with direct primaries may be first steps toward making a fuller participation possible. If direct primaries in the future are adopted in all the states of the Mexican union and are used for nominating candidates for all local offices, from mayor to state governor and federal deputy and senator, then it is likely that the two features of the Mexican polity this paper has dealt with will change rather drastically.

REFERENCES

Almond, Gabriel, *et al.*, *The Politics of Developing Areas,* Princeton: Princeton University Press, 1960.

Almond, Gabriel, and Sidney Verba, *Civic Culture,* Princeton: Princeton University Press, 1963.

Bermùdez, Antonio J., *The Mexican National Petroleum Industry,* Institute for Hispanic-American and Luzo-Brazilian Studies, Stanford University, 1963.

Brandenburg, Frank, *The Making of Modern Mexico,* Englewood Cliffs, N.J.: Prentice Hall, 1964.

Cronin, E. David, *Josephus Daniels in Mexico,* Madison: The University of Wisconsin Press, 1960.

Dore, Ronald, "Latin America and Japan Compared," in John J. Johnson (ed), *Continuity and Change in Latin America,* Stanford, California: Stanford University Press, 1964.

Durkheim, Emile, *The Division of Labor in Society,* New York: Free Press, 1964.

Emerson, Rupert, *From Empire to Nation,* Boston: Beacon Press, 1962.

El Dia, Mexico City Daily.

Excélsior, Mexico City Daily.

Flores, Edmundo, *Tratado de Economía Agrícola,* Fondo de Cultura Económica, Mexico-Buenos Aires, 1961.

Foster, George, *Empire's Children: The People of Tzintzuntzan,* Smithsonian Institution, Institute of Social Anthropology, Publication, No. 6. Mexico, 1948.

Friedrich, Paul, "A Mexican Cacicazgo," *Ethnology,* Vol. IV, No. 2 (April 1965), pp. 190–209.

Hispanic American Report. Published by the Institute for Hispanic-American and Luzo-Brazilian Studies, Stanford University.

Kling, Merle, *A Mexican Interest Group in Action,* Englewood Cliffs, N.J.: Prentice Hall, 1961.

LaPalombara, Joseph, "The Utility and Limitations of Interest Group Theory in Non-American Field Situations," *Journal of Politics,* Vol. 22 (February, 1960), pp. 29–49.

Poleman, Thomas, *The Papaloapan Project,* Stanford: Stanford University Press, 1964.

Política, Mexico City Weekly.

Scott, Robert E., *Mexican Government in Transition,* Urbana: University of Illinois Press, 1964.

Selznik, Philip, *TVA and the Grassroots,* Berkeley: University of California Press, 1949.

Shills, Edward, "The Military in the Political Development of the New States," in John J. Johnson (ed), *The Role of the Military in Underdeveloped Countries,* Princeton: Princeton University Press, 1962.

Siempre, Mexico City Weekly.

Siverts, Henning, "Political Organization in a Tzeltal Community in Chiapas, Mexico", *Alpha Kappa Delta,* Vol. III, No. 1 (Winter, 1960), pp. 14–28.

Vernon, Raymond, *The Dilemma of Mexico's Development,* Cambridge, Mass.: Harvard University Press, 1963.

—— (ed), *Public Policy and Private Enterprise in Mexico,* Cambridge, Mass.: Harvard University Press, 1964.

Whetten, Nathan, *Rural Mexico,* Chicago: University of Chicago Press, 1948.

Zelditch, Morris, Jr., and Bo Anderson, "On the Balance of a Set of Ranks," in Joseph Berger, Morris Zelditch, Jr., and Bo Anderson, *Sociological Theories in Progress,* Boston: Houghton-Mifflin, 1965.

Chapter 9

COERCION AND IDEOLOGY IN MEXICAN POLÌTICS

James D. Cockcroft

INTRODUCTION

In the previous chapter, we attempted to present parts of a structural model of the Mexican political system. The model postulates that the top decision-makers in the polity have in mind a *goal structure,* consisting of five national goals, between which positive or negative relationships obtain. In general it is not possible to pursue a maximizing policy on all five goals simultaneously. Shifts in policy occur over time when different weights are given to the elements in the goal structure.

The model furthermore incorporates six principles about the "operational code" of the ruling leadership of the dominant political party, the Partido Revolucionario Institucional (PRI). These principles are as follows:

1. *The national political leadership in Mexico is strongly committed to the goal structure and is cognizant of the interrelations between the various goals.*
2. *The political leadership in Mexico is committed to a substantial amount of pluralism, but is determined to preserve, for the foreseeable future, the* de facto *power monopoly of the PRI.*
3. *The top decision-makers in Mexican national politics act so as to minimize the overt conflicts between interest groups that give different priorities to the elements in the goal structure.*
4. *If conflict arises between two or more interest groups*

involving priority ordering of elements in the goal structure, then the top leadership and the government reserves for itself the right to make the final and binding decisions.

5. *The top leadership in the ruling party in Mexico systematically attempts to co-opt dissident groups into at least partial support of the PRI. The PRI is ready to make limited policy concessions to such groups in return for limited support.*

6. *If co-optation of dissident groups fails, then repression is likely to occur.*

In this chapter, I want to make some changes in and additions to the formulations in this analysis. First, I believe that the model presented exaggerates, to some considerable extent, the *stability* of the system. This is a bias common in "functionalist" formulations. Our model still captures some very important features of the system. Nevertheless, a realistic treatment of Mexican politics needs to pay close attention to some "built-in" sources of conflict. Second, an increased use of repression in recent years by the Mexican Government forces one to consider factors that were not dealt with in our earlier formulation, but that must be introduced if the complexity of the Mexican political system is to be more fully grasped: the consequences of economic "growth" obtained at the expense of continuing poverty among the rural and urban masses; inadequate channels of expression and influence for ever more conscious and maybe unco-optable sectors of the population (students, educated working-class youth); and the impact of foreign, primarily U.S., policies on Mexican domestic affairs. Third, the important role that ideology plays in Mexican politics is not at all considered in the previous chapter.

It should be emphasized that the formulations here are hypotheses rather than tested propositions and that a number of questions raised here do not yet have adequate answers. The aim here, as in the previous chapter, is to help develop an analytic perspective that can be of use for the comparative study of political institutions on the macro level.

SOURCES OF INSTABILITY IN TUTELARY SYSTEMS

Political power and authority in tutelary systems are typically wielded by "a unity party," interlocked with a centralized bureaucracy. Decision-making cannot be decentralized, because local communities are "not yet mature enough" and, therefore, have to be guided by the "modernized" political elite. In practice, this is likely to mean that important aspects of the welfare of peasants and local workers, often living in hinterland communities without direct access to the central decision-makers, are going to be sacrificed in the interest of the economic growth of the macrostructure, as conceived of by big business interests, central planners, and bureaucrats. In short, the policy becomes technocratic rather than populist.[1] If peasants and workers were socially insulated, they might submit to such politics. But, due to improved mass communications and facilities for travel, these groups are comparing their situation with those of other, more affluent groups in their own and other societies. They are coming to see possibilities for change.

Economic growth is for our purposes reflected in increased production and distribution of basic goods and in changes, over time, in the income distribution among different strata and groups of the population. There are two important and separate questions that the political analyst should keep in mind when looking at data dealing with changes in income distributions. First, he must ask what trends in real income there are for those various groups that are actual or potential actors in the political arena. (These groups may not coincide with the broad socioeconomic groupings used in statistical publications.) Second, he must at least try to guess at what such trends "mean" in terms of the welfare of the different groups. People's satisfactions with their income depend on social comparisons. Modest gains for a stratum, e.g., the

[1] A populist policy emphasizes the right of local communities or other groups affected by proposed policies to have a maximum influence over implementation.

metropolitan working class, might appear more and more unsatisfactory to the members of that stratum, the more the middle class is seen to be engaged in conspicuous consumption.

The first of these two questions can be answered, at least in principle, using available statistical techniques. For Mexico, there is information that appears to be fairly reliable about the changes in real income for different groups of the population.[2]

There is no need to go into detail here. Suffice it to say that income distribution is more unequal in Mexico than in some other underdeveloped countries,[3] and that the incomes of the poorest groups, the three lower deciles, declined somewhat between 1950 and 1963. For the other deciles the trend is upward, by and large.[4] According to Pablo González Casanova, between 1940 and 1960 industrial production increased 120 percent, agricultural production 100 percent, but average real income for workers decreased 6 percent and the minimum agrarian wage dropped 45 percent.[5]

The second question is more difficult to answer in any precise way. It would, however, seem peculiar if the relative deprivation felt among the poorest groups in Mexico were not either constant over the last twenty years, or increasing. Their real income has stayed constant or declined, while due to mass media, tourism, and improved communications, their opportunities for comparison to see how the other parts of

[2] Ifigenia M. de Navarrete, *La distribución del ingreso y el desarrollo económico de México* (Mexico City: Instituto de Investigaciones Económicas, Escuela Nacional de Economía, 1960), Tables 11 and 12. I am indebted to Professor Clark W. Reynolds for his generosity in showing me a chapter of his manuscript on the Mexican economy, before its publication as *The Mexican Economy: Twentieth Century Structure and Growth* (New Haven, Connecticut: Yale University Press, 1970).

[3] Reynolds, *op. cit.*, Chapter 2.

[4] Reynolds, *op. cit.*, Chapter 2, Table 9. This table shows the distribution of monthly personal income by decile, 1950, 1957, and 1963, in 1957 pesos. Reynolds lists his sources in the text under the Table.

[5] Pablo González Casanova, *La democracia en México* (Mexico City: Siglo XXI, 1965), p. 118.

the population live have become greater. But how does one assess the temper of, say, the lower middle class? Have their real incomes kept pace with their expectations regarding consumption?

The Mexican ruling party contained strong populist factions from the beginning, and during the Cárdenas administration (1934–40) people committed to populist beliefs and practices wielded great power. Technocratic elements have become rather dominant since the middle forties. And it is hard to see how it could have been otherwise. In a country that is promoting industrialization on the basis of privately owned enterprises, a "national bourgeoisie" has to develop. For various reasons, such as social origins, style of life, and location in the important cities, the bourgeoisie is going to have preferred access to the important decision-makers. It is also likely to control the mass media. Hence, it will be in a very good position to define the frame of reference and the premises used to analyze and conceptualize the problems to be decided upon. In Mexico, a contributing factor is the government control of the supply of paper for the press and consequent *de facto* censorship, which most Mexicans recognize. U.S. influence in the media is exemplified by the fact that *Selecciones del Reader's Digest* is the largest circulating publication in all of Mexico. When left-wing or radically dissenting publications appear, they usually do not last, as in the case of *Política*, which had to stop publishing in 1967, and whose founding editor was jailed.

The ideology of the "national bourgeoisie" does not have to conflict with that of the foreign (U.S.) bourgeoisie, especially in a developing country where the interests of the two bourgeoisies often overlap: industrialization, high profit rates, low wages, multinational corporations, etc. The ideology of the "national bourgeoisie" often ends up being viewed as a nonpolitical, "purely technical" and "expert" point of view. This process is, of course, not at all unique to Mexico, or limited to developing countries. It was called the "bourgeois embrace" by the radicals in the British Labour Party during the 1930s, after the split in the party and the formation of the national coalition government under Ramsay MacDonald.

In short, even in the absence of corruption, it will be hard to prevent the bourgeois strata from exercising ideological hegemony. Now, if the party system is operatively competitive, then it will be of at least some importance for each party to try to capitalize on populist discontent with the actions of capitalists and central planners. But in one-party states like Mexico this does not operate. This argument leads to another general hypothesis:

7. Ceteris paribus: *the more noncompetitive the political system (the less turnover in the composition of the administrative and political decision-makers), the more influence will socially dominant strata exert over policy; or, the more competitive the political system, the likelier it is that the interests of low-class or marginal groups will be taken into account by decision-makers.*

Populist policies, like the programs and actions of the Cárdenas administration, will become mere episodes in history as long as one leaves the economic positions of the bourgeoisie intact. And in "mixed economies," one has left bourgeois economic power intact, in spite of much rhetoric to the contrary. This argument is open for comparative empirical test. Several African states have been governed by regimes advocating and practicing populist policies, e.g., Kenya and Tanzania. Will these countries see a shift in emphasis in the direction of technocratic policies, as Mexico did in the middle 1940s?

Another important source of tension comes from within the elite groups. Tutelary systems conserve the power of entrenched elites. But a developing system through its educational institutions also trains new members of the elite, and it often seems that the ruling elite is unable to absorb many of these into the "system." Hence, tutelary systems keep producing potential challengers to their establishments. In a system that provides for circulation of elite groups through the political process, e.g., through elections, different groups can, to some extent, get a chance to wield power. Unless a tutelary system can invent some mechanism that gives po-

tential "counterelites" their pick of power, there is a danger
that these instead will ally themselves with the discontented
lower classes against the ruling elite. History has seen many
cases of coalitions between elite groups (which perceive their
access to power as blocked) and discontented and revolutionary groups in the "lower strata."[6]

It would be interesting to investigate the recent student
unrest in Mexico in this light. Students at the National University tend to come from elite families or middle-class ones.
How much do they feel blocked from either further advance
or meaningful participation in Mexico's development? Recognition of the corruption in the PRI, of the greed of the "national bourgeoisie" (*los coyotes,* as the more prosperous
businessmen are popularly called), of the sham of the "one-
party democracy," is widespread among Mexico's educated.
Many students were driven into the camp of the leftists in
1968 by the swiftness and brutality of the government's response. As one student informed me, "Smashed skulls, kids
choking on tear gas, and bullets coming right at us—that made
me a radical." More importantly, many of the protesting
students came from vocational high schools. It was against
these working-class students that the Army struck its hardest
blows. Once these students had linked up with the National
University students, and once rebellious labor-union elements
joined with the students in demonstrations in spite of the
official labor movement's condemnation of the student revolt, a significant multi-class coalition against the PRI may
have been a real, however nascent, threat. There may be
more than coincidence in the fact that the October 2, 1968,
massacre occurred at the Plaza of Three Cultures, a large,
low-income housing complex. Robert Freeman Smith
suggests:

. . . the government struck especially hard at this area
because it feared the explosive potential of lower income people, and perhaps believed that the sprawling
slums around Nonoalco were ripe for eruption. I would

[6] See Crane Brinton, *The Anatomy of Revolution* (New York:
Random House, Vintage Books, 1957).

also suggest that the vocational students were particularly resentful because they had been programmed into a socio-economic role with relatively fixed limits; one which has few defenses in a low-wage-rising-prices situation. Groups which have lost their traditional expectations in the midst of growing opulence may well experience a "new awareness of deprivation."[7]

Further investigation of the student revolt of 1968 should cast considerable light on the questions of sources of instability in tutelary systems and coalitions between diverse groups against ruling elites.

IS THE CO-OPTATION MECHANISM BREAKING DOWN?

Increasingly, co-optation was replaced by repression during the Presidency of Gustavo Díaz Ordaz (1964–70). This trend must be placed in the larger context of recent political developments in Mexico.

The experiment in local primaries and "democratization" of the PRI collapsed. The new president of the PRI during the Díaz Ordaz regime, Carlos Madrazo—the first civilian to hold that office in many years—lasted only a short time in his position. His nationwide speaking tour upon taking office, during which he appealed over the heads of many local caciques and state governors directly to the rank and file, elicited such a growing popular response, that many "old guard" leaders in the PRI began to complain to President Díaz Ordaz. Large audiences turned out at rallies for Madrazo, who was merely seeking to carry out his assignment: to drum up more active public participation in the PRI and to overcome widespread disbelief in the progressive and "revolutionary" character of the PRI. Increasing numbers of workers and peasants attended these rallies for Madrazo, coming on their own initiative without the usual free beer and breakfast customarily provided at PRI func-

[7] Robert Freeman Smith, "Repression: Origins of Social Unrest," in *Mexico, 1968* (New York: North American Congress on Latin America, 1968), p. 5.

tions. Madrazo was forced to resign and was replaced by an old-time party official. His speaking tours and subsequent resignation thus came to parallel in a striking fashion the Madero speaking tours of 1909–10, when Madero sought to democratize Mexico, then under the centralized rule of Porfirio Díaz and the Científicos. Madero too drew large audiences and was subsequently placed under house arrest. Madrazo was rumored to have been jailed or placed under house arrest in 1968. It was also alleged that the student movement was financed with funds from his supporters in the PRI and the bourgeoisie. (This sounds, however, characteristic of rumor-mongering in Mexican politics and should not be taken seriously without concrete, supportive evidence. Evidence on Madrazo's role may be hard to come by, since Madrazo died in an airplane crash in 1969.)

A second major crisis within the PRI occurred when the somewhat demagogic but popular mayor of the Federal District (Mexico City), Uruchurtu, who at times modeled himself after Madrazo, was replaced by General Alfonso Corona del Rosal, the military president of the PRI before Madrazo. It would be useful to know what deeper insecurity among Mexico's oligarchy led to such failures at democratization as the "progressive" but short-lived tenures of Uruchurtu and Madrazo. How do such failures, combined with obviously severe rifts within the PRI apparatus itself, affect the increased use of repression? To what extent is the military in Mexico—whose role has been exemplified by the tradition of a military president of the PRI and the use of troops in squashing unrest—itself a growing political force?[8]

[8] There is a myth in North American scholarship that the Mexican military is "nonpolitical," "professional," and relatively unimportant in a study of Mexican politics. It is true that the military's share of the national budget is not as large as it is in other Latin American countries (or the United States) and that relative to other budgetary items, such as education, it has gone down in Mexico. However, in absolute terms the military's share of the budget has gone up (the military has not suffered pay cuts, fewer munitions, etc.). This reflects the obvious fact that once a repression machinery is set up, its budget merely needs to be expanded to keep pace with cost expansion. In Mexico, the budgets reflect

Repression is not new within the Mexican system. However, the PRI was historically set up and maintained in significant part to reduce the necessity for violent repression. As was pointed out in the preceding chapter, repression against workers and especially against peasants has been common throughout Mexican history, as during the Alemán regime or with the crushing of the 1959 railroad strike. Prior to the events of 1968, peasants had been shot down many times (Veracruz, Oaxaca, Michoacán, Acapulco, Chihuahua), occasionally producing even attempted guerrilla warfare as a response (Chihuahua, also suppressed). Students had not been exempted from such repression, although not until 1968 were they killed and jailed in such large numbers. During the period 1966–68, students were jailed in Puebla; all schools in Sonora were occupied by the military when the PRI voided a local PRI primary; PRI reformers were purged from the party in Sinaloa; the military occupied the University of Morelia; the Governor of Durango sent troops into the mines to repress a student-worker movement; strikes at the agricultural and polytechnical schools were crushed; and scores of intellectuals, journalists, and alleged "Peking" and "Havana" conspirators were thrown into jail without "due process."

In order to understand the significance of these developments it is necessary to pursue research more thoroughly at two different, but overlapping, levels: first, at the general level of such areas as foreign investment, political imperi-

---

that the government has done more than that for the military. My field work has suggested to me that in Mexico there exist *two* parallel structures of political power and influence: the military, operating from the Secretary of Defense down through the various *zonas militares,* and the political, operating from the Secretary of Gobernación and the PRI national committee down through the state governments (governors). The two structures are kept somewhat separate by the prohibition against any state governor giving orders to the *jefe de la zona militar.* In this way, the military commander in a particular state or region has an autonomy of power vis-à-vis the state governor. To what extent these two parallel structures serve to check one another, or to supplement one another, is a question for further research.

alism, insecurity among Mexico's ruling oligarchy, factionalism within the PRI; and second, at the specific level of the co-optation process and its relationship to repression (the "carrot and stick" conceptualization spelled out in the previous chapter).

Co-optation is, as has been pointed out, an exchange process in which a group (party, movement, faction) "A" agrees to support another group "B" in return for certain favors, such as influence over policies, representation in legislative bodies, and so on. It is assumed that "A," at least at the beginning, is unfavorable toward "B," and that "A" would pursue its own policies in opposition to "B" were it in a position to do so. Co-optation represents a commitment on the part of "A" to support "B." This should produce *cognitive dissonance* in the minds of the articulate members of "A." It seems likely, however, that this dissonance is partly reduced in such a way that members of "A" come to feel that "'B' isn't so bad after all." Through this social-psychological process, "B" acquires a certain amount of legitimacy in the eyes of "A."

I would suggest that peasant opposition groups, like the Unión General de Obreros y Campesinos Mexicanos, can be co-opted by the PRI more easily than dissident student groups. A peasant league is co-opted when the leadership is co-opted. It has typically a shortage of personnel who can become effective leaders, and, often, due to an authoritarian organization structure, the leaders can bring the membership with them.

By contrast, student "leaders" are merely *spokesmen* for their "following," and if the membership perceives that the spokesmen have become co-opted, there will be many qualified individuals available to fill their roles. A co-opted student leader is much more likely than a co-opted peasant leader to be sacked by the membership, a new spokesman emerging in his stead. Also, contemporary student militants have an ideology that stresses the dangers of co-optation. It is these factors that explain why student dissidents to a considerable extent are unco-optable. Also, students find themselves in a more transient and "free" personal situation than do peasants, which makes them realistically more able to resist co-optation. When further research is completed, it should be possible in the case of Mexico to differentiate between upper-class students and lower-middle or working-class students (in the vocational and polytechnical institutes) in terms of co-optation-repression patterns. Similarly, it should be possible to distinguish the extent of blockage to "open careers" or "upward mobility" among students; the degree of formation of a "counterelite," for which there is no room among the already crowded upper echelons of the established elite; the feeling of "no outlet" among graduates in the social sciences, humanities, law; or the feeling of "middle-class poverty" among poorly paid vocational graduates faced with a rising cost of living.

An additional dimension to a more complete analysis of co-optation is, of course, the question of co-opted leaders who later "deco-opt" themselves, either for personal reasons or in response to rank-and-file pressure. For example, the popular peasant leader Jacinto López, whose co-optation we analyzed earlier, has recently proclaimed his resignation from the PPS and his decision to lead an independent, popular agrarian movement. This ostensibly suggests either López's personal dissatisfaction with the results of his co-optation, or his responding to pressure from the peasants whom he originally led and who feel he has not adequately "produced results." Both factors may be involved, of course.

Finally, the ability of the oligarchy, through the PRI, to "pay off" or "produce results" will seriously affect the degree of co-optation that is attempted or carried out. In a developing society faced with scarce resources, a delicately balanced goal structure, increased dependence upon foreign loans and investment, rapid population growth, and half the population rural and impoverished, it is never easy for the elite to reward those whom it co-opts in a consistent and lasting fashion. The degree of failure of the ruling oligarchy in Mexico to meet the most elementary demands of most peasants and some workers may be expected to correspond rather consistently with the degree of failure of co-optation.

We may summarize as follows: The increased willingness

of the PRI to resort to repression in later years may be due to a realization of (1) the unco-optability of student militants, (2) the inability of the ruling oligarchy to "pay off" beyond a fairly minimal level, and (3) the dangers to the regime which would arise were a counterelite to make common cause with the masses, who in a bourgeois society "have to suffer" if the country is to realize the long-term goals of economic development. Specifically, in 1968, it was very significant that the students' "political brigades" and "struggle committees" elicited increasing popular support from both lower-level government employees and working-class neighborhoods, as well as—in some instances—peasants. According to various reports, students linked up with peasants for five weeks in Topelejo, ten miles outside of Mexico City, in a struggle against government-appointed officials who regulated services and governance in the outlying agrarian region (total population, 250,000 peasants). The government officials were thrown out of Topelejo and, according to one student participant, "a student-peasant government" was established, leading to the creation of the political slogan ". . . two, three, many Topelejos." The Army put an end to this little-publicized insurrection.[9] Whether true in part or in whole, this report of the Topelejo insurrection suggests once more the importance of relating co-optation and repression patterns to ones of class conflict and class coalition.

The PRI has, over the years, acquired a fair amount of legitimacy as *"el Partido oficial"* precisely because of its ability to co-opt dissidents. However, skepticism about the PRI's legitimacy has spread widely throughout almost all strata of Mexican society. If the PRI resorts to oppression, it is likely to lose more of its political capital. It then becomes possible that the party has to resort to more naked use of force in a spiraling fashion.

To sum up, then, the discussions in this and the previous section, we might state the following hypothesis:

[9] "Students at War: Interview with Ricardo de la Luz," *Leviathan,* March 1969, p. 46; James D. Cockcroft, interview with political prisoners in Lecumberri Prison, Mexico City, 1969 (field notes).

8. *An important source of strain in the Mexican political system consists of popular discontent due to rising expectations and a shift away from populist policies, coupled with tendencies toward the emergence of unabsorbable and maybe unco-optable groups within the educated elite. The use of repression in this situation tends to weaken the hard-bought legitimacy of the ruling party.*

This hypothesis makes theoretical sense and fits the sociological facts presently available. It also provides a useful perspective from which one can study the dynamics of tutelatory political systems. They are all built on "alliances of order and progress," to use Eric Wolf's term,[10] and they probably all share the problem of coping with the trends discussed here.

THE ROLE OF IDEOLOGY

When asking officials of the PRI about how the party is organized and functions, one is likely to get a description very different from the picture given here. The party is depicted as consisting of three sectors that are independent of each other. Within each sector there is said to be a great deal of grass-roots participation in policy formation. Candidates for state and national offices are chosen by the rank-and-file members of the organizations making up the sectors through a consultative process. In short, the description given resembles very much that given in the official statutes of the party. There is a definite tendency to downplay the oligarchic features of the system.

The sociologically important facts about these descriptions by informants are, first, that they often are given in a vein of sincerity, and second, that the same informant later on, sometimes, will give rather vivid details about oligarchic control over party affairs. It is often clear that the informant sincerely

[10] Eric Wolf and Edward C. Hansen, "Caudillo Politics: A Structural Analysis," *Comparative Studies in Society and History*, Vol. IX, No. 2 (January 1967), especially p. 178 ff.

believes *in both pictures*. Observations such as these should, during our fieldwork, have given us clues as to the great importance of *myth* and *ritual* in Mexican politics.

The terms "ritual" and "myth" designate behavior, verbal or nonverbal, through which persons in a society express their ideas about "an ideal version of the social structure."[11] Leach continues: "It is a model of how people suppose their society to be organized, but it is not necessarily the goal toward which they strive."

The "idealized" pictures of the PRI given by informants were, then, normative models of political reality, and these can coexist, within the same mind, with an accurate descriptive model of sordid reality.[12] One must be careful to distinguish the normative picture from the cynical front, used by some to deceive themselves and others about the nature of the "facts of life." When one refers to normative models, one wants to separate them clearly (as much as can be done) from window-dressing and cant.

In the preceding chapter we mentioned a number of aspects of the system that indicate that there is a certain amount of pluralism in Mexican politics: the minority party representation in the parliament, the holding of presidential elections, with minority candidates, in spite of the fact that "everyone knows" that the PRI will win. We also noted that Díaz Ordaz went out of his way to consult with Jacinto López, the independent agrarian leader. Now, features and acts like these may have some operative or practical significance in making the system less oligarchic. But their true significance emerges if we *also* look upon them as parts of a ritual, designed to dramatize a normative version of the system. Another feature, which should be looked upon in the same dual manner, is the *junta popular de programmación*. This is an organization, set up in each state prior to major

[11] E. R. Leach, *Political Systems of Highland Burma* (Boston: Beacon Press, second edition, 1964), p. 286.

[12] For an interesting analysis of how people maintain two partly contradictory models of reality see Eva Hunt, "The Meaning of Kinship in San Juan: Genealogical and Social Models," *Ethnology*, VIII, No. 1 (January 1969).

elections, to conduct investigations into the problems of the various regions of the state. The aim is to bring the party to the grass-roots, to do some serious investigatory work, *and* to dramatize popular participation in the campaign, as part of the normative model of politics.

It is my contention that the various features of Mexican politics, from institutional arrangements like the minority party representation down to the minutiae of rhetorical invocations at public functions, serve to dramatize the normative model of the system. Tensions between the normative and the descriptive models make for a certain urgency in the elaboration of ritual and from time to time provoke at the local and national levels rather large-scale confrontations between groups (or coalitions) and the repressive forces of the ruling party (soldiers, police).

The point of view adopted here may be generally useful for the analysis of political, as well as other, institutions, not only in Mexico, but in other societies as well:

> 9. *Actors in political systems entertain simultaneously descriptive and normative models of their system. Frequently (if not always) these models are, at least in part, inconsistent. Political ritual serves to blur these contradictions, and to dramatize the moral conception of the system. The contradictions between normative and descriptive models of a political system contribute to periodic, large-scale confrontations between specific groups or coalitions and the military or police.*

The purpose of the normative picture of the political system is to help it gain and maintain *legitimacy*. In the previous section, I discussed a process that at least potentially threatens this legitimacy. This process and the tension that exists in the system between the normative and descriptive pictures might *interact*. That is, each time the system resorts to repression it points to the discrepancy between the two pictures, and makes the normative one slightly less plausible. The bullets made leftists out of some students.

The normative model of the political system is one major element in "official" Mexican political ideology. The Mexican Revolution of 1910–17 was, among other things, a revitali-

zation movement, or, rather, it contained several such movements.[13] The role of ideology in postrevolutionary Mexican
society has been very much neglected by scholars, especially
by North American ones. In fact, there is a general tendency
for students of the revolutionary process to neglect the role
of ideology or "culture-building" elements. Students of revolutions have tended to focus primarily on questions like the
social composition of various movements, power relations
between social strata, discrepancies between power and
wealth as a radicalizing factor, and so on. The role of ideology as a galvanizing force, the emergence of new world
views, and the discarding of old ones, in short, the "culture-
building" as opposed to the "nation-building" aspect of revolutions, tend to be neglected.

The study of ideology will probably be of great importance
in future Mexican studies. There are a number of sub-areas
which should handsomely repay both historical and structural analysis: the myths of the Indian past and the rejection
of the Spanish conquest (as depicted, for instance, by Diego
Rivera in the magnificent murals in the Presidential Palace);
the Agrarista Complex and its fate in an industrializing society; the emergence of the Presidency as a sacred office,
immune to public criticism, are a few examples.

Then there is the more difficult question of the "depth
structure" in Mexican ideology and culture. Sometimes, at
least, there is a remarkable continuity in style despite vast
changes. Is not the PRI with its operative emphasis on hierarchy, with the *jefe máximo* at the top, the heir of the Cien-
tífico Porfirista administration in some important respect?[14]
The pyramidical, oligarchic aspects of Mexican politics are
hardly just reflections of contemporary circumstances, but

[13] See A. F. C. Wallace, "Revitalization Movements," *American Anthropologist,* 58, 1956, and Bo Anderson, "Revitalization
Movements: An Essay on the Structure and Ideology in a Class
of Exclusive Underdog Systems," *Acta Universitatis Uppsaliensis*
(Skrifter rörande Uppsala Universitet, 17, 1968).

[14] The Porfirista system and its ideology is described in James
D. Cockcroft, *Intellectual Precursors of the Mexican Revolution,
1900–1913* (Austin: The University of Texas Press, 1968; Mexico
City: Siglo XXI, 1971).

also of a more ancient authority pattern. Ideological change often appears to be a matter of pouring new wines into old bottles (or, if the bottles are new, they retain the basic design features of the old ones). It is not hard to find examples of this in published ethnographic work. For instance, Friedrich has documented how an anticlerical agrarian leader has become the object of a cult that is partly expressed in religious symbolism;[15] and Rowland has shown in a valuable paper examples of how political events and figures get encoded into a traditional language of myth.[16]

Ideology, then, provides individuals and groups with a code and a vocabulary that they can use to conceptualize and speak about significant aspects of their world. How they come to conceive of events, persons, and groups will determine their sentiments toward them. Sentiments lead to actions. It is clear that much discontinuity in ideology would lead to cognitive chaos, but it is also obvious that the codes and vocabularies have to change as history moves on. It is the task of the sociology of knowledge to elaborate on and elucidate these basic facts, and here, as everywhere else, postrevolutionary Mexican history seems to highlight the intellectual problems of the sociology of rapid change.

IMPERIALISM AND REPRESSION

While the confidence of the foreign (U.S.) bourgeoisie in Mexico's economy has strengthened in the past two decades, as indicated by the tripling of U.S. direct investment in Mexico between 1950 and 1966 (from 400 million dollars to 1.3 billion dollars, according to the U. S. Department of Commerce), the national (Mexican) bourgeoisie has not been as consistently confident. For example, after the 1959 railroad strike was repressed and its leaders put in jail (one

[15] P. Friedrich, "Revolutionary Politics and Communal Ritual," in Marc J. Swartz *et al.*, (eds.), *Political Anthropology* (Chicago: Aldine Publishing Company, 1966).

[16] Robert Rowland, "Cantadores del Nordeste brasileño," *Aportes*, No. 3, 1957.

of the student demands in 1968 was to release these men),
flight capital swerved sharply upward as Mexican investors
chose Swiss banks instead of their own economy. By 1961,
flight capital from Mexico equaled one-third of the nation's
monetary reserve. A 1960 study by Mexican economist José
Luis Ceceña showed that of four hundred companies with
the largest incomes in Mexico, 54 percent were controlled
or strongly influenced by foreign capital, 21 percent by Mexican private capital, and 25 percent by the Mexican
government.[17]

Much attention has been given to the "Mexicanization"
policy, which requires that in certain areas foreign capital
be limited to 49 percent interest. However, enforcement of
this policy is left up to the executive. Many firms remain
100 percent foreign-controlled—General Motors, Ford, General Electric, Admiral Corporation, Monsanto Company, and
Anderson-Clayton, among others. U.S. business spokesmen
often endorse Mexicanization as part of a healthy and growing trend toward "multinational corporations," which continue to be dominated by U.S. interests. A financial analyst
recently stated in the *New York Times* (September 19, 1971)
that Mexicanization "is now seen as guaranteeing foreign investors against expropriation and providing access to essential raw materials." Bribery, corruption, and relentless pressure by foreign investors add to the ineffectiveness of
"Mexicanization" in actual practice.

For decades now, about two-thirds of Mexican trade (not
counting tourism) has been with the United States, and Mexico has suffered from a highly unfavorable balance of trade.
Tourism helps make up the deficit. In fact, tourism is
Mexico's No. 1 "export." How these trends of increased
dependence upon foreign interests affect Mexican politics
is an area of research that has been barely tapped by North
American scholars. For example, how important was the
scheduling of the Olympic Games in Mexico City in terms
of the government's response to growing social unrest in
1968, especially among students? Various government

[17] *Mexico, 1968,* p. 28; González Casanova, pp. 207–8.

spokesmen were blunt in asserting that any means necessary would be used to "maintain order" for the Olympics. Violent repression was used in 1968 in a situation where nonviolent efforts at co-optation might have been attempted in the past. How relevant was over-all U.S. policy, at home and abroad, of "law and order," development of Mace, crowd-control techniques, counterinsurgency training, military aid programs, and so on, for the Mexican policy of breaking up demonstrations swiftly and with overwhelming force in 1968?

It is important here to distinguish two forms of imperialism, which, however, in practice often occur together: "old-fashioned" *economic* imperialism and *political* imperialism. U.S. foreign policy is naturally geared to the protection of American economic interests in Latin America and elsewhere. It is in the interest of corporations to be able to open plants in Mexico where labor is cheap, and to capture the expanding domestic market for consumer and capital goods in Mexico. Political pressures may be used to achieve such ends. The goals of political imperialism are also tied to the security politics of the United States. Left-wing governments are perceived, whether correctly or not, as being in danger of Communist domination and as potential footholds in the Western Hemisphere of Russian (or Chinese) power. Even as the Soviet Union reserves for itself the right to intervene politically or, if need be, militarily in the border states from Finland in the north to Bulgaria in the south (the "Breshznev doctrine"), the United States will intervene if a Latin American country threatens to move in a radically leftist direction.

In brief, for an understanding of the Mexican political system, as well as other institutions, not only in Mexico but in other societies, *imperialism in all its forms* must be taken into account:

10. *Various forms of imperialism, which must be distinguished, affect the basic institutions of a society, and as foreign influence or pressure grows, repression is more likely to be used in order to maintain political stability, or "law and order."*

CONCLUSION

These formulations about Mexican political processes have been worked out in deliberate opposition to the "group theory" presented by Robert Scott and others. The group theory tends to view politics as a more or less constant struggle between interests, and political decision as results of more or less conflicting group pressures. Our model, to the contrary, tries to emphasize the *entrepreneurial* and dynamic aspects of politics.[18] Subgroups within the Mexican oligarchy have during several periods not only *responded to* pressures from interest groups and tried to work out compromises; *they have taken the lead* by creating interest groups, invigorating existing ones, and defining goals within the framework of the national goal structure. Thus, for example, the Cárdenas leadership in the 1930s helped create the Mexican Workers Confederation, CTM (labor), and the National Peasant Confederation, CNC (peasantry), and to keep those two organizations separate from one another as competing interest groups. Successful politics in a changing society must contain a "stream of innovations," just as the economy grows through the use of new techniques or the application of old ones to new problems or areas. A group that thinks it has a policy that should join the stream of innovations, first has to create effective demand for this policy within the party, in competition with other policies. Alliances are built through a complex series of transactions. Then it has to mobilize popular support for it, and finally it has to use the administrative apparatus to implement it or create new administrative organs.

This view implies a *dynamic* view of the political process, which seems lacking in the rather static "group theory" of Scott and others. The group theory sees politicians as *brokers*

18 For an interesting discussion of politics as entrepreneurship, see Herald Eidheim, "Entrepreneurship in Politics," in *The Role of the Entrepreneur in Social Change in Northern Norway*, edited by Fredrik Barth. Acta Universitatis Bergensis series humaniorum litterarum, 1963, no. 3, Bergen and Oslo, 1963.

between interest groups. It is suggested in these past two chapters, on the other hand, that while the broker function is of great importance in political systems, it is the entrepreneurial functions of political groups and leaders that are most strategic for understanding how a system evolves. In Mexico, Lázaro Cárdenas and Miguel Alemán were great political entrepreneurs. Advocates of "group theory" would have difficulty analyzing their careers. Furthermore, Cárdenas and Alemán operated in a larger and dynamic context of class conflict, economic crisis and change, foreign pressures and influence (imperialism), depression and war (or postwar), bourgeois control, and national planning in terms of an overarching goal structure subject to significant changes in emphasis. Our view goes far beyond the "group theory" model in taking into account these additional factors and insisting upon the need for further research into these other areas.

FURTHER PROBLEMS FOR RESEARCH

I would like to end this chapter by listing a few problems that I consider important research topics in Mexican studies. The list is obviously not exhaustive, but I do consider the problems important, not only for the further understanding of Mexican politics, but also because they might advance the comparative study of politics in developing nations. Let us face the fact that, for all the research that has been done on Mexican politics, the surface of the iceberg has barely been scratched.

1. Our model is of the national political system. This system contains subsystems, ordered in hierarchies. The states have political systems of their own: the State of Michoacán, for instance, is supposed to be largely controlled by a "Cárdenas machine."[19] Within the states there may be differ-

[19] See P. Friedrich, "The Legitimacy of a Cacique," in *Local-Level Politics,* Marc J. Swartz, ed. (Chicago: Aldine Publishing Company, 1968). While Friedrich's work is useful for the understanding of how *cacicazgo* works on the local level, it would be important to know how such local leaders tie in with the state "political machine."

ent kinds of local political systems on the *municipio* level. An important set of problems has to do with how such hierarchically ordered systems are related to one another. The transactions that produce power have to cross boundaries between the systems. What has to happen, for example, *on the local level*, for the governor of a state to be influential in the councils of the PRI on the *national* level?

2. Factionalism within the PRI obviously exists, but there is very little systematic knowledge of this phenomenon. How do factions arise, how do they persist, and how do they relate to one another? At the time when the official candidate for the Presidency is selected, a complicated bargaining game is played between the various factions, but there is no study, to my knowledge, that goes into this process in any detail.

3. Origins of the present system in the Calles and Cárdenas administrations, e.g., Cárdenas' deliberate separation of the CNC from the CTM, keeping peasants and workers in separate groups (today's two of three sectors in the normative model of the PRI).

4. The actual workings of institutions like the legislature, not as a parliamentary device, but as a functional component of the larger oligarchic and entrepreneurial political system.

5. The role of U.S. political, economic, and cultural imperialism.

6. The role of counterelites, especially as they emerge from the university and vocational school systems.

7. The role of ideology in the history of Mexican politics.

8. The role of the Mexican military.

9. The role of the "labor aristocracy," consisting of unionized, well-paid, skilled workers loyal to the CTM, who often oppose the strikes of less well-off workers, as well as those of doctors, nurses, and students; who are relatively indifferent to the needs of the peasantry; and who tend increasingly to aspire to "middle class" goals and life styles.

Chapter 10

ON OPPRESSED CLASSES*

Dale L. Johnson

The purposes of this chapter are to clarify the concepts of development, marginal underclass, and internal colony; to show the interrelationships between these concepts; and to clarify their usage in both industrially advanced and underdeveloped societies.

DEVELOPMENT

In Latin America about 25 percent of the population of major cities earn no regular income and are crowded into the most squalid of slums. Yet rural areas remain as destitute as ever. Thirty-five percent or more of the population in Latin American countries are peasants whose situation is no better, or even worse, than urban slum dwellers whose numbers are increasing at a rate of 10–15 percent annually. Ten percent of the income receivers earn about 50 percent of total personal income in Latin America—while the 40 percent of the population that is poorest earn only 8 percent of personal income.

In poor Bolivia and rich Brazil people live to an average of less than fifty years. In the United States people die at about sixty-eight years, except for blacks, who die at an average age of sixty-one, and American Indians, who live an average of forty-two years. In Brazil, 160 of every thousand

* This is a revision of a paper presented to a conference on "Social Science Research and Political Change in Latin America," Asilomar, California, May 9–11, 1969, sponsored by the Center for Latin American Studies, University of California, Berkeley.

babies die at birth; in the United States, twenty-two white and forty-two black babies of every thousand die.

In Latin America, people consume twenty-five hundred calories daily on the average (three thousand calories is considered an adequate diet). Of course, people do not eat averages any more than people die at an average age. The middle- and upper-income classes eat well and live long; the poor eat scanty quantities of corn and beans and die young. The poor consume little protein—and protein deprivation among children can result in permanent impairment of mental facilities. In Guatemala, a laborer may earn fifty cents a day—the price of a dozen eggs or a pound of meat.

Poverty is worldwide and is in part based on naked economic exploitation. In South Africa, a black mine worker produces about fifty-three dollars in value and receives cash wages of about fifty-three cents. In California, the Mexican and Filipino farm workers produce fruits and vegetables for one hundred million or more consumers, but don't themselves have an adequate diet and are forced to live below the poverty line. The Appalachian region of the United States, once rich with minerals, lies scarred—its mountains cavitied, its forests stripped, and its streams polluted, while its once proud miners subsist on welfare.

Everywhere the poor are excluded from access to the institutions through which they might improve their wretched material existence. They are shut off from education; labor unions shun them; the political system ignores, excludes, or represses them.

In sum, the poor everywhere are undernourished and sick and die young; they live in housing unfit for humans; they are exploited and subject to appalling social injustices; in their powerlessness they are excluded from the rights of citizenship; they become alienated from their own humanity and estranged from each other and from society; they are systematically excluded from participation in institutions that provide the opportunity for other members of society to reach something approaching a human level of material and social existence.

But the process of development, it is argued, eventually ameliorates the human condition. That is true, at least in terms of material well-being for some sectors of population in some countries during recent history. Half the population of the United States, for example, exists at a comfortable material level, and their situation improves over time. Yet another 30 percent live not far above subsistence levels, while 20 percent live at or below subsistence. "Subsistence," of course, is socially defined. The American poor are measurably less poor than the destitute of Latin America, Asia, Africa, or the Middle East. They have enjoyed an increase in the absolute level of their material existence in the twentieth century. Relatively, however, the American poor are poorer now than fifty years ago. In 1910, the bottom 20 percent of American wage earners gained 8.3 percent of total personal income; in 1959 the poorest 20 percent earned only 4 percent of total personal income. On the other hand, for sectors of the population in Latin America, development has probably meant absolute as well as relative deterioration. The distribution of income is more lopsided than it was forty years ago before the region began a process of industrialization. The poor have become poorer and the rich richer, and this is precisely a consequence of industrial development. It is possible that the poor in Latin America are worse off now than a century ago.

The process of "development" in capitalist societies has meant that rich countries get richer in part at the expense of the poor countries. The industrial countries of the West have appropriated a portion of the wealth of the poor countries whose "underdevelopment" has been structured through historical integration into the stream of world history. And the source of the stream has been Europe and North America, who today as yesterday control the diverse mechanisms of the world economy and the international stratification of power.

Everywhere the cities and their suburbs get rich at the expense of the country. The industrial and commercial centers of each country, developed and underdeveloped, act as huge syphons, draining the products, the natural resources, and human beings from rural and less-developed areas to the metropoles. Short of revolutionary changes, Appalachia, rural Latin America, the South of Italy, and other "depressed areas" will ossify as regional backwaters of underdevelopment.

The social change involved in development has meant that some human beings are constantly reshuffled into different social classes. Peasants become industrial workers, sons of workers become white-collar workers, sons of white-collar workers become technicians and professionals. But development has also meant that some classes change their function without changing their position at the bottom of the economic and social pile: black slaves became sharecroppers and sharecroppers became unskilled laborers and urban service workers. The blacks have been denied whatever benefits come from being reshuffled upward in the class structure over time. And the march of labor-displacing technology in the modern world, unparalleled in historical experience since the Industrial Revolution, appears to practically assure, short of revolutionary changes in society, that blacks will remain at the bottom; so too will Latin American Indians, peasants, and ex-peasants. In general, rural inhabitants and the urban poor throughout the capitalist world are likely to find themselves the more or less permanent *objects* of technological and social-political forces over which they have no control —until, that is, they and we say in all the world's languages, ENOUGH!

The term "development" has always implied a process of economic and social change for the better. Few analysts have stopped to ask themselves if these changes could be for the worse, or if changes could be better for some sectors of society and worse for other sectors.

It is useful to retain the positive value placed on the term *development,* and to formulate the proposition that *development is first of all the development of man out of conditions of exploitation, poverty, and oppression.*

The concept is thus based on the philosophical principles of humanism. But it also needs to be firmly grounded in social scientific theory. The second proposition, then, is that *development always involves changes in the basic institutions and structures of society.* Clearly, development is not simply a *continuous* expansion upon a previous base, such as an annual growth of national product of 2–3 percent; a steady increase in the rate of social mobility; or a gradual differentiation of roles, functions, authority, and social structure that tends toward greater pluralization and democratization of society. Development may, however, bring about a situation in which these desirable evolutionary changes in economic, social, and political spheres may occur. Development is basically a *discontinuous* process that involves changes in the fundamental institutions and structures of economy and society.

Not all structural changes, however, are necessarily developmental when development is seen from the humanist perspective that focuses upon the situation of man.[1] For example, changes in rural areas and the rapid industrialization of Lima have liberated thousands and thousands of Peruvian Indians from the shackles of essentially colonial domination by the landowners and their *mestizo* intermediaries. These Indians have been integrated into urban economic and social structures (and marginalized from others) in such a way that it is difficult to say they are any better off than before leaving the land. What has occurred in this situation is a basic structural shift from domination of an oppressed class by means of colonial relations to domination by means of class relations. The humanist postulate stated here permits the social scientist to analyze structural changes that are not developmental change—that is, those changes that do not necessarily improve the situation of man: *Development is the happy coincidence of structural change and improvement in the human condition.*

[1] The humanist definition of development is essentially a postulate from which to begin an analysis of development. The proposition that development always involves structural change has more the character of an empirical generalization, as economists from Schumpeter to Hirschman to the UN's Economic Commission for Latin America and sociologists from Marx to Barrington Moore have persuasively argued.

MARGINAL UNDERCLASSES AND INTERNAL COLONIES

Marginal underclasses. Marginality[2] and marginal under-classes are relatively new concepts that have their origin in the age-old concern for the plight of the poor urban classes uprooted from rural subsistence by economic forces and subjected to the vicissitudes of life as "lumpen proletariat," "masses," "surplus population," or as members of a "reserve army of the unemployed."[3] "The poor," "lumpen proletariat," and "surplus population" are descriptive terms without a great deal of analytical value. The term "masses" is very ambiguous, as it is sometimes used to refer to those at the very bottom of the social pile and at other times to everyone not of elite status. "Reserve army of the unemployed" is an analytical concept drawn from classical economics. Its value lies primarily in the implication that the process of economic change creates a class that performs certain functions within a capitalist economic and social order. While a reserve army of the unemployed is functional for dominant interests in a capitalist system, marginal underclasses can be afunctional or dysfunctional for the system as a whole. Unemployed labor is a factor in depressing wages in certain sectors and acts

[2] The concept of marginality does not have the meaning given to it by Robert Park, "Human Migration and Marginal Man," *American Journal of Sociology* XXXIII (May 1928), pp. 881–93; or Everett Stonequist, *The Marginal Man: A Study in Personality and Culture* (New York: Charles Scribner's Sons, 1937), or the literature on "status inconsistency" that has followed. As far as I know, this chapter represents the first time the concept of "marginal" has been combined with "underclass."

[3] For a clarification of concepts from traditional political economy, especially Marxism, see José Nun, *Superpoblación relativa, ejército industrial de reserva y masa marginal* (Buenos Aires: Instituto di Tella, 1969). It is a sad commentary on contemporary social science that "marginality" represents practically the first attempt in a century to develop a concept that is capable of theoretically analyzing (not just describing) the structural position of that sector of the population conventionally referred to as "the poor."

as a reserve for increases in demand for labor in periods of economic expansion without the consequence of bidding up the price of labor to "excessive" levels. Unemployment also gives employers a range of choice in investment in capital-intensive or labor-intensive technologies. Nevertheless, adoption of labor-displacing technology tends to march hand in hand with the inevitable process of increasing economic concentration. The consequences are the growth of afunctional (i.e., marginal) labor forces. Afunctional labor forces become dysfunctional for the system when it becomes necessary to divert resources for the subsistence of these unproductive populations and to strengthen the means of social control to deal with political instability caused by their revolt.

The problem is one of putting economic processes in a sociological context emphasizing class and power relations. Peruvian sociologist Aníbal Quijano has defined "social marginality" as ". . . a limited mode or inconsistent structuring of belonging and participation in the general structure of society, whether with respect to the total of structures in whole or in institutional sectors."[4]

Of course, in modern nation states no class of people is excluded from society, nor are we dealing with "dual societies." The problem has rather to do with the character and quality of participation in society by members of certain structural groupings created by economic changes. Marginal underclasses are excluded from participation, only minimally participate, or participate under discriminatory conditions in certain institutions, such as the political and educational. At the same time, participation in other institutions, such as the economy, is irregular and/or only yields minimal social rewards for roles performed. Moreover, marginal underclasses cannot claim, or find difficult access to, certain privileges,

---

[4] Aníbal Quijano Obregón, *Notas sobre el concepto de marginalidad social* (Santiago, Chile: CEPAL, División de Asuntos Sociales, 1966). On clarification of the concept see also José Nun, Juan Carlos Marín y Miguel Murmis, *La marginalidad en América Latina* (Santiago, Chile: Documento de Trabajo #2, 1967) and Nun, *ibid.*

advantages, or opportunities built into the social structure of
society that accrue to members of other social classes.

This conception is exceedingly broad, and it is useful to
limit the scope of the definition of marginality so as to refer
to concrete social phenomena, such as the position vis-à-vis
institutions and class structures of the poorest urban classes
(the "underclasses") in racially and culturally[5] *homogeneous*
societies. The position of peasants or of subordinated races in
ethnically dual or plural societies is structurally distinct from
that of urban underclasses, and different concepts may be useful in the analysis of the dynamics of relations between these
classes and the institutions and dominant classes of society.
"Internal colony" is one such concept that leads to new perspectives on the position of underdeveloped regions within a
national society and on national minorities.

Marginal underclasses, then, are those populations that
have not been integrated, or have been integrated under
highly disadvantageous conditions, into the institutions of society, but are not located in what will be termed "regionally
based internal colonies" or of allegedly "inferior" racial or
cultural origins. Categorized by the character of participation in the economy, these include the hard-core unemployed,
those employed in low-wage sectors of the urban economy
operating with labor-intensive technologies, and, the most important category, those whose skills are superfluous to a technologically geared society.[6] A marginal underclass would
include some but not all of the aged and those deprived of
regular or above-subsistence income because of physical or
mental incapacity.

Internal colonies. The concept of internal colony has its

[5] "Culturally" homogeneous meaning the absence of linguistic
or religious communities with a culture markedly different from
the dominant culture.

[6] An excellent portrayal of the enormity of the problem in
Latin America is André G. Frank, *Urban Poverty in Latin America* (New Brunswick, N.J.: Rutgers University Monograph Series
"Studies in Comparative International Development," II, No. 5,
1966); see also Richard Morse, "Recent Research on Latin American Urbanization: A Selective Survey with Commentary," *Latin
American Research Review* I (1965), pp. 35–74.

principal origin in two independent sources: the work of certain Latin American intellectuals,[7] and the black liberation movement in the United States. Economically, internal colonies can be conceptualized as those populations who produce primary commodities for markets in metropolitan centers, who constitute a source of cheap labor for enterprises controlled from the metropolitan centers, and/or who constitute a market for the products and services of the centers. The colonized are excluded from participation or suffer discriminatory participation in the political, cultural, and other institutions of the dominant society. An internal colony constitutes a society within a society based upon racial, linguistic, and/or marked cultural differences as well as differences of social class. It is subject to political and administrative control by the dominant classes and institutions of the metropolis. Defined in this way, internal colonies can exist on a geographical basis or on a racial or cultural basis in ethnically or culturally dual or plural societies. (Not all of these criteria need apply in order to classify a population as an internal colony.)

Regional internal colonies. The Northeast of Brazil, the Sierra region of Peru, rural areas of Guatemala, the Appalachia region and rural South of the United States, the southern region of Italy, all have one thing in common: They are underdeveloped regions functioning as internal colonies in relation to urban metropolitan centers.

An internal colony is first an economic phenomenon. The operation of the economic system generates colonies that function as satellites to national metropoles (and subsequently international metropoles, in the case of underdeveloped countries). The mass of the colonial population produce for sub-

[7] Pablo González Casanova, *Internal Colonialism and National Development* (New Brunswick, N.J.: Rutgers University Monograph Series "Studies in Comparative International Development," I, No. 4, 1965) and *La democracia en México* (México, D.F.: Era, 1965); Rudolfo Stavenhagen, *Classes, Colonialism, and Acculturation* ("Studies in Comparative International Development," I, No. 6, 1965); and Julio Cotler, *The Mechanics of Internal Domination and Social Change in Peru* ("Studies in Comparative International Development," III, No. 12, 1967–68).

sistence and export primary products to the metropolis for which they receive an exceedingly low proportion of the value of the products in the form of wages or wage substitutes. Profits from economic activity in the satellite are transferred to the metropolis or are reinvested principally in production of primary goods. Institutionally, the appropriation of wealth generated in the satellite takes place directly through capital transfers by landowners (often absentee) or mineowners to metropolitan centers (national and international) or indirectly through the terms of trade between products of the satellite and products of the metropolis and through metropolitan control of the commercial and financial sectors. There is little opportunity for capital accumulation by indigenous, nonoligarchic entrepreneurs.

At the same time, the economic system generates a rigid and polarized class structure in the satellite in which the owners of the means of primary production and a merchant and/or moneylending class are integrated into the upper ranks of a national class structure. The dominant class in the colony enjoys the privileges of participation in national institutions and a national class structure, while the mass of the colony are marginalized from participation in the benefits distributed among the classes of the metropolitan society. In conventional sociological terms, "the division between city and country dwellers is more pointedly a rift between 'classes' that inhabit the cities and 'masses' of disenfranchized peasants and rural laborers who live in the countryside."[8] (Recent urban developments have meant, of course, that the peasant mass is now located in both city and country.) The proposition that has been drawn from this conception is essentially correct with respect to the rural (and new urban) mass: ". . . instead of the classical Marxist or European pattern of struggle between classes, a struggle between class and mass takes place . . ."[9]

In this situation, change is not developmental change, even

[8] Irving Louis Horowitz, "Electoral Politics, Urbanization, and Social Development in Latin America," Glenn H. Beyer (ed.), *The Urban Explosion in Latin America* (Ithaca, New York: Cornell University Press, 1967), p. 216.

[9] *Ibid.*, p. 243.

though it may involve economic growth or transformation of structures. The process of economic change means a continuing, even sharpened, process of colonization. Economic transformations almost always mean increasing control of the satellite economies directly from the national (and subsequently international) metropolitan centers. Elements of the business classes of the satellites become absentee owners residing most of the year in the principal city, gradually expanding and diversifying their investments. Constant rationalization of marketing gives metropolitan merchants greater control over supplies and prices. Credit markets in the satellites disappear or are taken over by national banks. The class structure ossifies as an oligarchy-mass dichotomy. A process Frank has termed the "development of underdevelopment" occurs.[10]

Racially and culturally based internal colonies.[11] Amer-

---

[10] Frank has elaborated on metropolitan-satellite relations in his *Capitalism and Underdevelopment in Latin America* (New York: Monthly Review Press, 1967); on regional internal colonies and Latin American Indian populations. See Chapter 2 of this work.

[11] There are difficulties in retaining the concept of internal colony when the empirical referent is both an underdeveloped region whose resources are systematically appropriated by the metropolis and the underclasses of ethnically or culturally dual or plural societies. Thus, in the United States, poor whites of Appalachia, the white Crackers of rural Georgia, the Puerto Ricans of New York, the Chicanos of the Southwest, and urban and rural blacks are colonized populations. There is a serious question whether the concept may not be overinclusive. In Mesoamerica and the Andean regions the correspondence between regional colonies and Indian colonies is very high; presumably, poor mestizos and acculturated Indians of the urban areas have been mobile into the marginal underclasses. But what of Brazil, where racism and institutionalized discrimination (other than class prejudice and discrimination) are less institutionalized than in the United States, and the Indian countries of Central and South America? Are the blacks and Indians of Rio *favelas* colonial populations, while fellow *favela* dwellers of mixed racial origin and white complexion members of a marginal underclass? Probably not. In short, the concept does present some difficulties. Nevertheless, I believe the concept is worth retaining. Conceptual difficulties can be overcome by simply recognizing that the presence of racial minorities in a society does not necessarily mean the establishment of colonial relations and that each country has historically handled its "race problem" in distinct ways.

ican blacks, Chicanos, and Puerto Ricans; the blacks of South Africa; French Canadians;[12] the Catholics of Northern Ireland; and certain other racial and cultural minorities in different parts of the world can also be viewed as internal colonies. In Mesoamerica and the Andean countries, Indians are colonized racially *and* geographically.

Racially and culturally based internal colonies have a number of characteristics in common with marginal underclasses, particularly in the industrially advanced countries. Internal colonies are marginal with respect to participation in the institutions and class privileges of the dominant society in much the same way as underclasses. Both populations endure similarly severe social conditions. Both underclasses and internal colonies are predominantly classes of unskilled laborers. However, internal colonies possess a more differentiated social structure. The colony normally has a class of religious figures and political leaders, professionals and entrepreneurs (a "black bourgeoisie," for example) whose activities are usually confined to the colony, and often a *comprador* class carefully cultivated by the dominant society to administer the colony in the interests of the dominant powers of society. Both groupings are characterized by a "culture of poverty," but colonies possess a culture distinctive to the race that transcends the boundaries of class cultures.

CLASS RELATIONS AND COLONIAL RELATIONS

It could be argued that the differences in the structural position of underclasses and colonies are overwhelmed by the basic similarities, and, therefore, that the distinction is not

[12] "This is to say that French Canadian society was always a *minor society,* an inferiorized society; a colonial society where the role of colonizer was played first by England then by English Canada. . . . Collectively, we have never known freedom; we have always been a dependent, colonized people. We have never had a history. . . . This condition of being colonized and of being a minority has made of us what we are, and it is in this condition that we are able to discover the first reason of our alienation." Parti pris, *Les Québéçois* (Paris: François Maspero, 1967), p. 87.

particularly useful. It could also be argued that other concepts are more useful in dealing with extreme racial or religious-cultural divisions in society and the conflict these may engender. In conventional sociological terms, relations between the dominant and the dominated in racially divided societies can be conceptualized as a problem of "caste." Or, in Marxist terms, the problem can be seen as one of a "secondary contradiction" (the "primary contradiction" being an economic one of class). In certain racially stratified societies, the secondary contradiction (race) becomes a primary (class) or coprimary contradiction.

Neither of these concepts (caste or "secondary contradiction") seems to provide a framework for the understanding of the fundamental differences and variations in relations between dominant institutions and classes and dominated populations. The term caste best refers to strata within a relatively static, "traditional" society characterized by a high degree of hereditary occupational stratification. Caste societies, of which traditional India is the principal example, are also characterized by vast interstrata differences in language, religion, and culture. Relations between castes, however, are highly institutionalized and stable, which minimizes conflict. The Marxist conception of "secondary contradiction" is more attuned to the analysis of conflictive relations and change. But it is clear that race adds quite another dimension to class conflict. Historically, race contradictions have sometimes created even greater social divisions and conflict than class contradictions.

The distinction between marginal underclasses and internal colonies is particularly crucial in examining power relations. The major differences in the relations between the dominant classes and institutions of society and marginal underclasses on the one hand, and internal colonies on the other hand, revolve around different institutionalized practices of domination and different means of social control.

It is important to emphasize that *all* the classes of the dominant society rest upon the colonial population. Stavenhagen, González Casanova, and Cotler, among others, have described the manner in which the privileges and livelihood of the Ladino and mestizo populations depend upon domination and exploitation of the Indians of Mesoamerica and Peru.

> Ladinos and Indians hold different positions in the stratification scale, according to such well-known variables as income, property, degree of education, standard of living, etc. . . . Ladinos hold a higher position not only in the objective scale of socioeconomic characteristics, but they also consider themselves, *qua* Ladinos, as being superior to the Indians. They are contemptuous of the Indian as such. The latter, on the other hand, are conscious of their social and economic inferiority. . . .[13]

The economic exploitation inherent in these patterns of stratification are made clear by González Casanova:

> An exploitation of the Indian population by the different social classes of the Ladino population exists. . . . The characteristic of these social classes is the fact that they rest on the exploitation of the Indian as a worker or producer. The exploitation is combined—a mixture of feudalism, slavery, capitalism, forced and salaried work, partnerships, peonage, and gratuitous "free" domestic services.[14]

The population of internal colonies is subject to discriminatory practices over and above those characteristic of relations between dominant classes and underclasses. The colonized, very often including the *comprador* class, are discriminated against in the opportunity to participate in all institutional spheres. Institutionalized discriminatory practices create rationalizations of a normative character that place sanctions upon behavior contrary to the norms on the part of either the colonized or members of the dominant society. Racist ideologies evolve. The dominated adopt submissive attitudes and usually become subservient. Sectors of the business classes of society and the privileged sectors of the working classes are, or believe themselves to be, materially advantaged by the

[13] Stavenhagen, *op. cit.*, p. 67.
[14] González Casanova, *op. cit.*, 1965, pp. 34–35; on Peruvian Indians see Cotler, *op. cit.*

maintenance of internal colonies. Persons located in different strata in the social structure of the dominant society are motivated to move up the social hierarchy and are fearful of moving down. The ethnic pariah population at the bottom serves as a vent for the frustrations and personal hostilities of all the strata, especially those from the middle downward. This pattern is functional, in a kind of sociological "divide and rule" sense, for the dominant class in its power and status relations with the working and middle classes.

Individuals within the marginal underclass have opportunities for social mobility, depending upon opportunity structures, to the limited degree that they can shake off their class origins and become socialized into the skills, values, and attitudes of the mainstream society. The opportunities for social mobility for individuals within an internal colony are more sharply circumscribed. The colonized can be mobile within the stratification system of the colony or, with difficulty, pass one foot into the class structure of the dominant society while the other foot remains implanted in the colony. The individual is mobile under conditions strictly defined by the dominant society. He becomes stripped of his culture and values, losing his identity with the class of origin, but remaining uncomfortably "marginal" (to use the concept in the way that American sociologists have used it) in the dominant society. This is the case of the black bourgeoisie in the United States or the *cholo* of Peru.[15]

The institutionalization of dependence relations are a principal mechanism of domination. Dependence is a severe limitation of choices available to the dominated, regulated by alternatives set ultimately by the dominant group.

While paternalism is becoming less and less a pattern of class relations in underdeveloped countries, the population of internal colonies in Latin America are often locked into personalized dependence relations from which it is difficult

[15] On the *cholo*, see Cotler, *op. cit.*, and Aníbal Quijano, *"La emergencia del grupo cholo y sus implicaciones en la sociedad peruana"* (Lima: Universidad de San Marcos, Facultad de Letras, *tesis doctoral*, 1965).

or impossible to escape. Describing the situation of Peruvian Indians, Cotler notes that

> . . . the boss is perceived as the all-powerful source, whose good graces the Indian must woo in order to maintain his unstable position. Because the Indian has no other possibilities of livelihood within his reach he must accept the asymmetrical ties of reciprocity proposed by the landlord. Toward this end, he seeks to establish paternalistic ties with the boss and also with respect to the other tenants. . . . The landlord, for his own part, uses this paternalistic relationship to strengthen the tenant's ties of personal loyalty—highlighting the latter's exceptional status and thereby constituting himself as the single source of identification of his tenant-farmers—thus avoiding the formation of class identifications.[16]

But this type of relation does not end with landlords. The Indian is dependent upon the mestizo lawyer, judge, storekeeper, administrator, policeman, politician, and middleman.

The situation of urban marginal classes with respect to paternalistic dependence relations is quite distinct. In the case of Peru,

> . . . because of the existence of numerous spheres which compete to satisfy the requirements of the population of marginal slums (with the purpose of expanding their clientele), this group has avoided situations of dependence, since their members alternate between different power figures. Though the associations of dwellers seek to use influential middlemen in order to achieve their claims, the terms of reciprocity achieved through such links do not result in personal identifications or loyalties.[17]

In the industrial countries, personal dependence relations are not a principal mechanism of domination over internal colonies (but impersonal institutionalized dependencies are severe). The degree of dependence of the dominated upon the dominant is highly conditioned by the range of choice open to the dominated. Unlike what is common in under-

---

[16] Cotler, *op. cit.*, p. 233.
[17] Cotler, *op. cit.*, p. 242.

developed societies, the industrial society is characterized by an urban existential environment in which the oppressed individual can sometimes choose between various options that are institutionally created. The colonial subject in the advanced nations (much like marginal underclasses in underdeveloped countries) is dependent upon institutions—job markets, law-enforcement and probation agencies, welfare, etc.—rather than upon power figures of the dominant population.

Because mechanisms of domination over internal colonies are usually (but not always) less subtle than the mechanism of class relations, social control over the colony involves liberal application of force and repression. Extreme measures of social control of the colonial population come easier than control measures over marginal underclasses, because of racist sentiments widespread among the population of the dominant society. The danger of violent repression is particularly acute when colonies have lost many of their economic functions, such as provision of cheap labor to large enterprises. In this case, total containment, or the genocidal solution, is always an option in an extreme situation. Of course, the essentially functionless nature of marginal underclasses may also make extreme measures of social control possible when the marginals become defined as dysfunctional.

The dominant society attempts to impose its religion upon the colonized and to use it as an instrument of domination. Priests and ministers of colonial origin are assimilated into the *comprador* class and aid in the direct social control of the colony by the dominant powers. The socialization function of religion subordinates worldly consciousness of exploitation to other-worldly visions of the good life.

The colonized population is highly mobile, moving from rural areas and regional colonies to industrializing metropolitan centers. In the process of migration, colonies are ghettoized. *The change from rural to urban life suggests a structural shift from colonial to underclass status with urbanization.* It may very well be the case that black and mixedblood migrants from the Northeast of Brazil to Rio and São Paulo represent a shift from internal colonial to marginal underclass status. This, however, does not seem invariably to

be the case, as the situation of American blacks, who remain
colonized in urban ghettos, suggests.

American blacks have always constituted a colonial population: first as plantation slave labor, later as agricultural labor within the southern colony of the United States, and subsequently as unskilled labor in technologically backward
sectors of the urban economy and as a reserve army of the unemployed and underemployed for the industrial sector. The
great migration of blacks from the rural South to the nation's urban centers in the past three decades has an entirely
different character than the earlier immigration to American
cities. Successive waves of immigrants to the United States
in the late nineteenth and early twentieth centuries provided
cheap labor for the nation's expanding assembly lines, sweat-
shops, the elaborate distribution network, and an expanding
service sector. The Irish, Italians, Poles, and other immigrants
were never marginal classes and internal colonies except, if
at all, for limited periods. During and after the Second World
War blacks and browns from the rural backwaters of the
South and Mexico came by the millions to northern and western industrial cities. But the era of increasing absorption of
unskilled and semiskilled labor into the industrial system, and
thereby into the mainstream of the class society, was rapidly
drawing to a close. Blacks and browns were relegated to employment in the most technologically backward or labor-
intensive sectors (menial services, construction labor, corporate agriculture) and to unemployment, the squalor of
ghetto life, and welfare handouts. Today, the black, Chicano,
and Puerto Rican colonies remain indispensable sources of
cheap labor for the technologically backward and labor-
intensive sectors. They also provide a servant class to relieve
the affluent of the chores of ordinary living and to enhance
their status and feelings of superiority. For the highly technological corporate and the rapidly expanding public sectors
which require high skill levels, however, the minorities have
become superfluous labor. Moreover, the minorities do not
constitute an extensive and expanding market in a mass consumer economy—even subtracting from the buying power of
the working and middle classes, who bear the tax burden for
welfare.

Because minorities do not perform the traditional colonial functions as sources of cheap labor and markets for cheap manufactures to the benefit of the plantation owners or big corporations, does not mean that American minorities have entirely lost their character as internal colonies, though on the surface they appear more and more as urban marginals. The majority of the minorities serve local and regional enterprises and interests: the Mexican agricultural laborer's product is appropriated by the corporate farm (and indirectly by the supermarket and the suburban housewife), the denominational hospital squeezes the black orderly, the slumlord and ghetto merchant gouge the ghetto dweller, the white worker still can feel superior to someone, etc. In short, the ghetto is functional for a wide assortment of local interests that dominate local affairs. The American class structure does give rise to a pluralist set of interests operating on national, regional, and local levels. The corporate liberals of Domhoff's "Governing Class"[18] govern only at the national level, leaving local and regional vested interests firmly in control of urban and state politics and administration. These are the interests for whom cheap black and brown labor is by no means superfluous. Also, the means of social control remain essentially colonial in character. As nationalistic liberation movements gain strength, the institutions and power centers of the dominant center tighten control. As a matter of fact, *ghetto riots and the black liberation movement have generated very similar policies that U.S. corporations and the American government employ in their relations with external colonial dependencies when nationalist and revolutionary sentiments crystalize:* a combination of corporate investment in the colony, government aid and development programs (always designed as instruments of control), and custodial-counterinsurgent policies of repression.[19]

In Latin America rapid urbanization has brought disastrous

[18] William Domhoff, *Who Rules America?* (Englewood Cliffs, New Jersey: Prentice Hall, 1967).

[19] Beverly Leman, "Social Control of the American Ghetto," Michael Klare, "Urban Counterinsurgency," and Jill Hamberg and David Smith, "The Urban League in Action—Boston," all in *Viet-Report* III (Summer 1968).

human consequences for the internal colonies and marginal
underclasses of the region. Latin American economies show
high rates of technological advance, and the rate of labor
productivity climbs faster than the rate of absorption of new
workers into the productive labor force. The economies are
less expansive than the U.S. economy: Argentina, Uruguay,
and Chile, three of the most advanced countries, have been
virtually stagnant for fifteen years. The problem is also acute
in countries experiencing economic growth, such as Brazil,
Peru, Colombia, and Mexico. Being poor, the Latin American countries cannot even provide for minimal subsistence
and services (generally available to the American poor) to
the growing urban mass of superfluous unskilled laborers.
The polarization of society into a participant stable working
class (or "labor aristocracy," more narrowly defined) and
the entrenched middle class in alignment with the dominant
class, as against the marginalized and colonized populations,
accelerates each year.[20]

DOMINATION AND CHANGE

It is important to analyze change in the position of marginal underclasses and internal colonies from three perspectives: 1. that of the oppressed classes themselves, 2. that of
the dominant powers who must respond to the ferment for
change, and 3. that of the principal ideological currents that
structure the consciousness of all parties affected by, or involved in, the process of change.

1. In the analysis of the problem and in the search for
solutions, social science theory can ill afford to neglect the
way in which underclasses and internal colonies themselves
define their structural position in society and the strategies
and tactics they evolve in attempting to change their situa-

[20] See Glaucio Ary Dillon Soares, "The New Industrialization
and the Brazilian Political System," James Petras and Maurice
Zeitlin, *Latin America: Reform or Revolution?* (New York:
Fawcett, 1968).

tion. As is well known, the demands of urban underclasses have been for provision of those rudimentary social services that other classes enjoy and for access to the institutions of the larger society. These are reformist demands that have revolutionary implications if pushed long enough and far enough, because structurally the larger societies have not incorporated and, within the limits of the present system, probably cannot incorporate large numbers of new aspirants into the mainstream of society.

In many respects, the demands of internal colonies have been different from those of underclasses. The typical reaction to domination on the part of oppressed races is a "national" revolutionary movement demanding self-determination, as among American blacks, French Canadians, and certain Indian movements in Latin America. Regional internal colonies sometimes demand secession, as in the independent peasant "red republics" of Colombia.

"National" revolutionary movements have a strong cultural basis. The culture of the colonized has a quality lacking in underclass class culture: a sense of community and individual identity that can, under certain circumstances, give rise to racial consciousness and pride, the formulation of assertive ideologies, and action for change.

The "culture of poverty" among the colonized is not a product of traditional and allegedly "backward" peoples, but of the historical development of societies that subject the poor to social conditions over which they have no control.[21] The sense of despair and helplessness, the lack of self-esteem, the fiercely competitive struggle among the poor themselves, and all the characteristics of the culture of poverty described by Oscar Lewis, are produced by operations of the economic system and class and power structures

[21] The "culture of poverty" concept has been much abused; good criticisms have been formulated by Charles A. Valentine, *Culture and Poverty: Critique and Counter-Proposals* (Chicago: University of Chicago Press, 1968); Jack Roach and Orville Gursslin, "An Evaluation of the Concept 'Culture of Poverty,'" *Social Forces* XLV (March 1967), pp. 383–92; Jean Labbens, *La Condition Sousproletarienne* (Paris, 1966).

of capitalist societies in the modern world.[22] It is precisely
the remains of the "traditionalism" of indigenous cultures—
values of family, group solidarity, and community organization to survive in a hostile environment—that preserve the
colonized from absolute demoralization as human beings.
The other humanity-preserving institution that the colonized
have from time to time utilized is the act of rebellion.[23]
(Black is beautiful because black people are beginning to
stand up for themselves.)

> The act of rebellion requires a new appraisal of self,
> a rejection of the dominant cultural styles on behalf of
> more authentic or natural ones. It requires a realization
> that the blame for poverty falls not on oneself but on
> others who are responsible. It requires a sense that misery
> is not the result of God's inscrutable will but the re-
> sult of concrete power structure's priorities. The act of
> rebellion is the beginning of a man's making history and
> the end of his being its object.[24]

The position of the oppressed cannot be appreciated apart
from an analysis of changes that affect their structural position. One of the general patterns of change that may be identified is the transformation of internal colonies, or sectors
of the colonial population, to marginal underclasses, therefore bringing a shift from patterns of domination based on
colonial relations to patterns based on class relations. This
is the general argument of Stavenhagen.[25] Indians who break
with the community to migrate to urban areas learn Spanish,
perform new occupations, lose their self-identity as Indians,

---

[22] In French Canada the authors of *Les Quévéçois* note: "On
the cultural level, we are a depersonalized community because
we have been dispossessed from the beginning: and our depersonalization continually confirms and accentuates our condition
of being dispossessed. Dispossession and depersonalization make
up the two facets of the same alienation; they are its two major
characteristics . . . ," *op. cit.*, p. 96.

[23] Franz Fanon, *The Wretched of the Earth* (New York: Ever-
green Books, 1965).

[24] Tom Hayden, "Colonialism and Liberation in America,"
Viet-Report III (Summer 1968), p. 36.

[25] Stavenhagen, *op. cit.*

and are no longer identified by others as Indians or treated as such by the dominant classes. This is one pattern in the Indian countries of Latin America.

In Peru the *cholos,* a new class intermediate between the Indian colony and the urban marginals, has developed what represents another pattern.

> The *cholo* is characterized by an imcompatible status: due to his social origins and to the low prestige of his occupation, he resembles the Indian; yet in terms of his income and the occupational independence he enjoys with regard to the mestizo, he does not fit into these ethnic-social groups. His reference group is ambiguous for he maintains Indian cultural traits while adopting some of the mestizo's, impregnating them with a new, elusive element. While the *cholo* often settles in his own local area and engages in agricultural labor, he also undertakes new occupations which involve residential mobility, and which provide him with the means of obtaining a larger income and discovering new opportunities. He appears to be indifferent to the sacred character of agriculture and to the relations of communal solidarity—all of which occasions a loosening of ties with the extended family, typical of the Indian kinship structure.
>
> The *cholo* adopts an aggressive and mobile behavior which differentiates him from the "polite" mestizo, and from the "servile" and "apathetic" Indian.[26]

As the *cholo* moves away from the Indian position in the social structure he gravitates toward trade union and radical political activities. The *cholos* have been active in mobilizing the peasant indigenous colonized in land invasions and tenant strikes in certain areas of Peru. Under *cholo* leadership the Indians have not evolved "nationalist" perspectives emphasizing "Indianness." Their strategies of change have generally been to seize large blocs of land and attempt to hold them.

In general, the social scientist has an obligation to work out the implications of changes affecting the structural position of the oppressed and the direction of consciousness

[26] Cotler, *op. cit.,* p. 242.

among them. In so doing, the social scientist will likely also be contributing to the movement for change by working against false consciousness (such as racism among the underclasses) and by explicating concepts central to the development of ideologies and strategies of change.

2. Social science theory must also concern itself with the ways in which the dominant institutions and classes relate to changes in the consciousness, ideology, and strategies of change among the oppressed classes and populations. This is immanently a problem in power relations.

The institutionalized power structure, as Irving Louis Horowitz has observed, ". . . shapes up as a cupola in which classes alone engage in politics. The masses are simply not included by these classes in basic calculations concerning the distribution of power and wealth."[27] But changes in the structural position of the masses within underclasses and colonies often affect the consciousness of the dominated so that they act to place extra-institutional political pressures on the system of power and wealth distribution and upon institutions, that is to say, upon the system of domination. In this situation, something has to give.

In general, the pattern of change in class relations within ethnically homogeneous stratified populations (and *within* the class systems of the dominant population of ethnically dual or plural societies) is toward those changes that involve the least disruption of existing structures and institutions; namely, toward incorporation of sectors of the previously marginalized classes and their "neutralization" through extension of relative rewards and privileges. When groups of the powerless succeed in organizing themselves to provoke the power structure, the response is often to co-opt the moderate leaders into official structures, isolating them from their base, to repress the militant leaders, and to yield to the mass something of what they want: wage increases, city services,

[27] Irving Louis Horowitz, "Electoral Politics, Urbanization, and Social Development in Latin America." Horowitz, Josué de Castro, and John Gerassi, *Latin American Radicalism* (New York: Vintage Books, 1969), p. 140.

measured relief from police or administrative oppression.
. . . These benefits are often transitory, however, and the
struggle is continual and positive response reluctant.

François Bourricaud[28] and Julio Cotler have analyzed the
mechanisms involved in the "neutralization of participants"
in the case of Peru. Cotler notes:

> The "participant" sectors, or sectors integrated within
> the "national" society, namely, manufacturing, mining,
> and agricultural workers; governmental and private-
> sector employees; professionals, who live in urban sectors
> with access to education, to the polls, who are incor-
> porated to the internal market and participate in unions
> or political organizations; in sum, those who have means
> of representation, have achieved considerable gains with
> regard to the unorganized peasant mass, the Indian mass,
> and the unemployed population of the cities.
>
> The privileges of the system of domination are ex-
> panded by incorporating *segments of the population* to
> that system, extending the number of social sectors which
> directly or indirectly benefit from the peasant margin-
> ality. Thus it can be argued that, though the basic prob-
> lem "underdeveloped" societies confront is that of cre-
> ating ways and means for new population sectors to
> gain access to social and political resources—it might be
> added that to the extent that such incorporation is partial
> or in progressive steps, it favors the maintenance of the
> system of domination as it expands, neutralizing the ac-
> tivities of those "promoted" by alienating them from the
> marginal sectors.[29]

This is essentially the same argument that Marcuse has proposed to account for the pacification of classes in the advanced industrial societies,[30] with the difference that the
needs of newly incorporated sectors of the population in

[28] François Bourricaud, *Structure and Function of the Peruvian
Oligarchy* (New Brunswick, N.J.: Rutgers University Monograph
Series "Studies in Comparative International Development," II, No.
2, 1966).

[29] Cotler, *op. cit.*, pp. 238–39.

[30] Herbert Marcuse, *One Dimensional Man* (Boston: Beacon
Press, 1965).

Latin America are real human needs for the minimum material sustenance of life.

In most cases, however, the ability of dominant institutions and classes to incorporate and reward new entrants to the system is sharply limited by more or less "objective" conditions (i.e., technological developments, the operation of the economic system) and by subjective inhibitions (i.e., vested interests and reactionary consciousness). When "incorporation" and "neutralization" are structurally impossible or politically unfeasible, as is often the case, the response is violent repression.

3. Finally, the possibility of developmental change must be considered from the perspectives of different ideological currents that define the limits of imagination, and therefore of the possible.

On the most obvious level, to use the concept of marginal underclass implies that the strategy of liberation is the uplifting and integration of the marginal class into the mainstream of society. That is the liberal, social democratic, and Christian corporativist solution, as, for example, is implicit in the work of Goldrich, et al.[31] and DESAL;[32] or the corporativist policies explicit in the programs of Promoción Popular in Chile under the Christian Democrats,[33] and some programs of the War on Poverty in the United States. There is also the nationalist revolutionary solution. To use the concept of internal colony automatically implies a strategy of

[31] Daniel Goldrich, et al., Political Integration of Lower-Class Urban Settlements in Chile and Peru (New Brunswick, N.J.: Rutgers University Monograph Series "Studies in Comparative International Development," III, No. 1, 1967–68).

[32] Centro para el Desarrollo Económico y Social de América Latina (DESAL), América Latina y Desarrollo Social (Santiago, Chile: DESAL, 1966, Tomos I y II); DESAL, Seminarios de Promoción Popular (Santiago, Chile: DESAL, 1966).

[33] On corporativist policies in Chile, see James Petras, Chilean Christian Democracy: Politics and Social Forces (Berkeley: Institute of International Studies, University of California, 1967) and his Politics and Social Forces in Chilean Development (Berkeley: University of California Press, 1969).

"national" liberation. In practice, this means an attempt to build a more or less autonomous community within a larger society that can deal on a level of greater equality of power with established institutions and centers of power in the larger society in which the colony is doomed to be inextricably bound (secession from the mother country is rarely a viable alternative).

The liberal solution to the oppression of underclasses is a practical one if all that is required is a qualitative change in domination based upon class relations. Historically, the process of development has often permitted the incorporation of newly generated underclasses into the working class and the rights of citizenship.[34] Incorporation can be accomplished through extension of civil rights and political representation, by expanding job opportunities for unskilled or semiskilled labor, or by programs of qualifying unskilled labor such as extending educational opportunities or using the military or other institutions as an agency of socialization into appropriate skills, motivations, and attitudes. These are examples of policies that *act upon the situation* of marginal underclasses without necessarily implying basic changes in the institutions or social structures of society. The march of technology in the modern world, however, and the relative strength of the forces of domination (who normally use the extension of civil rights and provision of opportunities to participate as instruments of individual co-optation rather than for class incorporation) seem to suggest that incorporation of marginal classes implies the necessity of profound structural changes in institutions and stratification systems and the system of domination they reflect.

The problem is that it is precisely in the functioning of institutions and the dynamics of class relations in which marginal underclasses and internal colonies are generated. The system of domination functions to maintain, or even extend,

[34] T. H. Marshall, *Citizenship and Social Class* (New York: Anchor, 1964) and Reinhard Bendix, *Nation-Building and Citizenship* (New York: Wiley, 1964). Both of these books deal theoretically with the integration of new groups thrown up by industrialization into society.

the subordination of the classes in question. This is a particularly important problem when the most powerful groups in society *directly* derive their wealth and power from total domination of internal colonies. The extreme of this situation exists in South Africa. In contrast, the wealth and power of the corporate elite of the United States do not rest upon the exploitation of a black colony that has now become largely superfluous as a source of cheap labor for the big corporations and as an expanding market in a mass-consumer society. Guatemala or Peru may represent cases between South Africa and the United States, but as Aníbal Quijano has noted: "Available research concerning the problem of social marginality in actual national societies in Latin America immediately reveal that more is involved than a temporary maladjustment in the general structure of society."[35] The structural impossibility of mass incorporation of marginals and the colonized is built into highly technological industrialism of developed, and the industrialization of underdeveloped, societies.

Liberal reformist schemes of incorporation of marginal underclasses, and especially of internal colonies, are not likely to be viable solutions in any of the situations described above. The revolutionary solutions, on the other hand, are difficult to realize, to say the least.

The logical revolutionary strategy of marginal underclasses is sustained class struggle leading to a revolutionary seizure of power and a total transformation of society. Studies of Latin American underclasses have revealed the enormous obstacles that stand in the way of the development of revolutionary consciousness and action. Conditions of life among the underclasses are such that it is probable that underclasses will never form the vanguard of the revolution. At the same time, underclasses are not the lumpenproletariat of previous capitalisms in different stages of development. Certainly, they do not resemble Engels' description in his Prefatory Note to *The Peasant War in Germany:* "The *lumpenproletariat,* this scum of the depraved elements of all

---

[35] Quijano, *op. cit.,* p. 47.

classes, which established headquarters in the big cities, is the worst of all possible allies. This rabble is absolutely venal and absolutely brazen. . . . Every leader of the workers who uses these scoundrels as guards or relies on them for support proves himself by this action alone a traitor to the movement." The organization and mobilization of underclasses is central to revolutionary strategy. Yet, the revolutionary movement in Latin America, which is largely based upon students, intellectuals, assorted malcontents of the middle class, and the organized working class, has generally failed to direct its efforts toward the underclasses. Traditional Marxists have tended to concentrate their efforts in trade unionism among relatively privileged workers and electoral politics while the *Fidelista* forces, until very recently, plotted insurrectional movements in the countryside and urban disruptions lacking a mass base. This is now changing in countries like Chile and Colombia where it is still possible, though difficult, for revolutionaries to work aboveground among urban marginals and peasants. Nor do the present insurrectional movements in Uruguay and Brazil ignore the role of underclasses in making the revolution.

In the industrial countries, the immediate possibilities for revolutionary *action* (not revolution) seem to stem from oppressed races and cultural minorities, as well as an alienated class of youth, spun off the class society, who voluntarily marginalize themselves from the system rather than let themselves be channeled into roles they have no taste for. The concept of internal colony as a principal ingredient in an ideology of change propagated among racial minorities is most useful as a consciousness-building device. (Class consciousness among underclasses is difficult to generate, in part, because of the absence of a racial or cultural basis for community and solidarity that are actual or latent in colonies.) A conception of themselves as an internal colony by oppressed minorities normally comes about only after a "civil rights" struggle, as in United States ghettos and barrios, French Canada, and Northern Ireland, and readily becomes integrated into more sophisticated nationalist perspectives when it is perceived that extensions of civil rights do not end in social and economic equality.

Fervent nationalism, however, can lead to the adoption of self-defeating strategies of change and to serious tactical errors if the over-all aim of the movement is to force basic structural changes in society. If American blacks were to lock themselves into a ghetto and the only "white" faces there were policemen (even if the policemen were black), their basic *structural* position would not necessarily change. Certainly, it is foolish and dangerous to believe that American blacks or Central American Indians could achieve a genuinely autonomous community within the wider society, in the absence of profound structural changes within *that* society, though it may be possible to achieve concessions and partially control excesses of repression. At best, the demand for self-government in the ghetto can loosen the grip of the dominant institutions and power centers and force changes in power relations within the dominant society itself. The point is that raising demands for self-determination in the colony weakens the institutional mechanisms of domination through achieving concessions or by forcing the dominant to rely upon naked coercion, which may have the effect of further developing consciousness among the oppressed. The demands also generate the momentum for change in the dominant society. Ghetto insurrections and the black liberation movement in the United States have had these effects. This can also be seen at the level of particular institutions. The struggle, for example, of black students for autonomous black studies centers in American colleges and universities has illuminated the nature of power relations for all parties. Where the struggle has failed, authority retains less than its previous legitimacy. To the degree that black university students gain even partial self-determination and control over their education, the point is not lost on white students who create their own demands for control and institutional democratization.

The danger in nationalism based on racial or cultural identity is that the ideology of change ceases its further development with the growth of race consciousness, or what the Black Panthers term "pork chop" or "cultural nationalism." Huey P. Newton comments:

> Revolutionary nationalism is first dependent upon a people's revolution with the end goal being the people in power. Therefore to be a revolutionary nationalist you would by necessity have to be a socialist.
>
> Cultural nationalism . . . is basically a problem of having the wrong political perspective. It seems to be a reaction instead of responding to political oppression. The cultural nationalists are concerned with returning to the old African culture and thereby regaining their identity and freedom.[36]

Of course, it is precisely in cultural nationalism that the black movement began and continues to strengthen itself. As the movement grows and gains experience the ideology shifts and the possibility of political alignment of nationalist groups with a wider revolutionary movement, which flows from class relations within the dominant society, becomes feasible, however tenuous at any particular moment. Theoreticians of the Black Panther party now seem to be moving from revolutionary nationalism to revolutionary internationalism and toward a conception of blacks as a superexploited working class within a general framework of Marxist class analysis.

In Latin America the colonized Indians have barely begun to assert themselves, though peasant (primarily Indian) revolts in the 1960s in Peru were a significant factor behind the military coup of 1968 and the reformist programs of the regime that followed the coup. Latin American peasant movements, rising out of the colonized status of rural areas, in general have picked up considerable momentum during the past decade. Aníbal Quijano has analyzed traditional peasant revolts, messianic movements, and social banditry as these movements have evolved over time into modern reformist-

[36] Huey P. Newton, "Huey Newton Talks to the Movement About the Black Panther Party, Cultural Nationalism, SNCC, Liberals and White Revolutionaries," *The Movement* (August 1968) p. 8.

agrarianism, political banditry, and revolutionary agrarianism.[37] While rural trade unionism and peasant activities in alignment with class forces and political parties of the cities is common, advanced forms of peasant movements also act in an anticolonial manner by demanding a kind of internal independence. Quijano notes that "their strategies are mostly direct and often illegal including the seizure of land, the physical and social elimination of landlords, the destruction of the local political apparatus which is replaced by another power, and finally, armed defense or reprisal against the reaction of the landlord or the state."[38]

CONCLUDING NOTE

What has been said here has considerable implication for the role of the social scientist as scientist and as playwright-protagonist in the political drama of the modern world. It is not unreasonable to suggest that most contemporary social science theory and research has illuminated weaknesses in the system of domination, especially in the means of social control, *to the benefit of the dominant*. As Martin Nicolaus said at the 1968 convention of the American Sociological Association: ". . . the eyes of sociologists, with few but honorable . . . exceptions, have been turned downwards, and their palms upward."

I hope that this chapter may serve as an illustration that the social scientist as scientist, teacher, citizen, and human being can perform a particularly important role in forming public consciousness of the problems of human existence, of the need for developmental change, by carefully choosing the concepts he brings to bear on the problem. Concepts

[37] Aníbal Quijano Obregón, "Contemporary Peasant Movements," in Seymour Martin Lipset and Aldo Solari (eds.), *Elites in Latin America* (New York: Oxford University Press, 1967). Quijano, the author of an excellent paper on marginality, *op. cit.*, applies a class analysis framework to peasant movements and does not adopt a colonial analogy.

[38] *Ibid.*, p. 311.

such as those explicated here—development, marginal under-class, internal colony—are analytic constructs that refer to concrete social realities. The concepts can be operationalized and are valid as scientific constructs. But the concepts also have another quality—they contain a sense of magnitude and urgency that have the potential of awakening whatever humanity remains in man, of broadening consciousness, of stimulating action for developmental change. Conversely, if development is reduced to what happens to the GNP, if power is seen functionally as a facility available to society for achieving certain ends, if domination is stripped of its structural implication to refer to psychological phenomena, and if marginal underclasses and internal colonies are viewed simply as the poor who have "always been with us"— then the concepts become instruments in the domination of man's consciousness rather than instruments of his liberation.

PART III

SOCIAL SCIENCE AND
STRATEGIES OF DEVELOPMENT

Chapter 11

DECLARATION OF
LATIN AMERICAN ECONOMISTS*

André Gunder Frank and *Arturo Bonilla*

We Latin American economists who are concerned about
the inadequate ability of our science in its present state, and
consequently of our own ability, to offer the proper cooperation to the peoples of Latin America in their goal of attaining
economic and social development, consider it essential that
teaching and research in economic science in Latin America
use new approaches and take other directions. We are taking
advantage of the debates and resolutions of the Third
Meeting of Faculties and Schools of Economics of Latin

* This chapter originally appeared in Spanish in *Desarrollo In-
doamericano* (Colombia, 1966), and has been reprinted several
times elsewhere.

In a 1965 meeting of Latin American economists held in Mexico, professors André Gunder Frank of the National University
of Mexico, and Arturo Bonilla of the National School of Agriculture of Mexico, drew up and submitted for the consideration of
their colleagues a report which stated the need for new approaches in teaching and research in economic science in Latin
America. The authors later revised this document in order to submit it to Latin American economists for study and revision. Con-
currence was sought with the aim of presenting the document to
professors and students of economics as a set of formulations
which might stimulate the replacement of the inadequate techniques and methodologies which still prevail in our educational
and research institutions. Nearly 100 professional economists from
17 Latin American countries (whose names and institutional affili-
ations appear at the end of this chapter) signed the document before its publication and its subsequent use to reform the curricu-
lum in several Latin American economics departments. The
original title of the document was "Necesidad de Nuevos En-
foques en la Enseñanza e Investigación de la Ciencia Económica
en América Latina."

America to make available to our Latin American economist colleagues for their information and judgment our points of view on teaching and research in economics in Latin America.

The Third Meeting of Faculties and Schools of Economics of Latin America began its work under the following auspices:

> It is we, the economists of the underdeveloped countries, who have the duty to formulate a body of knowledge based on observation and experience by arranging these facts in a logical order which will permit us to derive conclusions of general validity. . . . The constant subordination to advances in economics in the Anglo-Saxon countries explains the apparent inability of Latin American economists to formulate a rigorous and logical body of knowledge applicable to the mechanics of growth, instead of limiting themselves to the rather thankless task of pretending that reality adapts itself to obsolete theoretical molds. . . . We must achieve a rational explanation of the fact that some countries grow and others do not, and that development occurs only at a particular historical juncture and not at another. . . . We must determine which are the mechanisms that prevent the international diffusion of economic development through trade and why this latter has turned into the instrument that most serves to accentuate the differences between rich and poor countries.

We agree with the general report of the Third Meeting of Faculties and Schools of Economics in its outline of the principal problems of Latin America, in that:

> The main obstacles that hinder and deform Latin America's economic development are of a structural nature and are therefore linked to basic aspects of the domestic economy and to the dependence vis-à-vis foreign power. Furthermore, both often influence each other reciprocally.
>
> The slow and unstable rate of Latin American economic development is due less to the lack or scarcity of productive resources than to the faulty utilization of investment potential, a substantial part of which is wasted

in the form of luxury consumption and unproductive investments and expenditures, and which escapes abroad because of an unfavorable rate of exchange and the negative effect of the international movement of capital.

Inflation and the disequilibrium in the balance of payments must be dealt with outside of orthodox monetary formulas; this does not imply an underestimation of the importance of financial problems or of the need for a good monetary and credit policy.

Direct foreign investments produce unfavorable effects on the balance of payments, on the integration of the economy, and on the formation of capital. They influence foreign trade unfavorably, encourage monopolistic competition, and displace and subordinate many domestic entrepreneurs.

Planning cannot be a substitute for structural reforms, which really should precede the former as well as emanate from it.

All these concerns are a consequence of the ever-graver problems faced by Latin American countries in their attempt to attain economic and social development.

Therefore, as was stated in the opening session of the Third Meeting of the Faculties and Schools of Economics: "It is for this reason that the fundamental task of this Conference must be to devise the basis which will permit the structuring of a specifically Latin American theory of economic development, which is the rallying cry of the younger generation."

We therefore consider it indispensable:

To construct by whatever means possible an economic theory for Latin America and other backward countries that can explain the causes and the phenomena which have brought about, and which maintain and generate, the stagnation of Latin America and its distorted development. This theory should be founded not so much on approaches, theories, and methodologies based on an alien reality, but rather on the historical experience and present-day reality of a Latin America which, ever since the Conquest, has been incorporated into the world expansion of the capitalist system. In its first phase this incorporation was mercantile and it subsequently generated the industrialization of the presently developed countries at the expense of inhibiting the industrialization of Latin America, Asia, and Africa, and of condemning their economies to a state of underdevelopment. Logically it devolves primarily on us, the economists and other scholars of Latin America and of other underdeveloped countries, to carry out the bulk of this task as an undeferrable scientific necessity and as a moral responsibility to our peoples.

The Third Meeting of the Faculties and Schools of Economics of Latin America has resolved that:

> The analysis of the problems of Latin American development requires its own theory, which without reflecting on the constructive contributions which it can gather from other countries, should arise basically from the systematic observation and analysis of Latin American problems. The theory of development formulated in highly industrialized countries does not adequately explain such problems, and consequently cannot serve as a basis for a strategy and a policy capable of dealing with them successfully.

We consider that in the teaching and research of economic science in Latin America there remain obstacles to the attainment of the proposed goals, such as:

—The indiscriminate and uncritical teaching of theories originating in a reality alien to that of Latin America.

—The existence of curricula in some faculties and schools of economics which do not yet include a chair in Economic Development; and where such chairs do exist they are not accorded the status that so important a subject merits. To make things worse, the fact is that in such courses of study the nature of underdevelopment is not rigorously analyzed.

—Departments, curricula, and even research programs generally divide the subjects up in such a way as to hinder both the scientific and didactic examination of the structural and dynamic relations among the various economic, political, social, and cultural characteristics of Latin America and an overall analysis of the structure and character of the capitalist system in Latin America.

—There is an inadequate treatment of the economic problems of each Latin American country; and, to make matters worse, no attention is paid to the situation in the other countries of the Latin American area, due to the lack of knowledge of what is happening in countries as a whole, which prevents seeing their similarities as well as their individual differences. In studying the underdevelopment of Latin America and the obstacles which hinder its economic and social development, either the analysis is based on economic theories alien to the Latin American reality which, furthermore, even contradict the facts cited above, or this Latin American reality is examined in a descriptive and superficial way, confusing its institutional manifestations with its nature and its structural character. Specifically, teaching and even research rely on static models of free competition which, even taking into account institutional rigidities such as those pointed out by the monopoly theory and the Keynesian theory, presuppose an equilibrating and rationalizing tendency, despite the fact that Latin American economies increasingly live in and suffer from an essentially monopolistic system which generates, in a dis-equilibrating and chaotic way, development for the few and underdevelopment for the many.

—Thus monopoly has yet to receive the attention it deserves as a problem of underdevelopment, even though it played a very important role in the colonial stage (foreign trade and a ban on the establishment of industry) and though in our day, in its new forms, it takes on ever-increasing significance as a factor of underdevelopment.

—The monetarist illusion often prevails, and inflation is studied as the cause of development in Latin America instead of considering it a consequence of underdevelopment. Neo-classical and Keynesian models are used, which, even if adapted as much as possible to our realities and needs, are not truly and adequately applicable to the economic and political structure in which the foreign trade and financial relationships of Latin America are evolving. The reason for this is that they take no notice of the penetration of direct and portfolio foreign investment in the economy and their impact on monetary and fiscal policy. Neither do they take into account the deformations which monetary and fiscal policy produce in the concentration of power and income and therefore in the growing obstacles to development.

—In teaching courses on international trade, business cycles, monetary and fiscal theories, agricultural economics, and other courses, as many theories are drawn on as there are authors. The courses begin with theories of developed countries; at most an attempt is made, at the conclusion of a course, to adapt the Latin American reality to these theories, rather than taking Latin American reality as the context and point of departure and then going on to look for and find wherever possible the necessary theoretical instruments for its analysis. Consequently neither international trade nor business cycles are seen as they were and are in underdeveloped countries.

—There is insufficient initiative and boldness in the revision of curricula overloaded with microeconomic and Keynesian analysis, the former already transcended and useful only in very specific cases, and the latter not applicable to our reality.

—As for demographic studies, Neo-Malthusianism, through the so-called theory of population explosion, plays an ever more important role in a false attempt to explain the causes of underdevelopment. In every way it evades the fact that if the population cannot earn a livelihood, it is not due to its rapid growth, but to the form of social organization which is to an ever-greater degree incapable of guaranteeing to the population forms and means which can guarantee and improve its standard of living.

—Economic planning is confused with sectoral or regional programming; and, moreover, an attempt is made to find in such programming the panacea for all the economic problems of our times, just as the free trade doctrine was regarded in the last century.

—The curricula do not sufficiently or rigorously prepare students in such subjects as economic research, statistics, mathematics, accounting, administration, and fiscal, monetary, and banking techniques. An attempt is frequently made to correct these deficiencies with remedies that contain deformations in economics, such as positivism and methodologism. The former attempts to reduce truth to the narrow framework of that which it is possible to show statistically or manipulate mathematically. The latter confuses methodology with theory, attempting to convert methods into objectives of knowledge instead of using them for the study of the historical and social background of the problems of underdevelopment, as well as of development, that the Latin American economies have.

—Thus inadequate courses of study in the subjects mentioned above serve to exacerbate the tendencies of positivism and methodologism. This leads to taking as parameters and fixed variables precisely those economic, political, and social factors which are changing or which should be modified if adequate Latin American economic development is to be attained, steering us away from the broad, structural, and historical approach which is fundamental to the elaboration of a theory of development based on Latin American reality. The deformations of positivism and methodologism have become more pronounced in teaching and are due to the conscious or unconscious intent of evading the responsibility which we, as intellectuals, have toward our peoples in regard to truths already discovered or yet to be discovered. Improved teaching of these subjects will only be significant, will only have meaning and potential, as a function of the approach which we are proposing in order to understand the causes of underdevelopment in Latin America, and it will have practical utility to the extent that it aids in finding the economic theory which must be constructed if Latin American development is to be attained.

—There is a tendency to follow the neo-classical pattern of isolating economic phenomena, minimizing the social character of classical political economy, and thus isolating the study and practice of the profession of economics from the life of our peoples and from our social responsibility to them.

—The growing foreign influence exercised through institutions, professors, curricula, research programs, scholarships for study abroad, and financing from certain developed countries, like other forms of technical assistance, encourage and contribute to the deformations we have pointed out, especially to positivism and methodologism in teaching and research in economics. Not only that: they frequently exert ideological influence and even interfere in political policy in Latin American universities.

From all the above we can deduce—as confirmed by the Second Commission of the Third Meeting of Faculties and Schools of Economics of Latin America—that "the studies which can best explain the process of our development will be those that include and give proper emphasis to factors of really fundamental importance, such as the manifold influence of foreign dependence, the effects of concentration of wealth and income on production, consumption, market formation, and the process of accumulating capital, as well as the inflexibility and inefficiency in economic policy which arise from the institutional structure."

Therefore, we, as Latin American economists who are conscious of these needs and defects in teaching and research in the faculties and schools of economics in Latin America, *recommend that:*

We economists and other Latin American scholars devote ourselves to elaborating an economic interpretation of Latin American history, inasmuch as in order to be able to understand, analyze, and overcome present Latin American underdevelopment, we must approach our problems in a totally new way, not based on the classic theory of international trade, but rather taking historical and present-day reality as its point of departure, objectively studying and analyzing in their totality the Latin American economic and political relations with now-developed countries, turning our sights to the objectives and goals of classical political economy, and dedicating ourselves as Latin American economists to the analytical and objective, rather than descriptive and emotional, study of the most important characteristics of Latin American underdevelopment and development which constitute its historical heritage and present reality, such as:

—The highly monopolistic structure of foreign and domestic trade.

—The extremely important but rarely studied role of the banking and financial sector in Latin American underdevelopment and development.

—Foreign investment and its economic and other implications in Latin America.

—The partially successful and frequently frustrated attempts of the present character of Latin American industrialization, especially in its monopolistic integration with overseas countries, its de-Latin-Americanization, and the impact these produce on small and medium industry.

—The concentration of land ownership and its ties to the oligopsonic and oligopolic character of trade in agricultural products and other sectors of economic activity.

—The continuing and growing deformation of the Latin American economic structure, particularly with respect to the alarming growth of the tertiary sector, which is generally unproductive, relating it to the underemployed population in this sector.

—The causes and consequences, for both development and underdevelopment, of the imbalances provoked by geographic centralization and regional impoverishment as signs of internal colonialism.

—The brakes on Latin American development caused by the social stratification and the class structure.

—To summarize, and this is decisive: it is necessary to study the nature and role of monopolies in the power structure, as related to the economic underdevelopment and development of Latin America.

Inasmuch as the goals indicated are difficult to reach, and in order to propose possible ways to attain them, *we recommend that the faculties and schools of economics of Latin America should:*

—Give first order of importance in their curricula and research programs to the historical interpretation of the Latin American economy, to economic underdevelopment, and to the present forms in which these phenomena appear in the various countries and in the area as a whole, so as to give students a better appreciation of the real problems.

—Assign a secondary status to Keynesian macroeconomics

and especially to neo-classical microeconomics, which is the rank they really deserve in the curricula, giving top priority to the introduction of studies of political economy.

—Take from orthodox macro- and microeconomics whatever they can contribute to the elaboration and teaching of a theory founded on experience and reality, for the explanation of development and underdevelopment instead of, as is frequently done, adding to the essentially static theories of classical macroeconomics and microeconomics a few afterthoughts on development, and few or none on the causes of Latin American underdevelopment.

—Be conscious of these theoretical needs, even at the risk of making mistakes sacrificing the minute precision of macro- and microeconomic theories and of methods such as mathematics, econometrics, and statistics; and instead have the courage to confront the reality of Latin American underdevelopment with their own intellectual and financial resources.

—Make use of their present courses and, where necessary, introduce courses in international trade, industrial economics, agricultural economics, economic history and geography, monetary and fiscal policy, etc., for the objective study and scientific analysis, rather than a merely theoretical treatment or superficial description, of these aspects of Latin American reality, beginning with an analysis in their historical and contemporary context of Latin America's foreign trade relations with today's developed countries and of the influence which these have had and continue to have on the distortion of these economies and in the underdevelopment of the area, as well as an analysis of other economic relations with developed countries of a financial, technological, and political character; a study of the dangers of foreign investment and foreign technological dependence, insofar as they bring with them growing de-Latin-Americanization, monopolization, and even industrial stagnation. At the same time it is necessary to study agricultural monopolization of land, water, technology, and of the commercialization of agricultural products, the interdependence among all of these, as well as their relations with so-called internal colonialism, which generates regional and sectoral polarization, resulting in the development of part of the economy at the cost of the ever more acute underdevelopment of many rural regions and some urban zones; and it is necessary to study the growing inequality in distribution of wealth and income, and the effects of all these tendencies on class structure, distribution of power, and social stratification.

—Include in their curricula more subjects in the fields of history and the other social sciences; strengthen their relations with the faculties and schools that teach these subjects, such as those of history or the political, geographical, social, anthropological, and psychological sciences, etc.; encourage these faculties and schools to revise their own curricula and research programs in the spirit of considerations and recommendations of this document.

—Promote round tables, conferences, meetings, studies, etc.; promote contacts with other universities in Asia, Africa, and Latin America, and also with those of developed countries, in order to analyze very doubtful theses which are nevertheless generally accepted in developed countries, such as:

(a) The so-called theory of the population explosion and its implications for economic backwardness.

(b) The thesis according to which only by receiving foreign capital is it possible to achieve economic development.

(c) The character and form of the so-called technical, economic, and financial aid from developed countries to underdeveloped countries.

(d) Free trade as the only formula which guarantees the development of backward countries.

(e) Unrestricted free enterprise as the necessary and only condition for industrialization.

In any case, these and many other doubtful theses which have originated in developed countries require a careful examination by us, in accordance with the purpose we have set forth.

—Link teaching with research to a much greater degree so as to bring the preparation and academic work of students and teachers closer to the reality and context of their countries and peoples, carrying out research sponsored by and in cooperation with government ministries and other public institutions in their countries, as an integral part of their study and research programs, but without prejudice to university autonomy or the principles which it involves, such as academic freedom and independence of research.

—The faculties and schools of economics in Latin America, in carrying out their long-overdue task of forming cadres to raise their own scientific and teaching level, must send to study abroad persons of such maturity and experience as to permit them judiciously to choose those studies that may be useful and to reject those which hinder the attainment of the goal of developing in their own countries a science of economics more adequate to the Latin American reality and *problematique,* thus sending abroad fewer inexperienced and immature young people who lack this capacity for judgment and selection.

The faculties and schools of economics in Latin America, as a part of their program for training cadres and for improving their own qualifications, must send more people to Asia, Africa, and of course Latin America for study, to profit from experiences and instruction springing from a reality more similar to our own. They must become acquainted with problems and efforts toward economic and social development carried out in these countries; this would mean sending fewer people to study in already developed metropolitan countries that are currently experiencing other problems and providing other lessons.

We support the proposal of the Second and Third Meetings of Faculties and Schools of Economics of Latin America to establish an Association of Faculties and Schools of Economics of Latin America as a permanent body.

We recommend that this Association establish permanent and special committees charged with:

—Promoting periodic meetings of faculties and schools.

—Facilitating an exchange of professors, students, and lecturers among the faculties and schools of economics of Latin America, in both regular and special courses, summer and winter.

—Establishing contacts with similar associations and with faculties and schools of economics in the countries of Asia and Africa with a view toward promoting a permanent exchange of professors, students, curricula, and above all of journals and other research works.

—Fighting for the defense of university autonomy and academic freedom, denouncing to the affiliated faculties any violation of this autonomy that might be inflicted on any one of them.

—Financing the Association and its activities principally through resources contributed by the faculties and schools of economy of Latin America and other Latin American sources.

A list of Professors and Researchers who have signed this declaration to signify their support, with names, country, and institutional affiliation (for identification purposes only) follows.

Argentina: Raúl Arturo Ríos (Universidad Nacional de Córdoba); Silvio Frondizi (Universidad Nacional de Buenos Aires).

Bolivia: César A. Vázquez (Secretaría Nacional de Planificación).

Brazil: Jairo Simoes (Universidad de Bahía); Caio Prado Junior (Universidad de São Paulo); Cid Silveira (Universidad do Brasil).

Colombia: Gumersindo Serje (Universidad de Cartagena); Iván Colorado (Universidad de América); Alfonso Delgadillo Parra (Universidad de América); Pedro Amaya Pulido (Universidad Distrital Francisco José de Caldas); Simeone Mancini (Universidad Nacional); José Consuegra (Universidad de Cartagena).

Chile: José Valenzuela Feijoo (Universidad de Concepción); Cristóbal Fasce Henry (Universidad de Concepción); Alexis Guardia Basso (Universidad de Concepción); Julio López Gallardo (Universidad de Concepción).

Dominican Republic: Marcio Mejía-Ricart (Universidad Autónoma de Santo Domingo).

El Salvador: Alejandro Dagoberto Marroquín (Universidad de El Salvador).

Guatemala: Raúl Sierra Franco (Universidad de San Carlos); Salvador Sánchez Aguillón (Misión Conjunta de Programación para Centroamérica).

Haiti: Gérard Pierre-Charles (Université de Haití).

Honduras: Jorge Arturo Euceda G. (Universidad Nacional Autónoma de Honduras); Marco Virgilio Carías (Universidad Nacional Autónoma de Honduras); Andrés C. Dávila (Universidad Nacional Autónoma de Honduras); Irma Roberta Díaz (Universidad Nacional Autónoma de Honduras); Diego I. Turcios L. (Universidad Nacional Autónoma de Honduras); Miguel Angel Funes Cruz (Universidad Nacional Autónoma de Honduras).

Mexico: Lucas de la Garza González (Universidad de Nuevo León); Sebastián Villanueva de la Rosa (Universidad Autónoma de Puebla); Juvencio Wing Shum (Escuela Nacional de Agricultura); Remigio Jasso (Escuela Nacional de Agricultura); Guillermo Garcés Contreras (Instituto Politécnico Nacional); Genero Arce (Universidad de Sinaloa); María del Refugio de Montero (Universidad de Sinaloa); Ismael Diarte Pérez (Universidad de Sinaloa); Rigoberto Elenes Bringas (Universidad de Sinaloa); Oscar González (Universidad de Sinaloa); Octavio Guerrero Bernal (Universidad de Sinaloa); Manuel Inzunza Sains (Universidad de Sinaloa); Silvia Millán Echegaray (Universidad de Sinaloa); Roberto de la Mora Zatarain (Universidad de Sinaloa); José Luis Ceceña Cervantes (Universidad de Sinaloa); Pedro Pérez Montes (Universidad de Sinaloa); Raúl Ramírez Quintero (Universidad de Sinaloa); María de la Luz U. de Cristerna (Universidad de Sinaloa); Félix Espejel Ontiveros (Universidad Nacional Autónoma de México); Eduardo Botas Santos (Universidad Nacional Autónoma de México); Juan Brom (Universidad Nacional Autónoma de México); Alonso Aguilar (Universidad Nacional Autónoma de México); Fernando Carmona (Universidad Nacional Autónoma de México); José Luis Ceceña (Universidad Nacional Autónoma de México); Rodolfo Puiggros (Universidad Nacional Autónoma de México); Manuel López Gallo (Universidad Nacional Autónoma de México); Graciela Wright (Universidad Nacional Autónoma de México); Gustavo

Cerna (Universidad Nacional Autónoma de México); Víctor Barceló (Universidad Nacional Autónoma de México).

Nicaragua: Raúl Castellón D. (Universidad Nacional Autónoma de Nicaragua); Fernando Robleto Marcenaro (Universidad Nacional Autónoma de Nicaragua); Eduardo Conrado Gómez (Universidad Nacional Autónoma de Nicaragua); Constantino Pereira (Universidad Nacional Autónoma de Nicaragua).

Panama: Rubén D. Herrera (Comisión Económica para América Latina).

Paraguay: Roberto Jadue Seba (Corporación de Fomento).

Puerto Rico: Paquita Pesquera de Mari (Universidad de Puerto Rico); Antonio J. González (Universidad de Puerto Rico); José Herrero (Universidad de Puerto Rico).

Uruguay: Samuel Lichtensztejn (Universidad de la República de Uruguay); Jorge Iristy (Universidad de la República de Uruguay); Carlos Quijano (Universidad de la República de Uruguay).

Venezuela: D.F. Maza Zavala (Universidad Central de Venezuela) Rafael Martínez Pérez (Universidad Central de Venezuela); Manuel Rodríguez Mena (Universidad del Zulia); Leticia Díaz de Zabala (Universidad del Zulia); Rafael Zabala (Universidad del Zulia); Diego Hernández D. (Universidad del Zulia); José Romero Coronel (Universidad del Zulia); Rubén Carlos Margheritti (Universidad del Zulia); Narciso Hernández Bravo (Universidad del Zulia); Gastón Parra (Universidad del Zulia).

Chapter 12

SOCIOLOGY OF DEVELOPMENT AND UNDERDEVELOPMENT OF SOCIOLOGY

*André Gunder Frank**

INTRODUCTION

This essay examines the sociology of development currently being produced in the developed countries, especially the United States, for export to and use in the underdeveloped countries. On critical examination, this new sociology of development is found to be empirically invalid when confronted with reality, theoretically inadequate in terms of its own classical social scientific standards, and policy wise ineffective for pursuing its supposed intentions of promoting the development of the underdeveloped countries. Furthermore, the inadequacy grows along with the development of the society which produces it. Like the underdeveloped society to which it is

* I am indebted, both for substantive and editorial help in the preparation of this study, to Nancy Howell Lee, Philip Wagner, Rodolfo Stavenhagen, Alonso Aguilar, Said Shah, and especially to Marta Fuentes Frank, David Aberle, and Barton Parks and other editors of *Catalyst*. I have full responsibility, however for the critique and critical tone of this essay, especially as concerns the theses associated with the Research Center in Economic Development and Cultural Change and its Journal, hereinafter referred to as *EDCC*, of which I am a former staff member and contributor. I have, perhaps mistakenly, not followed the good advice of some of the above named to try here to accompany my critique with a constructive alternative. But I have attempted to advance such an alternative in "The Development of Underdevelopment," Chapter 1 above, and in *Capitalism and Underdevelopment in Latin America: Historical Studies of Chile and Brazil* (New York: Monthly Review Press, 1967). This chapter originally appeared in *Catalyst*, Summer 1967, pp. 20–73. Reprinted by permission of the publisher.

applied, this sociology is becoming increasingly underdeveloped.

To permit a careful and detailed evaluation of this sociology of development, I shall examine the theoretical modes or trends represented by particular writings of selected social scientists. Nonetheless, my critique extends to the whole of this sociology of development. To avoid arbitrary selection, it is convenient to permit representatives of this sociology of development themselves to select the major modes and most of the authors to be examined here. Accordingly, they are given the first word.

Manning Nash, until recently editor of *EDCC,* has said,[1]

> There are, in my view, only three modes of attacking the problem of social change and economic development.
> The first mode is the index method: the general features of a developed economy are abstracted as an ideal type and then contrasted with the equally ideal typical features of a poor economy and society. In this mode, development is viewed as the transformation of one type into the other. Developed examples of this mode are to be found in Hoselitz's *Sociological Factors in Economic Development,*[2] or Parsons' *Structure and Process in Modern Societies,*[3] or in some of the work of the sociologist Marion J. Levy, Jr.[4] . . .

[1] Manning Nash, "Introduction, Approaches to the Study of Economic Growth" in "Psycho-Cultural Factors in Asian Economic Growth," (Issue Editors: Manning Nash and Robert Chin), *Journal of Social Issues,* Vol. 29, No. 1 (January 1963), p. 5.

[2] Bert F. Hoselitz, *Sociological Factors in Economic Development* (Glencoe: The Free Press, 1960). Hoselitz is the founder and editor of *EDCC.*

[3] Talcott Parsons, *Structure and Process in Modern Societies* (Glencoe: The Free Press, 1960).

[4] See especially, Marion J. Levy, Jr., "Contrasting Factors in the Modernization of China and Japan," *EDCC,* Vol. 2, No. 3 (October 1953); reprinted in S. Kuznets, W. E. Moore and J. J. Spengler, eds. *Economic Growth: Brazil, India, Japan* (Durham: Duke University Press, 1955). Levy refers to a related theme in his "Some Aspects of Individualism and the Problem of Modernization in China and Japan," *EDCC,* Vol. 10, No. 3 (April 1962).

The second mode is the acculturation view of the process of development. The West (taken here as the Atlantic community of developed nations and their overseas outliers) diffuses knowledge, skills, organization, values, technology and capital to a poor nation, until over time, its society, culture and personnel become variants of that which made the Atlantic community economically successful. Examples of this line of reasoning can be found in Moore and Feldman, *Labor Commitment and Social Change in Developing Areas*[5] [which also includes essays by Nash and Hoselitz], and in Lerner's *Passing of Traditional Society*,[6] or in the many accounts of how the Soviet Union and Japan 'did it'. . . .

The third mode . . . is the analysis of the process as it is now going on in the so-called underdeveloped nations. This approach leads to a smaller scale hypothesis, to a prospective rather than a retrospective view of social change, to a full accounting of the political, social, and cultural context of development. . . .[7]

Nash's discussion of these currents in contemporary American work on economic development and cultural change is found in his introduction to a collection of essays by, among others, Everett Hagen (who first introduced his thesis in the pages of *EDCC*),[8] David McClelland (who reviewed Hagen's book in the pages of *EDCC*),[9] and John H. Kunkel (who recently discussed the third approach in *EDCC*).[10] Nash describes these authors' essays as representative of the third approach and commends them for their "dialectic of social

[5] Wilbert Moore and David Feldman, *Labor Commitment and Social Change in Developing Areas* (New York: Social Science Research Council, 1960).

[6] Daniel Lerner, *The Passing of Traditional Society: Modernizing the Middle East* (Glencoe: The Free Press, 1958).

[7] Manning Nash, *op. cit.*

[8] Everett Hagen, "The Theory of Economic Development," *EDCC*, Vol. 6, No. 3 (April 1957); also see his *On the Theory of Social Change* (Homewood: Dorsey Press, 1962).

[9] David McClelland, "A Psychological Approach to Economic Development," *EDCC,* Vol. 12, No. 3 (April 1964); and *The Achieving Society* (Princeton: Van Nostrand, 1961).

[10] John H. Kunkel, "Values and Behavior in Economic Development," *EDCC,* Vol. 13, No. 3 (April 1965).

knowledge, of confrontation of bold assertion against fact in ever bolder more elegant assertion."[11] Robert Chin, co-editor of the collection, says that these writers "are performing a pioneering service."[12]

Nash's classification, summary, and evaluation of the "only three modes of attacking the problem of social change and economic development" can serve as a useful point of departure for our own examination and evaluation of these approaches which Nash is quite mistaken in claiming that these modes exhaust the possibilities of attacking the problems of social change and economic development. He is substantially correct, however, in observing that they virtually exhaust the approaches of American social scientists to these problems of vital contemporary concern.[13]

I propose, therefore, to examine and evaluate the empirical validity, theoretical adequacy, and policy effectiveness of these three approaches to the problems of development. In terms of their relative importance, we should begin with the criterion of policy effectiveness, and then consider theoretical adequacy, and empirical validity, in that order. For if the recommended policy is ineffective, it renders suspect the theory from which it is derived; if the theory used is inadequate, it matters relatively little whether the claims made about particular aspects of reality are in fact empirically accurate. Contrary to the logic of the case, however, expository convenience leads me to begin with an examination of the empirical validity of each approach, for this permits us to fa-

[11] Manning Nash, op. cit., pp. 5–6.

[12] Robert Chin, "Preface, A New Social Issue," Journal of Social Issues, op. cit., p. iii.

[13] A still unpublished 111 page essay by Seymour Martin Lipset, "Elites, Education and Entrepreneurship in Latin America," was unfortunately not available to me in time to be included in this review. In this essay, Mr. Lipset, who is probably the most technically skillful and influential contemporary American political sociologist, masterfully constructs an interpretation of Latin American development out of all the major and most of the minor empirical, theoretical, and policy errors criticised here. Since published as Chapter 1, "Values, Education and Entrepreneurship," in Seymour M. Lipset and Aldo Solari, eds., Elites in Latin America (New York: Oxford University Press, 1967).

miliarize ourselves with the approach under review. We will then proceed to the questions of theoretical adequacy and policy effectiveness in turn.

THE IDEAL TYPICAL INDEX APPROACH

The index method is an attempt to attack the problem of economic development and cultural change through the comparative statics of polar ideal types. Referring to the approach of economists generally, and to those of the World Bank in particular, Charles Kindleberger long ago labeled this mode the gap approach: you subtract the ideal typical features or indices of underdevelopment from those of development, and the remainder is your development program.[14] We may distinguish two major variants of this ideal typical gap approach: the pattern variable approach exemplified by Hoselitz, and the historical stage approach now mostly associated with Rostow. The second variant differs from the first in that it draws on the historical experience of the developed countries to interpose stages into the gap between development and underdevelopment. A further variant of the latter, the historical variations approach of Gerschenkron, which is not examined here, draws on this same historical experience to introduce the possibility of variation into the development stages of the underdeveloped countries. Common to all three variants is the assumption that underdevelopment is an original state which may be characterized by indices of traditionality, and that, therefore, development consists of abandoning these characteristics and adopting those of the developed countries.

PATTERN VARIABLES

This mode is derived not only from Max Weber's conception of the ideal type in general but also from some of Weber's

---

[14] Charles P. Kindleberger, "Review of *The Economy of Turkey; The Economic Development of Guatemala; Report on Cuba*," *Review of Economics and Statistics*, Vol. 34, No. 4 (November 1952).

particular ideal types, which were later elaborated and further systematized by Talcott Parsons. Hoselitz takes the pattern variables of Parsons' *Social System*[15] and applies them to the study of economic development and cultural change.

The pattern variables, according to the *Dictionary of Sociology*, are:

> types of choices open to purposive human beings; they are dichotomies . . . each representing polar extremes. *Universalism* and *particularism* are the names of one. In other words, any individual in a situation requiring choice in his relationships with others must ask himself if he is going to act in terms of a universally accepted precept or one particular to the situation in which he finds himself. Is he going to act according to rule or in terms of particular qualities of the person towards whom he is orienting his action. Another set is termed *achievement* and *ascription* (sometimes referred to as *performance* and *quality*) and here a person in deciding how to act focuses his attention on either the achieved aspects of the other person, e.g., his professional qualifications, or else his ascribed qualities, e.g., sex, age, social class. . . . Yet another set is known as *specificity* and *diffuseness*, and here the choice takes into account limited and specific factors, e.g., the contrast between a contract entered into, and wider diffuse obligations such as family loyalty. . . . The point of this scheme of pattern variables is to enable the sociologist to identify the typical choices made, especially of an institutionalized kind. . . . Pattern variable analysis may be used to identify similarities and differences between cultures, or it may be restricted in use to refer to aspects of society, to sub-systems of an institutionalized kind, such as political systems . . . —Jeffrey Duncan Mitchell, *Dictionary of Sociology* (London: Routledge and Kegan Paul, 1967), pp. 130–31.

Hoselitz first advanced his theory in 1953 under the title

---

[15] Talcott Parsons, *The Social System* (Glencoe: The Free Press, 1951).

"Social Structure and Economic Growth;"[16] and he repeated the same thesis again (more penetratingly, he says in a footnote) in 1963 under the title "Social Stratification and Economic Development."[17] He argues that developed countries exhibit the pattern variables of universalism, achievement orientation, and functional specificity, while underdeveloped ones are characterized by their opposites—particularism, ascription, and functional diffuseness. To develop, Hoselitz counsels, underdeveloped countries should eliminate the pattern variables of underdevelopment and adopt those of development. It may be added that *EDCC* has devoted many pages to the diffusion of this approach to the study of economic development and cultural change.[18]

Empirical Validity

Hoselitz characterizes the developed countries as universalist and not particularist. They are, as we shall see, normatively universalist. Yet the reality, the literature, and even the sociological treatment of many developed countries reveal substantial particularism. This is specifically the case for

[16] Bert F. Hoselitz, "Social Structure and Economic Growth," *Economia Internazionale*, Vol. 6, No. 3 (August 1953); reprinted in *Sociological Factors in Economic Development, op. cit.*, chapter 2. This is not to say, of course, that this approach exhausts the work of Hoselitz, which on the contrary ranges exceptionally widely over the fields of sociology, economics, history, etc. On the other hand this part of Hoselitz' work organizes and summarizes a very wide range of work by other social scientists.

[17] Bert F. Hoselitz, "Social Stratification and Economic Development," *International Social Science Journal*, Vol. 16, No. 2 (1964).

[18] In addition to the already cited article by Levy, see for instance, "India's Cultural Values and Economic Development: A Discussion," *EDCC*, Vol. 7, No. 1 (October 1958); Clifford Geertz, "Religious Belief and Economic Behavior in a Central Japanese Town: Some Preliminary Considerations," *EDCC*, Vol. 4, No. 2 (January 1956).

Japan,[19] France,[20] and of Europe in general,[21] where the existence of particularism has been demonstrated among both upper and lower classes. Particularism is deep and widespread especially in the working class in both Europe[22] and the United States, in recent migrants from the former to the latter, and among non-white, rural, or recent rural-urban migrant groups in the United States. Moreover, much of what flies a universalist flag in the United States and other developed countries is little more than the cover for unsavory particularist private interests. We will have occasion below to observe that the developed countries export particularism to the underdeveloped ones, wrapped in such universalist slogans as freedom, democracy, justice, the common good, the economic liberalism of free trade, the political liberalism of free elections, the social liberalism of free social mobility, and the cultural liberalism of free flow of ideas such as the ones we are examining here.[23]

Hoselitz also characterizes developed countries as achievement oriented. To examine the counterpart of this pattern variable in reality, it is important to divide it into three subvariables: reward, recruitment, and motivation. In the United States, reward within roles is indeed substantially dependent on achievement. But recruitment into roles, although perhaps substantially a matter of achievement among the middle classes, is very much based on ascription in both the high levels of business management, as Granick has shown in his

[19] James Abegglen, *The Japanese Factory* (Glencoe: The Free Press, 1958).

[20] Nicole Delefortrie-Soubeyroux, *Les dirigeants de l'industrie française* (Paris: Armand Colin, 1961).

[21] David Granick, *The European Executive* (Garden City: Doubleday, 1962).

[22] Ferdynand Zweig, *The British Worker* (Harmondsworth: Penguin Books, 1952); *The Worker in an Affluent Society: Family Life and Industry* (London: Heinemann, 1962); Raymond Williams, *Culture and Society 1780–1950,* (Harmondsworth: Penguin Books, 1961).

[23] Frederick Clairmonte, *Economic Liberalism and Underdevelopment—Studies in the Disintegration of an Idea* (Bombay and London: Asia Publishing House, 1960).

comparison of American and Soviet management,[24] and among the masses of poor in the Other America, as Michael Harrington has so dramatically demonstrated. The ascription of roles, and the consequent reward, to the American Negro speaks silently and eloquently for itself through his contemporary Freedom Movement. Harrington shows, moreover, that far from becoming less ascriptive, American Society, both at the top and at the bottom (and perhaps also in the middle), is becoming progressively more ascriptive.[25]

On the other hand, role recruitment in Japan is very much based on achievement, as Abegglen among others has pointed out.[26] However, the assignment of reward within the role, Abegglen argues, is highly ascriptive, being based on such factors as age, family obligations, etc. The important distinction between recruitment and reward (rarely made in discussions of achievement or ascription) and the obvious differences between Japanese and American practices in this respect would seem to explain a large part of the disagreement on this matter. For example, Bellah[27] and Levy,[28] who emphasize Japan's achievement orientation as a cause of its development, refer to role recruitment. On the other hand, Abegglen,[29] who emphasizes Japan's ascriptive pattern is apparently thinking of reward within roles. The other achievement variable, individual achievement motivation or n(eed for) achievement as David McClelland[30] calls it, while increasingly confused with the Weberian category of social role assignment and reward, is quite another matter and will be discussed when we come to examine the third mode.

[24] David Granick, *The Red Executive* (Garden City: Doubleday, 1960).

[25] Michael Harrington, *The Other America, Poverty in the U. S.* (New York: Macmillan, 1963); Gabriel Kolko, *Wealth and Power in America, an Analysis of Social Class and Income Distribution* (New York: Praeger, 1962).

[26] James Abegglen, *op. cit.*

[27] Robert Bellah, *Tokugawa Religion* (Glencoe: The Free Press, 1957).

[28] Marion J. Levy, *op. cit.*

[29] James Abegglen, *op. cit.*

[30] David McClelland, *The Achieving Society, op. cit.*

Thirdly, Hoselitz claims that in developed societies roles are functionally specific rather than diffuse, and that role specificity helps generate development while role diffuseness does the contrary. To assess this claim, we must first question the relevance of the specificity-diffuseness dichotomy to the structure of interaction which is being examined. Is it useful to distinguish the structure of interaction between ego and alter that is normatively defined in one diffuse role as a complex father-son, teacher-student, general-soldier, etc., relationship, from the structure of interaction in functionally specific roles which are integrated in such a way that ego is systematically father, teacher, general, etc., and alter is son, student, soldier, etc.? In a word, how important is the difference between role specificity and role diffuseness if the socially significant and dominant specific roles are collected together in one or a few individuals who wear many hats simultaneously or in quick and institutionalized succession? For the latter is the "functionally specific" role structure of the society in which, according to C. Wright Mills, the power elite dominates what President Eisenhower dubbed the military-industrial complex, and in which Douglas Dillon of Dillon and Reed & Co., comes to sit in the cabinet as Secretary of the Treasury; Robert McNamara, President of the Ford Motor Company, becomes Secretary of Defense—as successor to "Engine Charley" Wilson, who gave us the *bon mot*, "What's good for General Motors is good for the country;" and in which the bulk of military purchases are from a half dozen giant corporations who employ large numbers of retired high level military officers.[31]

Our own profession is not as isolated from this role structure as Hoselitz' characterization of role specificity might suggest: Roosevelt's and Kennedy's brain trusts co-opted all sorts of American social scientists. Harvard historian Arthur Schlesinger Jr.'s aid to the development of underdeveloped countries has so far consisted in writing the now famous

---

[31] C. Wright Mills, *The Power Elite* (New York: Oxford University Press, 1956); Fred J. Cook, *The Warfare State* (New York: Macmillan, 1962); also see Tristan Coffin, *The Armed Society* (Baltimore: Penguin Books, 1964).

White Paper on Cuba which was intended to justify the coming invasion of that country at the Bay of Pigs. He later admitted lying about the invasion in "the national interest." Stanford economist Eugene Staley wrote *The Future of Underdeveloped Countries*[32] and then planned it in the renowned Staley—(General Maxwell) Taylor Plan to put 15 million Vietnamese in the concentration camps they euphemistically christened "strategic hamlets." Since the failure of that effort at development planning, M.I.T. economic historian Walt Whitman Rostow has escalated the effort by writing *The Stages of Economic Growth: A Non-Communist Manifesto*.[33] He wrote of these stages at the CIA financed Center for International Studies on the Charles River and has been operationalizing them on the Potomac as President Kennedy's Director of Policy and Planning in the State Department and President Johnson's chief adviser on Vietnam. It is on behalf of Vietnamese economic growth that Rostow has become the principal architect of escalation, from napalming the south to bombing the North, and beyond. Then, doubtlessly due to universalist particularism and achieved ascription, Eugene Rostow moves from professing international law at Yale University to practicing it at his brother's side in Washington. Meanwhile, after performing his role as Dean of Humanities at Harvard University, McGeorge Bundy becomes W. W. Rostow's superior in Washington and goes on television to explain to the misguided and incredulous why this economic development theory and policy is humanitarian (after which he goes on to direct the Ford Foundation and

[32] Eugene Staley, *The Future of Underdeveloped Countries* (New York: Harper, 1964).

[33] Walt Whitman Rostow, *The Stages of Economic Growth, A Non-Communist Manifesto* (Cambridge: Cambridge University Press, 1962). The recent *New York Times* profile of Rostow observes: "Since McGeorge Bundy and Bill D. Moyers left the White House, Mr. Rostow, a former professor at the Massachusetts Institute of Technology, has been emerging as the White House spokesman on foreign affairs. . . . He now organizes and attends the President's Tuesday luncheon conferences. Secretary of State Dean Rusk, Secretary of Defense Robert S. McNamara and the White House Press Secretary, George Christian, are usually the only other guests." *New York Times,* April 13, 1967.

its influence on education and research). In the light of the manifest and institutionalized role summation and diffuseness of these deans of humane scholarship and professors of applied social science, the clandestine direction of Project Camelot by the Department of Defense and the financing of the United States National Student Association by the CIA pale into the shadows.

However, Hoselitz' and my concern is with the economic development and cultural change of the *underdeveloped countries.* It is therefore more important to examine the reality of underdevelopment and Hoselitz' ideal typical mischaracterization of it. Hoselitz characterizes the underdeveloped countries as particularist rather than universalist. Yet normatively, underdeveloped countries are also substantially universalist. A glance at the press, radio, and much of the educational ideology of any underdeveloped country exhibits just as much universalism as do their counterparts in the developed ones. Mexico's most influential newspaper publishes more column inches about the "universalist" United States than the *New York Times* does about the whole world outside of the United States; and one American magazine, the *Reader's Digest,* which excels in getting across the American "universalist" norms and ideology, has a higher circulation in Mexico than the eight largest Mexican magazines combined.[34] What makes Hoselitz right in a sense is that this kind of universalism goes no deeper in the underdeveloped countries than it does in the developed ones; for there too it is, instead, a cover for underlying particularism. On the other hand, there are forms of universalism in the underdeveloped countries apart from the superficial façade of the particularly interested organs of public opinion formation. There are general and political strikes, decried by so many of these same observers from the developed countries; militant nationalism, which the same observers frown upon as opposed to the universal good and therefore to the particular one of this or that underdeveloped country; and widespread support in under-

[34] Pablo González Casanova, *La Democracia en México* (Mexico: Era, 1965), p. 202.

developed countries for the anti-colonial and anti-neocolonial movements, which the developed countries are combatting by force of arms and universalistic sounding propaganda about freedom, etc., in Vietnam, Malaysia, the Congo, the Dominican Republic and elsewhere. This evidence suggests that universalism is after all quite widespread and deeply ingrained in the underdeveloped countries among groups which are not the privileged ones in command of the universalist organs of communication.

Hoselitz departs even further from reality when he says that social, economic, and political roles in the underdeveloped countries are distributed almost exclusively in terms of ascriptive norms. He specifically claims that the underdeveloped countries pay little attention to economic achievement in their determination of status and that political leadership is mainly determined by ascriptive norms.[35] Someone who had never lived in the universalist castle of American social science would be shocked to find that Hoselitz and many others characterize as ascriptive the national political leadership produced by the interminable military coups in Latin America,[36] and by the emerging "national" bourgeoisies all over Africa.[37] Yet the unreality of American popular and ostensibly scientific understanding of the world, permits Hoselitz and others to suggest that Latin American political power is in the hands of some traditional landed or even feudal oligarchy. They fail to see that in all capitalist underdeveloped countries the power behind the throne, be it military or civil, rests (if it is in national hands at all) with the

[35] Bert F. Hoselitz, "Social Stratification and Economic Development," *op. cit.*

[36] John J. Johnson, ed., *The Role of the Military in Underdeveloped Countries* (Princeton: Princeton University Press, 1962); *The Military and Society in Latin America* (Stanford: Stanford University Press, 1964); Edwin Lieuwen, *Arms and Politics in Latin America* (New York: Praeger, 1960); *Generals and Presidents, Neo-Militarism in Latin America* (New York: Praeger, 1964).

[37] Frantz Fanon, *Les damnés de la terre* (Paris: Maspero, 1961). Published and mistranslated as *The Wretched of the Earth* (New York: Grove Press, 1966).

people who occupy the top roles in the economic organization, and particularly with those who have commercial and financial ties to the developed metropolis.[38] This metropolis is increasingly the United States—precisely the vantage point from which these social scientists make their curious observations and characterizations of the underdeveloped part of the world. In supposedly ascriptive Asia, Africa, and Latin America, many present incumbents of these top economic and political roles have achieved their positions, and done so quite recently—often more so than in the achievement oriented developed countries of Europe and North America.[39] Thus, role assignment in the economically and politically most significant roles in underdeveloped countries is decidedly achieved and not ascribed.

It should be pointed out, however, that role assignment by achievement is also common among the lower level roles in the underdeveloped countries. This has been the case at least since mercantilist and capitalist penetration totally transformed these societies, often centuries ago. Only the social scientists from the invading metropolis seem unable to see how efficiently this penetration integrated these societies into the dominant world system and how universally the latter imposed its social organization and alienation on the people whom Frantz Fanon has called the damned of the earth.[40]

Evidently, the distribution of rewards in underdeveloped countries, at least in high level roles, is also determined by

[38] José Luis Ceceña, *El Capital Monopolista y la Economía de México* (Mexico: Cuadernos Americanos, 1963); Ricardo Lagos, *La Concentración del Poder Económico en Chile* (Santiago: Editorial del Pacífico, 1961); Carlos Malpica, *Guerra a la Muerte al Latifundio* (Lima: Ediciones Voz Rebelde, 1963); Jacinto Oddone, *La Burguesía Terrateniente Argentina* (Buenos Aires: Populares Argentinas).

[39] See for instance, José Luis de Imaz, *Los que Mandan* (Buenos Aires: EUDEBA, 1964).

[40] Frantz Fanon, *op. cit.* The degree of capitalist penetration of underdeveloped countries was observed long ago by Rosa Luxemburg in *The Accumulation of Capital* (New York: Monthly Review Press, 1964), especially Section Three, pp. 329–467. I have explored the same in *Capitalism and Underdevelopment in Latin America, op. cit.*

achievement, as Hoselitz uses that term. In the monopolistic underdeveloped economies, even more than in the developed ones, financial success is determined by successful speculation and extortion, and the resulting distribution of income is even more unequal. This suggests that, contrary to what Hoselitz says, ascription counts less, and achievement more, in the distribution of reward in the underdeveloped countries.[41] (This assumes that we may call this sort of success "achievement" by our universalist standards, which the present author would not wish to do.)

Finally, Hoselitz says that roles in underdeveloped countries are functionally diffuse rather than specific. This is true in part. The poor in the underdeveloped countries, whether classified as working in the primary, secondary, or tertiary sector, do indeed practice many professions at a time, such as farmer, trader, peddler, artisan, odd jobber, thief, and provider of social security to others, in the attempt to keep body and soul together.[42] The roles at the other end of the socioeconomic scale are no less diffuse. One need only read the daily press or suffer the consequences of monopoly control in underdeveloped countries to know that the controlling roles are indeed diffuse, as Hoselitz suggests, and also that economic roles predominate in that control, as Hoselitz denies. On the other hand, it is also well to observe that a whole series of intermediate roles in underdeveloped societies, occupied by such members of the middle classes as military officers, government bureaucrats, junior executives, administrators, policemen, and others, are functionally quite specific. Their incumbents serve specific functions of making the whole exploitative system function in the diffuse but particular interest of those who have achieved control, in the same sense that the plantation administrator runs the owner's slave plantation for him. It is perhaps not surprising that it is among

[41] United Nations Economic Commission for Latin America, *The Economic Development of Latin America in the Post-War Period* (New York: United Nations, 1963) E/CN.12/659.

[42] United Nations Economic Commission for Latin America, *The Social Development of Latin America during the Post-War Period* (New York: United Nations, 1963) E/CN.12/660.

precisely these middle role incumbents that universalist values are predominant.[43]

In a word, if we examine the patterns of social roles in the developed and underdeveloped countries, instead of being blinded by a hand-me-down ideal typical perspective of adulterated Weberian parentage, we conclude that the characteristics Hoselitz and others attribute to developed and underdeveloped countries present a distorted and inadequate conception of social reality. This is, however, the least of the deficiencies of Hoselitz' and allied approaches to economic development and cultural change. That it is so easy to challenge the empirical validity of Hoselitz' conception of development and underdevelopment—that Hoselitz can find some particularism, ascription, and diffuseness in underdeveloped countries, whereas we can easily find universalism, achievement, and specificity there—already suggests that probably neither the one nor the other of the patterns of variables Hoselitz selects for emphasis is important for characterizing, or crucial for determining, either development or underdevelopment. It raises the suspicion that the important determining factors of development and underdevelopment are not these but others: that is, the theoretical adequacy of Hoselitz' whole approach is cast in doubt.

Theoretical Adequacy

Having disposed of the empirical validity of Hoselitz' claims, we may examine the theoretical adequacy of his thesis in terms of, first, his selection of roles for study; second, his se-

---

[43] Theodore R. Crevanna, ed., *Materiales para el Estudio de la Clase Media en América Latina* (Washington: Unión Panamericana, 6 volumes, 1950–51); Marshall Wolfe, *Las Clases Medias en Centro-América: Características que Presentan en la Actualidad y Requisitos para su Desarrollo* (New York: United Nations) E/CN.12/CCE/Rev. 2; and United Nations, *The Social Development of Latin America, op. cit.;* John L. Johnson, *Political Change in Latin America: The Emergence of the Middle Sectors* (Stanford: Stanford University Press, 1958).

lection of a social system for analysis; and third, and most important, his treatment of the social structure of development and underdevelopment.

It may be best to begin by asking how Hoselitz and I can characterize the pattern of variables or roles in underdeveloped countries so differently. Part of the answer will be found in the difference between the roles we deem important for underdevelopment and development. It appears that in Hoselitz' analysis all roles have about the same weight in characterizing and determining underdevelopment. Thus Hoselitz' prescription for development is that the maximum number of roles, almost irrespective of which they are, change from being particularist, ascriptive, and diffuse, and become universalist, achievement based, and functionally specific. The greater this quantitative change of roles from one pattern to the other, it would seem, the greater the development. My review, on the other hand, has lent more emphasis to roles at the top and some at the bottom of the economic and political stratification systems, because they are more important for development than just roles-in-general.

If social roles do not all carry the same weight or importance for development and underdevelopment, as they evidently do not, then it is not legitimate to assign them the same weights in theory. If, like Hoselitz, we construct ideal type role patterns for development and underdevelopment (a dubious procedure to begin with) then in constructing the ideal-type we must surely assign more weight to the roles that in fact are more important for development or underdevelopment, even if they be less numerous. Yet in his characterization of both developed and underdeveloped societies, Hoselitz systematically evades the specific examination of the top economic and political roles. If Hoselitz lent these roles the weight they clearly have in the determination of development or underdevelopment, he would be unable to characterize as universalist, achievement based, and functionally specific a society in which the power elite of the industrial-governmental-military complex pursues particularist ends; or to characterize as particularist, ascriptive, and functionally diffuse those countries which are governed by oligarchies with economic, political, and military power that is derived from commercial monopoly privileges and the recurrent recourse to force of arms to protect and augment them. Still less would he be able to rest his theoretical case for development and underdevelopment on this empirical base.

Secondly, we may ask what social universe Hoselitz has in mind when he says that development is characterized by some pattern variables and underdevelopment by others. Hoselitz and many others associate particularism, ascription, and diffuseness in underdevelopment with the extended family, the primitive tribe, the folk community, the traditional sector of a dual society, and with the underdeveloped countries and part of the world in general. But the connection is never made with the developed part of the world nor with the contemporarily dominant social organization in the world taken as a whole. Indeed, he seems to be indifferent about where change should take place, since in discussing underdevelopment he moves quite easily and almost imperceptibly from referring to one of these units to talking about another (although never, of course, to the last two). Hoselitz leaves far from clear just which is the social whole whose role patterns he would change from one set of variables to another in order to effect development. Here the theoretical inadequacy is even more glaring, for it contravenes the generally accepted rule of social and all scientific theory to look for and refer to the systemic whole in terms of which the reality (in this case underdevelopment) can be explained and changed. The social system which is today the determinant of underdevelopment certainly is not the family, tribe, community, a part of a dual society, or even, as I shall argue below, any underdeveloped country or countries taken by themselves.

The folk characteristics which were studied by Robert Redfield, and which Hoselitz seems to associate with the pattern variables of underdeveloped society, do not characterize any whole society existing today. At best, they may characterize "tribal societies," few if any of which still remain independent. Redfield himself only spoke in terms of a nontribal folk society when he first studied Yucatan and Tepotzlan, and even then he entitled his book *The Folk Culture of Yucatan*.[44] When he later began to concentrate his attention on *Peasant Society and Culture*,[45] Redfield took great pains to point out that peasants with folk characteristics live only in *parts* of societies inasmuch as they are peasants only by virtue of their relation to the city, whose function complements theirs within the same wider social whole that incorporates them both. Furthermore, in his study of the Guatemalan peasant community, Cantel,[46] Manning Nash himself pointed out that the appearance of the universalist, achievement oriented, and functionally specific characteristics associated with labor unionism—and their renewed disappearance after the 1954 military coup of which John Foster Dulles was so proud—must be traced beyond the boundaries of the community to the national system. In view of the well known source of that military coup we might add that it should be traced further to the functioning and structure of the international system, which is never mentioned by Hoselitz, but of which Cantel, Guatemala, and all their inhabitants form integral if unhappily determined parts. Therefore, it is not a matter of empirical, theoretical, or policy indifference just which social system is selected for study and change with a view to promoting economic development. Hoselitz' selection is empirically unacceptable because he does not choose to study the system whose characteristics are the determinant ones for development and underdevelopment. Hoselitz' procedure is theoretically unsatisfactory because he does not address himself to the determinant social whole as Redfield counseled that social scientists must do.[47]

Thirdly, Hoselitz' treatment of economic development and

[44] Robert Redfield, *The Folk Culture of Yucatan* (Chicago: University of Chicago Press, 1941); "The Folk Society," *American Journal of Sociology,* Vol. 52, No. 4 (January 1941).

[45] Robert Redfield, *The Little Community and Peasant Society and Culture* (Chicago: University of Chicago Press, 1960); also see *The Primitive World and its Transformations* (Ithaca: Cornell University Press, 1955).

[46] Manning Nash, *Machine Age Maya* (Glencoe: The Free Press, 1958).

[47] Robert Redfield, *The Little Community, op. cit.*

cultural change is unsatisfactory on still more important theoretical grounds: his analysis belies its own title, "Social Structure and Economic Growth," by neglecting structure and especially the structure of underdevelopment. The previously discussed empirical and theoretical shortcomings in analyses such as Hoselitz' are of course part and parcel of this neglect. However, the failure of those using this approach to take adequate account of structure is of such far reaching importance that it requires more specific commentary of its own.

Hoselitz follows the lead of Talcott Parsons who, to commemorate the one-hundredth anniversary of the *Communist Manifesto,* explained the theoretical significance and political consequences of his own and "modern sociological theory":

> Marx, however, tended to treat the socio-economic structure of capitalist enterprise as a single indivisible entity rather than breaking it down analytically into a set of the distinct variables involved in it. It is this analytical breakdown which is for present purposes the most distinctive feature of modern sociological analysis. . . . It results in a modification of the Marxian view. . . . The primary structural emphasis no longer falls on . . . the theory of exploitation but rather on the structure of occupational roles. . . .[48]

The felicity of Parsons' analysis of this approach has already been empirically confirmed for us by Hoselitz' aforementioned practice of confining his attention to the arithmetic sum of social roles in general, and of forgetting about the social, political, and economic structure of a particular society under study.

Herein, Parsons, Hoselitz, and recent sociological theorists in general not only modify Marx but also depart from Weber. Parsons' structuralism and holism is confined to the analysis of a wholly abstract model of any and all real or imaginary societies and not with the study of any existing real society. However much Marx and Weber may have relied on theoretical models and ideal types, neither ever ventured to de-

[48] Talcott Parsons, "Social Classes and Class Conflict in the Light of Recent Sociological Theory," in *Essays in Sociological Theory* (Rev. ed.; Glencoe: The Free Press, 1954), p. 324.

part so far from reality. Other recent sociological theorists, mostly social anthropologists of the British structural-functionalist school, who have devoted themselves to the study of existing whole societies, fall short of the standards of classical sociology in other ways. They select small "societies" in Africa and elsewhere for study and analyze them as though they had an isolated existence independent from the imperialist system of which they formed an integral part at the time of study. Hoselitz abandons classical sociology and carries recent sociology still further. He leaves behind the structural holism of Parsons because it is not suited to any but abstract wholes. Yet he does not join the anthropologists on their field trips to study the social structure of social "wholes." Hoselitz is satisfied to abandon both holism and structuralism and to devote his attention to pattern variables. The above theorists deviate further from classical theory, which is a most serious handicap for those who would study economic development and cultural change. "Modern sociological theory" at best appeals to holism and structuralism to explain the existence of the parts, or merely to demonstrate the relations among them, but not to analyze or account for the existence of the social structure as a whole. Consequently, these theorists, who pretend to analyze economic *development* and cultural *change*, fail to direct their theoretical analysis to the past origins, the present transformations, or the future prospects of the existing social system as a system.

Yet Hoselitz and, as we shall see, also the advocates of the second and third modes of analysis all take another step beyond Parsons—and far beyond what would have occurred to Weber in his moments of wildest fancy. They argue that to eliminate underdevelopment and produce development it is only necessary to change particular variables, roles, or parts of the social system—that it is not necessary to change the structure of the system itself. Logically, Hoselitz and others can take this position only if they maintain one or the other of the following: (1) that underdevelopment and development are associated only with the characteristics of the simple majority of the society's roles, and not with the structure of that society; or (2) granted that development and underdevelopment are associated with the structure of the social system, the system's structure can be changed simply by changing some of its parts or their characteristics. The first violates all standards of social scientific theory; the second is contrary to all empirical reality.

The importance of the empirical and theoretical deficiency of the approach of Hoselitz and others cannot be stressed too much. The empirical evidence which has been discussed reveals that this criticism of Hoselitz' and related analyses on theoretical grounds is not based on an isolated appeal to arbitrary theoretical standards. That is, the weight of the scientific standards which such analyses fail to meet lies not so much in their universal acceptance as it does in their realism and efficacy: if Hoselitz and others had guided their observations and analyses of economic development and cultural change by these standards of structuralism and holism, they could not have come to the empirically erroneous conclusion that ascriptive role assignment in general is keeping underdeveloped countries underdeveloped. They would have seen not only that the crucial political and economic roles in underdeveloped countries are assigned and rewarded by achievement—which is the least of it, since it is not, after all, ascription or achievement which is really important—but also that these roles and their incumbents are no more than some of the manifestations of the real structure of development and underdevelopment of a world embracing system that gives rise to these roles and whose incumbents in turn serve to maintain the system and underdevelopment in particular.

Policy Effectiveness

Three examples may suffice to indicate that Hoselitz' policy prescriptions do not lead to the consequences he predicts. First, the existence, or the increase, if we would believe C. Wright Mills[49] or William H. Whyte,[50] of role ascription

---

[49] C. Wright Mills, *The Power Elite, op. cit.*
[50] William H. Whyte, Jr., *The Organization Man* (New York: Simon and Schuster, 1956).

and diffuseness in business, government, and military circles in the United States has not so far turned that country into an underdeveloped one. A second piece of evidence is that the supposed achievement of functionally specific roles and pursuit of universal standards among, for instance, the business magnates and their military executors in Latin America has not so far developed their countries and still gives no signs of doing so.

Although perhaps not the most important one, a third piece of evidence against Hoselitz' thesis is particularly interesting because it is supplied by Hoselitz himself. As we saw above, Hoselitz' pattern variables of development are associated particularly with the rise of the middle classes; and such students of Latin America as John Johnson[51] in the United States and Gino Germani[52] in Argentina, among many others, have argued that the greater the social mobility and the bigger the middle class, the more development. Yet Hoselitz recently took the initiative to test this thesis by confronting it with the hard facts of reality in Latin America. There he found and wrote that the countries with the largest middle classes, Argentina and Chile, are not at all the ones with the most development.[53]

Three things however are true of middle classes in Latin America. First, their social pattern closely corresponds to the one to which Hoselitz wishes to attribute economic development and cultural change. Secondly, as in Nazi Germany and Fascist Italy, it is precisely these groups which provide the principal "popular" support for the ultrareactionary military dictatorships, as these groups again demonstrated in an im-

[51] John J. Johnson, *Political Change in Latin America, op. cit.*; "The Political Role of the Latin American Middle Sectors," *The Annals of the American Academy of Political and Social Science*, Vol. 334 (March 1961).

[52] Gino Germani, *Política y Sociedad en una Epoca de Transición* (Buenos Aires: Paidós, 1962); *Política e Massa* (Belo Horizonte: Publicações de Revista Brasileira de Estudos Politicos, 1960).

[53] Bert F. Hoselitz, "Economic Growth in Latin America," *Contributions to the First International Conference in Economic History*, Stockholm 1960 (The Hague: Mouton & Co., 1960).

pressively manifest fashion in the 1964 military coup in Brazil.[54] A third fact, which is not unrelated to the foregoing one or to the unviability of the development prescriptions of Hoselitz, Johnson, Germani, and others, is that throughout the underdeveloped countries (as well as in the United States as Gabriel Kolko has recently shown[55]), when the income of these middle classes rises it does so not at the expense of the rich but at the expense of the large masses of the poor, whose relative and often absolute income in the underdeveloped countries is thereby forced still lower.[56] Economic development and cultural change of an underdeveloped country through the promotion and rise of the middle classes (or their pattern variables) has not occurred because, among other reasons, it is physically impossible for it to occur given the structure of the system: it only leads to the further underdevelopment of the majority.

STAGES OF GROWTH

Within the first ideal typical mode, which Nash calls the index mode and which I call the gap approach, we may distinguish a second variant. Here the identification of the gap between the characteristics of development and underdevelopment includes the specification of intermediate stages and their characteristics. Although Nash mentioned Rostow in connection with his earlier work on development propensities,[57] it is preferable to take Rostow's *Stages of Economic Growth* as the example of this variant of the first mode. My

[54] André Gunder Frank, "Brazil; The Goulart Ouster," *The Nation* (New York), April 27, 1964; reprinted as chapter 22 of André Gunder Frank, *Latin America: Underdevelopment or Revolution* (New York: Monthly Review Press, 1969).

[55] Gabriel Kolko, *Wealth and Power in America, op. cit.*

[56] Anibal Pinto, "Concentración del Progreso Técnico y de sus Frutos en el Desarrollo Latinoamericano," *El Trimestre Económico*, Vol. 32, No. 125 (January–March 1965). See also his *Chile: Una Economia Difícil* (Mexico: Fondo de Cultura, 1965).

[57] Walt Whitman Rostow, *The Process of Economic Growth* (New York: Norton, 1952).

review and evaluation of Rostow's and similar "stage" approaches will require less space because first, much of the criticism already made of Hoselitz applies to them as well and, second, Rostow's stages have already come in for much specific criticism from others.[58] Nonetheless, I submit that Rostow's *Stages of Economic Growth* deserves more fundamental criticism on empirical, theoretical, and policy grounds than it has thus far received.

According to Rostow,

It is possible to identify all societies, in their economic dimensions, as lying within five categories: the traditional society, the preconditions for take-off, the take-off, the drive to maturity, and the age of high mass-consumption. First, the traditional society. A traditional society is one whose structure is developed within limited production functions, based on pre-Newtonian science and technology, and on pre-Newtonian attitudes towards the physical world. . . . The second stage of growth embraces societies in the process of transition; that is, the period when the preconditions for take-off are developed; for it takes time to transform a traditional society in the ways necessary for it to exploit the fruits of modern science, to fend off diminishing returns, and thus to enjoy the blessings and choices opened up by the march of compound interest. . . . the stage of preconditions arise[s] not endogenously but from some external intrusion by more advanced societies. . . . We come now to the great watershed in the life of modern societies: the third stage in this sequence, the take-off. The

[58] Most of the criticism of Rostow's book has, however, been superficial and largely limited to quibbling about details in the characterization of his stages. This superficiality is notably evident in the "Appraisals and Critiques" of "The Rostow Doctrine" by Meier, Kuznets, Cairncross, Habakkuk, and Gerschenkron in *Leading Issues in Development Economics,* ed. Gerald Meier (New York: Oxford University Press, 1964). It is revealing of the narrowness of American economics that Meier, whose book has been very favorably reviewed for its purported breadth of issues and appraisals did not include the probably most penetrating criticism of Rostow so far by Paul A. Baran and Eric Hobsbawm, "The Stages of Economic Growth," *Kyklos* (Basel), Vol. 14, Fasc. 2 (1961).

take-off is the interval when the old blocks and resistances to steady growth are finally overcome. The forces making for economic progress, which yielded limited bursts and enclaves of modern activity, expand and come to dominate the society. Growth becomes its normal condition. Compound interest becomes built, as it were, into its habits and institutional structure. . . . [The] take-off is defined as requiring all three of the following related conditions: (1) a rise in the rate of productive investment from, say, 5 percent or less to over 10 percent of national income (or net national product (NNP)); (2) the development of one or more substantial manufacturing sectors, with a high rate of growth; (3) the existence or quick emergence of a political, social and institutional framework which exploits the impulses to expansion . . .[59]

Rostow's stages and thesis are incorrect primarily because they do not correspond at all to the past or present reality of the underdeveloped countries whose development they are supposed to guide. It is explicit in Rostow, as it is implicit in Hoselitz, that underdevelopment is the original stage of what are supposedly traditional societies—that there were no stages prior to the present stage of underdevelopment. It is further explicit in Rostow that the now developed societies were once underdeveloped. But all this is quite contrary to fact. This entire approach to economic development and cultural change attributes a history to the developed countries but denies all history to the underdeveloped ones. The countries that are today underdeveloped evidently have had a history no less than have the developed ones. None of them, for example India,[60] is today the way it was centuries or even decades ago. Moreover, reference to even any schoolboy world history confirms that the history of the now underdeveloped

[59] W. W. Rostow, *The Stages of Economic Growth,* pp. 4, 6, 7, 39.

[60] R. Palme Dutt, *India Today and Tomorrow* (London: Lawrence & Wishart, 1955); A. R. Desai, *Social Background of Indian Nationalism* (Bombay: Popular Book Depot, 1959); Jawaharlal Nehru, *The Discovery of India* (New York: John Day, 1946); V. B. Singh, *Indian Economy Yesterday and Today* (New Delhi: People's Publishing House, 1964).

countries has been most intimately related to the history of the now developed ones for at least several centuries.

Indeed, the economic and political expansion of Europe since the fifteenth century has come to incorporate the now underdeveloped countries into a single stream of world history, which has given rise simultaneously to the present development of some countries and the present underdevelopment of others. However, in their attempt to construct theory and policy for the underdeveloped countries, Rostow and others have examined the developed countries as if they had developed in isolation from this stream of world history. It stands to reason that any serious attempt to construct theory and policy for the development of the now underdeveloped countries has to be based on the examination of the experience of the underdeveloped countries themselves—that is, on the study of their history and of the world historical process which has made these countries underdeveloped. Yet this task of constructing a realistic theory and policy of development has not been pursued by any of the students of economic development and cultural change who employ the modes of approach to the problem which, according to Nash, exhaust all possibilities. We see again, then, that these three approaches to studying and solving the problems of economic development and cultural change only exhaust what is done; but they do not exhaust what can be done, and least of all what must be done.

It is impossible, without closing one's eyes, to find in the world today any country or society which has the characteristics of Rostow's first, the traditional, stage. This is not surprising since the construction of Rostow's stages takes account neither of the history of the now underdeveloped countries, nor of their crucial relations with the now developed ones over several centuries past. Rostow's approach obliterates the fact that through these relations, the now developed countries have totally destroyed the pre-existing fabric of these societies (be it "traditional" or not). This was most notably the case in India which was de-industrialized;[61] Africa, where the slave trade transformed society long before colonialism

[61] *Ibid.*

did so again;[62] and Latin America, where the high civilizations of the Incas and the Aztecs were wiped out altogether.[63] The relationship between the mercantilist and capitalist metropolis and these colonies succeeded in supplanting the pre-existing—or, in the case of the *tabula rasa* situations of Argentina, Brazil, the West Indies and elsewhere, in implanting —the social, political, and economic structure they now have: that is, the structure of underdevelopment.[64]

This long relationship between the now underdeveloped and now developed countries within the same historical process did not affect only the export enclave in the underdeveloped countries, as the almost universally accepted and just as empirically and theoretically erroneous "dual" society or economy thesis has it.[65] On the contrary, this historical relationship transformed the entire social fabric of the peoples whose countries are now underdeveloped, just as in the developed countries.[66] (I shall return to this problem of the dual society or economy in the section on diffusionism below.)

[62] Basil Davidson, *The African Slave Trade* (Boston: Atlantic-Little, Brown, 1961); and Jack Woddis, *Africa, The Roots of Revolt* (London: Lawrence & Wishart, 1960).

[63] Eric Wolf, *Sons of the Shaking Earth* (Chicago: University of Chicago Press, 1959).

[64] Sergio Bagú, *Economía de la Sociedad Colonial. Ensayo de Historia Comparada de America* (Buenos Aires: Ateneo, 1949); Celso Furtado, *The Economic Growth of Brazil* (Berkeley: University of California Press, 1963); Aldo Ferrer, *The Argentinian Economy. An Economic History of Argentina* (Berkeley: University of California Press, 1967); Anibal Pinto Santa Cruz, *Chile, Un Caso de Desarrollo Frustrado* (Santiago: Editorial Universitaria, 1958); André Gunder Frank, *Capitalism and Underdevelopment in Latin America, op. cit.;* Ramiro Guerra y Sanchez, *Sugar and Society in the Caribbean* (New Haven: Yale University Press, 1964).

[65] J. H. Boeke, *Economics and Economic Policy of Dual Societies* (New York: Institute of Pacific Relations, 1953); Jacques Lambert, *Os Dois Brasis* (Rio de Janeiro: Ministerio da Educação e Cultura, n. d.). See also footnote 121.

[66] Paul A. Baran, *The Political Economy of Growth* (New York: Monthly Review Press, 1957); André Gunder Frank, *Capitalism and Underdevelopment in Latin America, op. cit.* See also footnote 120.

If Rostow's first, traditional, stage cannot be found in any underdeveloped country today, his second stage, which contains the pre-conditions for take-off into economic development, is even more conspicuous by its absence. Characteristic of Rostow's second stage is the penetration of underdeveloped countries by influences created abroad—mostly in the developed countries—and diffused to the underdeveloped ones, where they destroy traditionalism and simultaneously create the pre-conditions that will lead to the subsequent take-off in the third stage. (This, too, is examined in the section on diffusionism.) The factual error of the second stage in Rostow's thesis is so glaring that it may be discussed briefly. As we observed with respect to the first stage, the now underdeveloped Asian, African, and Latin American parts of the world, even if they were traditional in the Rostowian sense before their contact with Europe—a dubious thesis, considering the high civilizations and technological development that had been achieved on all three continents—certainly have been and still are affected by conditions in, and penetrated by influences emanating from, the now developed metropolis. Yet these same metropolitan conditions and influences, which already have a history ranging from one to several centuries, have not brought about economic development, or even led to a take-off into development, in a single one of the "75 countries," as they came to be called in the 1964 Geneva Conference on World Trade and Development.

This Conference was called because the nearly two-thirds of the world's population living in these countries feel and know that these metropolitan imposed second stage conditions, far from furthering their economic development as Rostow and other metropolitan pundits claim, not only hinder their economic development, but even increase their underdevelopment.[67] The reason for all this is that the reality of underdevelopment, which Rostow's first and second stages obscure and even deny, is that the incorporation of these

[67] See United Nations Conference on World Trade and Development (Geneva: 1964); U. N. Document Series, E/CONF. 46, and especially the Report by the Secretary-General cited in footnote 92.

lands and peoples into the expanding mercantilist and then capitalist world system first initiated their underdevelopment; that, furthermore, their continued participation in this same system still maintains and even aggravates that underdevelopment.[68] As Prime Minister Jawaharlal Nehru said, in his *The Discovery of India,*

> . . . nearly all our major problems today have grown up during British rule and as a direct result of British policy: the princes; the minority problem; various vested interests, foreign and Indian; the lack of industry and the neglect of agriculture; the extreme backwardness in the social services; and, above all, the tragic poverty of the people.[69]

Rather than countering the authority of Rostow and most of his colleagues from the developed countries only with an appeal to the authority of Nehru and his colleagues from the underdeveloped countries, we may also appeal to empirical evidence, which is devastating for the Rostowian thesis. The evidence is from the *tabula rasa* countries that had no population at all before they were incorporated into the developing mercantilist and capitalist system. Today, more than half of both the area and the population of Latin America—especially Argentina, Uruguay, Brazil, and all of the West Indies—occupies regions which, at the time of their incorporation into the European centered mercantile system, were either entirely unpopulated or were repopulated after the rapid extermination of the pre-contact population. None of these countries ever experienced Rostow's first stage: the mercantile metropolis did not conquer and settle these regions to insti-

[68] Paul A. Baran, *The Political Economy of Growth, op. cit.;* Gunnar Myrdal, *Rich Nations and Poor* (New York: Harper & Brothers, 1957), also issued under the title *Economic Theory and Underdeveloped Regions;* Yves Lacoste, *Les pays sous-developés* (Paris: "Que Sais-Je?," France Universitaires Presses, 1959); Frantz Fanon, *Les damnés de la terre, op. cit.;* André Gunder Frank, *Capitalism and Underdevelopment in Latin America, op. cit.*

[69] Quoted in Paul Baran, *The Political Economy of Growth, op. cit.,* pp. 149–50.

tute Rostow's traditionalism, but to exploit them through the establishment of exclusively commercial mines, sugar plantations and cattle ranches. If anything, these regions and peoples entered world history by stepping right into Rostow's second stage. But after more than four centuries, Rostowian second stage conditions and contact have not led to the third stage take-off in these regions, much less to the fourth or fifth stage of development. Today these previously unpopulated regions are just as underdeveloped as are the previously populated ones which were similarly incorporated into the world embracing capitalist system. Indeed, contrary to Rostow's conception of the second stage—and, as we will see below, contrary to most of the diffusionist thesis—the more intimate the past contact of these regions with the metropolis, the more underdeveloped they are today. Among the many examples are the ex-sugar exporting regions of the Caribbean and the Brazilian Northeast and the ex-mining export regions of Minas Gerais in the center of Brazil, of Bolivia and Peru in the Andean Highlands and of the famous Zacatecas and Guanajuato mining regions in the center of Mexico.[70]

Abundant historical evidence from the underdeveloped countries shows that Rostow's first two stages are fictional. Contemporary evidence from them shows that his last two stages are utopian. After all, if these countries now were to find themselves in the fourth stage of drive toward maturity or in the fifth one of high mass consumption, we would not call them underdeveloped—and Rostow would not have to invent his stages. What is more, while in Rostow's rendition of reality his utopian last two stages are the mere mechanical summation of the fictitious first two stages plus the third, in the unfortunate reality of the underdeveloped countries it is precisely the structure of their underdevelopment—which Rostow whitewashes with his traditionalism and externally created pre-conditions—and their structural relations with the developed countries, which Rostow fails to mention at all, that have for so long prevented the realization of the last two stages. By Rostow's count, we are then left only with the

[70] Cf. Chapter 1 above.

third stage and by my count with the second crucial flaw in Rostow's entire argument.

Rostow would have us believe that in his third stage, the take-off, he has theoretically synthesized the dynamic qualitative change between the structure of underdevelopment and that of development. However, his theory is not dynamic and he does not isolate structural characteristics or change. Least of all, does he incorporate the real structure of underdevelopment and development into his theory. On the contrary, he fails to consider it altogether. Like most, but not all, stage theories of history, Rostow's is an exercise in comparative statics. While he identifies stages of development, he does not say anything about how to get from one to the other. This is no less the case for the third stage than it is for the four others. The unreality of Rostow's dynamic should not surprise us: for as we have seen, even his statics are entirely unreal; his stages correspond to no reality in the underdeveloped countries at all. How, then, could his development from one stage to another correspond to the underdeveloped world's reality?

That Rostow does not argue from structure is already suggested by the fact that he places the major burden for development in the third stage, on the mere rate of investment and growth. The conclusive evidence of the theoretical inadequacy of Rostow's stages for understanding and eliminating the structure of underdevelopment goes far beyond that, of course. In completely ignoring the history of the underdeveloped countries, Rostow necessarily completely ignores the structure of their underdevelopment. The changes in institutions and investment he posits as the take-off out of underdevelopment do not begin to affect the real structure of underdevelopment. The proof is that countries such as Argentina,[71] which Ro-

[71] Aldo Ferrer, *op. cit.;* and "Reflexiones Acerca de la Política de Estabilización en la Argentina," *El Trimestre Económico,* Vol. 30, No. 120 (October–December 1963). "Two Argentinian scholars have recently written doctoral dissertations under Professor Walt Rostow at the Massachusetts Institute of Technology, attempting to identify in the economic history of their own country his series of stages of economic growth. The period of Pre-Conditions, they thought, was completed by 1914 when the railway net was finished and the entire rich area of the Pampas had

stow claims to be taking off into development, are becoming ever more structurally underdeveloped and that, indeed, no underdeveloped country has ever managed to take off out of its underdevelopment by following Rostow's stages.

Rostow's empirical and theoretical errors extend beyond his analysis of the underdevelopment of the underdeveloped countries to his characterization of the development of the developed ones. While the developed countries are not our topic here, it is necessary at least to point out this faulty characterization of development because, like Hoselitz and others, Rostow bases so much of his policy for the underdeveloped countries on his picture of the developed ones. Rostow is particularly explicit in claiming that England was the first country to industrialize and that it did so by domestically mobilizing its own resources after having experienced certain internal structural changes. Others among the now developed countries, he says, also developed on their own except insofar as the prior development of England and others helped to create the pre-conditions for their take-off. Again, Rostow is wrong both on empirical and theoretical grounds. That England and other countries did not develop by relying only on their own efforts has been exhaustively proven. The English

---

been brought into pastoral or agricultural use. But somehow development did not follow, and the Take-Off did not occur, again by their reckoning, until 1933. What they did in this situation was to invent a wholly new stage of growth, or rather nongrowth, for the Argentinian case, which they called The Big Delay. Even their Take-Off, moreover, has not been followed by rapid progress. Writing in 1959, the experts of the United Nations Economic Commission for Latin America [said], '. . . Since the time of the great world depression . . . per capita production has increased at an average rate scarcely half the rate of the increase registered between the beginning of the century and the onset of the depression.' It appears, then, that Argentina had in fact attained a relatively high level of income by the earlier part of the century and that in more recent decades . . . the Argentine experience has been characterized by delay, stagnation, and—to take another word from the ECLA economists—'strangulation'." Carter Goodrich, "Argentina as a New Country," *Comparative Studies in History and Society,* Vol. VII (1964–65), pp. 80–81.

Mercantilists such as Thomas Mun,[72] had no doubt about it. Neither did Cantillon[73] or Marx.[74] Among our contemporaries, Earl Hamilton,[75] Eric Williams,[76] now Prime Minister of Trinidad and Tobago, and Basil Davidson,[77] have again demonstrated the crucial role played by the underdeveloped countries in financing the capitalization of the now developed ones. If the now underdeveloped countries were really to follow the stages of growth of the now developed ones, they would have to find still other peoples to exploit into underdevelopment, as the now developed countries did before them.

This misrepresentation of reality by Rostow must, of course, lead to (or does it follow from?) a theoretical error of the first magnitude and of vital importance for development theory and policy. This error is common not only to both variants of the first mode but also to all three modes of approach to economic development and cultural change reviewed here.[78] They each view the characteristics of devel-

---

[72] Thomas Mun, *England's Treasure by Forraign Trade, or the Balance of Our Forraign Trade is the Rule of Our Treasure* (Oxford: Basil Blackwell, 1959), first published in 1664.

[73] Richard Cantillon, *Essai sur la nature du commerce en général*, edited, with an English translation and other material, by Henry Higgs (New York: A. Kelley, 1964).

[74] Karl Marx, *Capital*, Vol. III (Moscow: Foreign Languages Publishing House n. d.).

[75] Earl J. Hamilton, "American Treasure and the Rise of capitalism," *Economica* (London), No. 27 (1929); *American Treasure and the Price Revolution in Spain, 1501–1650* (Cambridge: Harvard University Press, 1934); *War and Prices in Spain 1651–1800* (Cambridge: Harvard University Press, 1947). See also the extension of this work by P. Vilar, "Problems of the Formation of Capitalism," *Past & Present*, November 1956.

[76] Eric Williams, *Capitalism and Slavery* (Chapel Hill: University of North Carolina Press, 1944); reprinted by Russell & Russell, New York, 1963; and issued in paperback by Andre Deutsch, London, 1964.

[77] Basil Davidson, *The African Slave Trade, op. cit.; Old Africa Rediscovered* (London: Gollancz, 1959).

[78] The same error also applies to a further variant which is associated particularly with Alexander Gerschenkron, *Economic Backwardness in Historical Perspective* (Cambridge: Belknap Press of Harvard University, 1962). Gerschenkron introduces variations into the ideal types of development. He reasons that

opment and underdevelopment as *sui generis* to the country concerned. When they proceed to the study of any structure at all, as we have already seen in the case of Hoselitz, they confine themselves to examining only parts of the domestic structure of the country concerned. In none of these modes is there an examination of the actual structure of development and underdevelopment—of the structure of the historical system which gave rise to and includes them both. As to the efficacy of the policy recommended by Rostow, it speaks for itself: no country, once underdeveloped, ever managed to develop by Rostow's stages. Is that why Rostow is now trying to help the people of Vietnam, the Congo, the Dominican Republic, and other underdeveloped countries to overcome the empirical, theoretical, and policy shortcomings of his manifestly non-communist intellectual aid to economic development and cultural change by bombs, napalm, chemical and biological weapons, and military occupation?[79]

---

since the pattern of development of the latecomers, such as Germany, differs from that of those which developed earlier, it is only reasonable to suppose that the pattern of those still later —that is the still underdeveloped countries—will differ even more from the already established pattern and stages of growth. This analysis might indeed seem to be a major advance over the others. But it is not. As with the other proponents of the first mode, there is no hint in Gerschenkron that the underdeveloped countries also have a history which requires study; nor is there any hint that their history and their relations with the now developed countries are much more important for any serious attempt to understand and remove the causes of underdevelopment than is the study of the history of the developed part of the world, whose experience has been quite different. Gerschenkron's variety of the first mode must, therefore, also be judged inadequate.

[79] The *New York Times* profile comments: "Mr. Rostow is an architect of the United States policy in Vietnam, and proud of it." *New York Times*, April 13, 1967. "W. W. Rostow once explained the State Department's rationale behind the arms race in the 1950's as forcing the USSR to 'waste' her resources for military purposes and thus denying her the use of these resources to sustain her growth rate." Two Labor Economists, "Tasks of the American Labor Movement," *Monthly Review*, Vol. 18, No. 11 (April 1967), p. 12. Is this also the rationale for the stages of growth Mr. Rostow is proud to impose on Vietnam and China in the 1960's?

The first or ideal typical mode of approaching problems of economic development and cultural change turns out upon examination to be empirically invalid, theoretically inadequate, and ineffective policy-wise. The fundamental reason why the whole approach must be rejected by those who would meaningfully understand and solve the problems of economic development and cultural change is that the approach, in all its variations, ignores the historical and structural reality of the underdeveloped countries. This reality is the product of the very same historical process and systemic structure as is the development of the now developed countries: the world embracing system within which the now underdeveloped countries have lived their history for centuries; it is the structure of this system which constitutes the historical cause and still contemporary determinant of underdevelopment. This structure is ubiquitous; it extends from the most developed part of the most developed country to the most underdeveloped part of the most underdeveloped country. Even if the first approach were to study the structure of underdevelopment on the domestic level of the underdeveloped countries, which as we have seen it does not, it would be unable adequately to analyze and understand that domestic structure—let alone to permit policy formulation adequate to change it: Those engaging in the first mode of analysis, and as we will see the second and third ones as well, resolutely avoid the study of the international structure of development and underdevelopment of which the domestic structure of underdevelopment is only a part. On all grounds then, empirical, theoretical, and policy, the first approach to economic development and cultural change must be rejected as inadequate.

THE DIFFUSIONIST APPROACH

The second mode identified by Nash views development as occurring through the diffusion of cultural elements from the developed to the underdeveloped countries. This involves, of course, acculturation to these elements on the part of the underdeveloped countries. The diffusion is seen to spread from the metropolis of the advanced capitalist countries out to the national capitals of the underdeveloped ones, and from these in turn out to their provincial capitals and finally to the peripheral hinterland.

According to this view, since development consists of and is promoted by diffusion and acculturation, underdevelopment remains because of obstacles or resistance to this diffusion. Underdevelopment is taken to be the original "traditional" state as much as it is in the first mode. There is even less inquiry into the causes and nature of underdevelopment than in the first mode. In effect, the diffusionists do not suggest to the peoples of the underdeveloped world that they inquire into and remove the causes of underdevelopment; instead they advise them to await and welcome the diffusion of developmental aid from the outside.

Empirical Validity

Nash emphasizes the diffusion of "knowledge, skills, organization, values, technology, and capital" as the primary factors in the second mode's view of economic development and cultural change. For expository convenience, we shall reclassify these as 1) capital, 2) technology, including knowledge and skills, and 3) institutions, including values and organization.

Capital: With respect to the diffusion of capital, the thesis of the second mode begins with the proposition that, being poor, the underdeveloped countries lack investment capital and therefore find it difficult or impossible to develop and thereby escape from their poverty. Therefore, the richer developed countries can, should, and do diffuse capital to the underdeveloped ones, thereby promoting their economic development. The acceptability of the initial proposition—that it is poverty which hampers the underdeveloped countries' efforts at investment and development—has been strongly challenged on theoretical grounds by Paul Baran in *The Political*

Economy of Growth, op. cit.; and this writer has supplied further theoretical and empirical evidence which discounts this proposition.[80] I shall say no more about this proposition here since it is the assumption—or justification—which serves only as the starting point for the diffusionist thesis. Instead, I shall go on to examine the thesis itself, namely that the developed countries diffuse capital to the underdeveloped ones and thereby aid in their development. This thesis is upheld in the pages of *EDCC* by, among others, Martin Bronfenbrenner,[81] and by Daniel Garnick,[82] who challenges Bronfenbrenner's argument. Whatever the disagreement between them, however, they both agree that the developed countries actually contribute capital to the underdeveloped ones. The variety of views on foreign aid and investment presented under Gerald Meier's editorship in *Leading Issues in Development Economics,*[83] by Raymond Mikesell in *U. S. Private and Government Investment Abroad,*[84] or by Benjamin Higgins, in his chapter on "Foreign Investment and Foreign Aid" in his *Economic Development,*[85] exhibit a variety of sharp disagreements. But all these writers, as well as others in *EDCC,*[86] seem to be in full agreement with the proposition that the flow of capital is from the developed countries to the

[80] André Gunder Frank, *Capitalism and Underdevelopment in Latin America, op. cit.*

[81] Martin Bronfenbrenner, "The Appeal of Confiscation in Economic Development," *EDCC,* Vol. 3, No. 3 (April 1955); "Second Thoughts on Confiscation, *EDCC,* Vol. 11, No. 4 (July 1963).

[82] Daniel H. Garnick, "'The Appeal of Confiscation' Reconsidered: A Gaming Approach to Foreign Economic Policy," *EDCC,* Vol. 11, No. 4 (July 1963); and "Further Thoughts on Confiscation," *EDCC,* Vol. 12, No. 4 (July 1964).

[83] Gerald Meier, *op. cit.*

[84] Raymond F. Mikesell, ed., *U. S. Private and Government Investment Abroad* (Eugene: University of Oregon Books, 1962).

[85] Benjamin Higgins, "Foreign Investment and Foreign Aid," in his *Economic Development* (New York: Norton, 1959).

[86] Chi-Ming Hou, "External Trade, Foreign Investment, and Domestic Development: The Chinese Experience 1840–1937," *EDCC,* Vol. 10, No. 1 (October 1961).

underdeveloped ones. Again, the only disagreement seems to stem from the facts.

The conservative estimates of the United States Department of Commerce show that between 1950 and 1965 the total flow of capital on investment account from the United States to the rest of the world was $23.9 billion, while the corresponding capital inflow from profits was $37.0 billion, for a net inflow into the United States of $13.1 billion. Of this total, $14.9 billion flowed from the United States to Europe and Canada while $11.4 billion flowed in the opposite direction, for a net outflow from the United States of $3.5 billion. Yet, between the United States and all other countries, that is mainly the poor, undeveloped ones, the situation is reversed: $9.0 billion of investment flowed to these countries while $25.6 billion profit capital flowed out of them, for a *net inflow from the poor to the rich* of $16.6 billion.[87]

Other available statistics show exactly the same pattern of net capital flow from the underdeveloped countries to the developed ones.[88] The only trouble with these data is that they very much understate the actual flow of capital from the poor underdeveloped countries to the rich developed ones. First of all, they understate the capital flow from poor to rich on investment account.[89] Secondly, they obscure the fact that the largest part of the capital which the developed countries own in the underdeveloped ones was never sent from the former to the latter at all but was, on the contrary, acquired by the developed countries in the now underdeveloped ones.

[87] Harry Magdoff, "Economic Aspects of U.S. Imperialism," *Monthly Review*, Vol. 18, No. 6 (November 1966), p. 39.

[88] Keith B. Griffin and Ricardo French-Davis, "El Capital Extranjero y el Desarrollo," *Revista Economia* (Santiago), Vol. 83–84 (1964), pp. 16–22; and André Gunder Frank, "On the Mechanisms of Imperialism: The Case of Brazil," *Monthly Review*, Vol. 16, No. 5 (September 1964), reprinted as chapter 9 in *Latin America: Underdevelopment or Revolution, op. cit.*

[89] *Ibid.*; José Luis Ceceña, *El Capital Monopolista y la Economía de México* (Mexico: Cuadernos Americanos, 1963); and Michael Kirdon, *Foreign Investments in India* (London: Oxford University Press, 1965).

Thus, according to the United States Department of Commerce, of the total capital obtained and employed from all sources by United States operations in Brazil in 1957, 26 per cent came from the United States and the remainder was raised in Brazil, including 36 per cent from Brazilian sources outside the American firms.[90] That same year, of the capital in American direct investment in Canada, 26 per cent came from the United States while the remainder was also raised in Canada.[91] By 1964, however, the part of American investment in Canada that entered from the United States had declined to 5 per cent, making the average American contribution to the total capital used by American firms in Canada during the period 1957–64 only 15 per cent. All the remainder of the "foreign investment" was raised in Canada through retained earnings (42%), depreciation charges (31%), and funds raised by American firms on the Canadian capital market (12%). According to a survey of American direct investment firms operating in Canada in the period 1950–59, 79 per cent of the firms raised over 25 per cent of the capital for their Canadian operations in Canada, 65 per cent of the firms raised over 50 per cent in Canada, *and 47 per cent of the American firms with investments in Canada raised all of the capital for their Canadian operations in Canada and none in the United States*. There is reason to believe that this American reliance on foreign capital to finance American "foreign investment" is still greater in the poor underdeveloped countries, which are weaker and more defenseless than Canada. This, then, is the source of the flow of capital on investment account from the poor underdeveloped countries to the rich developed ones.

Thirdly, these data take account neither of the well known decline in the underdeveloped countries' relative participation

90 Claude McMillan, Jr., Richard F. Gonzales, with Leo G. Erickson, *International Enterprise in a Developing Economy. A Study of U.S. Business in Brazil*, M.S.U. Business Studies (East Lansing: Michigan State University Press, 1964), p. 205.

91 This and the following data on Canada are taken or computed from A. E. Safarian, *Foreign Ownership of Canadian Industry* (Toronto: McGraw-Hill Company of Canada, 1966), pp. 235, 241.

in world trade, nor of the deterioration of the terms of trade which is currently costing the underdeveloped countries far more capital than their net or gross receipts of investment and loans from developed ones.[92] (Net receipts, as was noted above, are negative to begin with.) Fourthly, these data on the flow of investment capital leave out of account the still larger flow of capital from the underdeveloped countries to the developed ones on other service accounts. In 1962 Latin America spent fully 61 per cent of its foreign exchange earnings on services that were supposedly rendered to it by the developed countries. Half of this, or 30 per cent of the total, was accounted for by officially registered profit remittances and debt service. The other half was composed of Latin American payments to the developed countries, which means mostly the United States, for transportation and insurance, travel, other services, donations, transfer of funds, and errors and omissions (in registered capital flows). Moreover, Latin America's loss of capital on service accounts is increasing over time: while in 1961–63 it was 61 per cent, in 1956–60 it had been only 53 per cent.[93] This capital outflow amounts to 7.3 per cent of Latin America's Gross National Product, or 10 per cent if we add the 3 per cent of GNP

[92] Report by the Secretary-General of the Conference, "Towards a New Trade Policy for Development," *Proceedings of the United Nations Conference on Trade and Development* (New York: United Nations, 1964), E/CONF.46/141, Vol. II, pp. 9–13, 42, and other documents of the Conference. It should be noted (cf. p. 13) that in comparing the underdeveloped countries' loss of capital due to declining terms of trade with the "net inflow of all types of finance (loans, investments and grants-in-aid)," the United Nations calculate the latter "including private reinvestment," that is, including the investment capital that does not flow in at all, net or gross, but is generated in the underdeveloped countries themselves.

[93] André Gunder Frank, "Services Rendered," *Monthly Review*, Vol. 17, No. 2 (June 1965); André G. Frank, "Servicios Extranjeros o Desarrollo Nacional?" *Comercio Exterior* (Banco Nacional de Comercio Exterior, S.A., Mexico), Vol. 16, No. 2 (febrero 1966); and the English translation and slight revision of the latter, "Foreign Invisible Services or National Economic Development?" in chapter 11 of André Gunder Frank. *Latin America: Underdevelopment or Revolution, op. cit.*

lost by recent years' deterioration in the terms of trade; and this equals two and three or more times the capital that "capital poor" Latin America devotes to net investment for its own development.[94] Other kinds of capital loss by the underdeveloped countries are not included in these calculations, such as the notorious brain drain, or outflow of human capital that was financed by the poor countries for the subsequent benefit of the rich. Who, we may ask, is diffusing capital to whom?

Beyond the question of the amount and direction of capital diffused, there is the problem of the kind and consequences of foreign aid and investment in underdeveloped countries. That metropolitan investment in and control of primary sector production in underdeveloped countries (in, for example, sugar, bananas, minerals, and most spectacularly petroleum) has notably failed to develop the underdeveloped countries, but has instead interposed a whole series of obstacles to their development, has by now surely been sufficiently documented to be obvious even when viewed from the developed countries themselves.

Foreign investment in the industrial and service sectors of underdeveloped countries raises further questions. It is far from clear that even this investment helps underdeveloped countries to develop. Nonetheless, with few exceptions, writers from the developed countries have failed to question, much less to analyze, the supposed benefits of this foreign investment to underdeveloped countries. Economists and statesmen from the underdeveloped countries, on the other hand, are increasingly challenging these supposed benefits and are going on to analyze the obstacles to industrialization

---

[94] The 7.3% are computed from the $6,195 million service expenditures in *ibid.* as a percentage of the $84,458 million GNP in 1962 reported in United Nations Economic Commission for Latin America, *Estudio Económico de America Latina 1963* (New York: United Nations, 1964), E/CN.12/696/Rev. 1, p. 6. This document is also the source of all the data used in the computations of the articles cited in footnote 93. The 3% are computed from United Nations Commission for Latin America, *El Financiamiento Externo de America Latina* (New York: United Nations 1964), E/CN.12/649/Rev. 1, p. 33.

and economic development created by foreign investment. For example, a congress representing thirty-four Schools of Economics in Latin America recently concluded that:

> Direct foreign investment has many unfavorable effects on the balance of payments, on economic integration and on capital formation in our countries; it determines in great measure the character and direction of our foreign trade, stimulates monopolistic competition, absorbs or subordinates weaker national firms, etc. For all these reasons it is necessary to adopt ways and means that can impede these negative effects.[95]

Arturo Frondizi wrote during his successful electoral campaign for the presidency of Argentina:

> It is not amiss to remember that foreign capital usually acts as an agent which perturbs the morality, the politics, and the economy of Argentina. . . . Once established thanks to excessively liberal concessions, foreign capital obtained bank credits which permitted it to expand its operations and therefore its profits. These profits are immediately sent abroad as if all of the investment capital had been imported by the country. In this way, the domestic economy came to strengthen foreign capitalization and to weaken itself. . . . The natural tendency of foreign capital in our country has been, in the first place, to settle in areas of high profits. . . . When Argentinian effort, intelligence, and perseverance created an independent economic opportunity, foreign capital destroyed it or tried to create difficulties for it. . . . Foreign capital had and has a decisive influence in the social and political life of our country. . . . The press is usually also an active instrument of this process of submission. . . . Foreign capital has had special influence in the political life of our nation, allying itself with the conservative oligarchy . . . those who are tied to foreign capital

---

[95] Relatorio de la III Reunion de Facultades y Escuelas de Economia de America Latina, Mexico, June 21–25, 1965. Published in *Presente Económico* (Mexico), Vol. 1, No. 1 (July 1965), p. 63 and in *Comercio Exterior* (Mexico), Vol. 15, No. 6 (June 1965), p. 439; and *Desarrollo* (Colombia), No. 1 (January 1966), p. 7–9.

by economic ties (directors, bureaucratic personnel, lawyers, newspapers that receive advertisements etc.) and
those who, without having economic relations, end up
being dominated by the political and ideological climate
created by foreign capital.[96]

Octaviano Campos Salas, before he became Minister of
Industry of Mexico, summarized the consequences of foreign
investment:

(a) Private foreign capital takes over high profit sectors
permanently, expelling or not permitting the entry of
domestic capital, by relying on the ample financial resources of its home office and on the political power
which it sometimes exercises. (b) The permanent take-
over of important sectors of economic activity impedes
domestic capital formation and creates problems of balance of payments instability. (c) Private direct foreign
investment interferes with anti-cyclical monetary and
fiscal policy—it comes when there are expansions and
withdraws during depression. (d) The demands by private foreign investors for concessions to form a 'favourable climate' for investment in the receiving countries
are unlimited and excessive. (e) It is much cheaper and
more consistent with the underdeveloped countries' aspirations to economic independence to hire foreign technicians and to pay royalties for the use of patents than
to accept the permanent control of their economies by
powerful foreign consortia. (f) Foreign private capital
does not adapt itself to development planning.[97]

It is not, then, indisputably obvious that the underdeveloped
countries would be still more underdeveloped if they were not
visited by foreign capital.[98] Evidently, not any and all diffu-

[96] Arturo Frondizi, *A Luta Antiimperialista* (São Paulo: Editora Brasilense, 1958); a translation of *Petróleo y Política*
(Buenos Aires: Editorial Raigal, 1955).

[97] Quoted in Camara Textil del Norte, "Las Inversiones Ex-
tranjeras y el Desarrollo Económico de México," *Problemas
Agrícolas e Industriales de México*, Vol. 9, No. 1–2 (1957).

[98] For more detailed analysis of this problem, see: José Luis
Ceceña, *El Capital Monopolista y la Economía de México, op.
cit.*, Fernando Carmona, *El Drama de América Latina, El Caso*

sion, even of capital, let alone of other things, is an aid to economic development.

Technology: Technology is diffused only in part. However, the problem is not, as the diffusionists would have us believe, one of insufficient quantity of technology diffused, and still less one of cultural resistance to its acceptance and employment in technologically backward areas. The problem of technology and its diffusion arises out of the same monopoly structure of the economic system on the world, national, and local levels. During the course of the historical development of the capitalist system on these levels, the developed countries have always diffused out to their satellite colonial dependencies the technology whose employment in the colonial and now underdeveloped countries has served the interests of the metropolis; and the metropolis has always suppressed the technology in the now underdeveloped countries which conflicted with the interests of the metropolis and its own development, as the Europeans did with the irrigation and other agricultural technology and installations in India, the Middle East, and Latin America; or as the English did with industrial technology in India, Spain, and Portugal.[99] The same is true on the national and local levels in which the

---

de México (Mexico, Cuadernos Americanos, 1964); Arturo Frondizi, *op. cit.;* Silvio Frondizi, *La Realidad Argentina* (2nd ed.; Buenos Aires: Praxis, 1967), Vol. I; Hamza Alavi, "U. S. Aid to Pakistan," *Economic Weekly* (Bombay), Special Number, July 1963; and André Gunder Frank, "Brazil: Exploitation or Aid?" *The Nation* (New York), Nov. 16, 1963; "On the Mechanisms of Imperialism," *Monthly Review,* September 1964; and reprinted as chapters 8 and 9 of *Latin America: Underdevelopment or Revolution, op. cit.;* and *Capitalism and Underdevelopment in Latin America, op. cit.,* especially chapter V on "Foreign Investment in Latin American Underdevelopment."

[99] Analysis of this process may be found for instance for India in the work cited in footnote 60; for Africa in footnote 62; for Latin America in footnote 64; for China in footnote 132; for Spain, in José Larraz, *La Epoca del Mercantilismo en Castilla (1500–1700)* (2nd ed.; Madrid: Atlas, 1943); for Portugal in Alan K. Manchester, *British Preeminence in Brazil, Its Rise and Decline* (Chapel Hill: University of North Carolina Press, 1933).

domestic metropolis promotes the technology in its hinterland that serves its export interests and suppresses the preexisting individual or communal agricultural and artisan technology that interferes with the use of the countryside's productive and buying capacity and capital for metropolitan development.

Throughout this historical process the metropolis has maintained a high degree of monopoly over industrial production and technology which it has relinquished only when it had already established an alternative source of monopoly in heavy industry; this latter it is slowly beginning to relinquish in our day now that it has developed a still newer source of technological monopoly in electronics, synthetics, cybernetics, and automation in general. Far from diffusing more and more important technology to the underdeveloped countries, the most significant technological trend of our day is the increasing degree to which new technology serves as the basis of the capitalist metropolis' monopoly control over its underdeveloped economic colonies.

Some of the facts of technological diffusion, which sharply contrast with most of the diffusionist faith, were recently analyzed by the American business magazine, *Newsweek,* under the title "The U. S. Business Stake in Europe":

> To knowledgeable Europeans, in fact, the technical lead of the big U. S. companies is the most disturbing facet of the dollar invasion. In the future, a French study committee recently concluded, competition over prices will give way to competition in innovations, and the pace will be so hot that only firms of international size—that is, American ones, chiefly—will survive. . . . European industries will function more and more under foreign licensing agreements; they will become subsidiaries of U. S. parent companies, which will sell them their know-how and manage Europe's production. . . . French politicians and publications of the right, left, and center have been accusing the U. S. of economic colonization, satellization, and vassalization. . . . A company chairman in Brussels sums up: "We are becoming pawns manipulated by U. S. giants". . . . An Olivetti executive discussing alternatives to the GE [General Electric]

deal . . . [declared] "But even if we had merged with Machines Bull in France and Siemens in Germany (which later signed a licensing agreement with RCA [Newsweek]), we still would have been dwarfed and eventually put out of business by the U. S. giants. . . . Research costs are too high. The transatlantic technological gap is a fact of life. . . . We studied a European solution very carefully. . . . There is no European solution to these problems."[100]

Contrary, then, to what the diffusionist would have us believe, the hard fact of technological diffusion, as these members of the developed European business community are well aware, is not the essentially simple matter of diffusing technological development aid from the more developed to the less developed countries. Still less, of course, is the problem of technological diffusion and economic development one of cultural resistance derived from traditionalism or from Hoselitz' pattern variables. If these strong and developed European economies cannot find a European solution to the real developmental problem posed by the technological gap (rather than to the fancied one of the diffusionists), what hope do the weak and underdeveloped economies caught in the same system have to find such a solution?[101] It is surely no accident that among European and previously underdeveloped countries, it is only in the socialist countries—the Soviet Union and China—that a "solution to these problems" has been found.

Institutions: The past, present, and future diffusion of institutions and values from developed to underdeveloped areas is a fact beyond question. The construction of an entire theory

[100] "The U. S. Business Stake in Europe," *Newsweek*, March 8, 1965, pp. 67–74.

[101] See André Gunder Frank, articles on Brazil, *op. cit.*, and particularly the last part of "Capitalism Development of Underdevelopment in Brazil" in *Capitalism and Underdevelopment in Latin America, op. cit.* Also see "The Growth and Decline of Import Substitution in Brazil," *Economic Bulletin for Latin America* (New York: United Nations), Vol. 9, No. 1 (March 1964).

of economic development on this foundation is another matter. In addition to Manning Nash, who is probably best classified in this category—although he rejects diffusionism in its crudest "pitchforking" form as he calls it—theorists concerned with the developed countries' diffusion of institutions and values, and the underdeveloped recipients' resistance to them, have been well represented in the pages of *EDCC*.[102] Technically, diffusionist theory might deal with the diffusion of any kind of institutions or values. In practice, however, the diffusionist school has concentrated its attention on the diffusion of old fashioned or new fangled liberalism (though they rarely call it this)—which is, indeed, most of what has been diffused from the metropolitan to the now underdeveloped countries during the last century. Consequently, I shall concentrate attention on the diffusion of liberalism, in its economic, political, and social forms. Moreover, the pattern variables of universality, achievement orientation, and functional specificity with which Hoselitz identifies economic development are little more than liberalism recast into technical sounding jargon. This is what Hoselitz apparently would like to see diffused to transform underdevelopment into development. Does diffusionism constitute an adequate development theory, and does the diffusion of liberalism or of anything else serve as an effective economic development policy?

Economic liberalism was and is diffused, not in general, but under very specific and particular circumstances. Its exportation from the metropolis is an expression of the particular interests of those who diffuse it, as its importation by the underdeveloped countries is an expression of the particular interests of those who are acculturating to it. The specific

---

[102] Manning Nash, "Social Prerequisites to Economic Growth in Latin America and South East Asia," *EDCC,* Vol. 12, No. 3 (April 1964), Burkhard Strümpel, "Preparedness for Change in Peasant Society," *EDCC,* Vol. 13, No. 2 (January 1965); S. N. Eisenstadt, "Breakdowns of Modernization," *EDCC,* Vol. 12, No. 4 (July 1964); William N. Parker, "Economic Development in Historical Perspective," *EDCC,* Vol. 10, No. 1 (October 1961); S. N. Eisenstadt, "Sociological Aspects of the Economic Adaptation of Oriental Immigrants in Israel—A Case Study in the Problem of Modernization," *EDCC,* Vol. 4 (April 1956); and others.

circumstances of and particular interests in the diffusion and acculturation of liberalism, like anything else, were and still are determined by the structure and development of the economic, social, and political system within which it occurs. The German economist Friedrich List reported in the 1840's that an American Supreme Court Justice had observed, in regard to one of liberalism's most important tenets, that like most of Great Britain's other products, the free trade doctrine was produced primarily for export.[103] A few years later, U. S. President, General Ulysses S. Grant observed,

> . . . for centuries England has relied on protection, has carried it to extremes, and has obtained satisfactory results from it. There is no doubt that it is to this system that it owes its present strength. After two centuries, England has found it convenient to adopt free trade because it thinks that protection can no longer offer it anything. Very well, then, Gentlemen, my knowledge of my country leads me to believe that within two hundred years, when America has gotten all it can out of protection, it too will adopt free trade.[104]

President Grant only erred by a century; since World War II, that is, since it achieved the unrivaled industrial supremacy and near monopoly in the world which Britain had attained a century before, the United States both directly and through its controlling influence in international agencies, such as GATT, the International Monetary Fund and the World Bank, has been most adamant in exporting free trade. Free trade, like free enterprise, is protective monopoly under another name—as Frederick Clairmonte has so well shown.[105]

The circumstances and interests leading to the underdeveloped countries' ready acculturation to international free

[103] Friedrich List, *National System of Political Economy* (Philadelphia, 1856).

[104] Quoted in Pedro Santos Martinez, *Historia Económica de Mendoza durante el Virreynato* (Madrid: Universidad Nacional del Cuyo, 1959), p. 125 and retranslated from the Spanish by the author.

[105] Frederick Clairmonte, *Economic Liberalism and Underdeveloped Countries . . .* , *op. cit.*

trade and domestic economic liberalism in the nineteenth century—and to free trade in technology and free enterprise in the twentieth—can be summarized just as clearly:

> The doctrine of liberalism, imported from Europe, thus found fertile ground in our country [Chile] and grew vigourously. It constituted the theoretical basis to re-enforce the interest of the controlling forces, inasmuch as it represented and expressed its desires.[106]

Another more specific and thorough observation is worth quoting at length:

> The pressure groups who controlled the economic policy of the country were decidedly freetraders: they were more freetrader than Courcelle-Seneuil, the famous and respected leader of doctrinaire freetradism: they were definitely more Catholic than the Pope. . . . The mining exporters of the North of the country were freetraders. This policy was not fundamentally due to reasons of doctrine—though they also had these—but rather to the simple reason that these gentlemen were blessed with common sense. They exported copper, silver, nitrates and other minerals . . . they were paid in pound sterling or dollars. . . . It is hard to conceive of an altruism or a farsighted or prophetic vision which would lead these exporters to pay export and import duties with a view to the possible industrialization of the country.

Veliz goes on to describe how the agricultural and livestock exporters and the big import houses operated in terms of the same logic. He adds,

> Here then is the powerful coalition of strong interests which dominated the economic policy of Chile during the past century and part of the present one. None of these three had the very least interest in Chile industrializing. They monopolized the three powers at all lev-

[106] Max Nolff, "Industria Manufacturera," in *Geografia Económica de Chile* (Santiago: Corporación de Fomento de la Producción), Vol. III, pp. 162–63.

els; economic power, political power, and social prestige.[107]

Aldo Ferrer finds the same pattern in nineteenth century
Argentina:

> The merchants and livestock owners, who were the dy-
> namic forces in the development of the Litoral, were
> chiefly interested in the expansion of exports. Free trade
> thus became the philosophy and practical policy of these
> groups. . . . Free exports also meant freedom to im-
> port.[108]

Ferrer returns to discuss the Argentina of our day after its
supposed take-off into industrialization during the 1930's and
1940's, and after the expulsion of Perón and the abrogation
of his policy in the 1950's by these same groups and their
foreign, now primarily American, allies who instituted the
policy of the International Monetary Fund instead:

> In January of 1959, Argentina began the application of
> a stabilization plan. . . . At the same time the exchange
> rate structure was liberalized, and the peso was deval-
> ued. . . . Devaluation has become, moreover, a tool of
> economic policy explicitly designed to change the do-
> mestic price structure in favor of the export sector. . . .
> The difficulties of this kind of readjustment, in view of
> the objective conditions obtaining in the Argentinian
> economy as well as in the world market, are reflected in
> the fact that stagnation has not been overcome and that
> the rigidities of the economic system which determine it,
> far from being on the way to solution, have become even
> more serious. . . . The financial and monetary policy
> . . . has been accompanied by a strongly regressive re-
> distribution of income. . . . There has been a strong
> business contraction. . . . The deficit in the balance of
> payments and the government budget and the rise in
> price have not been resolved. . . . In fact, the stabiliza-
> tion plan and the recommendations received from abroad

[107] Claudio Veliz, "La Mesa de Tres Patas," *Desarrollo Económico* (Buenos Aires), Vol. 3, No. 1–2 (April–September 1963),
pp. 237–42.

[108] Aldo Ferrer, *The Argentinian Economy, op. cit.*, p. 56.

have simply served as a tool in the hands of the sectors who saw their immediate and long term interests served by the impact of the policy followed on the distribution of income and the *backward* structural adjustment of the Argentinian economy.[109]

Two additional well known examples are instructive as to how economic liberalism in the domestic economies of the underdeveloped countries promotes monopoly and thereby the underdevelopment of the majority. One example is the nineteenth century breakup, in the name of liberalism, of communally held Indian land, its distribution into private ownership and consequent monopoly concentration during the epoch of liberal reform—a concentration which far exceeded that of the autocratic colonial times.[110] Another example is the currently ever greater monopoly concentration of finance, commerce, industry, and (still) of land in underdeveloped countries under the aegis of the "free" world's "free" enterprise.[111] It is clear then that the diffusion and acculturation of economic liberalism between the developed (or developing) metropolitan countries and their underdeveloped satellites—as well as that within the underdeveloped countries—is a response to interests, and produces consequences which can be summed up in a single word: monopoly. Contrary to the elaborate classical and neoclassical theoretical economic edifice that was carefully built up in Manchester (the first city to enter the modern industrial age!) and which

[109] Aldo Ferrer, "Reflexiones acerca de la Política de Estabilización en la Argentina," *op. cit.,* pp. 501–14. Emphasis in the original.

[110] Antonio Garcia, *La Democracia en la Teoria y en la Práctica, Una Tercera Posición Frente a la História* (Bogota; Editorial Iqueima, 1951), and *Bases de la Economía Contemporanea, Elementos para una Economía de Defensa* (Bogota, 1948); Moisés Gonzáles Navarro, ed., *Vallarta en la Reforma* (Mexico: Ediciones de la Universidad Nacional Autónoma, 1956); and *La Colonización en México, 1877–1910* (Mexico, 1960); Jesús Reyes Heroles, *El Liberalismo Mexicano* (México: Universidad Nacional Autónoma, Faculdad de Derecho, 3 Vols., 1957–61); chapters 2 and 3, above.

[111] See works cited in footnotes 38, 56, and 66.

is still being assiduously exported and imported by interested parties, the diffusion of economic liberalism has quite consistently contributed its significant share to the establishment, maintenance, and strengthening of economic monopoly, both on the national and international levels. Through this monopoly, economic liberalism has contributed to the economic development *of those who diffuse it;* to, as the United Nations Economic Commission for Latin America calls it, the limited "outward-oriented development"[112] of the capitals of the underdeveloped countries; and to ever more underdevelopment for the world's majority who were and are liberally forced to suffer its consequences.

The diffusion of political liberalism which accompanied and followed the spread of economic liberalism cannot be said to be very different. Since the consequences of the diffusion of political liberalism are clear in the above analysis of economic liberalism, and since they are explicit in our daily newspapers, it is unnecessary to rely on Lenin's analysis of the relations between economic and political power and institutions in his *The State and Revolution,* or to go into it here.[110] The only remark that needs to be made is that the relations between economic and political power—again discussed by President Eisenhower in terms of the "military industrial complex"[114] and by C. Wright Mills in the *Power Elite*[115] are even more intimate in the underdeveloped countries than they are in the developed ones which are discussed by Lenin, Eisenhower, and Mills.

Although it does not go by that name, we may also observe the diffusion of and acculturation to "social liberalism." This modern liberalism takes the form primarily of promoting "social mobility" and "middle classes" in the underde-

112 United Nations Economic Commission for Latin America, *The Economic Development of Latin America in the Post-War Period, op. cit.,* and other publications.

113 V. I. Lenin, "The State and Revolution," in *Selected Works in Two Volumes* (Moscow: Foreign Languages Publishing House n. d.), Vol. II, Part 1.

114 Quoted in Fred J. Cook, *The Warfare State, op. cit.*

115 C. Wright Mills, *The Power Elite, op. cit.*

veloped countries. Like the others, social liberalism is adver-
tized as leading to a more open, democratic society capable of
greater and faster economic development. We have observed
above that Hoselitz' pattern variable approach lends support
to this thesis, and that Johnson and Germani, among many
others, propose the promotion of middle classes and of social
mobility as development theory and policy. Johnson diffuses
it from the United States,[116] and Germani acculturates to
it in Argentina when he writes under the title of "A Strategy
for Promoting Social Mobility."[117] Like economic and political liberalism, social liberalism is, however, more aptly described as individual liberalism. It is the liberty of a few individuals to move, to monopolize, and thereby restrict the
development of the economic, political, and social whole.
Those persons in underdeveloped countries who have mi-
grated from country to city or moved from a lower economic
and social status to a higher one often say in one way or another that they have made their own individual reform or
revolution. In so doing they express not only the conservatism
which reflects their desire to maintain their newly gained
position but also a fundamental social scientific truth which
seems to escape the attention of diffusionists and others: "social" mobility is really *individual* mobility and does not
transform social structures: rather, a change in the social
structure may render possible *social* mobility and economic
development.

As with the other liberalisms, the evidence is accumulating (supplied in part by Hoselitz himself, as we saw above[118]
that the diffusion to the underdeveloped countries of the institutions and values of social liberalism is highly selective
at both the diffusing and acculturating ends. The selective
diffusion is determined by the structure of the international

---

[116] John J. Johnson, *Political Change in Latin America: The
Emergence of the Middle Sectors, op. cit.*

[117] Gino Germani, "Estrategia para Estimular la Movilidad
Social," *Desarrollo Económico* (Buenos Aires), Vol. 1, No. 3
(1962).

[118] Bert F. Hoselitz, "Economic Growth in Latin America,"
op. cit.

system, including the structural relations of the sending and receiving societies and sub-societies within it. Far from aiding the development of the underdeveloped countries, social liberalism hinders it. As we noted above, social mobility and the rise of the middle classes in the underdeveloped countries renders the distribution of income not more but less equal;[119] and it provides economic and political support not for changing but for maintaining and reinforcing the structure of the economic, political, and social status quo.[120]

Theoretical Adequacy

As with our examination of the first mode, our review of the empirical validity of propositions in the second mode offers a good vantage point from which to evaluate their associated theoretical formulations. Like the first mode, the diffusionist approach suffers from serious theoretical shortcomings because of its failure to take adequate account of the determinant structure and development of the social system within which diffusion, acculturation, and economic development and cultural change take place. Perhaps the most important theoretical fault of diffusionism is that it is premised on dualism instead of on structural and developmental holism. In the pages of *EDCC*, the theory of dualism itself

[119] Anibal Pinto S. C., *Chile: Una Economia Dificil, op. cit.*, and his "Concentración del Progresso Técnico y sus Frutos en el Desarrollo Latino-americano," *op. cit.* Also see Gabriel Kolko, *op. cit.*, for the United States.

[120] André Gunder Frank, "Not Feudalism: Capitalism," *Monthly Review*, Vol. 15, No. 8 (December 1963) reprinted as chapter 23 of *Latin America: Underdevelopment or Revolution, op. cit.*; Rodolfo Stavenhagen, "Seven Erroneous Theses about Latin America," *New University Thought*, Vol. 4, No. 4 (Winter 1966/67). Claudio Veliz, "Social and Political Obstacles to Reform," *World Today* (London), January 1963, reprinted in Oscar Delgado, ed., *Reformas Agrarias en La América Latina* (Mexico: Fondo de Cultura, 1965).

has been most explicitly advanced and defended by Benjamin Higgins,[121] who rejects the social dualism of Boeke[122] only to argue that dualism has a technological and economic basis. Reflecting its widespread acceptance, dualism is explicitly expressed in *EDCC* by writers and reviewers who span the globe.[123]

Although explicit reliance on the dual society or economy thesis is usually reserved for the analysis of underdeveloped countries alone, the dualist thesis is implicit in the entire analysis of development reviewed here.

All three modes of analysis seek to analyze both the differences between developed and underdeveloped countries as well as the inequalities within the latter by attributing separate and largely independent economic and social structures to the developed and underdeveloped sectors, each with its own separate history and dynamic, if any. (Frequently, as we have seen, the one part is denied any history at all.) Jacques Lambert for example argues in his *Os Dois Brasis* (The Two Brazils),

> The Brazilians are divided into two systems of economic and social organization. . . . These two societies did not evolve at the same rate . . . they are separated by centuries. . . . The dual economy and the dual social structure which accompanies it are neither new nor charac-

[121] Benjamin Higgins, "The 'Dualistic Theory' of Underdeveloped Areas," *EDCC*, Vol. 4, No. 2 (January 1956); also see his *Economic Development, op. cit.*

[122] J. H. Boeke, *The Structure of the Netherlands Indian Economy* (New York: Institute of Pacific Relations, 1942); *The Evolution of the Netherlands Indies Economy* (New York: Institute of Pacific Relations, 1946); and the definitive *Economics and Economic Policy of Dual Societies, op. cit.*

[123] P. T. Ellsworth, "The Dual Economy: A New Approach," *EDCC*, Vol. 10, No. 4 (July 1962); Walter Elkan, "The Dualistic Economy of the Rhodesias and Nyasaland," *EDCC*, Vol. 11, No. 4 (July 1963); Samir Dasgupta, "Underdevelopment and Dualism—A Note," *EDCC*, Vol. 12, No. 2 (January 1964); Tsunehiko Watanabe, "Economic Aspects of Dualism in the Industrial Development of Japan," *EDCC*, Vol. 13, No. 3 (April 1965).

teristically Brazilian—they exist in all unequally developed countries.[124]

In this sense, the plantation or mining sector of an underdeveloped country is viewed as an enclave of the developed metropolitan economy on foreign soil. The "enclave" is presumed not to be a real part of the supposedly isolated subsistence economy of the underdeveloped country itself; and it is thought to exercise little if any economic and social influence on this isolated sector in the present, and none in the past.[125] Similarly, in a supposedly somewhat less underdeveloped country, part of the population, usually the indigenous inhabitants, are said to be outside the market economy and marginal to the national society and to the world as a whole.[126] This conception of a dual economy and society, whether the duality be attributed to cultural, social, technological, economic, or other causes, then gives rise to the diffusionist theory and policy regarding the diffusion of capital, technology, and institutions.

The dualist theory and the diffusionist and other theses based on it are inadequate because the supposed structural duality is contrary to both historical and contemporary reality:[127] the *entire* social fabric of the underdeveloped countries has long since been penetrated and transformed

[124] Jacques Lambert, *Os Dois Brasis, op. cit.*; see also his new book, *L'Amérique latine* (Paris: Presses Universitaires de France, 1963).

[125] The classic argument of the enclave economy is that of J. H. Boeke, *op. cit.*

[126] Pablo Gonzáles Casanova, *La Democracia en México, op. cit.*, and many other works. The Guatemalan government's "Seminario de Integración Nacional" carries the entire idea in the organization's very name.

[127] See Review of Rostow's work above, and André Gunder Frank, *Capitalism and Underdevelopment in Latin America, op. cit.*, especially the chapter entitled, "Capitalism and the Myth of Feudalism in Brazilian Agriculture." For further criticism of dualism in general and of the particular dualist theses of Jaques Lambert and Celso Furtado about Brazil and of Pablo Gonzáles Casanova about Mexico, see my Chapters 14, 20 and 21 of *Latin America: Underdevelopment or Revolution, op. cit.*

by, and integrated into, the world embracing system of which it is an integral part. The facts of this penetration have been presented and the thesis of the consequent transformation and integration has been persuasively argued for Meso-America by Eric Wolf;[128] for India by Marx,[129] Dutt,[130] and Desai;[131] for China by Owen Lattimore;[132] for Africa by Woddis,[133] Suret-Canale,[134] and Mamadou Dia;[135] and even for Indonesia, the birthplace of dualism, by Wertheim and Geertz,[136] the latter formerly a research associate of Higgins and now a colleague of Hoselitz.

More specifically, as Eric Wolf[137] has taken great pains to point out for Meso-America and this writer for Brazil,[138] it is not true, as diffusionists and others implicitly or explicitly maintain, that the isolation of indigenous peoples, peasants, and others declines over time until they are completely integrated in the national society, which then is no longer dual. On the contrary, the degree of integration and other aspects of the relationship which these peoples have with others at

[128] Eric Wolf, *Sons of the Shaking Earth, op. cit.*

[129] Karl Marx, "British Rule in India," in *On Colonialism* (Moscow: Foreign Languages Publishing House n. d.).

[130] R. Palme Dutt, *India Today and Tomorrow, op. cit.*

[131] A. R. Desai, *The Social Background of Indian Nationalism, op. cit.*

[132] Owen Lattimore, "The Industrial Impact on China 1800–1950," *First International Conference of Economic History,* Stockholm 1960 (The Hague: Mouton & Co., 1960).

[133] Jack Woddis, *Africa, The Roots of Revolt, op. cit.*

[134] Jean Suret-Canale, *Histoire de l'Afrique Occidentale* (Paris: Edicions Sociales, 1961).

[135] Mamadou Dia, *Réflexions sur l'economie de l'Afrique noire* (Paris: Présence Africaine, 1960).

[136] W. F. Wertheim, *Indonesian Society in Transition, A Study of Social Change* (2nd revised edition; The Hague and Bandung: W. van Hoeve Ltd., 1959); and Clifford Geertz, *Agricultural Involution, The Process of Ecological Change in Indonesia* (Berkeley: University of California Press, 1963).

[137] Eric Wolf, *Sons of the Shaking Earth, op. cit.,* and "Types of Latin American Peasantry," *American Anthropologist,* Vol. 57, No. 3 (June 1955).

[138] André Gunder Frank, *Capitalism and Underdevelopment in Latin America, op. cit.*

home and abroad varies in ways which are determined primarily by the structure and development of the national and international capitalist system, and secondarily by these peoples' own very partially successful efforts to defend themselves against the exploitative consequences of this system.

Dualism is not only theoretically inadequate because it misrepresents and fails to analyze the capitalist system on the international, national, and local levels, but also because it fails to adhere to the standards of holism, structuralism, and historicity. Dualists contravene holism in explicitly setting up two or more theoretical wholes to confront a single social whole which they can not or will not see. As for structuralism, dualists fall far short because if they see and deal with any structure at all it is at best the structures of the parts. They do not deal with, and even deny the existence of, the structure of the whole system through which the parts are related—that is, the structure which determines the duality of wealth and poverty, of one culture and another, and so on. As to the historical development of the social phenomena they study, dualists and diffusionists either deny any history to one part altogether or, observe its ongoing social change without the historical perspective necessary to interpret it adequately; and they steadfastly abstain, of course, from giving any consideration whatsoever to the historical development of the social system of which diffusing donor and acculturating recipient are but parts. Little wonder then that diffusionists and other dualists who only look at appearances misunderstand their significance and misjudge their consequences for economic development and cultural change.

As Marx said, science would be pointless if the outward appearance of things were to correspond to their inner significance. Thus the task of social scientific theory, which dualist and other advocates of the three modes reviewed here fail to pursue, is not to see how different the parts are, but on the contrary, to study what relates the parts to each other in order to be able to explain why they are different or dual. If the policy of economic development and cultural change is really meant to eliminate these differences—or the undesirable ones among them—then its task must be to change the relationships that produce these differences: that is, it must change the structure of the *entire* social system which gives rise to the relations and therefore to the differences of the "dual" society.

The unfortunate, though not inexplicable, fact is that the theory and policy reviewed here is moving away from this task. With their supposedly structural and historical ideal typical approach, the disciples of Weber are leaving their teacher's scientific scope and method behind and dedicating themselves to no more than its cruel caricature. Similarly, dualists and diffusionists-acculturationists are corrupting the vision and work of one of their principal teachers of recent times, Robert Redfield. In creating the ideal type of the folk community, and in analyzing diffusion along the folk-urban continuum,[139] as well as in his later works on the relations between high and low culture,[140] Redfield, no doubt unintentionally, encouraged contemporary students of economic development and cultural change to adopt a dualism and diffusionism, which he himself rejected in his later years.

Redfield taught that in situations of culture contact diffusion is never a one way affair. In this respect, then, the diffusionist emphasis on diffusion from the metropolis to the periphery, and the virtual exclusion of the reverse is a departure from Redfield, as well as being unacceptable on other theoretical grounds. Moreover, although Redfield was far from being a structuralist (although he spared no pains to emphasize the need for holism in social scientific theory), he did call our attention to the structural determination of mutual diffusion between, for instance, high and low culture within a single social system. Nonetheless, Redfield's lessons seem not to have come to the attention of that majority of diffusionists who employ his terminology while distorting his ideas.

[139] Robert Redfield, *The Folk Culture of Yucatan, op. cit.,* and *The Little Community and Peasant Society and Culture, op. cit.*
[140] Robert Redfield, *Human Nature and the Study of Society, Papers of Robert Redfield,* ed. Margaret Park Redfield (Chicago: University of Chicago Press, 1962).

Finally, it was Redfield more than anyone else in recent times who insisted that there are no peasants without the city to which they are tied and which defines them as peasants, and that there can be no city without its peasants or their equivalent.[141] It is clear, then, that at least the later Redfield himself recognized and emphasized the *holistic interdependence and unity* of the dual ideal typical poles and social sectors he made so popular. It may be lamentable that Redfield did not extend this holism to the larger social system and to historical evolution, although his concern with the relations between high and low culture in his last years may have been a step in that direction. It is certainly more than lamentable, however, that so many of his diffusionist and dualist followers have abandoned their mentor's empirical realism and scientific holism and have substituted the most simplistic and crassly nonholistic diffusionism.

Policy Effectiveness

As a policy of economic development and cultural change diffusionism has been largely ineffective. The centuries long contact and diffusion between the metropolitan countries and the now underdeveloped ones has failed to result in the economic development of the latter. Nor has any diffusion from the capitals to the provinces of the underdeveloped countries brought about the development of these hinterlands. New technology may have increased diffusion beyond that of certain times in the past but surely not beyond the diffusion of initial contact times which, far from initiating the development of, initiated the underdevelopment of the now underdeveloped countries. More diffusion, per se, does not generate more development. Moreover, the diffusion which follows in the train of new roads, buses, transistor radios, etc., is not increasing the economic development of the recipient regions. Often it has helped to sink them into even deeper and more hopeless underdevelopment.

[141] Robert Redfield, *Peasant Society and Culture, op. cit.*

Conceived in its present form, diffusionism is inherently ineffective as a policy of economic development and cultural change. For it is not so much diffusion which produces a change in the social structure as it is the transformation of the social structure which permits effective diffusion. Development, underdevelopment, and diffusion are all a function of the social structure. In order for the underdeveloped parts of the world to develop, the structure of the world social system must change—on the international, national, and local levels. This structural change, however, cannot be brought about by diffusion. On the contrary, the structure of the system itself on all these levels determines the amount, nature, direction, and consequences of the past and present diffusion —a diffusion which has so far produced development only for the few and underdevelopment for the many, and by all indications will continue doing so. Consequently, the structure of this system has to change in order to permit development for all and to permit diffusion to contribute to that development.

THE PSYCHOLOGICAL APPROACH

Nash introduces the third approach as the one "most profitably pursued," and which leads to "smaller scale hypotheses, to a prospective rather than a retrospective view of social change." Furthermore, Nash writes:

These papers I commend to your attention as examples of the dialectic of social knowledge, the confrontation of bold assertion against fact, and the incorporation of more general fact in ever bolder, more elegant assertion.[142]

Nevertheless, a year later, comparing the psychological (and to some extent the first) mode of approach with his own second mode as published in *EDCC,* Nash seems to have had second thoughts:

[142] Manning Nash, "Introduction . . . ," *op. cit.,* pp. 5–6.

The 'specific factor' analysis of social requisites (like lack of entrepreneurship, low achievement motivation, particularism, capital shortage, etc.) are not likely to provide anything systematically relevant to an understanding of growth. . . .[143]

When Nash says that this mode of analysis leads to smaller scale hypotheses, he is quite right, as we will see below. However, it should be noted here that the first two modes were seen to be inadequate precisely because the scale of their theory and hypotheses is already too small to adequately treat the dimension and structure of the social system which gives rise to both development and underdevelopment.

As any historian of social thought will recall, Marx turned Hegel on his head and substituted historical materialism for idealism. Further, he worked with relatively large-scale theory and hypotheses which he derived from his examination of the capitalist system as a whole as he saw it. Being a true holist, Marx was led—inevitably as Parsons pointed out above—to the observation that exploitation is a necessary basis of this system and to the conclusion that such a basis generates the polarization of the system. Since this conclusion was not palatable to Social Democrats such as Weber and Durkheim, whose disciple Parsons became, they set out to construct an alternative theory of the social system by starting with its parts rather than with the whole—a procedure which, as Parsons says, inevitably de-emphasizes exploitation and makes the system appear to be not polarizing or disintegrative but integrative instead. Nonetheless, although Weber and Durkheim intentionally and explicitly abandoned the approach, conclusions, and policy of Marx, they still retained strong emphasis on the determinative importance of social structure, and in the case of Weber especially, of history as well. Even Hoselitz, being directly as well as via Parsons a disciple of Weber, and an advocate of the first mode of analysis, retains considerable interest in the role of social structure (he even puts it in his title) despite the attraction that the third

[143] Manning Nash, "Social Prerequisites to Economic Growth . . . ," *op. cit.*, p. 242.

mode approach of David McClelland, although apparently not of Everett Hagen, holds for him.[144]

The pioneering service, as Nash's co-editor, Robert Chin calls it, of these latter students of economic development and cultural change is precisely that they drop all pretense and practice of social scientific structuralism. They "Freudianize" Weber to such an extent that they no longer follow him at all. In fact, they specifically deny the importance of social structure and reject structural analysis. Although Hagen puts the word "social" into his title, he is quite frank in his preface in explaining that his theory is not social at all but rather psychological—or really psychiatric.[145] McClelland, reviewing Hagen's book in *EDCC*, agrees: He calls it "A Psychological Approach to Economic Development," albeit one which he finds to be not up to his own standards.[146] Not to be outdone, McClelland is quite explicit in telling his readers that not the social structure as Weber had it, nor even assignment of and reward in social roles based on achievement (as in Hoselitz' view), but only a high degree of individual motivation or need for achievement is the alpha and omega of economic development and cultural change:

> In its most general terms, the hypothesis states that a society with a generally high level of *n* Achievement will produce more energetic entrepreneurs who, in turn, produce more rapid economic development . . . it must satisfy us to have learned that high *n* Achievement leads people to behave in most of the ways they should behave if they are to fulfill the entrepreneurial role successfully as it has been defined by economists, historians, sociologists. . . . The whole view of history shifts once the importance of the achievement motive is recognized. For a century we have been dominated by Social Darwinism, by the implicit or explicit notion that man is a creature of his environment, whether natural or social. Marx

[144] Bert F. Hoselitz, "Role of Incentives in Industrialization," *Economic Weekly* (Bombay), Vol. 15, Nos. 28, 29, & 30, Special Number, July 1963.
[145] Everett E. Hagen, *On the Theory of Social Change, op. cit.*
[146] David McClelland, "A Psychological Approach . . . ," *op. cit.*

thought so in advocating economic determinism, in arguing that man's psychology is shaped in the last analysis by the conditions under which he must work. Even Freud thought so in teaching that civilization was a reaction to man's primitive urges and to the repressive force of social institutions beginning with the family. Practically all social scientists have in the past generations begun with society and tried to create man in its image. Even Toynbee's theory of history is essentially one of environmental challenges, though he recognizes that states of mind can create internal challenges.[147]

In his contribution to the volume edited by Nash and Chin, McClelland goes on to be even more explicit.

What is needed is a glacial shift in Western and particularly American social thinking. Ever since Darwin, social scientists have almost unconsciously started with the premise that the environment is primary and that the human organism somehow learns to adapt to it. . . . Consequently if one wants to change anything really fundamentally, he must start by modifying material arrangements in the environment which in turn will gradually re-shape institutions and eventually ideas. Yet the evidence, as in the present instance, is very strong that it is just as often and perhaps more often initiated the other way around. . . . This is just one more piece of evidence to support the growing convictions among social scientists that it is values, motives, or psychological forces that determine ultimately the rate of economic and social development. . . . *The Achieving Society*, suggests that ideas are in fact more important in shaping history than purely materialistic arrangements.[148]

We have returned full circle to Hegel. Except that McClelland's prescriptions for progress are not quite Hegel's. In his book's final chapter entitled "Accelerating Economic Growth," McClelland summarizes his prescriptions in his

[147] David McClelland, *The Achieving Society, op. cit.,* pp. 205, 238, 391.
[148] David McClelland, "Motivational Patterns in Southeast Asia with Special Reference to the Chinese Case," *Journal of Social Issues, op. cit.,* p. 17.

sub-titles: "Increasing Other-Directedness and Market Moral-ity;" "Increasing n Achievement;" "Decreasing Father Dominance;" "Protestant Conversion;" "Catholic and Com-munist Reform Movements;" "Effects of Education on n Achievement;" "Reorganizing Fantasy Life;" "Utilizing Ex-isting n Achievement Resources More Effectively;" and he offers a final recommendation:

> So we end on a practical note: a plan for accelerating economic growth through mobilizing more effectively the high n Achievement resources of a developed coun-try to select and work directly with the scarcer high n Achievement resources in underdeveloped countries par-ticularly in small and medium scale businesses located in provincial areas. . . .[149]

This new pioneering service was undoubtedly inspired by Weber's emphasis on values in *The Protestant Ethic and the Spirit of Capitalism*[150] and reinforced by Schumpeter's em-phasis on entrepreneurship in *The Theory of Economic De-velopment.*[151] The post World War II revival of academic interest in economic development was soon followed by a return to the letter if not to the spirit of Weber and Schum-peter. Books and articles on the role of religion and values in economic development appeared in great numbers, not a few of them in *EDCC,* as cited above.[152] Simultaneously, Harvard University set up a Research Center in Entrepre-neurial History and a journal, *Explorations in Entrepreneur-ial History.* Papers on entrepreneurship as a crucial factor in economic development and cultural change were pub-lished in *EDCC* and elsewhere.[153] The increasing evidence

[149] David McClelland, *The Achieving Society, op. cit.,* pp. 391–437.

[150] Max Weber, *The Protestant Ethic and the Spirit of Capi-talism* (London: G. Allen & Unwin, 1930).

[151] J. A. Schumpeter, *The Theory of Economic Development* (Cambridge: Harvard University Press, 1934).

[152] See footnote 18.

[153] For recent examples see, Alec P. Alexander, "Industrial Entrepreneurship in Turkey: Origins and Growth," *EDCC,* Vol. 8, No. 4, Part I (July 1960), and Arcadius Kahan, "Entrepreneur-ship in the Early Development of Iron Manufacturing in Russia," *EDCC,* Vol. 10, No. 4 (July 1962).

against the supposed role of the Schumpeterian entrepreneur in economic development, not only in underdeveloped countries but even in the nineteenth century United States,[154] has not prevented the psychological idealizers of economic development from going on to advance theories such as those of Hagen and McClelland. Nor has it prevented *EDCC* from following in their footsteps to publish an entire series of studies reinterpreting the world to show the supposed importance of the achievement motive.[155] Furthermore, *EDCC's* reviewer of *The Achieving Society,* S. N. Eisenstadt, concludes:

> . . . the fact that in discussing this book, we are confronting it with Weber's work, is the measure of the importance of the problems raised by McClelland's endeavor. . . . McClelland has given a very stimulating and important work which anybody interested either in the broader problem of the impact of motivational orientation on society or in the more specific problem of economic development cannot ignore.[156]

To his and *EDCC's* credit, John H. Kunkel has recently evaluated this "pioneering service":

> As long as man's activities are considered to be a function of values or personality, little attention need be directed to the immediate surrounding social environment, since it is not so much the present social structure as that of the past which is most involved in the formation

---

[154] W. Paul Strassman, *Risk and Technological Innovation: American Manufacturing Methods in the Nineteenth Century* (Ithaca: Cornell University Press, 1959); and "The Industrialist," in John J. Johnson, ed., *Continuity and Change in Latin America* (Stanford: Stanford University Press, 1964).

[155] Norman N. Bradburn and David Berlew, "Need for Achievement and English Industrial Growth," *EDCC,* Vol. 10, No. 1 (October 1961); Juan B. Cortes, "The Achievement Motive in the Spanish Economy Between the 13th and 18th Centuries," *EDCC,* Vol. 9, No. 1 (October 1960); James N. Morgan, "The Achievement Motive and Economic Behavior," *EDCC,* Vol. 12, No. 3 (April 1964).

[156] S. N. Eisenstadt, "The Need for Achievement," *EDCC,* Vol. 11, No. 4 (July 1963), p. 431.

of values and personality. The delineation of societal prerequisites of economic development, according to this view, can accomplish no more than prepare the ground for industrialization years, if not decades, in the future. However, as soon as behavior is considered to be a function largely of the surrounding social structure, both past *and* present, which affects behavior through the continuously operating determination of reinforcing and discriminative stimuli, the present social system takes on great importance. The behavioral prerequisites of economic development can be created only through alterations of the social structure, or certain elements of it, viewed broadly and including the economic system of a society. . . . There is no foundation, on theoretical grounds, for the pessimistic outlook concerning the capacity of the underdeveloped countries to industrialize in a short period of time. Pessimistic conclusions regarding the time necessary for the preparation of the right psychological conditions for economic development are based, essentially, on an incorrect conception of man and on the disregard of principles of behavior formation and maintenance derived from experimental psychology.[157]

Nevertheless, in his contribution to the collection of papers edited by Nash and Chin which exemplify this third mode approach, Kunkel's criticism is based largely on psychological principles and limited essentially to methodological criticism of the third mode's empirical assertions.[158] So is Eisenstadt's criticism in his review of McClelland's book.[159] Furthermore, Kunkel's proposed alternative in his contribution to *EDCC* is limited to suggesting that behavioristic methodology can overcome the methodological shortcomings of the approach exemplified by Hagen and McClelland.[160] In this connection, Kunkel rightly observes:

[157] John H. Kunkel, "Values and Behavior in Economic Development," *op. cit.*, pp. 276–77.
[158] John H. Kunkel, "Psychological Factors in the Analysis of Economic Development," *Journal of Social Issues, op. cit.*
[159] S. N. Eisenstadt, "The Need for Achievement," *op. cit.*
[160] John H. Kunkel, "Values and Behavior . . . ," *op. cit.*

Hagen makes much use of personality as an 'internal state' of individuals. The characteristics of the 'internal state' are derived from psychoanalytic theory, and then used to support the theory and the hypothesized relations among observed facts and inferred characteristics. When psychoanalytic concepts and theories are used in the study of economic development, problems of validating the concepts make any casual generalization difficult to test and accept on bases other than faith. . . . The casual analysis is inadequate. Hagen infers causes from effects, but no evidence is presented to validate the inference made. . . . McClelland postulates a variety of needs as components of a person's 'internal state', but this method of analysis involves inferences from behavior (e.g., the writing of stories based on TAT pictures) which are difficult to validate, in order to explain the data collected by McClelland and his associates.[161]

Both Kunkel and Eisenstadt find that the work of these students of economic development and cultural change is deficient in that it fails to establish a methodologically adequate efficient cause between the supposedly causative psychological states and the supposedly derivative economic development. Kunkel's purpose in his contribution to *EDCC* is to provide such an efficient causative relation which is not dependent on untestable inferences about internal states of mind.[162]

Whatever the methodological merits or demerits of Kunkel's resort to behaviorism, it is as limited to generating small

[161] John H. Kunkel, "Psychological Factors . . . ," *op. cit.,* pp. 72–73, 82. For a similar criticism also see S. N. Eisenstadt, "The Need for Achievement," *op. cit.*

[162] This effort is reminiscent of the famous but unsuccessful attempt to remedy functionalists' accounting for the existence of institutions through reliance on teleology by George C. Homans and David M. Schneider in their *Marriage, Authority, and Final Causes. A Study of Unilateral Cross-Cousin Marriage* (Glencoe: The Free Press, 1955). Rejecting the final cause of societal equilibrium as an explanation for an institution's existence, Homans and Schneider sought to substitute an identifiable efficient cause, though strangely their "efficient cause" was an internal state—that is, another final cause similar to the ones criticised here.

scale hypotheses, as Nash calls them, and to recommending small scale changes as is the methodology it seeks to substitute. Kunkel himself concludes:

> If it is true that striving behavior, like any other, is shaped through differential reinforcement [such as reward and punishment by parents, as Kunkel tells us elsewhere], there is no reason why an internal state . . . should have to be postulated as an essential element in the analysis of economic development. . . . Various selected elements of the societal environment are amenable to change today, thereby making possible the shaping of behavior patterns necessary for economic development. . . . Since usually only a few aspects of the societal environment can be altered, present efforts to create behavioral prerequisites must begin on a small scale.[163]

This suggests that, to evaluate the theoretical adequacy of the third mode approach, we must bring still other criteria to bear, such as the historicity and holistic structuralism by which we already examined the first two approaches.

As editor of a collection of works which exemplify the third mode, Manning Nash holds that of the three modes he is able to visualize, this third one is "most profitably pursued." One of its profitable aspects is that it leads "to a prospective rather than a retrospective view of social change." That is, as we may infer, Nash thinks that the social scientists working in terms of the third mode are performing a pioneering service not only because they abandon Weber's structuralism, leaving behind as well Bert Hoselitz—who after all not only retains some structuralism but also is world renowned as an economic historian—but also because in not looking back, these pioneers leave behind them Weber's retrospective and historical approach and analysis as well.

However, Nash does not confine himself simply to lauding this effort and to recommending that students of economic development and cultural change forget about the past history of the underdeveloped countries concerned. Instead, he

[163] John H. Kunkel, "Values and Behavior . . . ," op. cit., pp. 275, 277.

goes on to deny that the underdeveloped countries have any history. The third approach he says, poses three main theoretical problems:

> 1. to systematically take account of the varieties of *traditional* societies, 2. to seek out the sources of resistance . . . among the various species of *traditionality,* 3. [to study why a society may or may not come] to rest somewhere between its *initial base* and modernity.[164]

In other words, underdeveloped societies have no history, they have traditionally been the way they are now, which is underdeveloped. This is indeed a "bold assertion;" but once it faces "confrontation with fact" this claim is clearly revealed to be a falsification. How could Nash make such an assertion after having done the fieldwork for his doctoral dissertation in a community descended from a people who are world renowned for their history, the last seventy years of which he studied, and after having entitled his book *Machine Age Maya?*[165] How is it a pioneering service for the practitioners and champions of the third mode to take less and less account of the history of the underdeveloped countries they presume to study (especially after having delved into it here and there themselves), and finally to end up denying that the underdeveloped countries and underdevelopment even have history? For whom is this a pioneering service?

The answers emerge if we apply the criterion of structural holism to the question of the theoretical adequacy of the third mode approach and if we inquire into the effectiveness of the policy of economic development and cultural change to which this approach gives rise.

Kunkel correctly notes in regard to both the theory and the policy of the third mode that "little attention need be directed to the immediate surrounding social environment since it is not the present social structure which matters." But the critic of this approach is hardly as explicit and clear as its exponent, McClelland himself: "ideas are in fact more im-

[164] Manning Nash, "Introduction . . . ," *op. cit.,* p. 4. Emphasis supplied.
[165] Manning Nash, *Machine Age Maya, op. cit.*

portant in shaping history than purely materialistic arrangements . . . of his [man's] environment, whether natural or social." The third mode of approaching economic development and cultural change, then, represents perhaps the ultimate step in pioneering progress away from classical scientific structural holism. The present economic, social, and political structure does not matter at all: There is no need to change the contemporary status quo.

What, then, according to these purveyors of dialectic social knowledge (as Nash terms their service) is to be done; and how effectively and for whom does their policy of promoting economic development and cultural change work? McClelland tells us what is to be done: "Increasing *n* Achievement . . . Protestant Conversion . . . Education . . . Reorganizing Fantasy Life." As McClelland himself recognizes, not only Marx, but even such progressive students as Spencer, the father of Social Darwinism, Toynbee, the father of neo-Thomism, and Freud, the father of individual psychiatry, and all of their intellectual children, never were progressive enough to believe and maintain that so deeply ingrained a social and economic condition of society could be changed simply by having more of its individuals taught to get a hold of themselves and raise their need for achievement, as McClelland would have it; or by not letting themselves be beaten down by adversity, as Hagen would have it; or even by having teachers and parents tell children more hero stories so that when the latter grow up they might be heroic developers themselves. This degree of progress and progressiveness had to await the coming of David McClelland and his disciples.

McClelland gives credit to one source of co-revelation of his vision of economic development and cultural change: the Communists, particularly the Chinese ones.[166] They receive no credit for following the teachings of Marx or other social scientists, the validity of whose theory McClelland denies; no credit for changing any economic, social, or political structure, the need for which change McClelland denies;

[166] David McClelland, "Motivational Patterns in Southeast Asia . . . ," *op. cit.*, and *The Achieving Society, op. cit.*, pp. 412–413.

nor any credit for making a revolution, which McClelland does not deem worthy of mention. Instead, they receive credit for realizing and putting into practice the truth that ideas and *n* Achievement promote economic development: the Chinese are achieving faster economic development than the Indians, McClelland points out.[167] On the basis of what economic, social, and political structure, he doesn't say: the Chinese have more *n* Achievement and *n* Power.[168] According to McClelland, it does not matter how that structure determines the distribution of power and the direction of achievement. Despite this generous bow to the Chinese Communists, we need no great insightfulness to discern the allegiance and effectiveness of an economic development policy which—following the example of such highly motivated members of the Cambridge, Massachusetts, academic community as W. W. Rostow,[169] McGeorge Bundy, Arthur Schlesinger, Jr., and perhaps David McClelland himself—promotes *n* Achievement and reorganization of fantasy life within the existing economic, social, and political structure, at home or abroad.

In complimenting the Communists, McClelland fails to give due credit where it really belongs. It is Frank Buchman and his world wide movement for Moral Rearmament (MRA) who preached precisely the policy of economic development and cultural change now clothed in academic gown by David McClelland. His policy advice to developers is to take their eyes off and leave as is the economic, social, and political structure of the status quo; prepare instead each man for himself, to rearm morally and spiritually to face the difficult road of economic development, cultural change, and social progress that lies ahead. The political character and effectiveness of this development policy is amply demon-

---

[167] David McClelland, *The Achieving Society, op. cit.,* p. 423.
[168] David McClelland, "Motivational Patterns . . . ," *op. cit.*
[169] "Mr. Rostow's former university colleagues on the old Kennedy White House staff . . . are savagely critical of his increasing influence, and they condemn his aggressive intellectualism as self-serving opportunism that consoles the President but tends to mislead him, particularly on Vietnam." *New York Times,* April 13, 1967.

strated by its practitioners who include such renowned practical dialecticians, progressive servants, and self-declared MRA supporters as ex-Chancellor Adenauer of Germany, ex-Premier Kishi of Japan, ex-Prime Minister Tshombe of Katanga and the Congo, and the second President of Brazil after the 1964 military coup, General Costa e Silva.

CONCLUSION

Having examined the three modes of approach to and analysis of the problems of economic development and cultural change separately, we can briefly evaluate them conjointly. What first forces itself into view is the wide and deep similarity in the extent of the three modes' empirical inaccuracy, theoretical inadequacy, and ineffectiveness of policy. Yet this similarity should not surprise us. It is no more than the reflection of their fundamental similarity in points of departure, both ideologically and analytically. Thus, the first mode is ideal-typical in that it sets up the supposedly typical characteristics of development. The second mode concerns itself with how these typical characteristics of the first mode are supposedly diffused from the developed countries to the underdeveloped ones. Finally, the third mode, and herein lies its pioneering service, tells us how the typical characteristics that are identified in the first and diffused according to the second mode are to be acculturated by the underdeveloped countries if they wish to develop. This, in a nutshell, is the sum total of this received theory and analysis of economic development and cultural change; it is the alpha and omega of the possibilities that Manning Nash can visualize: it is thanks to this limitation of his, if not of theory and reality, that Nash manages to arrive at the third mode, as he says, "via the argument of residue."

The pioneers of these three modes have progressed; to social dualism, they have added sociological dualism. Their whole theory and theorizing is split down the middle. They see one set of characteristics, take note of one social structure if any; construct one theory for one part of the what has been one world economic and social system for half a millenium, and construct another pattern and theory for the other part. And all that in the name of universalism. They argue that one part of the system, Western Europe and Northern America, diffuses and helps the other part, Asia, Africa, and South America, to develop. They similarly argue that those national metropolises of these three continents that have already received the benefits of this diffusion in turn help pull up their own hinterland behind them. They argue that the take-off by the underdeveloped countries and their national metropolises is hindered by the drag on them of their slow and backward hinterlands. Curiously, though fortunately, except for the most irresponsible among them, they do not argue similarly that the take-off and development of the world capitalist metropolis in Europe and North America is hindered by the drag of its underdeveloped hinterland in Asia, Africa, and Latin America. They ask where the capital for the development of the national metropolises of the underdeveloped countries is to come from and say it must and will come from the developed countries; which is wrong, since in fact it comes from the domestic internal colonies of these national metropolises. They ask where the capital for the development of the already developed countries came from and say it came from themselves; which is also wrong since much, and at the time the critical part, of it came from the consequently now underdeveloped countries. As with most of the remainder of the developed countries' universalism, the theoretical universalism of their social science is a pretense and a sham. If we may borrow something from the arsenal of this mode's pioneers, the theorists of all three modes of economic development and cultural change who like to call themselves universally theoretical dualists, are intellectual and political schizophrenics.[170]

To render the real significance and value of this highly

---

[170] Further theoretical limitations of the functionalist part of this social science theory are examined in my "Functionalism, Dialectics, and Synthetics," *Science & Society*, Vol. 30, No. 2 (Spring 1966), reprinted as chapter 3 in André Gunder Frank, *Latin America: Underdevelopment or Revolution, op. cit.*

developed conventional wisdom still clearer, we may characterize it—no less exhaustively than Nash summarizes it—by the caricature of the twin methodological supports of the society that produced it, which Steinberg put on the cover of a *New Yorker*: Santa Claus and Sigmund Freud. American society rests on and revolves around these twin gods, Steinberg suggests, and we may add, so does the ideology of economic development and cultural change which that same society produces and exports. How are the people in the underdeveloped countries to achieve economic development? By waiting for Christmas and then accepting the gift of diffusion from Santa Claus in the North. What gift does Santa Claus bear for the peoples of the underdeveloped countries? The latest message from Sigmund Freud. If only the people of the mythically characterized underdeveloped world will, like we did, learn to worship at the altar of these twin Gods, they too will change culturally and develop economically. Can it be any wonder that the people of the real underdeveloped world must, and will, look beyond what some others dream possible to find a theory of economic development and cultural change which is empirically congruent with, theoretically adequate for, and politically acceptable to their reality, needs, and desires?

The direction in which to look for an alternative theory of economic development and change that is more adequate for the underdeveloped countries is suggested by the common shortcomings of the three-part approach of received theory reviewed here. Firstly, where this approach is empirically wrong about the past and present reality of the underdeveloped part of the world, the developed part of the world, and the world as a whole; an adequate alternative theory will have to come to terms with the history and contemporary reality of development and underdevelopment. Secondly, where the approach is theoretically inadequate because it cannot identify the determinant social whole, because it takes account neither of the history of the underdeveloped part nor of its relations with the developed part, and least of all of the world as a whole, and because it does not conform to the structure of that world's social system; an alternative theory must reflect the structure and development of the system which has given rise to, now maintains, and still increases both structural development and structural underdevelopment as simultaneous and mutually produced manifestations of the same historical process. Thirdly, where the development policy of this approach is ever more politically conservative and counsels accepting the structural status quo with folded hands while waiting for others' gifts with open hands, an alternative policy for economic development and cultural change will have to be politically ever more revolutionary and help the peoples of the underdeveloped countries to take the destruction of this structure and the development of another system, into their own hands. If the developed countries cannot diffuse development, development theory, or development policy to the underdeveloped countries, then the people of these countries will have to develop them by themselves. These three modes of approach are the emperor's clothes, which have served to hide his naked imperialism. Rather than fashioning the emperor a new suit, these people will have to dethrone him and clothe themselves.

Chapter 13

THE CONCEPT
OF POLITICAL DEVELOPMENT

José F. Ocampo and *Dale L. Johnson*

"Political development" is a concept of recent origin that has become central to political science, especially within the United States, in the discipline's effort to come to grips with politics in underdeveloped countries. The usage of the concept unfortunately has the effect of systematically diverting attention from both the problems of development and the nature of politics. We are therefore hesitant to use the concept at all and do so here only to gain a point of departure for a critical analysis of the assumptions that underlie its conventional usage.

We contend that the major considerations that any theory of politics in a developmental context in capitalist societies must deal with are as follows:

1. The basic institutional framework of capitalist societies—private property, private initiative, and inequalities in the distribution of wealth and income—generate class structures grounded in inequalities of power and privilege and therefore of antagonistic relations between classes.

2. The fundamental political entity of capitalist society is the state. Any theory of politics and development must take into account the manner in which power vested in control of the economy and power resources of social classes are reflected in the state. The major problem here is identification of the various mechanisms by which the economic power of dominant social classes is translated into institutionalized political power.

3. A crucial problem for the analysis of politics and development is the nature of objective, patterned relations between economy, society, and the state. This involves an identification of the functions, basically of system-maintenance, of the state in and for society. Developmentally, the activities of the state are subject to the structural constraints, which analysis must identify, imposed by the system of capitalism.

4. The different forms of the state—liberal-democratic, authoritarian, fascist, populist, and others—are determined by economic transformations and changes in class relations in historical and cultural contexts characteristic of different countries and regions.

5. Development involves the liberation of man from conditions of exploitation and oppression. Politics is the means of human liberation.

We contend that contemporary political science, as practiced in the United States and diffused to other parts of the world, denies, avoids consideration of, ignores, or refuses to accede to any of these five fundamental propositions regarding politics and development.

There are two basic sets of working assumptions that most contemporary political scientists use in analyzing "political development." These are (a) that power relations in capitalist societies are, or tend toward, and ought to be "pluralistic" and (b) the concept of evolutionary functionalism. The former involves the notion that with development, power becomes dispersed or widely diffused in different sectors of society. The latter involves an assumption of continuous change borrowed from the classic evolutionary faith in "progress," combined with the theoretical apparatus of modern functionalism (which in turn has been adopted from sociology and anthropology and the equilibrium analysis of macroeconomics).

POLITICS AND DEVELOPMENT FROM THE PLURALIST PERSPECTIVE

ORIGINS OF PLURALIST THEORY

Proposition 1: The basic institutional framework of capitalist societies—private property, private initiative, and inequalities in the distribution of wealth and income—generate class structures grounded in inequalities of power and privilege and therefore of antagonistic relations between classes.

Modern pluralist theory has its historical origin in the nineteenth and early twentieth centuries' theoretical and ideological confrontations with the Marxian version of the above proposition. Marx viewed the class structure as directly related to the modes of production. Politics and development in turn are a direct consequence of antagonistic class relations. Underlying Marx's sociological theory of politics and historical change is a humanist perspective. The philosophical and ethical foundations of the scientific work of Marx derive from his concern for human liberation. For Marx there is no possibility of bettering the human condition while a privileged minority maintains decisive control over the means of production.[1] Political reality is determined and dominated by economic forces. In a capitalist society, the minority that monopolizes direct access to the means of production has the capacity to dominate and exploit the majority. The Marxist critique of capitalist society postulates the necessity of eliminating the domination of a propertied minority by means of revolutionary abolition of the system of private property

[1] Karl Marx, *Early Writings*, T. B. Bottomore (ed.) (New York, 1964); Marx and Engels, *Basic Writings on Politics and Philosophy*, Lewis S. Feuer (ed.) (New York, 1959); Jean-Ives Calvez, *La Pensée de Karl Marx* (Paris, 1956); Roger Garaudy, *Humanismo Marxista* (Buenos Aires, 1959); Herbert Marcuse, *Reason and Revolution* (Boston, 1960); Lezek Kolakowski, *Toward a Marxist Humanism* (New York, 1968); Henri Lefevre, *The Sociology of Marx* (New York, 1968); T. B. Bottomore, *Elites and Society* (New York, 1964).

in favor of social property. There is no other manner of restoring freedom and achieving the liberation of man.

The classical European theorists, Vilfredo Pareto and Gaetano Mosca, reject this theory of Marx. For these predecessors of contemporary pluralist theory, the elimination of a dominant minority would be impossible because their power is a consequence of superior personal qualities which the elite possess by nature. Rule by a minority has always existed historically. The organization of society itself, they contend, is only possible given the existence of a limited ruling elite which is entitled to enjoy social, economic, and political privileges. A society without classes is not possible. For these reasons, it is necessary to accept political domination exercised by a minority that bases its power in the force of its economic resources. In contradiction to Marx, Pareto and Mosca not only accept the power of minority but also justify it as the only possible mode of human existence.[2]

It is ironic that the antidemocratic perspective of Pareto and Mosca later formed the basis of a theory of democracy. In spite of being antidemocratic, Mosca did suggest that it was possible to harmonize the ideals of the theory of the ruling class with those of liberal democracy. Subsequently, Joseph Schumpeter and Raymond Aron took the classic elite theorists a step farther and proposed a "pluralist" solution to the problem of the elite.[3] Aron concludes that a synthesis

[2] Gaetano Mosca, *The Ruling Class*, Arthur Livingstone (ed.) (New York, 1939); T. B. Bottomore, *op. cit.*, pp. 1–17; James Burnham, *The Machiavellians* (Chicago, 1963); Peter Bachrach, *The Theory of Democratic Elitism: A Critique* (Boston, 1967), pp. 10–26.

[3] Seymour Martin Lipset gives the following definition of democracy based upon Schumpeter and Weber: ". . . a political system which supplies regular constitutional opportunities for changing the governing officials, and a social mechanism which permits the largest possible part of the population to influence major decisions by choosing among contenders for political office." *Political Man: The Social Bases of Politics* (Garden City, New York, 1963). See also Raymond Aron, "Social Structure and the Ruling Class," *The British Journal of Sociology* I (March and June 1950); Joseph Schumpeter, *Capitalism, Socialism, and Democracy* (New York, 1947), pp. 232–302.

is possible between a united elite and the "circulation of elites" proposed by Pareto as a solution to the problem of renovation of power. This synthesis is the idea of representative government. According to Aron, a representative (i.e., democratic) government incorporates different elites to the exercise of political power and gives rise to loyal competition between them. Representative government permits a constant renovation of the governing figures and of those elites that decay with the use of power. Thus, the system makes it possible to avoid the danger of a government directed by a decadent elite that perpetuates itself in power. Nor is it necessary to postulate revolution as the only form of progressive political change. In this way, Aron believes that he has surmounted two impasses posed by Marxist theory: that of the monopoly of power by a minority and that of the need for revolution in order to renovate power.

The theory of pluralist democracy based upon European theory and today accepted by the majority of United States political scientists (and citizens) derives from this formulation. These principles are the bases of the numerous political analyses centered on pressure groups and political parties; the necessity of a value consensus, an opposition, elections, and a representative system; and, most importantly, the existence of an equilibrium in the exercise of economic and political power.[4]

In his historical analysis of North American democracy, Robert A. Dahl, the foremost pluralist theorist, has spelled out the implications of the pluralist-democratic theory of power. Dahl concludes that contemporary democracy is characterized by the command not of the minority but of *minorities*.

> Elections and political competition do not make for government by majorities in any very significant way,

---

[4] See, among others, V. O. Key, Jr., *Politics, Parties, and Pressure-Groups* (New York, 1958); Robert A. Dahl (ed.), *Political Oppositions in Western Democracies* (New Haven, Connecticut, 1966); Talcott Parsons, "The Distribution of Power in American Democracy," *Structure and Process in Modern Societies* (New York, 1960); Arnold M. Rose, *The Power Structures; Political Process in American Society* (London, 1967).

but they vastly increase the size, number, and variety of minorities which preference must be taken into account by leaders in making policy choices. I am inclined to think that it is in this characteristic of elections—not minority rule but minorities rule—that we must look for some of the essential differences between dictatorships and democracies.[5]

The "minorities" that pluralists are particularly concerned with are the "elites" from different sections of society. Walker has appropriately termed this "the elitist theory of democracy."[6] Political scientists of this persuasion speak of the very nature of political systems in democratic elitist terms. For example, instead of social classes or interest groups, Gabriel Almond (one of the pioneers in extending pluralist and functional theory to political development in underdeveloped countries) analyzes "interest articulation" and reduces the analysis of political parties to a function, the "aggregation of interests"; instead of dealing with political consensus or legitimacy as such, Almond introduces the terms "political culture" and "socialization."[7]

Pluralists generally avoid consideration of the concentration of economic power, except when directly engaged in polemics with Marxist or "power elite" theorists. When they do deal with this, they accept as a fact (presumably an inevitable fact) the concentration of economic power in the hands of a few, but roundly deny that this is an obstacle to the equalitarian distribution of political power in society. The pluralists hold that it is possible to construct a political system in equilibrium and of genuine popular representation, as if the political system were one of free markets and competition wherein elites compete for the favor of the citizenry. Economic monopoly is conveniently neutralized in the politi-

[5] Robert A. Dahl, *A Preface to Democratic Theory* (Chicago, 1956), p. 132.

[6] Jack L. Walker, "A Critique of the Elitist Theory of Democracy," *The American Political Science Review* LX (June 1966), pp. 285–95; Robert A. Dahl, "Further Reflections on 'The Elitist Theory of Democracy,'" *ibid.*, pp. 296–306.

[7] Gabriel Almond and G. Bingham Powell, Jr., *Comparative Politics: A Developmental Approach* (Boston, 1966).

cal sphere by the competition that is established between the different minorities or elites.[8] In this way, the theoretical disassociation of economic power from political power is justified. As long as a variety of economic and institutional forces exists, political power remains free of any predominant control.

An upper class of the wealthy and privileged may exist, but it is divided into competing elites or interest groups, and therefore no community of interests exists within the class. At the same time, this class receives the pressure of political mechanisms that are in the hands of other classes, especially the middle class, and the "countervailing" or "veto" power of the working class organized into unions.

The pluralists often hold that power is an available means (similar to money in the economy) that permits a society to mobilize its resources in order to achieve collective ends. In contrast, we hold that power is a tangible substance rooted in the economic, social, and institutional structure of society. Pluralists assume that shared values—rather than control and distribution of property and income—within a society determine its social stratification and permit those with greater capacity to occupy the elite positions of greatest responsibility. In no way does this break the equilibrium of power in society as a whole. If an "upper class" exists in society, this only facilitates the organization of society to achieve a high level of economic production, to elevate technology and science to the maximum, with the end of increasing productivity, and to promote acceptance in pragmatic form of an authority more or less in contact and consonant with economic power.

[8] See Robert A. Dahl, *Who Governs? Democracy and Power in an American City* (New Haven, 1961); Dahl, "The Concept of Power," in Sidney Ulmer (ed.), *Introductory Readings in Political Behavior* (Chicago, 1961); Dahl, *Modern Political Analysis* (Englewood Cliffs, New Jersey, 1963); Nelson W. Polsby, *Community Power and Political* (New Haven, 1963); Pendleton Herring, *The Politics of Democracy* (New York, 1966); William Knornhauser, "'Power Elite' or 'Vote Groups'" in Reinhard Bendix and Seymour Martin Lipset (eds.), *Class, Status, and Power* (New York, 1966), pp. 210–18.

PLURALISM IN LATIN AMERICA

The fundamental fact in Latin American societies is that political systems have been dominated historically by the propertied minority and their servants in power, and continue being so dominated. This permits the minority to maintain its situation of privilege, while the great majority of the population are poor and subjugated.

We assume that political power cannot be analyzed in separation from economic power and that those classes that hold economic power exercise domination over other classes. Only empirical analysis can reveal the mechanisms and limits of such domination in particular cases. The pluralists, on the other hand, assume that "human conduct is governed in great part by inertia."[9] This means that if the lower classes of society are less politically or socially active, it is because they do not want to participate, and consequently values must not be imputed to them that they do not wish to accept. For the pluralist, each actor and every class has its role in the community and, ordinarily, no one tries to manipulate in the realm of the other, unless he wishes to risk the high price that an action of this type could bring. Political participation is "voluntary," because it implies risks and responsibilities. According to pluralist theory, the resources of power in a society are or can be more or less at the disposition of all, and their diversity is not exhausted in economic resources. While the rich have money, the poor have numbers, etc. That a few have a greater access to resources of power is a consequence of their "activity" and of their will to participate. For this reason, modern democratic society is well structured as it is. What is needed in underdeveloped countries is simply more "civic participation" by "low status" groups. Underdeveloped systems may also need a greater dosage of rationality and secularization, and elites need to be more pragmatic in order to adapt different elements to society and to maintain intact an indispensable system of compromise and understanding.

[9] Polsby, *op. cit.*, p. 60.

According to the interpreters of pluralism in the Latin American case, then, the weak point in Latin American society is basically a lack of institutional rationality, secularization, and political pragmatism. Some political scientists have gone even farther. What Charles W. Anderson calls the "prudence model" of politics has been operative and effective, according to Anderson, in achieving social and economic development in Latin America. For the political system to respond to the present and future imperatives of development, the established "power contenders" in pluralistic Latin American systems need only be prudently rational and pragmatic and yield a bit of ground to the "underrepresented masses." Prudent politics for change-minded social groups would consist of the formulation of demands that do not fundamentally disturb existing "power contenders" or threaten their "power capabilities."[10] In his review of Anderson, David Felix prudently comments:

> The book . . . has certain features common to current U.S. academic studies of Latin American politics: preference for moderate solutions, pretentious formalization, normative appeals which paper over weak spots in the positive analysis, and reluctance to call an *espada* an *espada*.[11]

Even stranger than Anderson's propositions that Latin American societies are pluralistic and that power distribution is no obstacle to development is James Payne's conclusion that there is no such thing as an oligarchy in Peru because labor sometimes manages to gain wage demands through strikes, street violence, and political activity.[12] R. H. Dix surpasses the conventional pluralists in reducing Colombian politics to a status game between individuals, families, and groups.[13]

[10] Charles W. Anderson, *Politics and Economic Change in Latin America: The Governing of Restless Nations* (Princeton, 1967).

[11] David Felix's review of Anderson, *Economic Development and Cultural Change* XVII (October 1968), p. 120.

[12] James Payne, *Labor and Politics in Peru.*

[13] R. H. Dix, *Colombia: The Political Dimensions of Change* (New Haven, Connecticut, 1968).

REPRESENTATIVE SYSTEMS

Proposition 2: The fundamental political entity of capitalist society is the state. Any theory of politics and development must take into account the manner in which power vested in control of the economy and power resources of social classes are reflected in the state. The major problem here is identification of the various mechanisms by which the economic power of dominant social classes is translated into institutionalized political power.

Whether the reference is to Latin America or to the United States, the notion of pluralistic power structures and the "democratic-elitist" idea of competing or plural elites serves explicit ideological functions—to mystify and obfuscate the nature of power relations and to deny the existence of a dominant class in capitalist societies.

Pluralistic power structures are normally seen as reflected in a state organized around representative political systems. Pluralist theorists take particular delight in the analysis of representative systems complete with political parties, legislatures, and elections. Where such systems exist, democracy prevails; where they do not exist, say the pluralists, their achievement is the essence of political development.

Representative systems are said to be based upon the "conciliatory model," which involves a minimum of coercion of citizens and a maximum of articulation and aggregation of diverse social interests. In other words, private initiative and free enterprise reign with a maximum of liberty possible in all fields, while flexible mechanisms exist that maintain communication throughout governmental levels and between government and private interests.

Pluralists see the diffusion of power as inherent in representative systems. Moreover, this diffusion of power permits a commitment to and achievement of development goals. This is possible because the state stands above the pluralism of society and can pursue the general public interest. The government, of course, gears its policies and decisions to the degree of popularity or support that it has among "the people"—that is to say, to the approval of the groups that compete in the system. We maintain elsewhere in this chapter that under these circumstances groups do not compete over development goals as such, but over distribution of the social product. When the pie is small, organized groups act to maintain or increase the relative size of their piece. They are not usually concerned to increase the size of the pie. Yet, even supposing *a priori* that what passes for politics within representative systems is more than a struggle over the social product and that the government is conscious of the goals of development that it attempts to obtain, it is clear that it is not primarily a vision of the future or a plan based upon a conception of the general interest of all the people that determines or specifies development goals. At best, goals are the result of a mutual communication between government and interested groups. Ideally, in a pluralist, representative system, "goals are in a very direct relation with resources and with the desires of the public . . ."[14] But such a political system, David Apter notes, "is frequently a prisoner of society."[15] This is precisely what has happened in Latin America. However, the government is a prisoner, not of a structure wherein power is widely dispersed, but of a structure in which a few monopolize economic resources and control or heavily influence institutions both within and outside of the formal political system. These interests determine development goals and policies.

The control of the state in a conciliatory system in Latin America operates through the bureaucracy and the political process. Issues, questions to resolve, policies to formulate, etc., are fed into the bureaucracy and political process by those in the private sphere who control information media and channels. In this sense, direct participation of powerful interest groups in government is not necessary, because it is always possible to obtain favorable decisions, or to put

[14] David Apter, *The Politics of Modernization* (Chicago, 1965), p. 384.
[15] *Ibid.*, p. 399.

obstacles in the way of adverse decisions when circumstances require it. The political power of social groups within a representative system cannot be measured by the level of direct group participation in the government. It is not necessarily the politicians who maintain power, nor are government posts necessarily effective centers of power. It is also important to analyze this in relation to legislatures that are the indicated bodies to control the executive and represent diverse social interests.

The issues that enter legislative bodies are determined by the legislators themselves. They are the ones that search out, discriminate, and accept information and definitions of problems for policy formulation from that which the political system makes available. Legislatures are the result of a political process that bases itself in an electoral system. And it is exactly in this system where dominant economic and political forces exercise all of their techniques in order to manipulate the electoral system: the control of parties, the selection of candidates, the financing of the process, the annulling of independent groups, and the manipulation of the elections themselves. Information at all levels in the political system is the result of the same forces. Legislation is principally directed to those problems that are of interest to the minority or that are necessary to deal with in order to maintain control over the majority and to integrate the majority into the system of political manipulation.

Much of the pluralist argument constitutes an ideological affirmation of the neutrality of the state. Since the political system contains the means of articulating and aggregating diverse social interests, the state can only compromise the various interests in order to serve the general interest. Political development, then, constitutes the institutionalization of the means for strengthening interest articulation and aggregation in the body politic and the rationalization and departicularization of the state bureaucracy, so that it can be more effectively neutral of vested interests and can act in the public interest.

The fact is, of course, that even in the most "legitimate" and "effective" (to borrow the terminology of Seymour Martin Lipset[16]) representative political systems, such as in Venezuela, Uruguay, Costa Rica, and Mexico, the distribution of the resources of power is such that the overwhelming majority of the population have no meaningful way to "articulate" their interests, while the "aggregation" of popular interests, even under progressive governments, actually constitutes a means of manipulation and social control. Of course, the state must take into account all those interests that are articulated and backed up by power. This is a game of "who gets what, when, and how." In other words, what passes for politics in normal situations in capitalist societies is a struggle over the distribution of the social product. This is almost always a *defensive* game for all organized groups except those with a near monopoly on the resources of power.

The "neutrality" of bureaucracy is a myth. The heads of bureaucratic agencies of the state are typically recruited from the uppermost social ranks or are compliant individuals from lesser classes co-opted by the dominant powers. While the literature on the role of the bureaucracy in political development emanating from universities in the United States is voluminous, it does not address itself to the objective functions, largely of system maintenance and control, of the state bureaucracy under capitalism; and it refers only indirectly to the mechanisms of class control over the bureaucracy. Because of the objective functions of the bureaucracy and class control of key bureaucratic posts, the interests that are aggregated and the interests compromised and served are those of the dominant class. In its most effective form, perhaps best exemplified by military dictatorships such as those in Argentina and Brazil, the bureaucracy does achieve a certain "neutrality": It stands above the conflicts within the dominant class, prepared to act decisively in order better to facilitate the hegemony of the class as a whole.

Authoritarian systems are imposed in Latin America when the mechanisms of domination of representative systems begin to fail, that is, when the system actually begins to give some degree of representation to popular interests. Neverthe-

[16] Lipset, *op. cit.*

less, all the legitimating ideology of the representative system usually remains more or less intact, because this system normally responds rather well to the aspirations and interests of the propertied minority. Only recently in the general drift toward the politics of reaction, most notable in Brazil, Bolivia and Argentina, have the principles of representative government been under attack over a period of years.

Thus we conclude that the pluralist argument is little more than an ideological affirmation of the neutrality of a state that is anything but neutral. This is in fundamental contradiction to our proposition No. 2, which states that any theory of politics and development must take into account the manner in which power vested in control of the economy and in social classes is reflected in the state.

Moreover, the doctrine of pluralism does not respond to our third proposition:

A crucial problem for the analysis of politics and development is the nature of objective, patterned relations between economy, society, and the state. This involves an identification of the functions, basically of system-maintenance, of the state in and for society. Developmentally, the activities of the state are subject to the structural constraints, which analysis must identify, imposed by the system of capitalism.

The bureaucracy and all other agencies of the state actualize the functions that are defined by the institutional imperatives of capitalism. This is true in capitalist societies whether reactionaries, conservatives, or reformers are in power. The basic functions of the state—the maintenance of private property and other institutions fundamental to capitalism, the preservation of law and order, the over-all coordination and administration of economic policy, the formation of consensus around fundamental values and legitimating doctrine, the adjudication of conflict between conflicting interests—are fulfilled, to be sure, with varying degrees of efficiency, by governments of whatever political persuasion. The pluralists, on the other hand, see the functions of the state as more or less confined to conflict resolution between conflicting interests, consensus formation, and the achievement of development goals. They assume that the state can independently pursue development goals, without recognizing the structural constraints imposed by both the objective functions of the state and the controls, direct and indirect, that dominant classes exercise over it.

POLITICS AND DEVELOPMENT FROM THE EVOLUTIONARY FUNCTIONAL PERSPECTIVE

Proposition 4: The different forms of the state—liberal-democratic, authoritarian, fascist, populist, and others— are determined by economic transformations and changes in class relations in historical and cultural contexts characteristic of different countries and regions.

By itself, pluralist doctrine is sadly inadequate to explain either politics or development, much less the interrelations of the two phenomena. Conceptually, it recognizes only two forms of the state: democratic and authoritarian. Moreover, pluralist theory involves a static conception of society. It makes no particular, and certainly no systematic, attempt to analyze the impact of economic transformations or technological changes upon social structure, and consequently upon class and power relations in society. Most contemporary political scientists have recognized the limited and static nature of conventional political theory and, therefore, have increasingly turned to attempts to combine pluralist theory with more sophisticated social scientific modes of analysis. In fact, United States political scientists have been in the forefront of an attempt to reformulate functional theory so that its traditional static bias is overcome and so that different types of societies in different stages of economic-social-political evolution can be identified and analyzed.

Most political scientists now hold the view that underdeveloped regions are simply at a lower stage of social evolution than that characteristic of the industrial democracies of the West. The means to further development are those attributed to the historical evolution of Western Europe and the United States. The present state of economic underdevelopment is due to a deficient application of capitalist economics and to only a superficial penetration of structures such as the free market, free competition, free enterprise, modern tax systems, and the rational organization of the state. Socially and culturally, underdevelopment is viewed as having its roots in insufficient social mobility and the absence of certain values. Politically, underdevelopment comes from the lack of necessary prerequisites for a representative democratic system. This is the case because underdeveloped political systems do not possess the civic cultural participation of the industrialized democratic countries, nor the interest articulation necessary for advanced systems, nor a sufficient degree of autonomy in secondary systems.[17] In general, the literature of political development considers development only in terms of a capitalist economy, social mobility, cultural values, and pluralist democracy—and the essence of political development is the institutionalization of these phenomena. Theoretical categorization in political science revolves around these "empirical" absolutes.

The absolutization of these categories involves several important considerations: First, a methodology is adopted which converts the comparative method into the only means of investigation of political development; second, the categories represent a reification of the ideological doctrines of liberalism; third, a theoretical stance is taken that involves a static conception of change; fourth, this absolutization leads to a practical deficiency that conceives of goals of development as simple transformations of social organization that do not affect the situation of man.

[17] See principally Gabriel Almond and James S. Coleman (eds.), *The Politics of Developing Areas* (Princeton, 1960); Gabriel Almond and Sidney Verba, *Civic Culture: Political Attitudes and Democracy in Five Countries* (Boston, 1965); Gabriel Almond and G. Bingham Powell, Jr., *Comparative Politics: A Developmental Approach* (Boston, 1966); Lucian W. Pye and Sidney Verba, *Political Culture and Political Development* (Princeton, 1966).

THE COMPARATIVE METHOD
AND THE REIFICATION OF LIBERAL DOCTRINE

The comparative method[18] has become a substitute for dialectical analysis. The method is presented as "objective" analysis which, it is claimed, does not originate in *a priori* deductive or subjective concepts. At the same time, the comparative method attempts to be empirical, that is, subject to the data extracted from reality and to the exactitude of statistical indices. The comparative method appears as a system of classification. Ostensibly, this provides a basis for studying change from one state of the system to another state. Actually, analysis often begins and ends with simple classification of phenomena into functional categories. Unfortunately, the objectivity of the comparative method ends where the ideological bases that give origin to the premises of all its analyses become manifest. Gabriel Almond and G. Bingham Powell, for example, attempt a comparative analysis of political systems. All the functions and roles of systems are constructed and classified in such a way that only the democratic systems of the United States and England score high on the indices of political development.

Empirically, the models of political systems constructed do not transcend the data collected in the study of existing systems. If democracy is under consideration, this refers to systems that actually exist and call themselves democratic. If communism is under consideration, the presumed traits of present systems that officially call themselves communist are the model. In this way, the possibilities for realization of certain ideals implicit in democratic or communist conceptions that transcend the raw empirical data are unimagined or denied. The Western democratic model concludes in the identification of human freedom with free enterprise, social democracy with social mobility, and representative

---

[18] See Harry Eckstein, "A Perspective on Comparative Politics: Past and Present," in David Apter and Harry Eckstein (eds.), *Comparative Politics* (New York, 1963).

government with political democracy. What can be no more than relative, what is simply limited to historical moments, and what is subject to all the imperfection of the real is converted into an absolute. All the range of possible political systems are reduced to existing systems. The capacity of man begins and ends in the imperfections of systems of a given historical moment.

The best of these political theorists, such as David Apter, have departed somewhat from the conventional model of political development. For Apter, the best system of modernization is a "mobilist system" with strong central control, little "information," and a large dose of "consummatory" values. But even in this case, the ideal type toward which systems should—and tend to—evolve is the secular libertarian model that consecrates utilitarian liberal principles and places emphasis upon mechanical harmony and equilibrium.[19]

Although Frank has, in the preceding chapter, analyzed the bias inherent in functional theory, these distortions warrant further analysis here. In this framework, development is the gradual evolution of social systems characterized by "universalistic norms," "achievement orientation," and "functional specificity."[20] This approach, which manifests a classic evolutionary faith in progress (progress=imminent change, always for the better) through gradualist responses to change (which normally consist of a political or cultural response to accommodate change after technology has forced it), can be termed "evolutionary functionalism." This approach is consistent only with liberalism functioning as legitimating ideology for prevailing systems of domination. Universalism is just another term for the preference for the rule of law and bureaucratic order—which are principal instruments of system maintenance in the modern world.

[19] Apter, *op. cit.*, p. 29.
[20] Specificity refers to the specialization of functions and roles in society; universalism has to do with the predominance of norms applied to the entire society without consideration of particular privileges; achievement is a motivational category that refers to the preparation and capacity of an actor as a reference point for social evaluation, not to his social position.

Achievement is a set of motivations to be infused into the culture of "ascriptive" societies and socialized into "traditional" personalities. This amounts conveniently to individualizing inequality of opportunity, thus avoiding the problem of analytically confronting the *structure* of inequality. Functional specificity presumably gives rise to a differentiated institutional and social structure more conducive to "pluralism"—the liberals' favorite concept. Thus, the concepts actually represent those ideal-typical states American academics cherish. This might be acceptable if they constituted useful scientific constructs. But surely development is more than defining the desirable from the liberal ideological perspective.

Those who utilize functional theory in the Latin American case consider that the problem of underdevelopment does not relate to power distribution but rather to the values that all societies must adopt and institutionalize in order to become modern.[21] Seymour Martin Lipset, for example, contrasts Anglo-Saxon with Latin values and attributes Latin American underdevelopment to the latter: Catholic are opposed to Protestant values and aristocratic ways are contrasted to the values of the innovating entrepreneur.[22] In effect, Lipset's analysis reduces the blame for underdevelopment to Latin Americans, for their incapacity to become real capitalists and imitators of North American culture, which motivates people to accept the search for wealth as the maximum instrumental value.

In general, the "culturalist" theory, apart from the class and racial prejudices that it often contains, can be construed as a justification for the social, political, and economic state of the world that benefits the countries that enjoy economic and political as well as cultural hegemony. Though the terminology is far more subtle these days, as in the ideas of a

[21] Seymour Martin Lipset, "Values, Education, and Entrepreneurship," in Lipset and Aldo Solari (eds.), *op. cit.*, pp. 3–61. See also Everett Hagen, *On the Theory of Social Change* (Chicago, 1962); David McClelland, *The Achieving Society* (New York, 1961).

[22] *Ibid.*

"culture of poverty" and "traditional society," it seems that the ideas of the Anglo-Saxon white man's civilizing burden and manifest destiny are still with us.

For the "culturalist" the poverty of man is only one datum among others. Exploitation, the immediate cause of poverty, nowhere fits into the conceptual scheme, nor does the solution necessarily require any basic structural change in society: The solution will come through the adoption of proper values. For some "culturalists," poverty is simply an inevitable datum of human reality that is governed by inertia, and it is therefore realistic to think that no solution exists to eliminate it. The abstractness of the "culturalist" solution comes from the fact that man has been converted into a Platonic being subject to ideas and values but not to concrete realities. The man who suffers, who does not have enough to permit him to reflect on ideas and values, who is the product and the object of overwhelming economic and power systems, who remains in a state of misery precisely because a minority enjoy the privileges that a value system of universalism, achievement, and specificity have brought them—this man remains absent from "culturalist" theories like that of Lipset, and even more so in the cases of Parsons, McClelland, Hagen, and Hoselitz, which provide the conceptual model for conventional political development theory.[23]

In practice, Parsonian universalism, long institutionalized in Latin America, actually means the perpetuation of norms that the propertied minority consider applicable to all, because such norms favor the minority's interests and mechanisms of domination. Each individual's ability, magnified by the value of achievement, is actually a function of the prevailing opportunities for education and work that a society controlled by a propertied minority permits a person to enjoy. The fact that some people are "better endowed" and

[23] Talcott Parsons, *Structure and Process in Modern Societies* (New York, 1960); "On the Concept of Political Power," in Bendix and Lipset, *op. cit.;* "Power, Party, and System," in Sydney Ulmer (ed.), *op. cit., Toward a General Theory of Action* (New York, 1962); *The Social System* (Glencoe, Illinois, 1951). McClelland, *op. cit.;* Hagen, *op. cit.;* Bert F. Hoselitz, *Sociological Perspectives on Economic Growth* (New York, 1960).

some have "greater capacity" than others is not a consequence of innate inequality that the "culturalists" devine,
but of a system that permits some to advance in work and in
culture while others are prevented from doing so because
of institutionalized economic and social inequality and political powerlessness. The specialization of roles in the context of specificity reflects patterns imposed by the same minority through control over economic and other institutions.
Evolutionary functionalism, then, reduces the problem of
development to one of acquiring relative values. Man and
the structures that exploit and oppress him remain relegated
to a secondary plane or are totally erased from consideration.
This misplaced focus of functional theory derives directly
from a conception of power that ignores the situation of man
and that sustains the possibility of development without challenging or changing the economic bases of political power.
This is an ideological position that implies not only a particular conception of social reality, but also attempts to justify
existing social systems. Moreover, the problematic nature of
human existence becomes determined, in one or another
form, ideologically, thus destroying the scientific objectivity
that functionalism pretends.

Evolutionary functionalism involves, to use José Nun's
terminology,[24] an "abstract" conception of man, and therefore cannot readily orient theoretical endeavor or empirical
analysis to problems of the development of man out of structural conditions of oppression. Evolutionary functionalism
also has great difficulty in identifying structures and, particularly, in analyzing the dialectical forces built into structures
that cause change. Denying both the dialectic as a tool for the
analysis of change and the humanistic assumptions of social
theory in favor of a supposed "value free" social science,
evolutionary functionalism forsakes man and observes social
systems evolving—invariably toward the "modern," "industrial," "democratic" society—without being able to explain
why and how they evolve.

[24] José Nun, "Notes on Political Science in Latin America"
in Bryce Wood and Manuel Diegues (eds.), *Social Science in
Latin America* (New York, 1968).

Finally, we suggest that the weaknesses and errors indicated are not merely a case of intellectual failure, but are an effort, conscious for the most part, although unconscious in some cases, to extend the supremacy of industrial capitalism, American style, on the social science front. This is a form of "cultural imperialism," whose ideological offensive is manifested in the diffusion of the theories of pluralism, culturalism, and functionalism, and whose practical application is manifested in operations like the Peace Corps, Project Camelot, and the provision of grants and scholarships to researchers and students at home and abroad who show promise of furthering the ideological hegemony and practical applicability of these theories.

THE STATIC NATURE OF CHANGE

The object of functional analysis is a given system with its functions, structures, and roles, with its input and output, with its values, and with its institutional organization.[25] In this context, change refers to the greater differentiation of the system, or to a greater degree of secularization that appears within it, or to the autonomy that secondary or sub-systems manage to attain. Evolution in a process of development or modernization is conceived of in relation to system states or stages that grow out of each other and that pass from one to another, owing to determined transformations (which cannot be causally explained) that operate within the preceding system or to exogenous events. The end result of the evolutionary process is the "modern" society with the

[25] Neil J. Smelser, "Mechanisms of Change and Adjustment to Change" in Bert F. Hoselitz and Wilbert Moore (eds.), *Industrialization and Society* (The Hague, 1963); Talcott Parsons, "A Paradigm for the Analysis of Social Systems and Change," in Demerath and Peterson, *System, Change, and Conflict* (New York, 1967), pp. 189–213; S. N. Eisenstadt, "Social Change, Differentiation, and Evolution," *ibid.*, pp. 213–31; David Easton, *Systems Analysis of the Political Life* (New York, 1965); Don Martindale, *Functionalism in the Social Sciences* (Philadelphia, 1965).

characteristics previously analyzed. A process of evolutionary maturation of social forms and institutions occurs through the functions of adaptation, integration, and goal-attainment.[26] Determined forms of industrialization, technology, efficiency, bureaucracy, and democracy become ideal types and expressions of the highest level of development toward which to aspire. Stages and processes are constructed that lead in one form or another to the idealized and absolutized ends. The means to development are a continuous application of economic rationality and political moderation that yield indefinite progress toward these ends.

The concept of "modernization," which is central to political development theory, is a typical case of the problems that this conception of change presents. Modernization is taken as progressive increments to the functions of the community, or as constant innovation within a social system that adapts itself to conditions of the world, or as a series of dimensions that involve "equality," "capacity of mobilization," and "differentiation."[27] Here "equality"—rather than being a measure of the unequal distribution of income, wealth, social prestige, and power—becomes a political concept that refers to culture, to the legitimation of the system, and to participation in elections. "Capacity" and "differentiation" are related to authoritative and nonauthoritative structures of the government.[28] But there is no analysis of the structure and function of the state in relation to power relations in society. Pye converts political modernization into a process of responding to a series of crises identified as identity, legiti-

[26] Talcott Parsons, "Some Highlights of the General Theory of Action," in Roland Young (ed.), *Approaches to the Study of Politics* (Evanston, 1958), pp. 282–301.

[27] See Apter, *op. cit.;* Lucion W. Pye, *Aspects of Political Development* (Boston, 1966); Almond and Powell, *op. cit.;* Almond and Coleman, *op. cit.;* Joseph La Palombara, "Bureaucracy and Political Development" in La Palombara (ed.), *op. cit.;* Reinhard Bendix, *National-Building and Citizenship: Studies in Our Changing Social Order* (New York, 1964); Clark Kerr, *et al., Industrialism and Man* (Cambridge, 1960); Rostow, *A World of Nations* (Washington, D.C., 1967).

[28] Pye, *op. cit.*

macy, penetration, participation, integration, and distribution.[29] But he does not seek the roots of these crises in the structure of society.

THE SITUATION OF MAN

As a method, functionalism is incapable of dealing with human problems directly because principal interest is rooted in the variables of the system and its functions. As a theory, functionalism suffers from a philosophical blindness that sees not man but only his mechanical processes. The empiricism and positivism that pervade functional thinking ignore the historical and dialectical conditioning of man in society. The social and economic realities that the existential situation of man in the contemporary world implies become formalistic theoretical problems.

When functional theory does move from the world of highly abstract systems to deal with "actors" (never men or women) or collectivities of actors, the question becomes one of motivation. The extreme of this position leads to an absurd psychological reductionism, as in McClelland's reduction of economic development to the number of actors with a high need for achievement. The popular variant of psychological reductionism in political science is the literature that deals with political behavior in terms of the personal pathologies of political actors. Revolutionaries, for example, are seen as "extremists" or "deviants" motivated by abnormal factors in their personal life histories. Psychological reductionism of course has an ideological function in maintaining prevailing systems of domination: The problem becomes one of individual pathologies rather than institutional deficiencies.

We submit that political analysis involves the search for power relationships that reside in the structural relations between economic and social institutions, social classes, and the state. In this way, actors are *agents* of objective institutional, class, and power relationships that exist in society.

[29] *Ibid.;* see Rostow, *op. cit.*

The roles that individuals perform in various institutional involvements and in the political sphere are not determined merely by their personal motives nor by interpersonal-situational factors. Roles are fundamentally shaped by institutional arrangements and by basic structures of class and power.

In the evolutionary functional framework, development has been reduced to a mechanical process related to normalization and equilibrium. This concept of development has nothing to do with the dignity of man and his potential, with contemporary men and women, afflicted, anguished, and continuously subjected to the inevitable imperfection of dominant institutions. Not exploitation, nor misery, nor hunger, nor ignorance, nor economic inequality, nor colonialism, nor domination of one people by another people, nor control by a minority over the majority, nor any other social fact of this nature receive consideration as crucial variables in the functional approach to political development. What, then, is really the object of political development? If the problems of the ordinary man and his situation are not considered important, can any theory, any political analysis, any social study, be relevant to the solution of human problems? Is theory at the service of man or is man a function of theory? Political theory cannot remain at the margin of the primary problems of man without converting itself into an inhuman theory, empty of content.[30]

Pluralism, culturalism, and functionalism are different aspects of the same ideological current. On these bases the modern theory of political development has been constructed. This ideological current is based on conceptions

[30] The tendency toward dehumanization is not exclusive to political science. It is possibly a consequence in part of the dehumanization of other social sciences from which political scientists have borrowed perspectives, particularly sociology and anthropology. John Horton has illustrated how the use of the concepts of anomie and alienation are a reflection of the dehumanized ideology characteristic of dominant American sociology: "The Dehumanization of Anomie and Alienation: A Problem in the Ideology of Sociology," *The British Journal of Sociology* (December 1964), pp. 283–300.

of political power and of man that do not take into account the economic and social conditions of determined structures of social organization. Ignoring the social and political implications of economic concentration, they arrive at the absolutization of existing, or reification of desired forms of economic, social, and political organization. The fact that political development theory ignores the fundamental structural aspects of underdevelopment is not simply an accident. Methodologically, the approach cannot overcome the limitations of the comparative method, positivism, and excessive empiricism. Theoretically, it considers change as a process of abstract systems and not of man liberating himself from exploitation and oppression. Practically, it suffers a blindness that cannot see the real problems of man. These factors make contemporary political science an inhuman science, whose research tends to become abstract irrelevance or, worse still, a contribution to the means of imposition and control of one part of the society over another, of one people over another.

Thus, we conclude with our fifth and final proposition:

Development involves the liberation of man from conditions of exploitation and oppression. Politics is the means of human liberation.

Chapter 14

WHO IS THE IMMEDIATE ENEMY?*

André Gunder Frank

Tactically, the immediate enemy of national liberation in
Latin America is the native bourgeoisie in Brazil, Bolivia,
Mexico, etc., and the local bourgeoisie in the Latin American countryside. This is so—in Asia and Africa included—
notwithstanding that strategically the principal enemy undoubtedly is imperialism.

The Latin American class structure was formed and transformed by the development of the colonial structure of international capitalism, from mercantilism to imperialism.
Through this colonial structure, the consecutive metropolises
of Spain, Britain, and North America have subjected Latin
America to an economic exploitation and political domination that determined its present class and sociocultural structure. The same colonial structure extends throughout Latin
America, where national metropolises subject their provincial centers, and these the local centers, to a similar internal
colonialism. Since the structures are completely interpene-
trated, the determination of the Latin American class structure by the colonial structure does not prevent the fundamental contradictions of Latin America from being
"internal." The same is true for Asia and Africa.

Today the anti-imperialist struggle in Latin America must
be carried out through class struggle. Popular mobilization
against the immediate class enemy on the national and local
levels produces a stronger confrontation with the principal
imperialist enemy than does direct anti-imperialist mobilization. Nationalist mobilization through political alliance

* Synthesis and translation from Spanish of the paper presented
at the Cultural Congress of Havana in January 1968.

of the broadest anti-imperialist forces does not adequately challenge the immediate class enemy, and generally it does not even result in a real and necessary confrontation of the imperialist enemy. This also applies to the neocolonial countries of Asia and Africa and perhaps to some colonial countries, unless they are already militarily occupied by imperialism.

The strategic coincidence of class struggle and the anti-imperialist struggle and tactical precedence of class struggle in Latin America (over the anti-imperialist struggle) against the metropolitan bourgeoisie is obviously valid for guerrilla warfare, which must begin against the national bourgeoisie of the country; and it is also valid for the ideological and political struggle that must be directed not only against the imperialist and colonial enemy but against the native class enemy.

The tactical precedence of the class struggle over the strategic anti-imperialist struggle appeared in the Cuban Revolution and in the October Revolution among others, and also in the recent constitutionalist struggle in Santo Domingo, where the initial attack of the popular forces against their own bourgeois class immediately led to a real confrontation with imperialism; because the interpenetration of the colonial and class structure makes the survival of imperialism depend on the maintenance of capitalist class structure in Latin America as well as in Asia and Africa (although the reverse is also true).

The purpose of this chapter is to suggest how in Latin America the scientific study of the interpenetration of the colonial and class structures in the historical development of capitalism, in bourgeois nationalism, in imperialism, and in the ideological field permits the discovery of the weak links in the class and colonial chain so that they can be broken through revolution; and to raise questions for further research.

Such scientific study must be undertaken first and foremost by the Latin American intellectuals themselves and by those of other underdeveloped countries. The social scientists from the capitalist metropolis and almost all Marxists

have looked at the capitalist system in its metropolitan mani-
festation. They have considered Asia, Africa, and Latin
America as mere annexes, without adequately considering
the integral part that the peoples—and the bourgeoisies—of
these continents play in the world capitalist system. This has
deformed the scientific representation of the colonial and
class structure of the capitalist or imperialist system as a
whole, especially in its underdeveloped part, but also in its
developed part. The necessary perspective is to be found
among the colonized themselves. But these can develop the
necessary perspective only by active confrontation of this
class and colonial structure through active and organized
political militancy.

The Latin American class structure and especially the
rural class structure has since the conquest been formed by
external and internal colonialism, which converted Latin
America into an export economy that provides the metropolis with raw materials *and capital* in exchange—a very unequal and exploitative exchange—for manufactures. The
productive relations in the *latifundios* of prerevolutionary
Cuba, Argentina, coastal Peru, São Paulo, and postrevolutionary and postagrarian reform Mexico of the nineteenth
and twentieth centuries are evidently due to this colonial
imperialist relation and not to the supposed transfer of a
feudal class structure from Spain or Portugal during the
sixteenth or seventeenth centuries. Examination of Chile,
Mexico, Peru, and other regions during the sixteenth to
eighteenth centuries show the same process there as well.

If we must look for the bourgeois democratic revolution
in Latin America at all, we should do so approximately during the years from 1830 to 1880. During this period almost
all of Latin America experienced a series of civil wars that
confronted at once federalists, provincialists, manufacturers,
economic and political nationalists, and liberals (but not
freetraders) on the one side; against unitarists, national
metropolises (in general port cities), exporters, importers
and agriculturalists, Latin American freetraders and the
English or French metropolis, on the other side. The latter
triumphed first in the political and military field and then

in the economic one. They thus diverted what might be called the bourgeois democratic revolution of Rosas (before this Federalist changed to what in essence became a unitarist and give-away policy) in Argentina, of Dr. Francia and the Lopezes in Paraguay, Rengifo and Balmeceda in Chile, Mauá and Nabuco in Brazil, etc. This frustrated the development of national capitalism under the auspices of the Argentine provinces, Paraguay, parts of Chile, Antioquia in Colombia, Puebla and Querétaro in Mexico, etc.

The next upsurge of national capitalism and of bourgeois capitalism was between 1930 and 1955, and arose as a result of the economic *and political* necessities and possibilities generated by the Great Depression and the Second World War in the imperialist metropolis. The weakening of the imperialist ties within the colonial structure resulted in changes in the Latin American class structure and in the economic, political, and ideological movements associated with Vargas, Perón, Cárdenas, Haya de la Torre, Aguirre Cerda, Betancourt, Figueres, Arévalo-Arbenz (and in another part of the same world capitalist system Gandhi and Nehru). All these movements (and those leaders like Betancourt and Figueres who survived) lost their economic and political nationalist impulse with the recovery of imperialism and with the reintensification of its colonial ties. Under present conditions it is utopian for the bourgeoisie, and politically disastrous for the people, to hope for the continuation or renovation of this bourgeois nationalist movement.

The renewed strengthening of the colonial ties brought with it foreign investment and "aid" in the Latin American and other neocolonial countries, where it came importantly to modify foreign trade and the national economic structure. The flow of Latin American capital toward the metropolis that is generated by these new colonial relations is several times greater than the sum of two billion U.S. dollars a year that is mentioned in the Second Declaration of Havana and by Fidel Castro in some of his recent speeches. Latin America's expenditure on service account alone (profit remittance, foreign debt service, donations, transport, and others) exceeds six billion U.S. dollars annually, which accounts   for

61 percent of Latin America's foreign exchange earnings or 7 percent of its Gross National Product (GNP). This may be compared, for instance, with the total expenditure for education of only 2.6 percent of GNP. The deterioration of the terms of trade since the early 1950s accounts for an additional 3 percent of GNP, and the exploitation included in the most favorable of these terms represents a further incalculable loss. Most of the profits remitted to the imperialist metropolis are not earnings on capital that was brought to and invested in Latin America, but on national capital that Latin America put at the disposal of the imperialist enterprise by reinvestment, bank loans, the stock market, "mixed" companies, etc.

Nonetheless, far more important still than the drain of capital from Latin America to the metropolis is the structure of underdevelopment that these imperialist colonial ties and especially foreign investment impose on Latin America. Because of their political consequences, the "mixed" companies (where the Latin American entrepreneur and even his government—witness "Chileanization"—combine with the American monopoly), require further study, due to the increasing economic, political, and ideological dependence of the Latin American bourgeoisie that they create. The American technological monopoly plays an increasing and inadequately studied role in this colonial relationship.

All these and other factors combine to create a situation in which the so-called national bourgeoisie does not even have any existence, let alone independence, in Latin America. The export-import and agrarian bourgeoisie was and remains a colonized or *comprador* bourgeoisie. It does not appear possible that any sector of the Latin American bourgeoisie could react with any degree of independence in case of a renewed imperialist crisis, or that it could even take political advantage of an interimperialist struggle. But it does seem that the Brazilian great bourgeoisie can become a junior or "subimperialist" partner of American imperialism in Latin America. The political implications for the Latin American and Brazilian revolution remain to be studied.

The industrial proletariat has been unionized by the bourgeoisie and has been politically tied to the same, especially to its nationalist sector during its upsurge; and the labor movement, often including its Communist sector, has been an ally of this bourgeoisie. But lately the nationalist sector has lost power and the economic crisis provoked by imperialist penetration has obliged the bourgeoisie to reduce the real wages of the workers. Will the bourgeoisie be able to maintain its control over the labor movement, or will the latter become more revolutionary?

How do productive relations determine the political potential of the "floating" or "marginal" population, which often constitutes the majority of the urban population of Latin America? Is this population really an unorganizable "lumpenproletariat"? Often the most reactionary sector of the bourgeoisie has managed to get the support of many so-called "marginals." But in Caracas in the early 1960s these were mobilized by the left, and in Santo Domingo they came to mobilize Colonel Camaño.

The petit bourgeoisie has also been politically very volatile. Will its various sectors be more progressive when their economic and social horizons narrow, or will they become more reactionary when they feel themselves threatened by proletarianization?

The rural class structure—given the rural sector's internal colonial status—is an integral part of the national and international capitalist class structure. It is necessary to investigate the commercial, financial, and political relations of the *latifundium* sector of the bourgeoisie with other sectors, given the fact that many *latifundistas* derive their income perhaps less from agricultural production than from the commercial, financial, and political exploitation that their monopoly over the land affords them. No sector of the Latin American bourgeoisie, evidently, can have a real economic or political interest in changing the essence of that colonial and class structure.

In all of Latin America those who work the land are distinguished by having little or no property in the means of production, which permits their exploitation by the bourgeoisie who own these means. The forms, but not the essence, of this relationship vary. In what proportion—in each particular region—are these people who work the land peasants, agricultural proletarians, or whatever, and with what variations? Large regions of Brazil, Argentina, the Caribbean, and even of the Indo-American countries are characterized by what in reality is an agricultural proletariat, which is very mobile among *latifundia*, regions, and even countries. Much of this proletariat cannot even aspire to a piece of land and seeks better and more secure working conditions and wages. There and in other regions each one of millions of "peasants" combines in himself various "capitalist," "semifeudal," etc., relations of production. Small peasants and even tenants often employ proletarian labor. What implications does so complex a colonial and class structure have for the political mobilization of these exploited—and small exploiters—and on the basis of what grievances and worries? Some have maintained that it is easier to organize the small owner and tenant than the agricultural wage worker. Others deny it. Some say that it is not yet possible to mobilize the Indian for the revolution because they consider him "isolated" from the society and the culture. But the Indian sector is the most exploited one in the class and colonial structure. In Guatemala he has recently been mobilized, and in Bolivia he has shown himself able to mobilize even his leaders. Where is the truth or truths?

The socialist revolutions have taken place in the weak links of the colonial structure of the imperialist system (and not where the industrial proletariat has seen its greatest development). It is necessary to study the interpenetration of the class structure and the colonial structure in order to find the weak points on the continental, national, regional, and local levels. How can we, on the basis of an analysis of the interpenetration of the colonial and class structure, combine the rural struggle with the urban, the military with the political and the ideological ones? It will be necessary to put Marxist analysis of the Latin American society at the service of the revolutionary struggle.

The task and the responsibility of Marxists from Latin America and other underdeveloped countries is scientifically to criticize and to reject not only the ideology and "science" of imperialism (which at the moment is very much on the offensive on the Continent), but also the revised version that is propagated by the Latin American bourgeoisie, no matter how nationalist or progressive it may appear. In recent years nationalist sectors of the bourgeoisie—at a time when its economic base was already disappearing—sponsored the ideology and the economic and social science created by ECLA, ILPES, ISEB, the Instituto Torcuato di Tella and associated with the names of Prebisch, Furtado, Sunkel, Pinto, Germani, González Casanova, and others. This view revises the imperialist version insofar as it recognizes some colonial relationship between the metropolis and Latin America. But it does not recognize imperialism and its colonial *structure* (it welcomes foreign investment and "aid," asking only for "safety measures"); it does not recognize the internal colonial structure (given that it considers Latin America "a dual" economy and society, part feudal and part capitalist); and of course it diverts all attention from the class structure in Latin America. The Latin American Marxist and revolutionary intellectual necessarily must combat this ideology as well, however progressive and clothed in Marxist language it may appear. But he will not be able to do so in terms of traditional "Marxist" and "reformist" models, according to which Latin America has a dual society in which a "feudal" sector is still awaiting its liberation by a "national and anti-imperialist" bourgeoisie. Marxists will have to create the leading revolutionary ideas which, as Fidel Castro says, the Latin American revolution needs. Ideological clarity about these problems becomes especially essential when the revolutionary movement is temporarily slowed down, because it is at that time that ideological firmness is necessary in order to resist the temptations—that the bourgeoisie always offers—to recede toward a reformist policy, suggesting, for example, the supposed possibility and necessity of a "democratic peace," as the Communist Party of Venezuela is doing at this time. To reach this ideological and theoretical clarity, Marxists will have to work intellectually, but more than intellectually as well, inspired by the example of Che Guevara, who was revolutionary first and then intellectual.

To pursue this ideological and revolutionary objective, which is the real responsibility of the Latin American intellectual, and of the Marxists especially, will mean—as Che also found—leaving the institutional bounds of the Latin American and imperialist bourgeoisie. The Latin American intellectual—and this is true as well for the artist or writer as for the social scientist—will have to become conscious of the fact that he has been working for the bourgeoisie. He will have to realize also that, the more acute the contradictions become and the more the revolutionary process advances, the less will the bourgeoisie permit the Latin American intellectual to take advantage of its bourgeois institutions —universities, publishing houses, press, etc.—for the development of a really revolutionary Marxist theory and practice. In some parts of the continent, the hour at which the doors of the bourgeois institutions close to the Marxist has already come; in the remaining parts that time will come soon. The Latin American intellectual and Marxist will have to decide if he will remain inside, pursuing reformism, or outside with the people, making the revolution.

INDEX